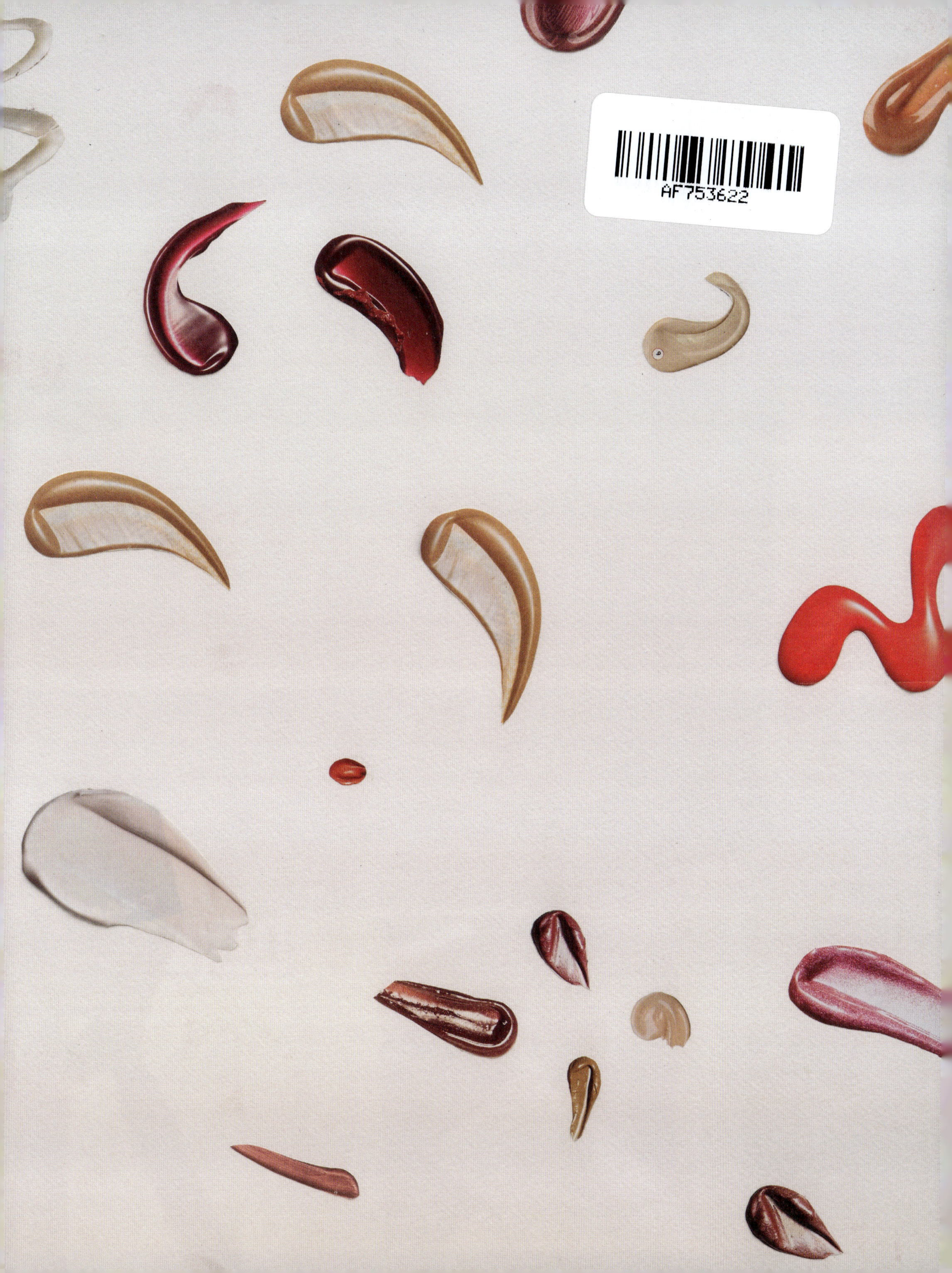

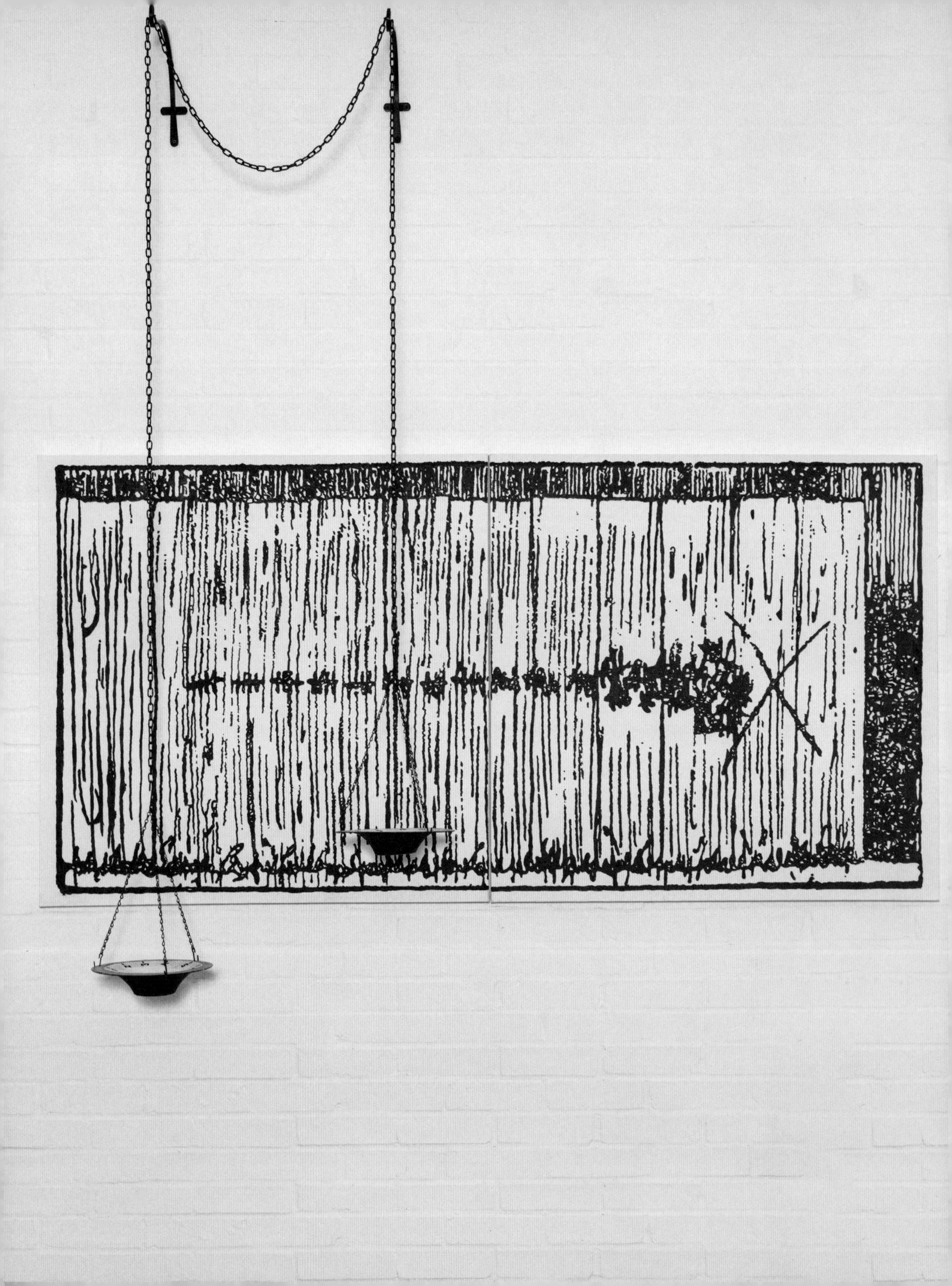

ANDY HOLDEN

Weight of Imagination

Jennifer Higgie

Foreword by JARVIS COCKER

HENI Publishing, London

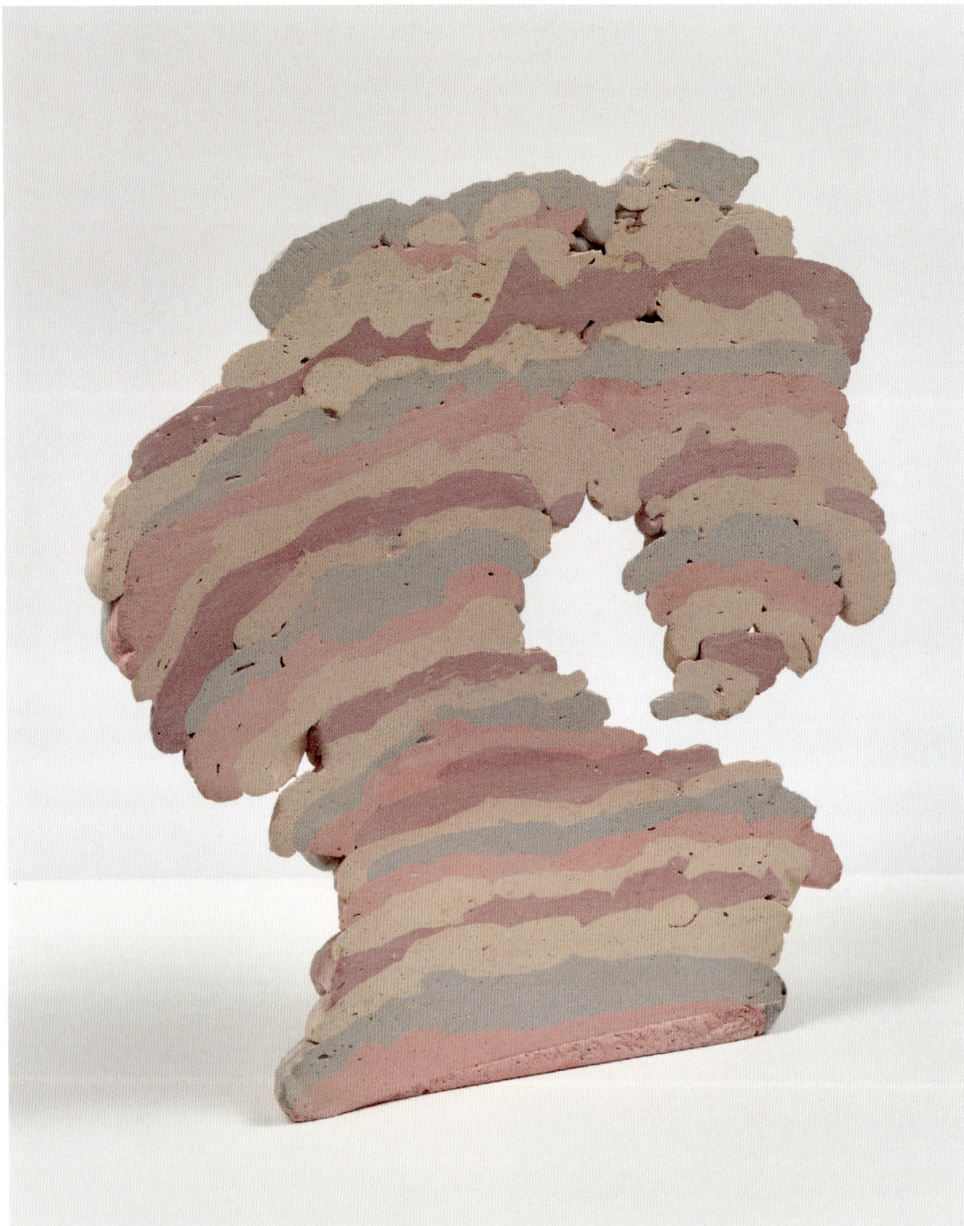

Ghosts in the DNA, 2020,
plaster and emulsion paint,
10 × 40 × 10 cm (3 ⅞ × 15 ¾ × 3 ⅞ in.)

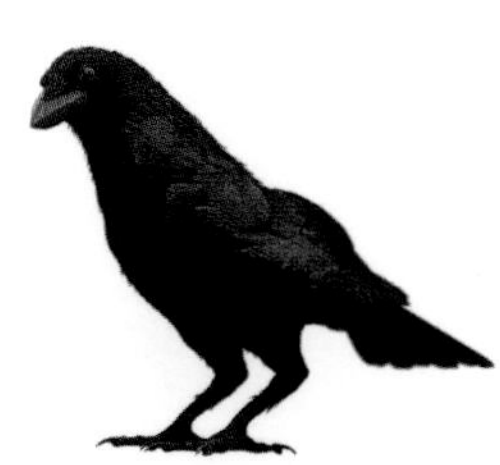

FOREWORD

Jarvis Cocker

Who is Andy Holden?

Good question.

I first became aware of him in 2017, when I went to see his 'Natural Selection' show in a disused library near Elephant & Castle in London. From that I surmised that he knew a lot about birds & that his dad had been the bird expert on *Blue Peter*.

The next encounter was at the Cinema Museum in London where I saw an animated version of Andy Holden narrate his film *Laws of Motion in a Cartoon Landscape*.

Next, I received an invitation to go to Brixton during the Covid lockdown & visit his *Structure of Feeling*, whilst riding around a warehouse on a mobility scooter transformed into a dodgem car.

Then there was an experience in Holland where I encountered the film he had made about stealing, then returning, a small fragment of the Great Pyramid whilst on a trip to Egypt as a child. He had also made a very large, knitted replica of the stone.

I began to realise that Andy Holden was a complex character. He is a man looking for answers. He is a man who uses his art to ask the questions that he is looking for the answers to. His art speaks to you. But it is also the sound of him talking to himself.

He has a work entitled *The Origin of the Work of Art (Bower)*. It is a recreation of the mysterious structures made by bowerbirds. Bowerbirds build these nest-like sculptures & then decorate them with objects they find in the surrounding area. Scientists can find no practical reason for why they do this. Some people say this is the only example in the entire animal kingdom of a creature that decorates its abode just for fun. Just because they like the look of it. Andy made this oversized replica of the bowerbird's nest himself. I think that's significant.

Rather than ask, 'Who is Andy Holden?' perhaps I should have asked, 'What is Andy Holden?'

Well... Andy Holden is a human being. A human being who realises he is also a part of the animal kingdom. A human being who wonders what exactly a human being is. Who wonders what art is – & what function it performs for the people who make it.

Big questions.

I have seen Andy use his art, at times of great personal distress, as a shield against the cosmos. As a way of navigating his way through a dangerous, life-threatening landscape. That's a very important function of art. One that is perhaps a little overlooked in our current Capitalist Phase.

This art is not an Investment Opportunity – it's an Enlightenment Opportunity: an opportunity to understand where the creative urge comes from & what it can do for you.

It's an education.

So start learning.

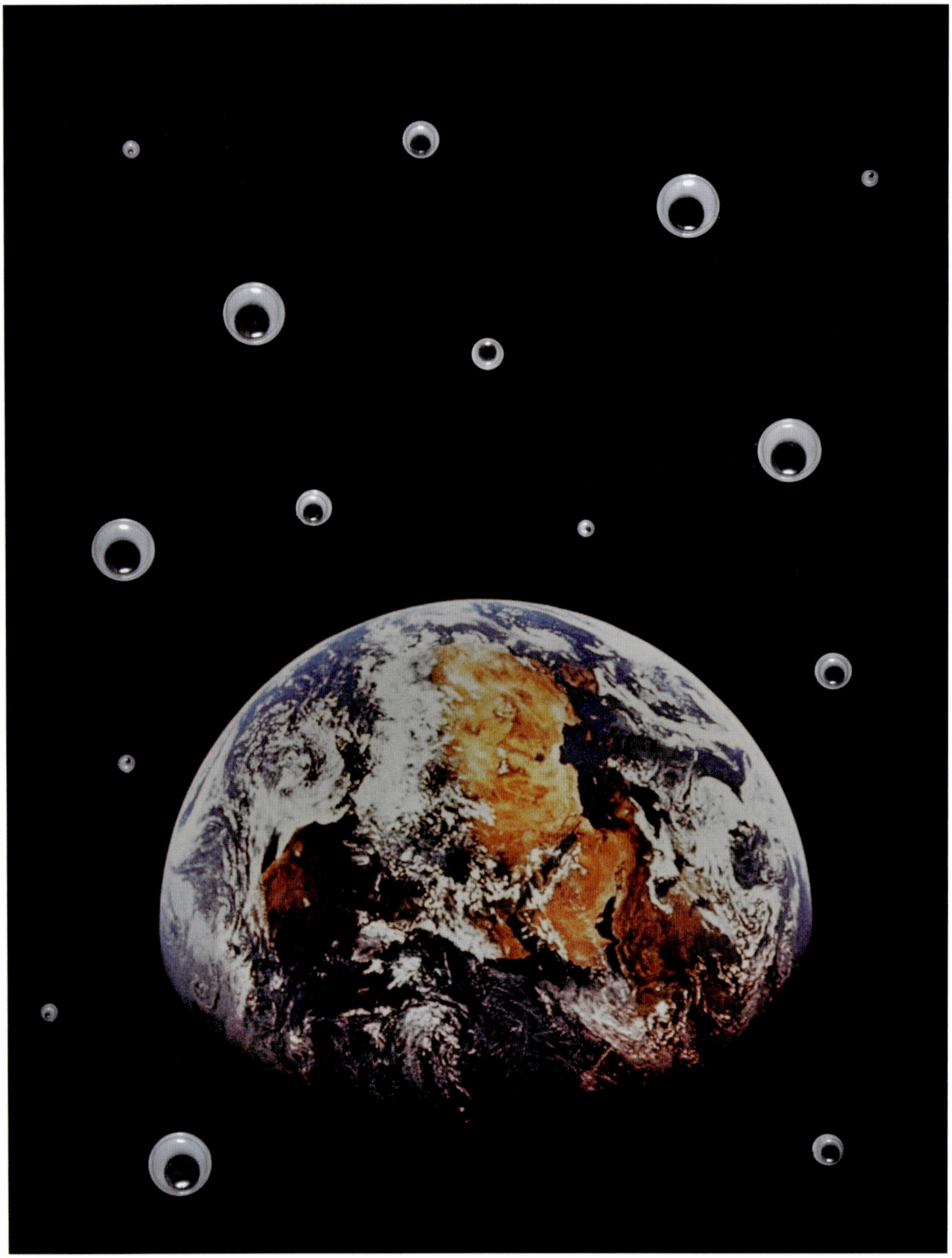

↑ *Untitled (Eyes in Space)*, 2012, plastic eyes on book plate, 25 × 14 cm (9 ⅞ × 5 ½ in.)
↗ *The Mountain & I*, *c.* 2007, collage, 29 × 16 cm (11 ¾ × 15 ¾ in.). Private collection

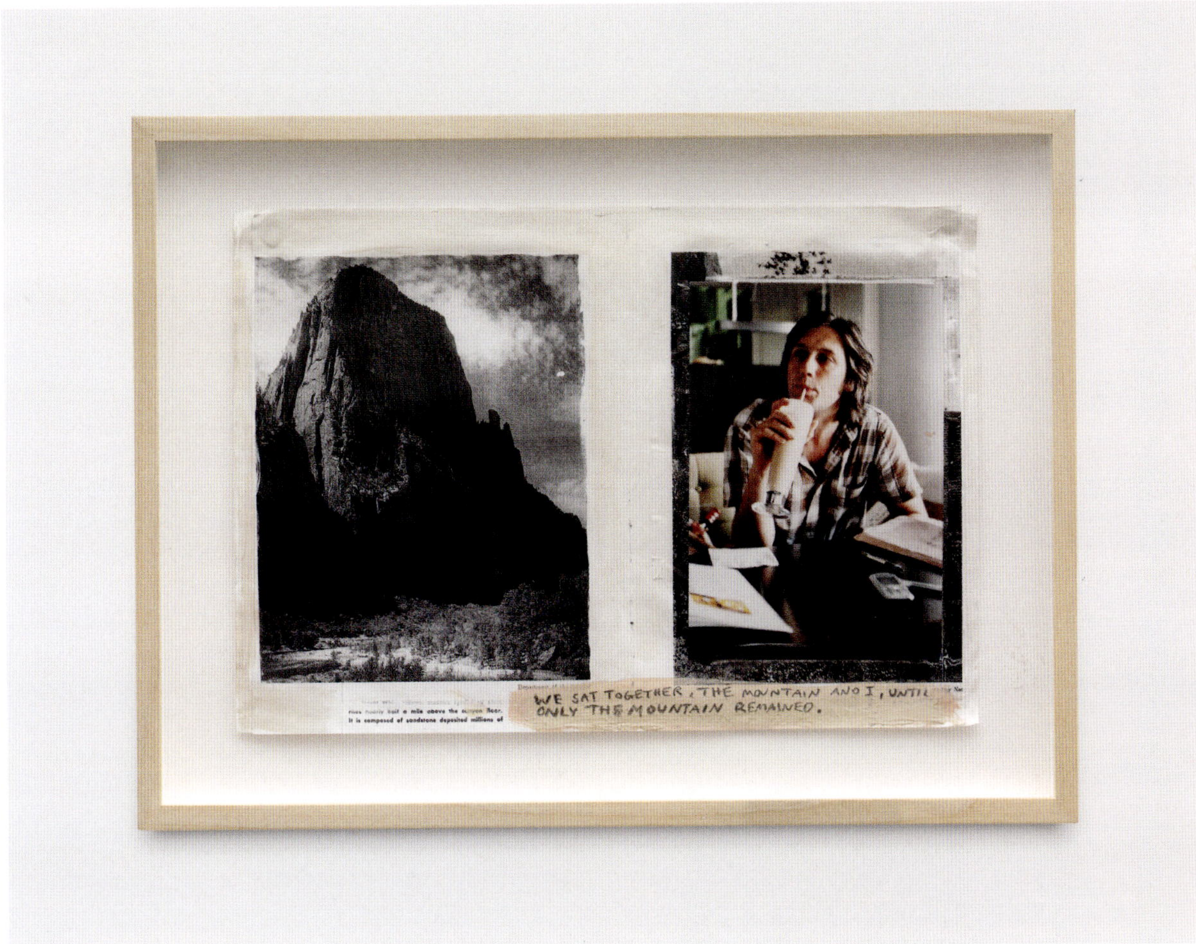

Weight of Imagination: Andy Holden's Worldview

Jennifer Higgie

Andy Holden was born and still lives in Bedford, an historic English market town some 50 miles north of London. For some artists, their place of birth is not important, but Holden is an artist for whom the imaginative and philosophical potential of the everyday is central to his thinking. His home, friends, family and wider community continue to shape who he is and what he creates.

For Holden, the intertwining of the physical world and metaphysical realms – a space each of us navigates daily – poses a seemingly infinite set of questions. These can range from the momentous – what constitutes time? – to the very personal, such as the significance of his late grandmother's ceramic cat collection. His attempts at answers, some of which are inflected with absurdity or humour, range across the thin skin between comedy and tragedy, irony and sincerity, nature versus culture, nostalgia and love, amateurism and value, and more. Defying, at every turn, a signature style, Holden has explored

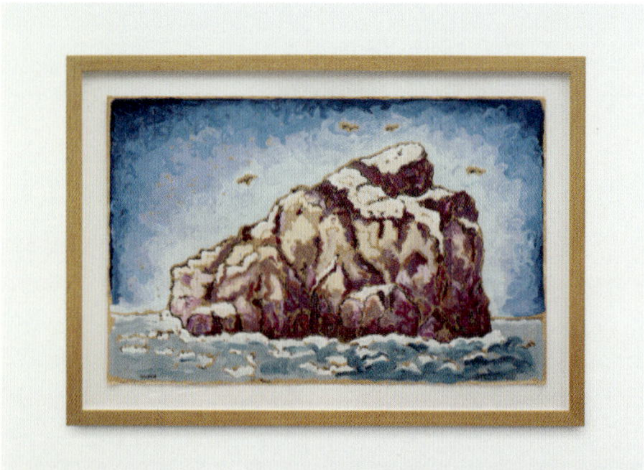

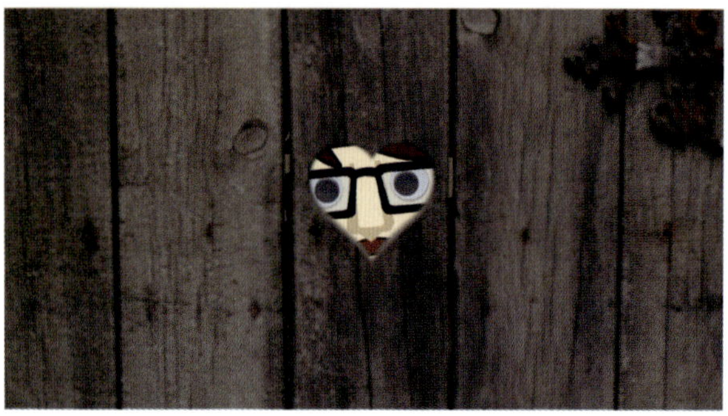

↑ *Bastion of Empire*, 2009, emulsion paint on brown paper, 90 × 120 cm (35 ⅜ × 47 ¼ in.). Collection Hidde van Seggelen
↑ *What Is Love?*, 2018, animated video, 4 mins.
↓ *What a Time to be Alive*, 2017, animated video, 7 mins.

a vast array of approaches – from delivering lectures and shaping theoretical frameworks, to writing, creating animations, installation, painting and sculpture. His artworks can be as tangible as a giant knitted pyramid, as modest as an amateur painting bought in a charity shop, or as subtle as a query about the relationship of physics to cartoons.

Holden often inserts himself into his artworks, playing a version of himself as a kind of baffled everyman – someone who is curious to not only know more about himself and his place in the world but what the world actually is and how to best navigate it. His approach – which combines a formidable amount of analysis tempered by the vagaries of the creative mind – is not dissimilar to that of a physicist trying to understand time: a universe of possibility dictated by a set of seemingly incontrovertible rules that must, paradoxically, be challenged in order to move forwards.

In 2021, *Andy Holden, Collected Free Labour: Blog Interviews 2010–2021* was published by Slimvolume. It was conceived as a means of compiling the many responses Holden had provided to a decade-long, dizzying range of queries from various specialist online platforms – from art and craft to science and music. The result – what the editor, Tyler Woolcott, describes as a 'whirlwind of metonymical references'[1] – is both a compilation and a portrait of sorts, of an artist for whom the accrual of knowledge is, and will forever be, a work in progress. As well as questions about the motivation and meaning behind his various creations,

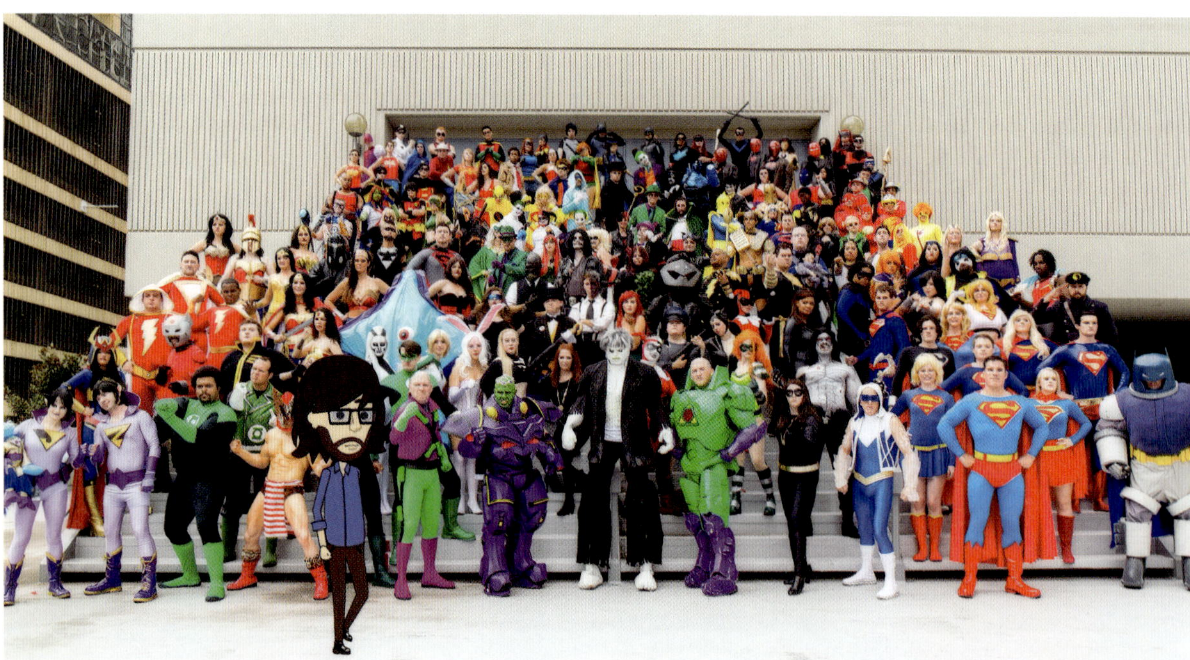

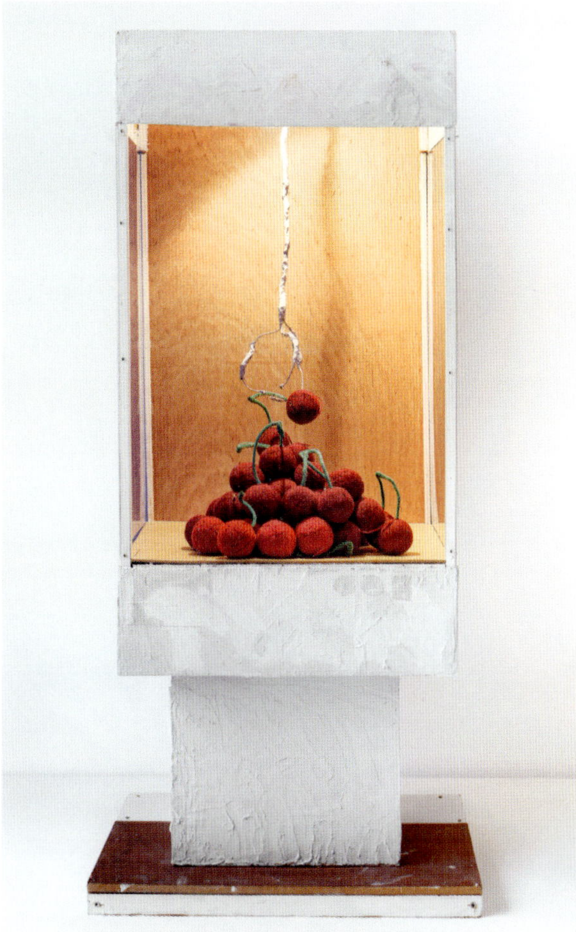

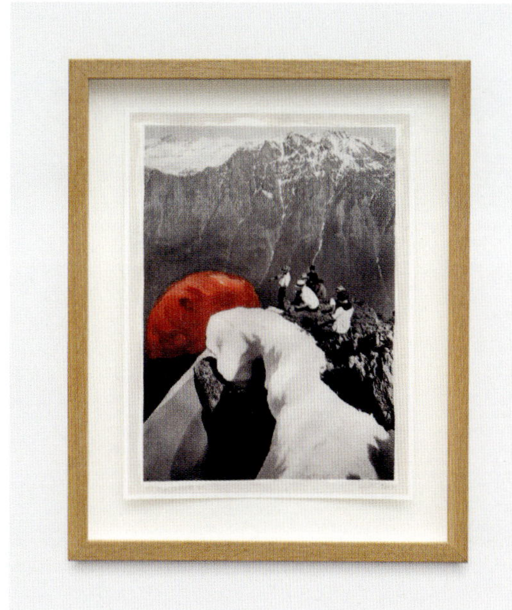

← *Untitled (Cherry Picker)*, 2006, wood, plaster and knitted fruit, 50 × 50 × 180 cm (19 ¾ × 19 ¾ × 70 ⅞ in.). Private collection

↑ *Unquiet Grave*, 2006, print on Somerset Rag, 38 × 27 cm (15 × 11 in.), edition of 10

the artist was quizzed about issues that beat at the restless, inquisitive heart of his work: 'How would you describe love?'; 'are you interested in linguistics?'; 'does interpretation get us closer to knowing the thing?'; 'do you subscribe to the multi-worlds theory?'. His answers are unfiltered, open, vulnerable; Holden is clearly less interested in propounding his knowledge than in dissecting his own ignorance. A throughline is his indifference to the hierarchical categories that have long dominated traditional art history – the assumption that paintings and sculptures made by professional artists are the pinnacle of human achievement. He is as fascinated by works by the great masters as he is by cartoonists and the passion of hobbyists. A case in point: asked by Rosanna Head 'what or who inspires you?', Holden cites 'the best cartoons by Chuck Jones, such as Duck Amuck' and 'some paintings by El Greco that I will always love – I like paintings of saints, I've noticed.'[2]

For this book, a loosely chronological cross-section of works that encapsulate the breadth of his artistic and philosophical enquiry has been selected. Each of them evolved from what he describes as a 'formative moment in the construction of subjectivity':[3] moments transformed into artworks that have helped him to better understand the present and prompted a new set of enquiries that will, no doubt, accompany him on his journey into the future.

Accompanying Holden on his pursuit of knowledge as he weaves from the English suburbs to the Egyptian pyramids, gazing up at the infinite variations of the night sky, tripping through cartoon landscapes and contemplating the 'gooey space' of 'thingly time' is nothing short of exhilarating; a journey of discovery which might well prompt the reader to look afresh at this strange, often contradictory, demanding and often wondrous world we share.

1 Tyler Woolcott quoted by Andy Hunt, 'The Critic as Artist as Cartoon', in *Collected Free Labour: Blog Interviews, 2010–2021*, Slimvolume, 2021, p. 84.
2 *Andy Holden, Collected Free Labour: Blog Interviews, 2010–2021*, Slimvolume, 2021, p. 3.
3 Andy Holden, email to Jennifer Higgie, 30 January 2025.

Pyramid Piece and Return of the Pyramid Piece

2008

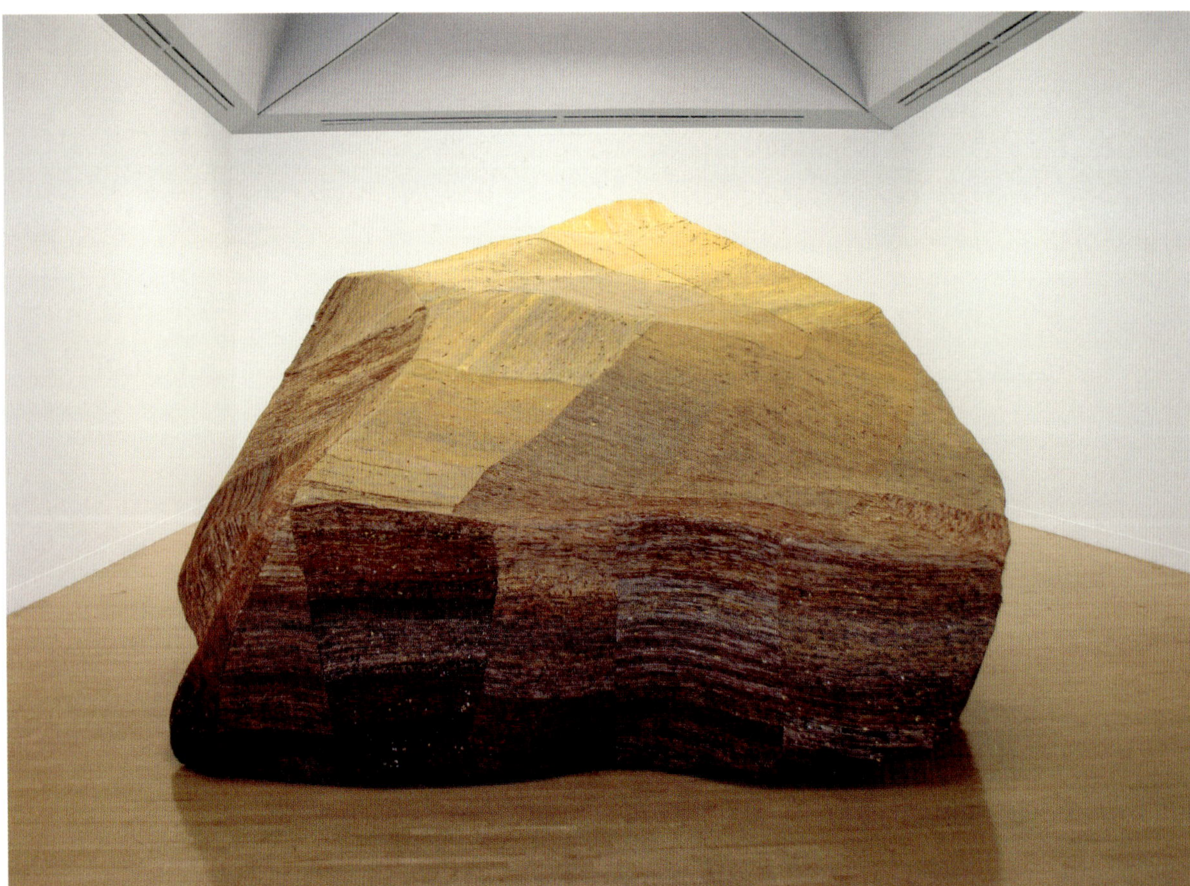

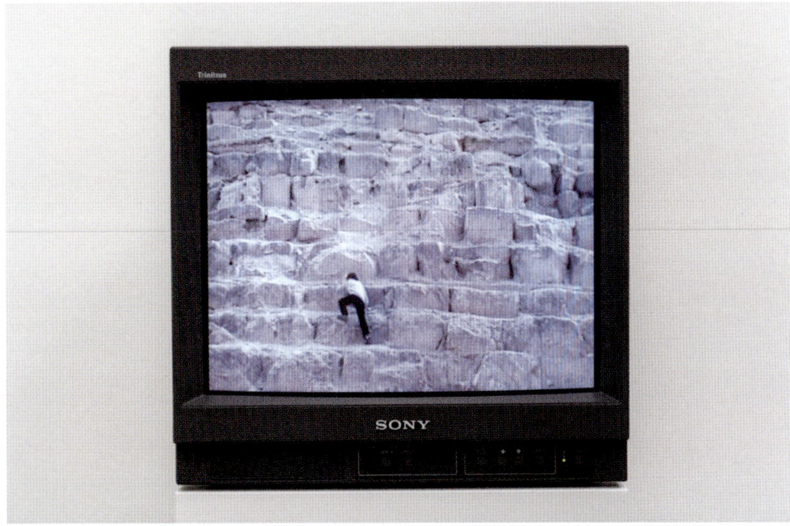

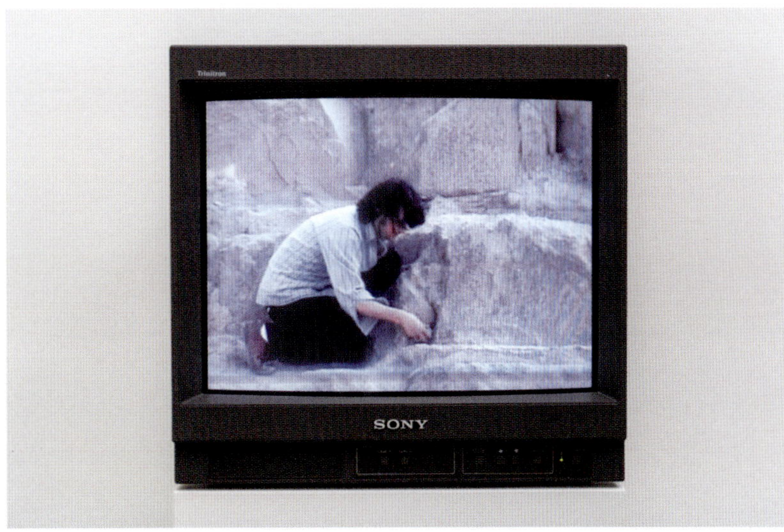

← *Pyramid Piece*, 2008, knitted yarns, foam and steel frame, 4.5 × 3.8 × 3 m (14 ¾ × 12 ½ × 9 ¾ ft.), installation view, *Andy Holden: Art Now*, Tate Britain, London, 2010
→ *Return of the Pyramid Piece*, 2008, video, 6 mins 50 secs., installation view and collection Kröller-Müller Museum, Netherlands

Guilt can be manifested, and exorcised, in many ways. In 1992, when Andy Holden was ten, he stole a small piece of rock from the Great Pyramid of Giza in Egypt, where his father was lecturing on bird migration. When they returned to England, his father discovered his son's crime and, annoyed, made clear that if everyone took a piece of the pyramids, they would eventually cease to exist – words that, over the years, haunted the young Holden. Overwhelmed with a need to redeem his youthful crime, in 2008 he travelled back to Egypt to find the exact spot he'd taken the rock from and put it back.

By chance, in a Cairo café Holden met a man called Hassan. Despite the fact that Hassan had never used a video camera before, Holden asked him to film him returning the rock to its rightful place. Hassan obliged; his inexperience resulting in a series of shaky zooms, which aptly lends the resultant four-and-a-half-minute film *Return of the Pyramid Piece* (2008) a slapstick mood of urgency, anxiety and instability. Holden, a small, baffled figure on the flank of the pyramid, scrabbles across giant boulders, his memory refusing to divulge the rock's original resting place. The enormity of the pyramid, its antiquity and its erosion, render Holden's need to make reparations at once absurd and moving. The sense of futility is intensified by the soundtrack, performed by Holden's nine-piece 'art pop group' The Grubby Mitts, which evokes the percussive sound of a marble dropping through the wooden rings of a child's toy.

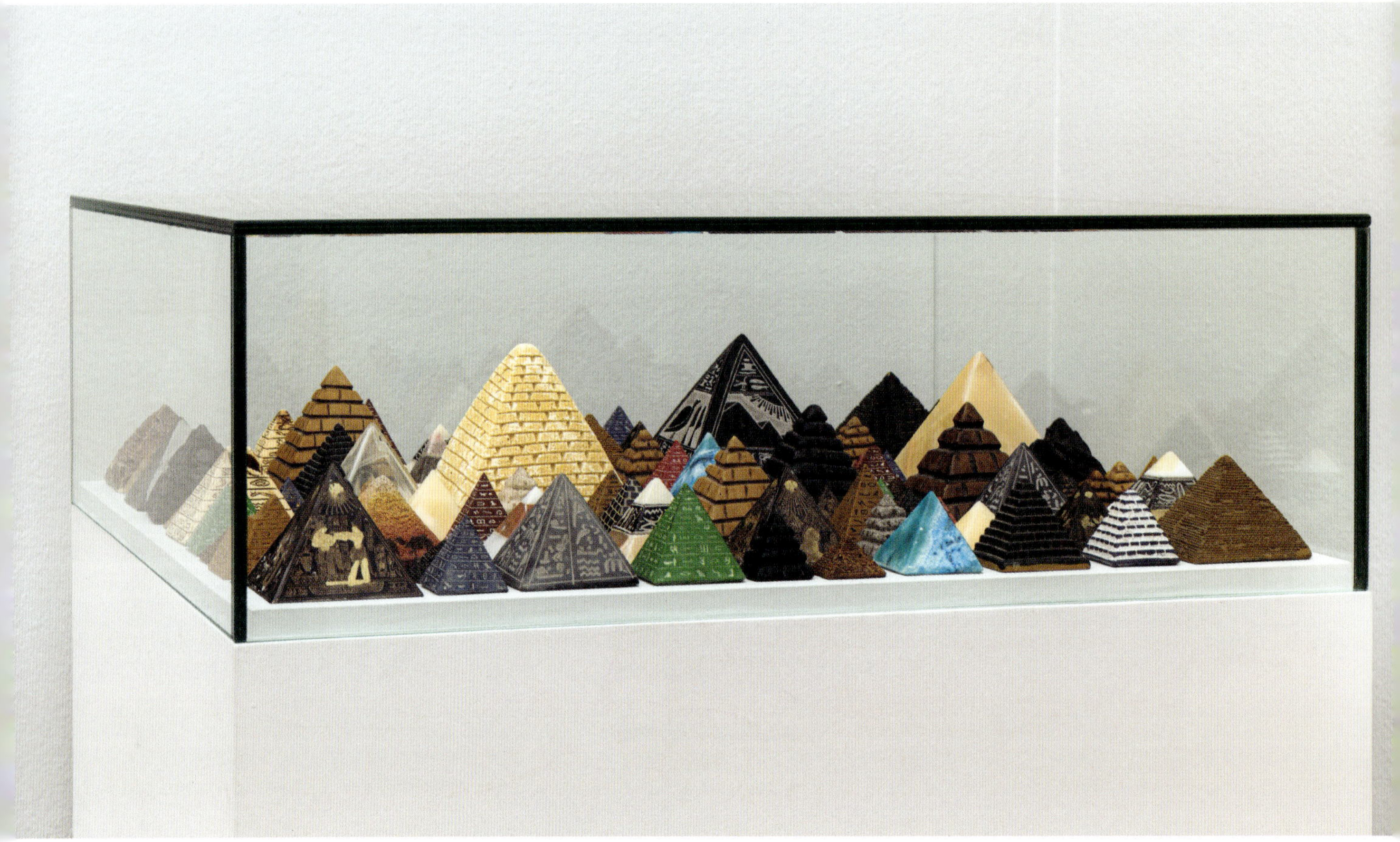

Back in Cairo, Holden became fascinated by the amount of pyramid souvenirs on sale. It made him realise how important it had been to him as a child to have an authentic piece of the pyramid. To reiterate the absurd gulf between reality and representation, the artist decided to collect as many versions of the souvenir as possible – a unique monument reimagined as a cheap, mass-produced object. The collection became *In Search of an Ending* (2008).

The work has a wider symbolic meaning, beyond a youthful transgression. Alongside his personal exorcism, Holden was, in his words, trying to 'tap into the collective unconscious of the British guilt around the taking of cultural artefacts, touching a nerve about what should go back.... I hoped it could describe a movement between the microcosmic and macrocosmic. It is a work about guilt, first personal, then colonial.'[1]

Return of the Pyramid Piece was the starting point for a vast new work. Back in England, Holden decided to make what he describes as 'a monument to the piece of the monument'.[2] Over the course of a year, he created a model of the stolen stone, enlarged 100 times in length and 100,000 times in volume – a size approximate to his sense of guilt. According to Lizzie Carey-Thomas, who curated the work when it was presented at Tate Britain in 2010, the artist's aim was to 'convey the childish, awestruck incomprehension he experienced during his first encounter with the pyramids, "an unknowing confrontation with material" untouched by any real understanding or historical context'.[3]

↑ *In Search of an Ending*, 2008, collected pyramid souvenirs, variable dimensions. Collection Kröller-Müller Museum, Netherlands

→ *Pyramid Piece*, 2008, knitted yarns, foam and steel frame, 4.5 × 3.8 × 3 m (14 ¾ × 12 ½ × 9 ¾ ft.), installation view and collection Kröller-Müller Museum, Netherlands

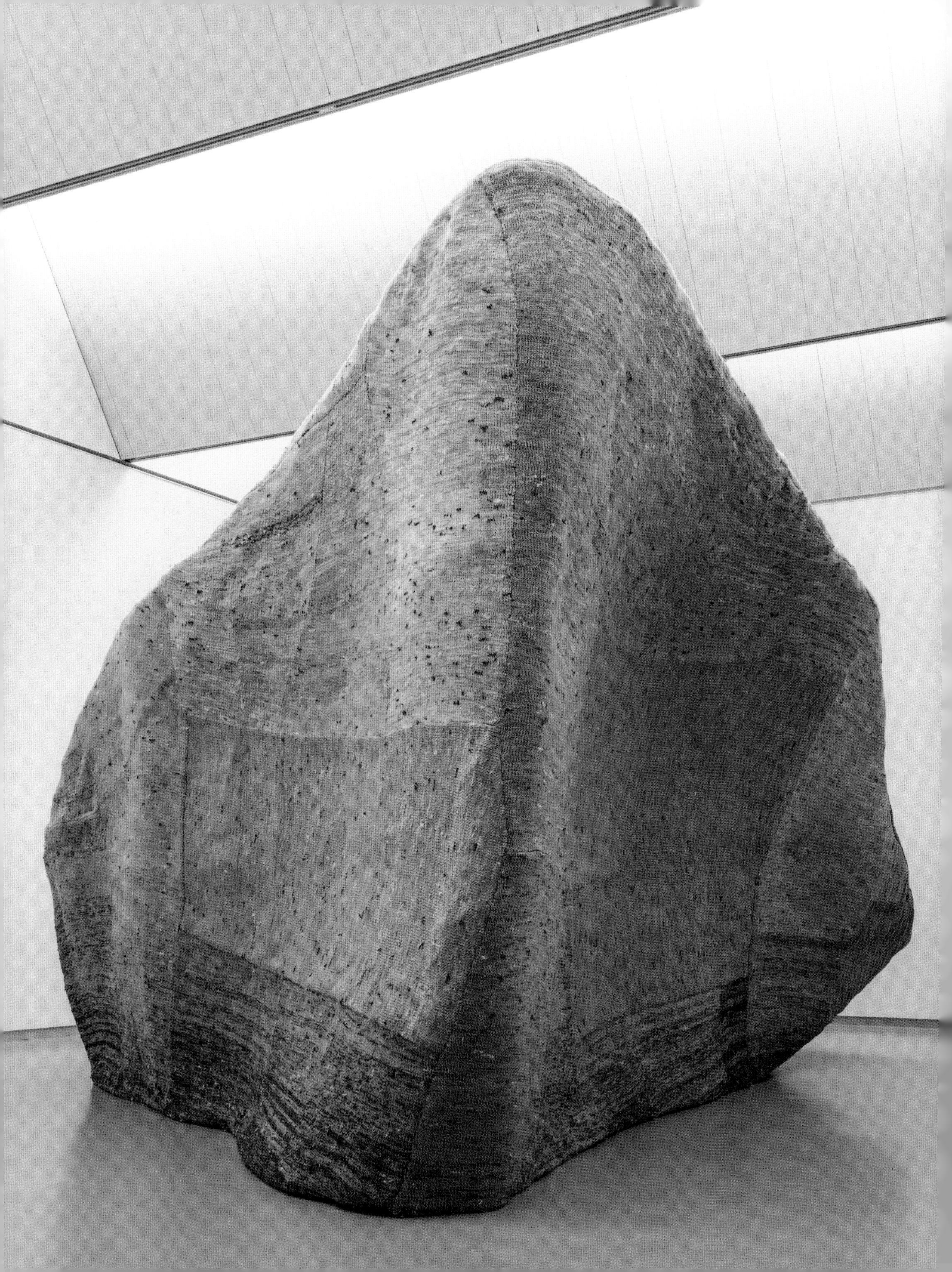

To transform his memory and his guilt into something concrete, Holden stretched upholstery foam over a steel framework and, using a small knitting machine, created a cover that ripples in undulating patchworks of colour, like sunshine hitting a rock, from light yellow to dark brown. Holden's use of knitting is an inversion of sorts: knitted objects are usually worn, intimate, easily held. (The suggestion of 'spinning a yarn' also springs to mind.) The creation of the *Pyramid Piece* sculpture was a long, laborious, repetitive process that resulted in a work that is as absurd and enigmatic as it is moving – a testament to the fact that, in art, the significance of an object is often greater than the sum of its parts.

The artist's desire to prompt a debate around the return of cultural artefacts was successful. The press seized upon the work, and it was mentioned in discussions around repatriation. A spokesperson from the British Museum's Egyptian department said: 'The removal of any material from an archaeological site is damaging and we hope that this artwork showing the artist returning this piece will encourage other people to be more responsible when they visit such sites.'[4] Dr. John DeSalvo, the Director of the Great Pyramid of Giza Research Association, remarked: 'Breaking a piece off the pyramid is definitely not the right thing to do, but I can understand why he felt overpowered by the magnificence of the pyramids and wanted a memento. I applaud his attempt to make reparations and hope his work will encourage interest in the pyramids.'[5]

1 Andy Holden, email to Jennifer Higgie, 30 January 2025.
2 'Art Now*:* Andy Holden', Tate Shots, *Pyramid Piece*, 2010, https://www.tate.org.uk/whats-on/tate-britain/art-now-andy-holden. Accessed 2 Mar 2026.
3 Lizzie Carey-Thomas, exhibition text, 'Andy Holden*:* Pyramid Piece and the Return of the Pyramid Piece', Art Now, Tate Britain, London, 2010.
4 Royanikkhah, 'Tate show reveals artist's pyramid theft', *The Daily Telegraph*, 10 January 2010.
5 Ibid.

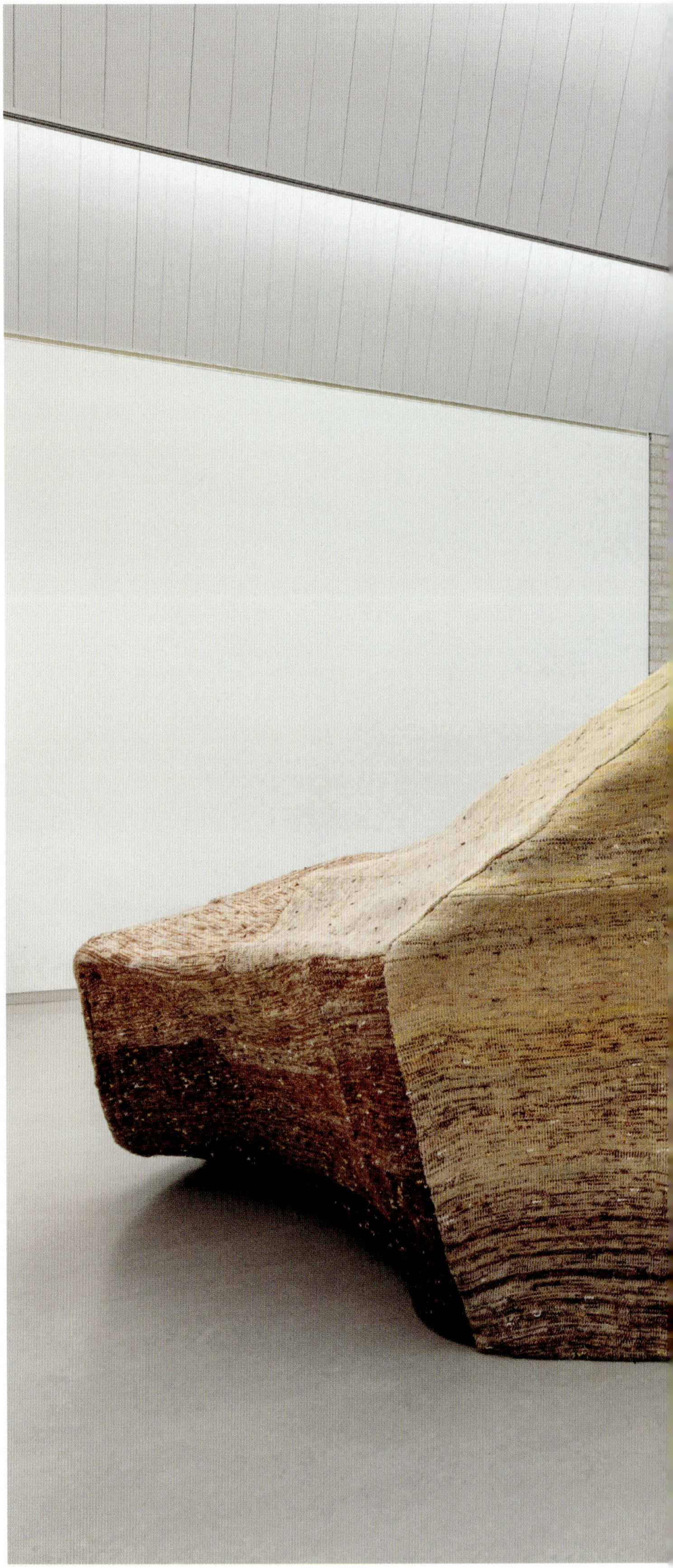

→ *Pyramid Piece*, 2008, knitted yarns, foam and steel frame, 4.5 × 3.8 × 3 m (14 ¾ × 12 ½ × 9 ¾ ft.), installation view and collection Kröller-Müller Museum, Netherlands

↠ (Overleaf) *Pyramid Piece*, 2008, knitted yarns, foam and steel frame, 4.5 × 3.8 × 3 m (14 ¾ × 12 ½ × 9 ¾ ft.), installation view, Kunstfort Vijfhuizen, Netherlands. Collection Kröller-Müller Museum

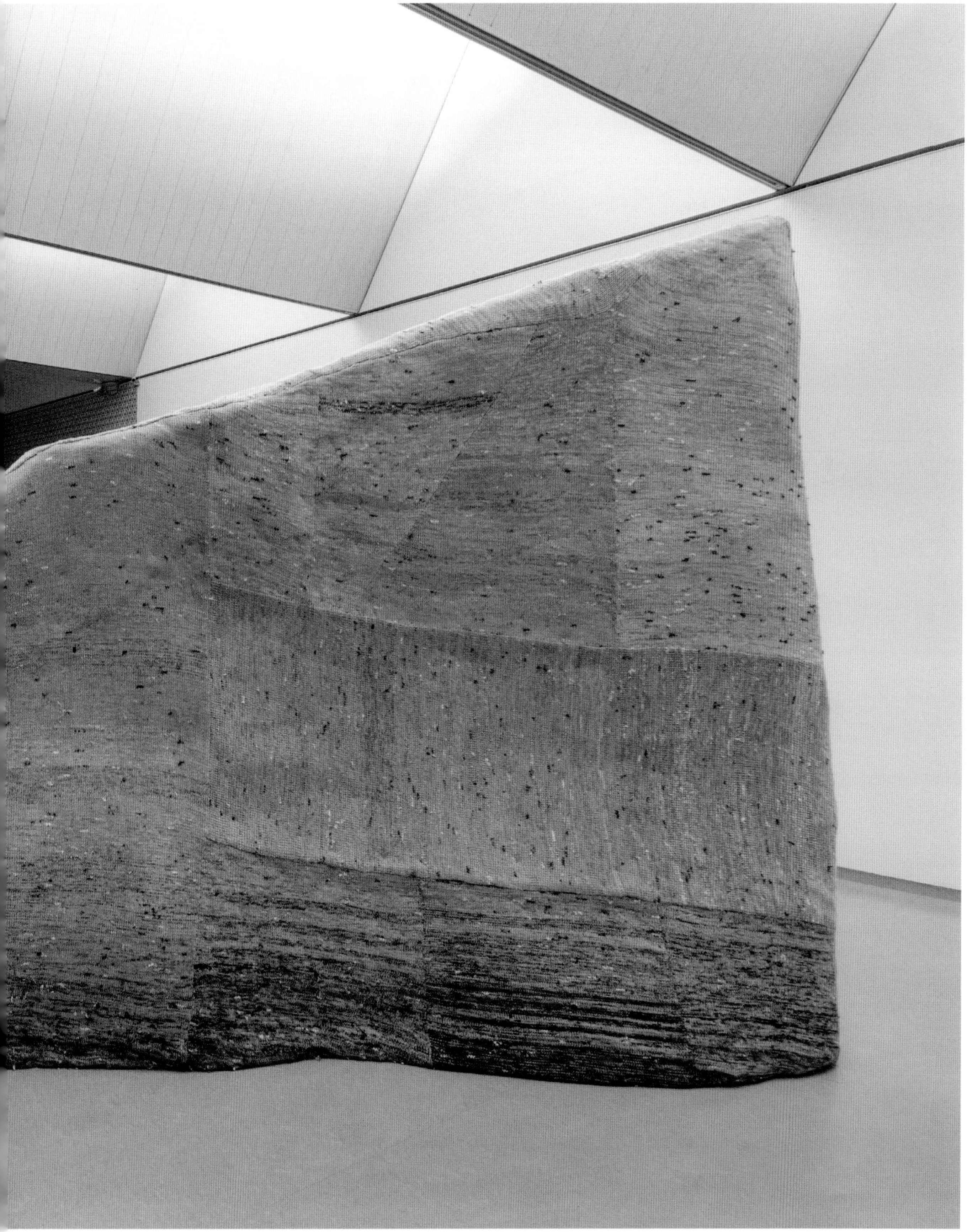

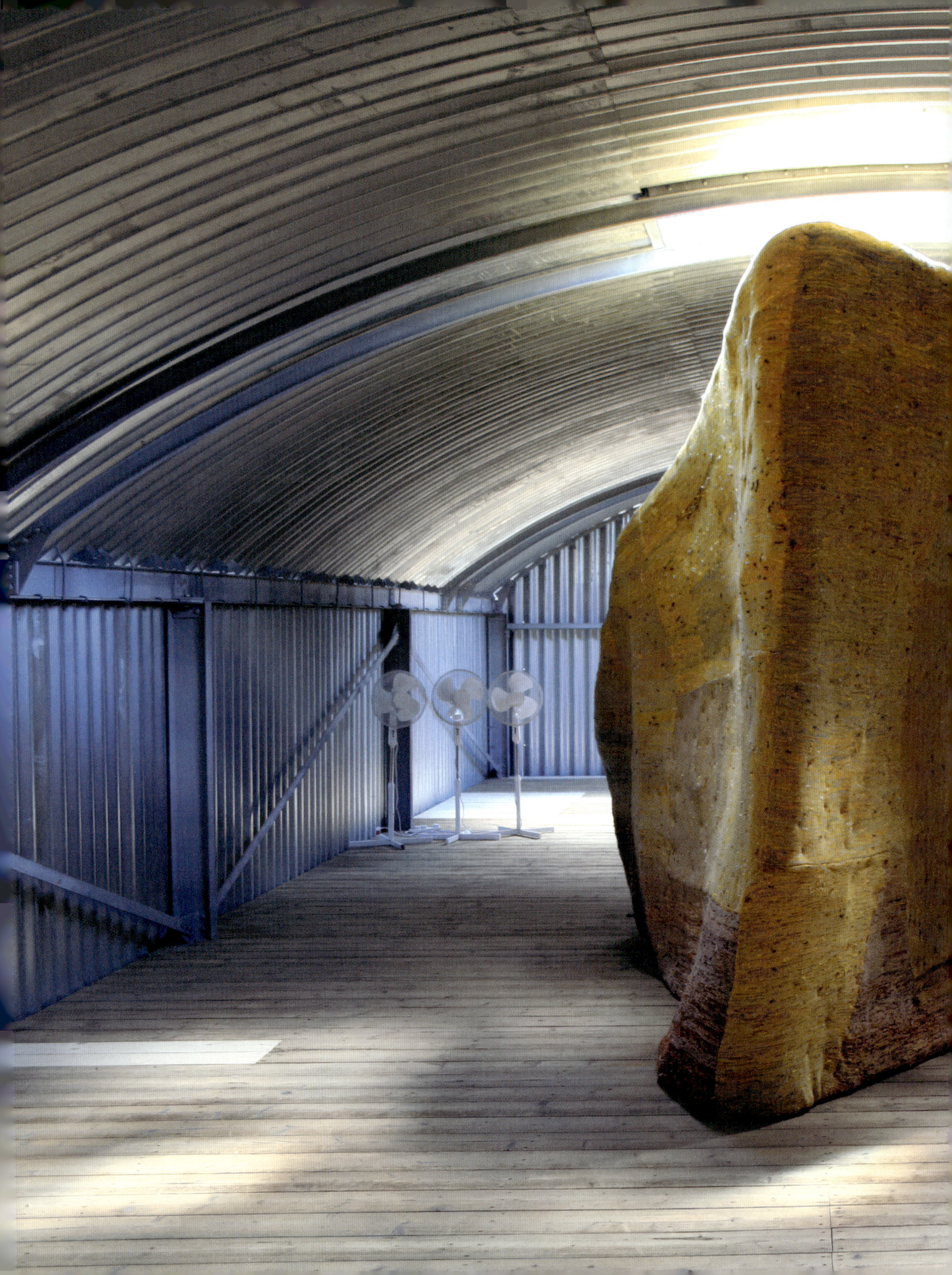

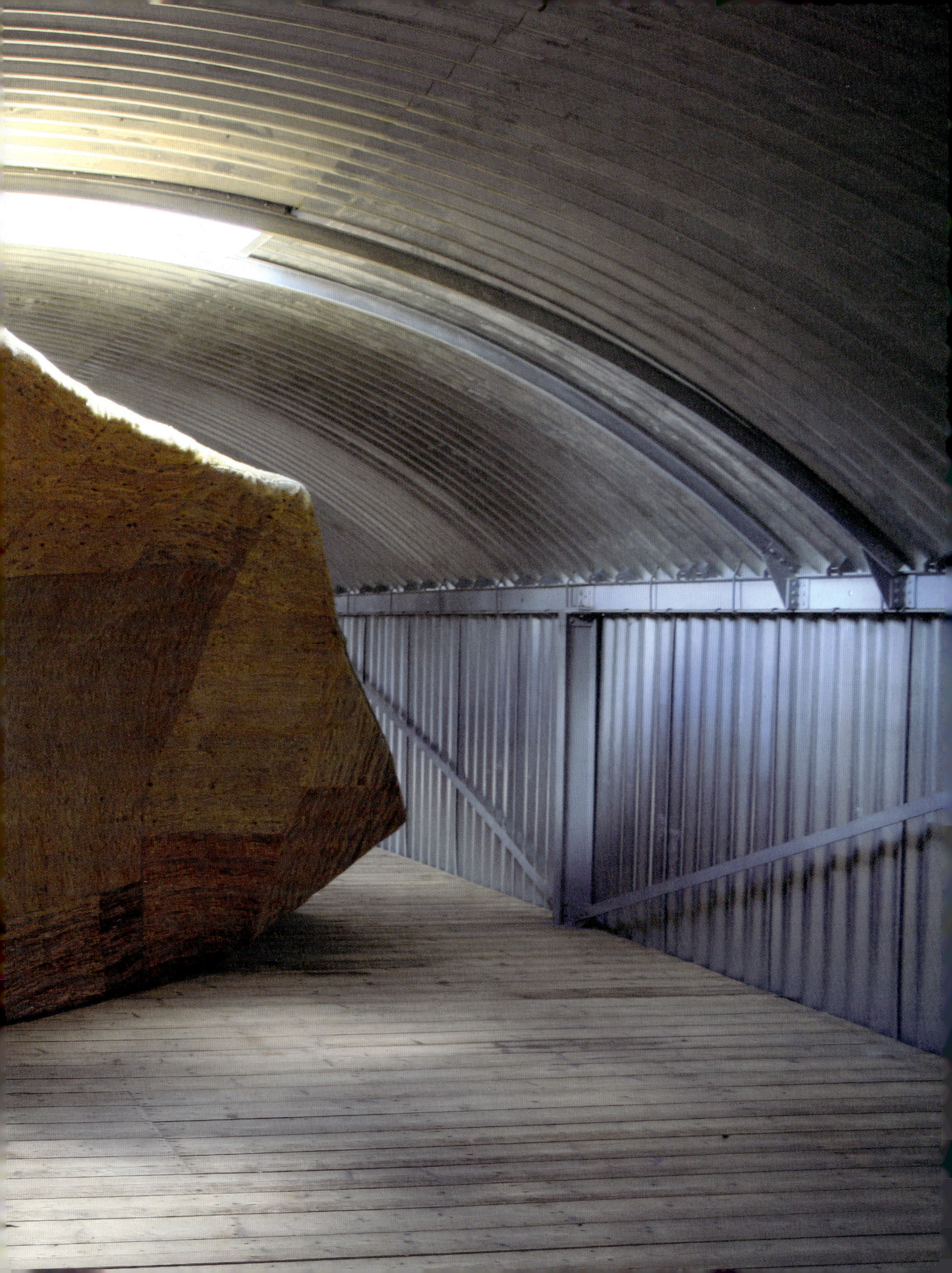

The Dan Cox Library for the Unfinished Concept of Thingly Time

2011, revised 2023

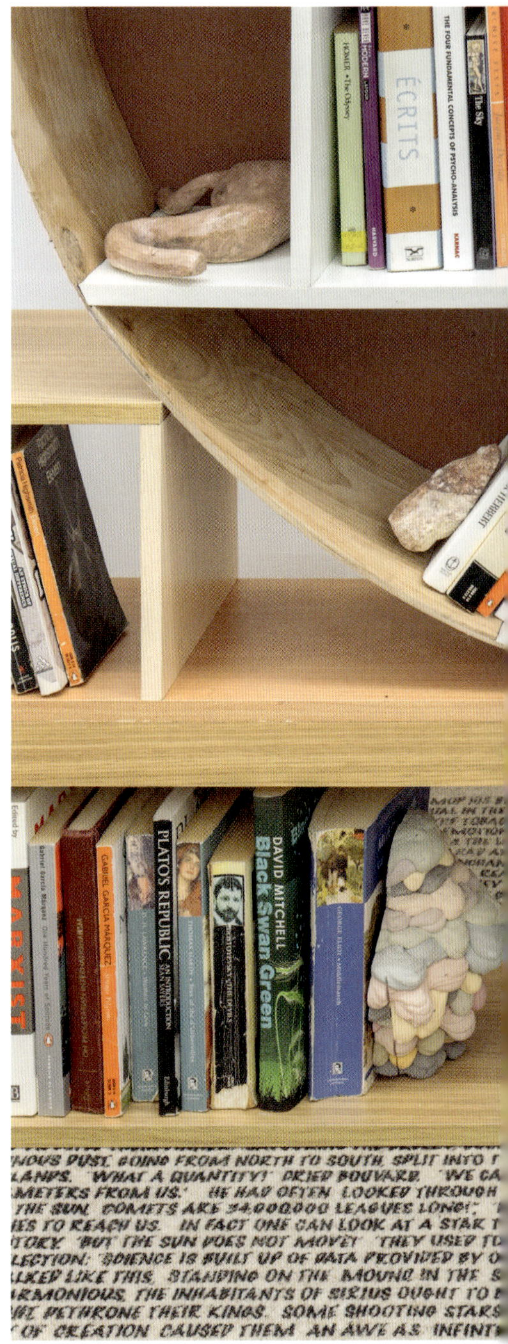

The Dan Cox Library for the Unfinished Concept of Thingly Time came about because of a tragedy. Andy Holden's close friend Dan Cox was the 'theoretical advisor' for the artist's 2011 exhibition at Kettle's Yard in Cambridge, UK but, during preparations for the show, he was knocked off his bicycle and died. The pair had been recording their conversations, using two books as springboards to shape their thinking: Gustave Flaubert's unfinished satirical novel *Bouvard et Pécuchet* from 1881 – in which two bumbling clerks try and fail to master agriculture, science, archaeology, literature, gardening, politics, love, philosophy, religion, pedagogy and more – and Thomas Pynchon's experimental and anti-authoritarian *Gravity's Rainbow* (1973), which pivots on the design and dispatch of V-2 rockets by the German military during World War II. Holden wrote:

> We saw the dialogue as horizontal, a metonymic unfolding, from Charlie Brown's round head to the Boulder to the Cherry, which would then be annotated with moments of interruption, close readings, contradictions, metaphoric moments that paused the movement for a minute. These would be extensive footnotes, digressions, attempted conclusions, by writers both Dan and I hoped could shed more light on subjects which were, after all, their subjects and not ours.[1]

↓ *Library for the Unfinished Concept of Thingly Time*, 2011–ongoing, books, furniture, plaster, bronze, natural materials, soft-furnishing and collected works, variable dimensions, installation view, Seventeen, London, 2023

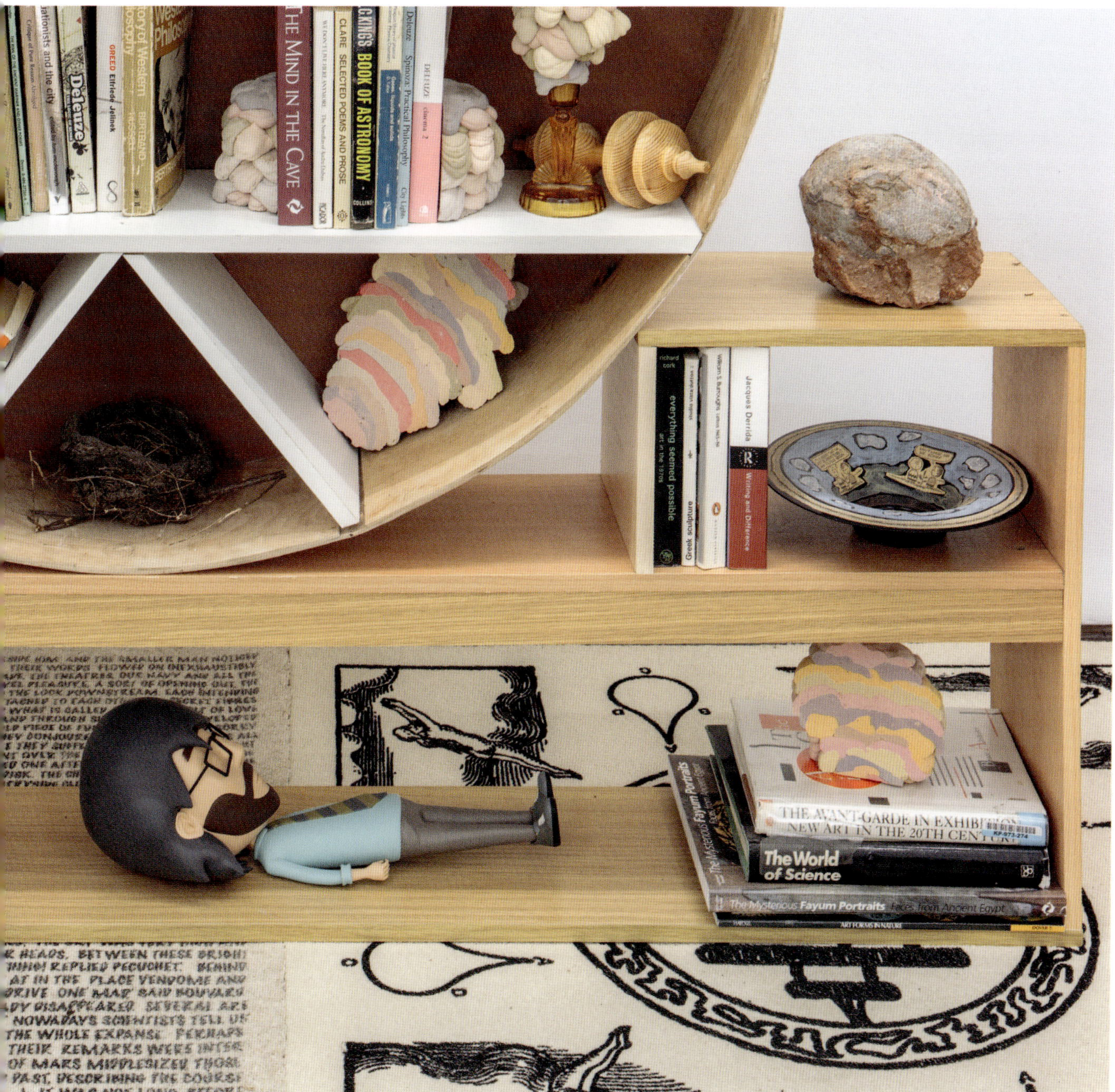

Cox had suggested a title for the project, 'Chewy Cosmos Thingly Time', after spotting the slogan 'a chewy cosmos of peanuts and caramel' on a Cadbury Starbar. His concept of 'Thingly Time' is, in the artist's words, 'a description of how an object can communicate something that is absent; how an object can make a duration visible'.[2] It was to be Cox's 'Great Theory', a three-part division of Time as 'Intensive, Extensive, and Thingly' but at the time of his death, its conception was incomplete.[3]

Holden dedicated the central installation of the Kettle's Yard exhibition to his friend, titling it *The Dan Cox Library for the Unfinished Concept of Thingly Time*. It is an expanded memorial that houses myriad objects: sculptures in bronze and wood, 'totemic geological plaster works', a Peanuts cartoon about art, 3D-printed pieces that refer to older works by the artist and a reproduction of a drawing by Jean Cocteau of a semi-naked youth with a scythe inscribed with words that translate as 'time itself looks at the time of a universal watch'. The bookshelves, which are designed and made by Holden, display the books in Cox's possession at the time of his death – novels, notebooks and treatises on philosophy, art and politics. The installation also includes carpets printed with passages from *Bouvard et Pécuchet* and correspondence between Holden and the science fiction writer Ursula K. Le Guin, who wrote a text for its inception.

↓ *Library for the Unfinished Concept of Thingly Time*, 2011–ongoing, books, furniture, plaster, bronze, natural materials, soft-furnishing and collected works, variable dimensions, installation view, Cubitt, London, 2012
→ (As above) installation view, Seventeen, London, 2023

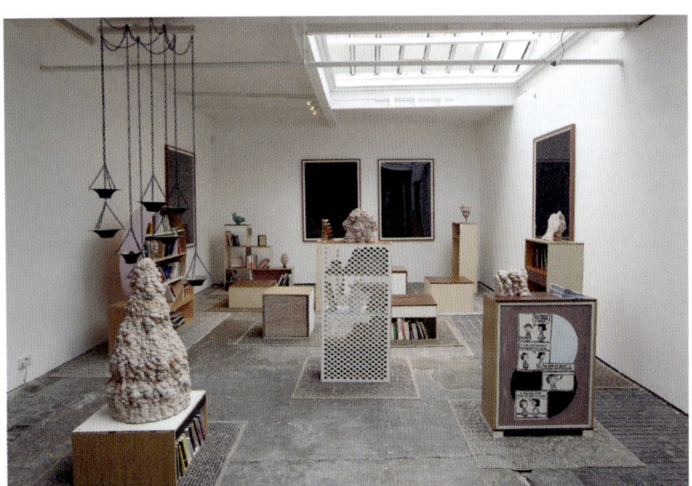

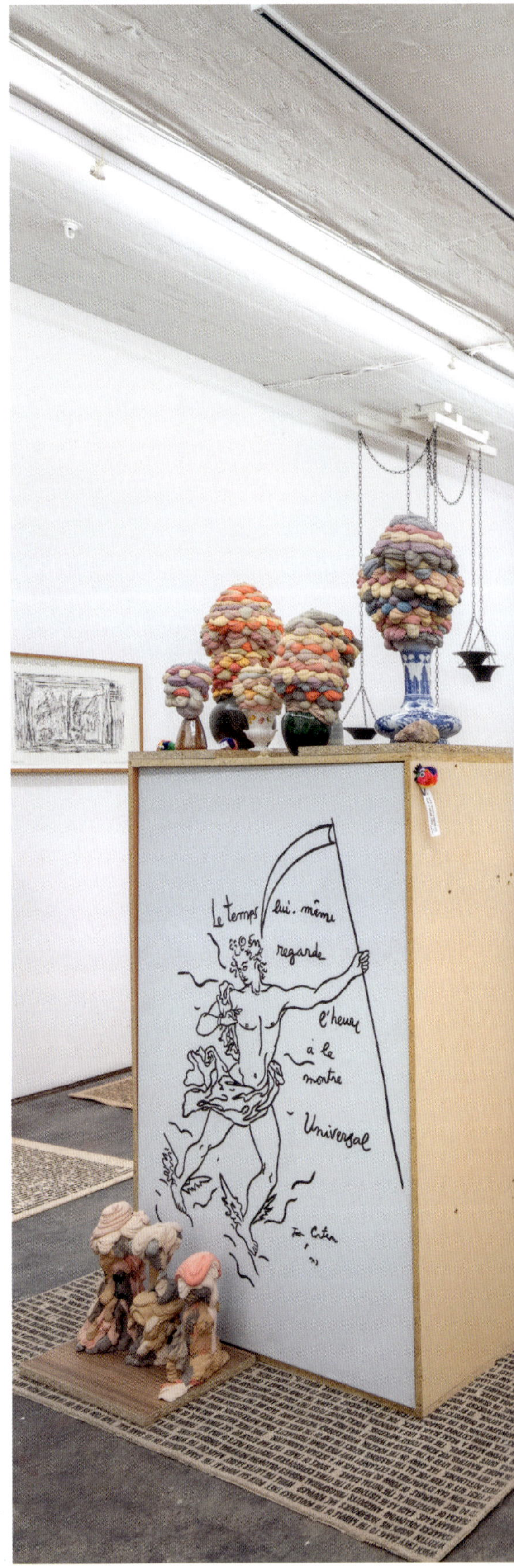

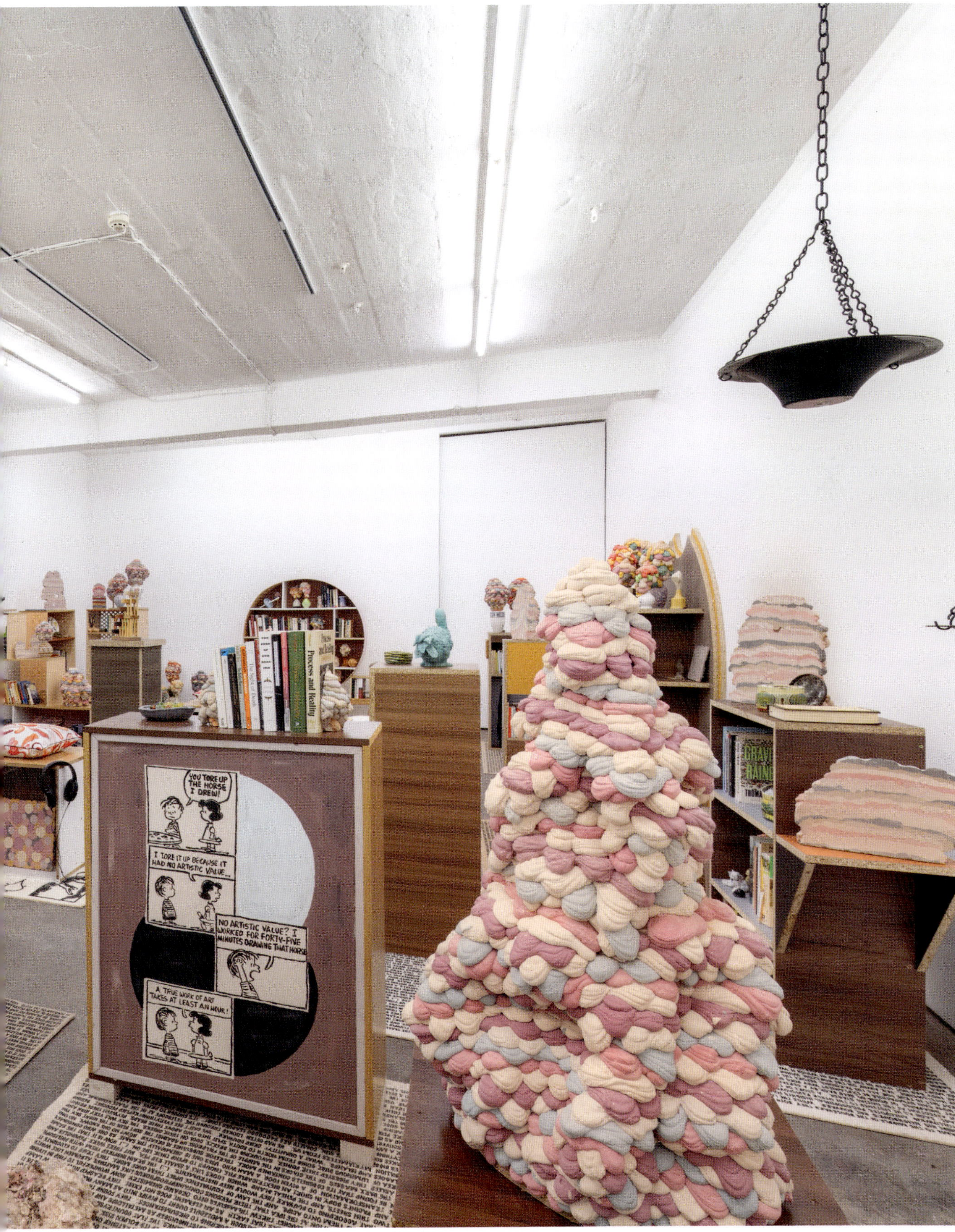
Process and Reality
YOU TORE UP THE HORSE I DREW!
I TORE IT UP BECAUSE IT HAD NO ARTISTIC VALUE...
NO ARTISTIC VALUE? I WORKED FOR FORTY-FIVE MINUTES DRAWING THAT HORSE!
A TRUE WORK OF ART TAKES AT LEAST AN HOUR!

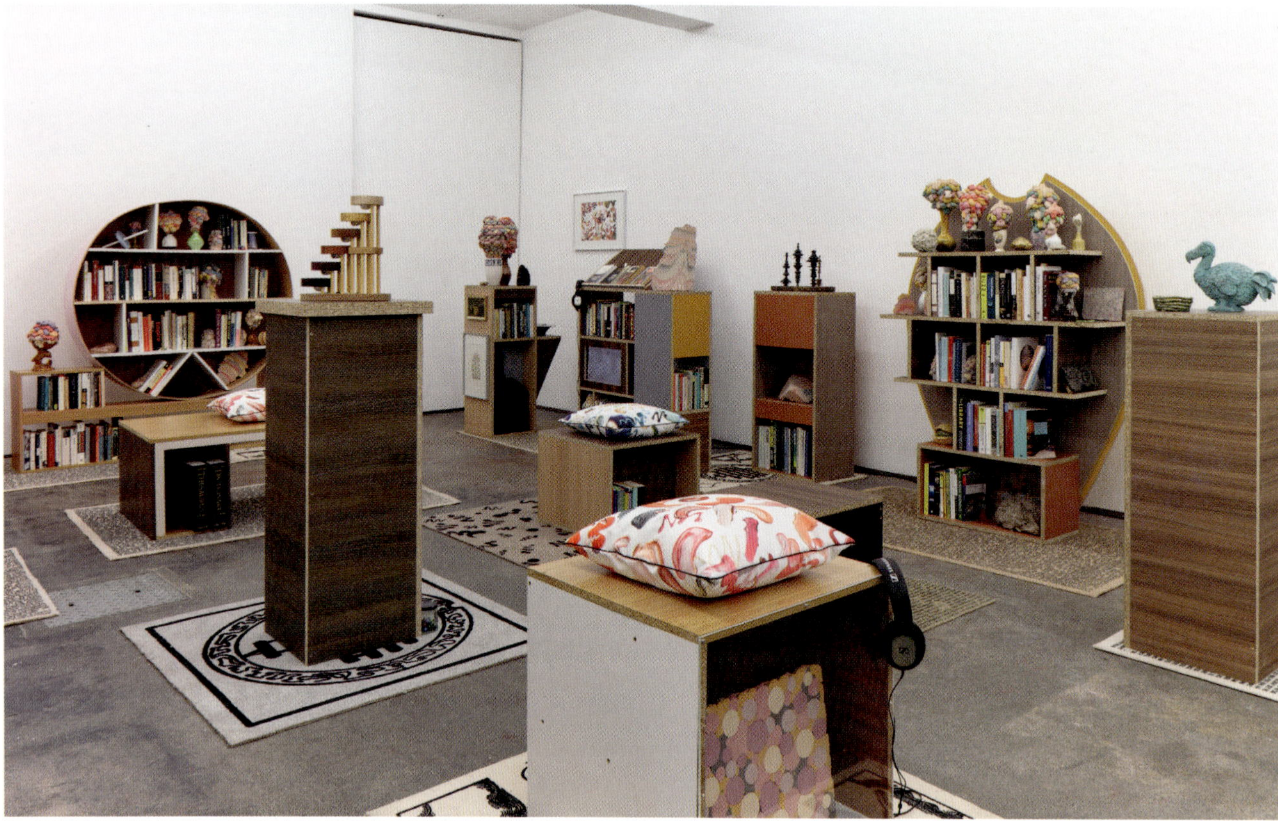

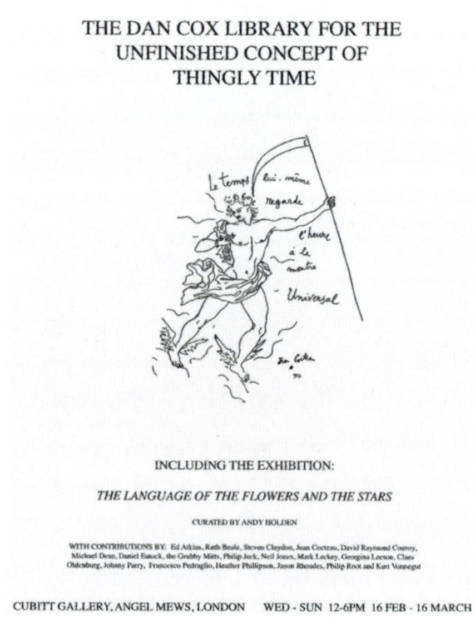

↑→ *Library for the Unfinished Concept of Thingly Time*, 2011–ongoing, books, furniture, plaster, bronze, natural materials, soft-furnishing and collected works, variable dimensions, installation view, Seventeen, London, 2023

↓ *The Dan Cox Library for the Unfinished Concept of Thingly Time, Poster for Cubitt, London*, 2012, screenprinted poster, 51 × 39 cm (20 1/8 × 15 3/8 in.)

The library is part of the long tradition of the Wunderkammer – a wonder room in which texts and objects are placed together to spark new associations, meanings and conversations. It embodies the great art historian Aby Warburg's 'law of the good neighbour' – the idea that when browsing shelves or catalogues for a particular work a reader might be drawn to the ones on either side of it, which might then in turn prompt new ways of thinking. However, solitary reading is not the only activity in *The Dan Cox Library for the Unfinished Concept of Thingly Time*. Over the years, it has hosted reading groups, exhibitions and performances by artists who are interested in exploring what 'Thingly Time' might be.

In 2023, the library was included in Holden's solo exhibition 'Song of Songs' at Seventeen gallery in East London. Committed to the idea that it is a living, evolving entity, the artist expanded it to accommodate new books and sculptures. Alongside the library's original collection of sculptures, books, posters and furniture, Holden designed four new cabinets – one based on a diagram of a beehive – to house books the

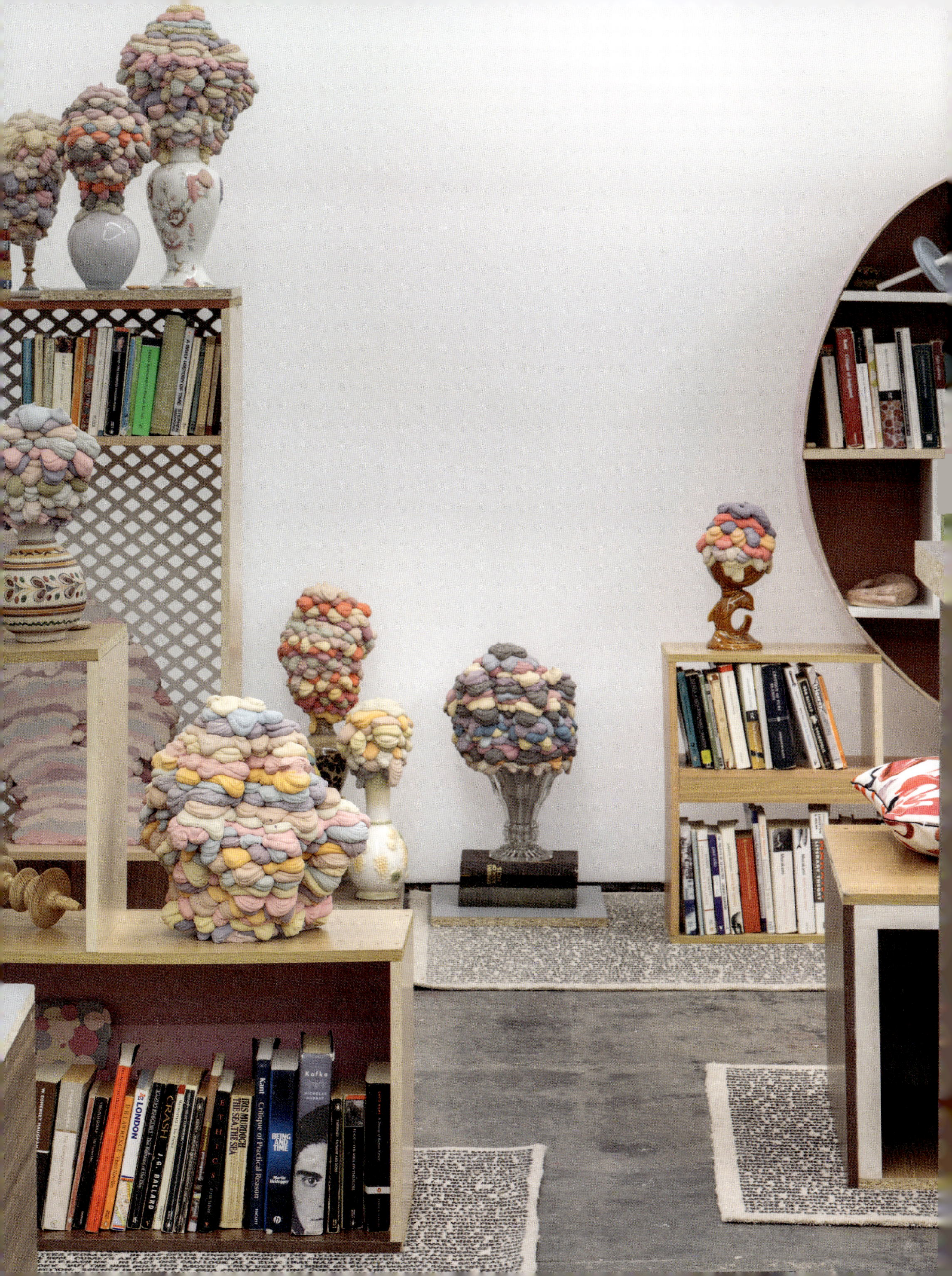

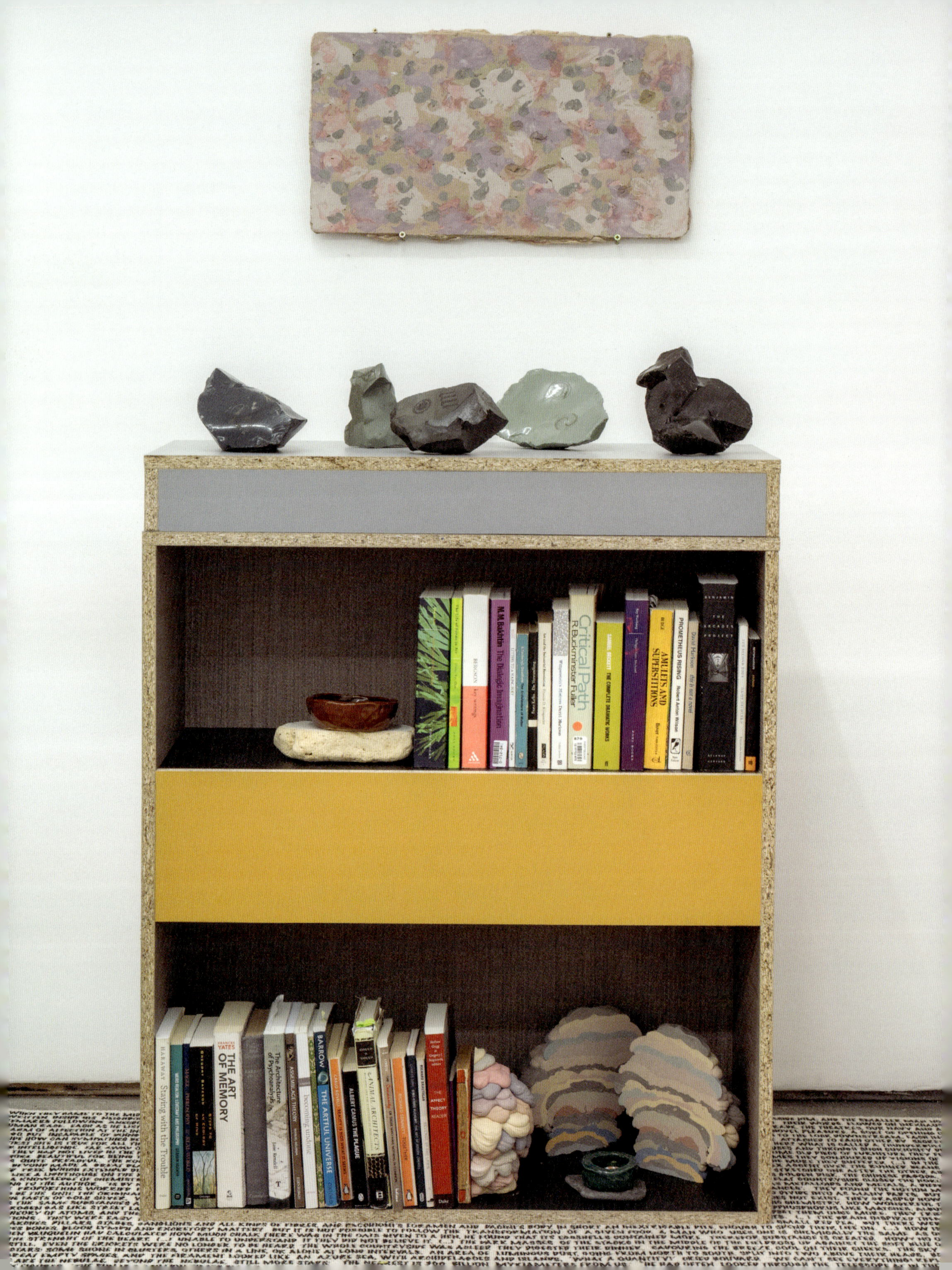
M.M.Bakhtin The Dialogic Imagination
Critical Path
R.Buckminster Fuller
SAMUEL BECKETT THE COMPLETE DRAMATIC WORKS
AMULETS AND SUPERSTITIONS
PROMETHEUS RISING
Robert Anton Wilson
THE ARCADES PROJECT
HARAWAY Staying with the Trouble
FRANCES YATES
THE ART OF MEMORY
The Architecture of Psychoanalysis
becoming undone
BARROW
THE ARTFUL UNIVERSE
ALBERT CAMUS THE PLAGUE
ANIMAL ARCHITECTS
THE AFFECT THEORY READER

artist had read over the previous year on poetry, philosophy, psychoanalysis and physics. Many of them were themed around death and suicide, while relating to alternative notions of or reflections on time, exploring how the process of mourning affects the experience of time, lifting a veil and revealing its illusion.

Holden also added new bookends, made by slicing plaster pieces in half – like a cross-section of rocks – and new sculptures, including a number of *Ornamites* (a portmanteau of 'ornament' and 'stalagmite'), which comprise bulbous arrangements of coloured plasters in matte pinks, purples, blues, greens, beiges and lilacs that erupt, like lava, from various found ceramic vases. Objects from other series also entered the library: a small resin version of the *Auguries (Last Calls)* (2023), dedicated to birds on the edge of extinction; mosaics made from acrylic teeth; and four rocks that Holden took from the Thames embankment on a walk with his late partner, Mira Calix, a few weeks before she took her own life, which he had engraved with various diagrams taken from books in the library. The earlier carpet, which had been printed with lines from *Bouvard and Pécuchet*,

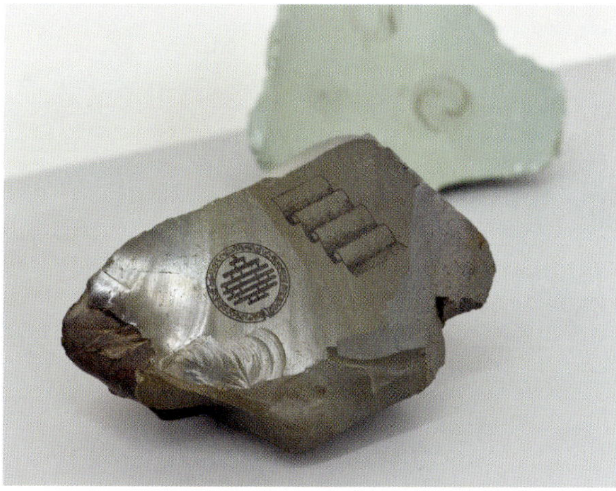

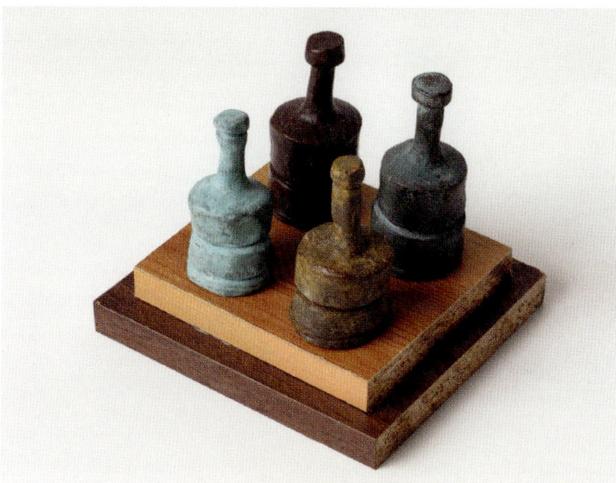

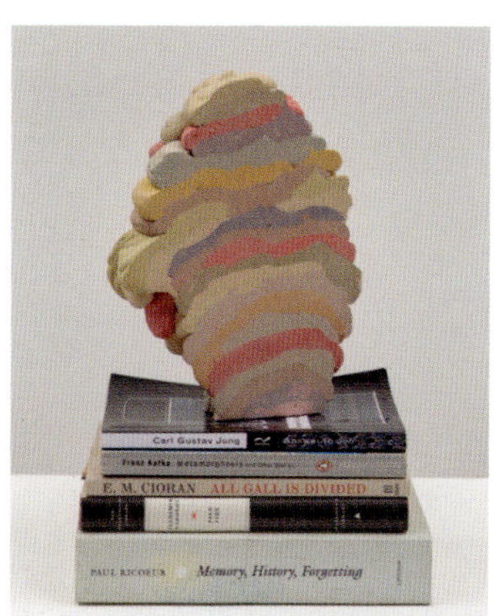

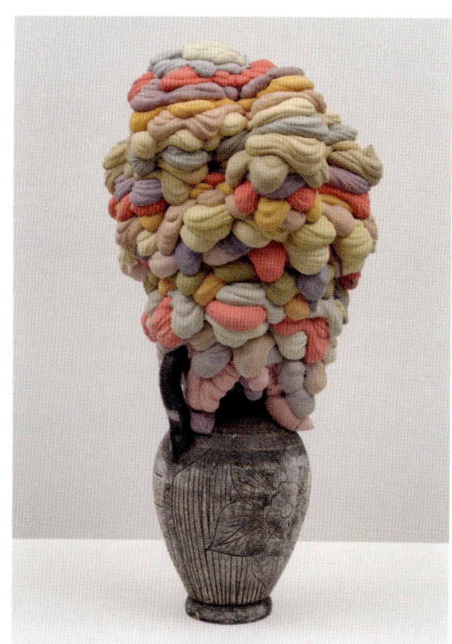

← *Library for the Unfinished Concept of Thingly Time*, 2011–ongoing, books, furniture, plaster, bronze, natural materials, soft-furnishing and collected works, variable dimensions, installation view, Seventeen, London, 2023
↑ *Library for the Unfinished Concept of Thingly Time*, 2011–ongoing, slag found in the river Thames with laser engraving, 20 × 13 × 12 cm (7 ⅞ × 5 ⅛ × 4 ¾ in.), installation view, Seventeen, London, 2023
↑ *Holden Family*, 2011, patina bronze and laminate wood, 15 × 15 × 12 cm (5 ⅞ × 5 ⅞ × 4 ¾ in.)
→ *Book End*, 2023, plaster and emulsion paint, 23 × 13 × 9 cm (9 ⅛ × 5 ⅛ × 3 ½ in.) and books
→ *Ornamite*, 2012, plaster and emulsion paint on vase, 40 × 15 × 15 cm (15 ¾ × 5 ⅞ × 5 ⅞ in.)

↓ *Pessimism of the Intellect, Optimism of the Will*, 2011, melted gramophone records with emulsion paint and collage, each: 22 × 22 × 8 cm (8 ⅝ × 8 ⅝ × 3 ⅛ in.), installation dimensions variable, installation view, Seventeen, London, 2023
↘ *Last Stop for the Good Old Times (Marble Run)*, 2011, wood turning by Geoffrey Leeson, 34 × 14 × 10 cm (13 ⅜ × 5 ½ × 3 ⅞ in.)
→ *Library for the Unfinished Concept of Thingly Time*, 2011–ongoing, books, furniture, plaster, bronze, natural materials, soft-furnishing and collected works, variable dimensions, installation view, Seventeen, London, 2023
↘ *Chewy Cosmos*, 2011, collage, 60 × 40 cm (23 ⅝ × 15 ¾ in.)

had worn out and was replaced with rugs printed with diagrammatic images. Holden writes:

> It remains an ongoing library that is both sculpture and resource. [It embodies] the idea that knowledge in books needs to be supplemented with a more haptic knowledge contained in objects. The work is permanently unfinished – and can only be finished by the presence of an observer. It invites people in to complete it.[4]

Talking about the importance of Flaubert's novel to the project, Holden remarked: 'It suggests that in the end, after all the research and experimentation with different kinds of knowledge, the only thing that was important was their friendship.'[5]

The conversation continues.

1 Andy Holden, introduction to the catalogue published on the occasion of 'Chewy Cosmos Thingly Time', Kettle's Yard, Cambridge, UK, 14 May–10 July 2011, p. 5.
2 *Andy Holden, Collected Free Labour: Blog Interviews, 2010–2021*, Slimvolume, 2021, p. 38.
3 Press release for 'The Dan Cox Library for the Unfinished Concept of Thingly Time', Cubitt gallery, London, 16 February–16 March 2012, https://andyholdenartist.com/dancoxlibrary. Accessed 2 Mar 2026.
4 Andy Holden, email to Jennifer Higgie, 6 November 2024.
5 *Andy Holden, Collected Free Labour: Blog Interviews, 2010–2021*, Slimvolume, 2021, p. 39.

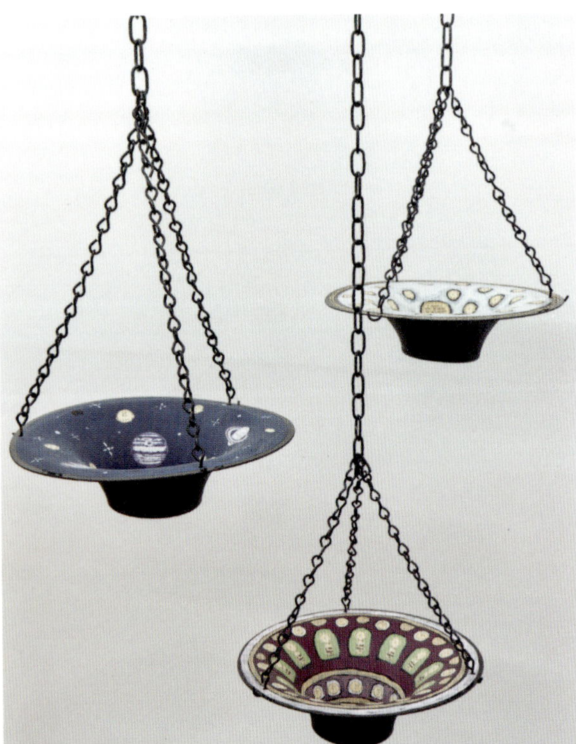

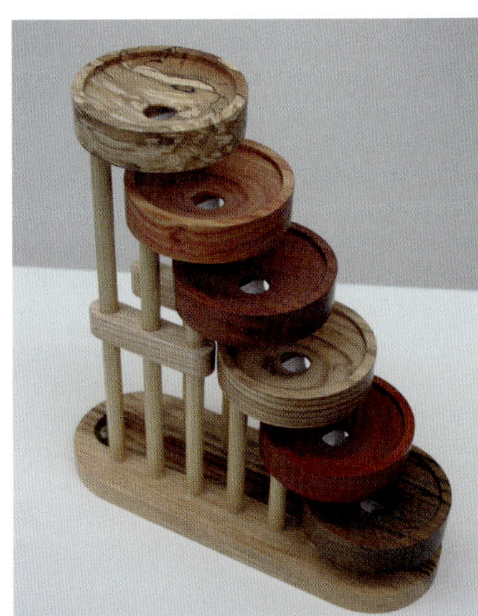

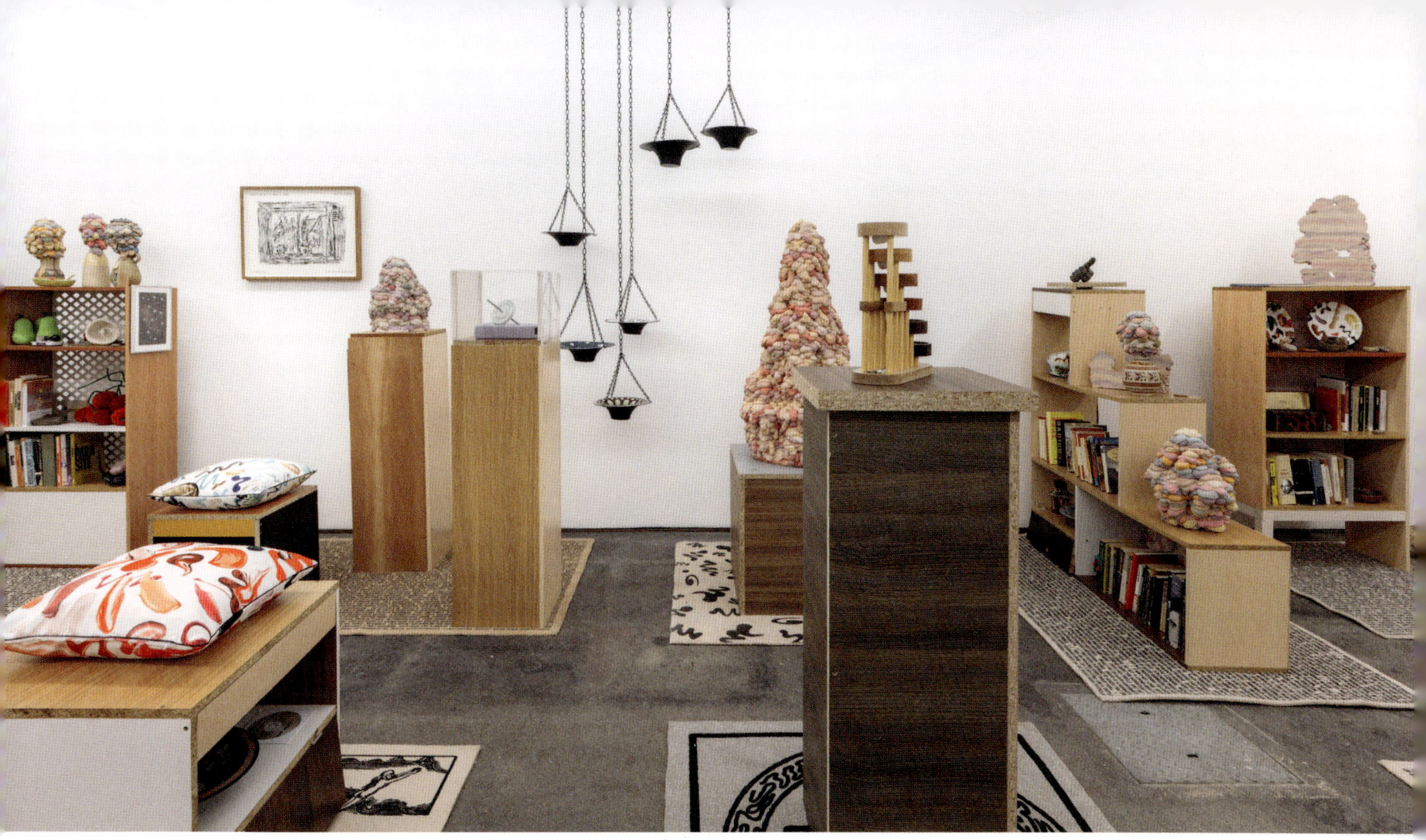

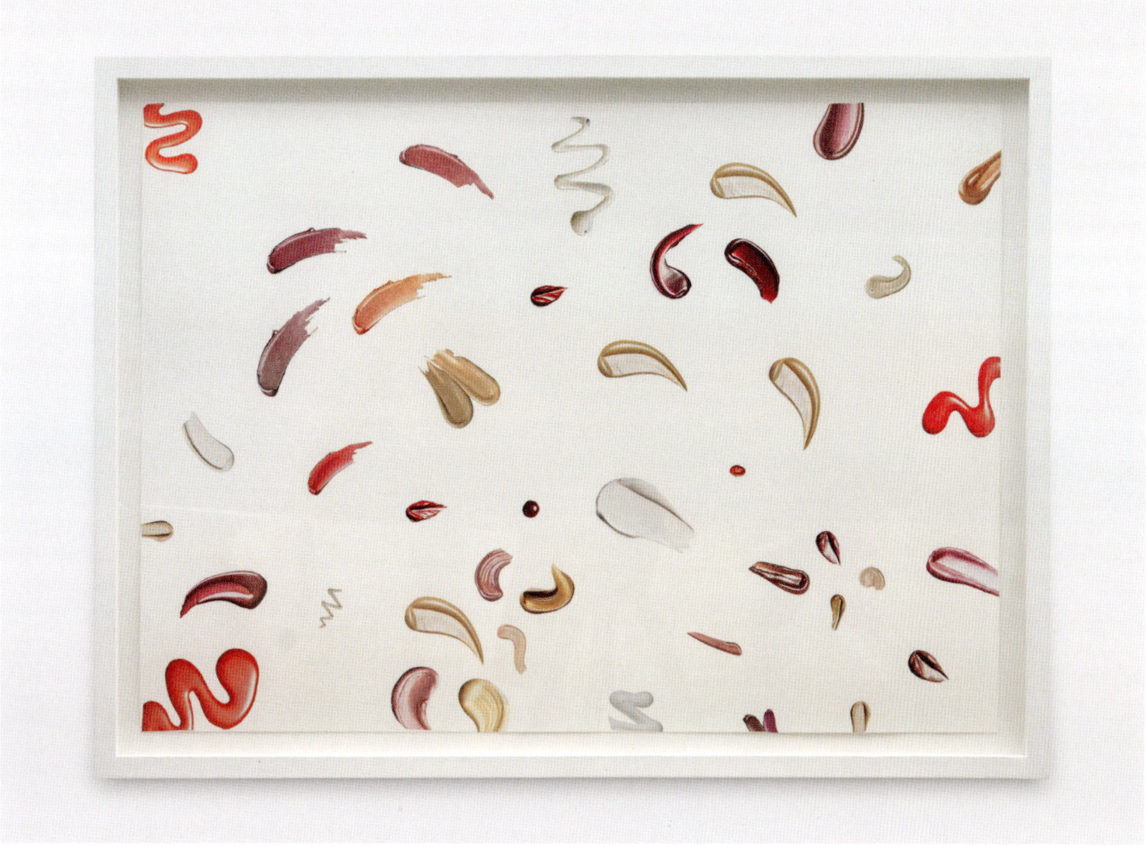

Totems for Thingly Time

2008–24

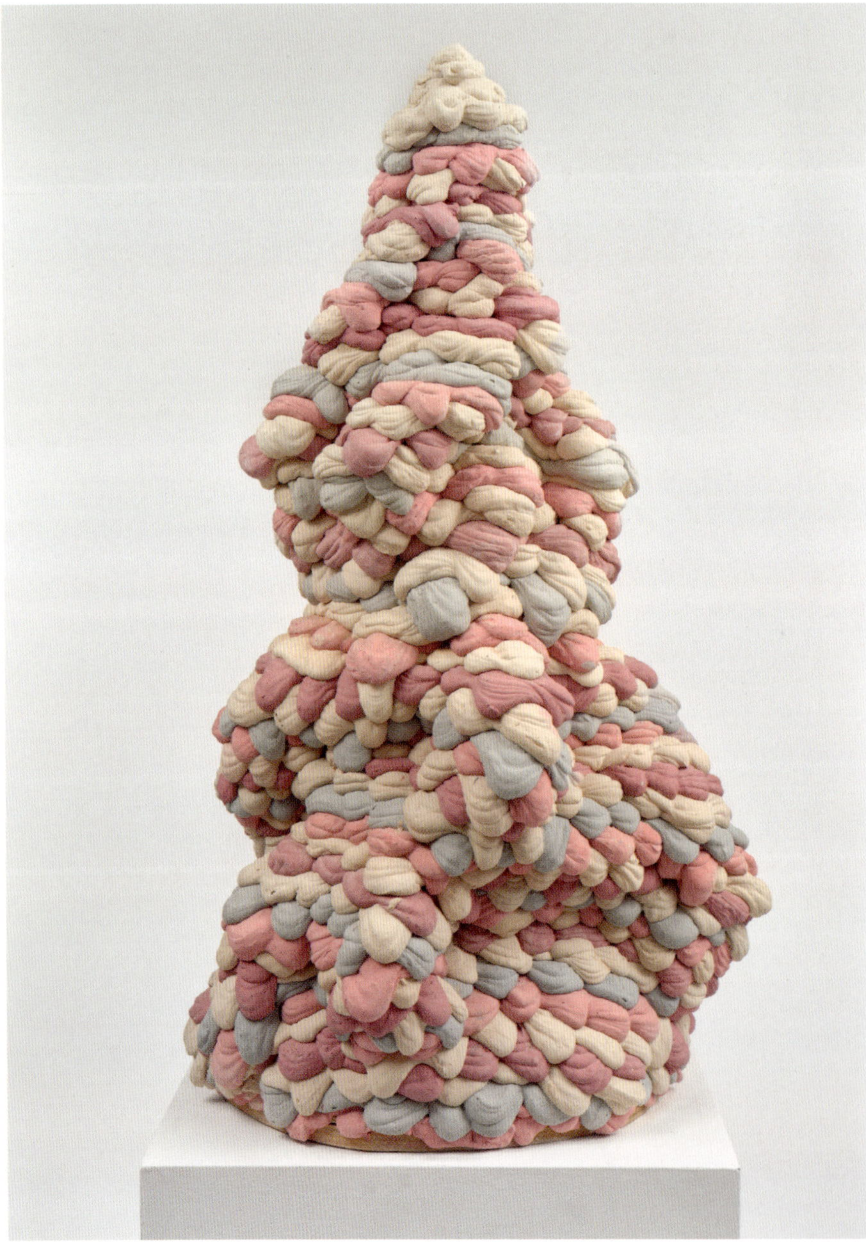

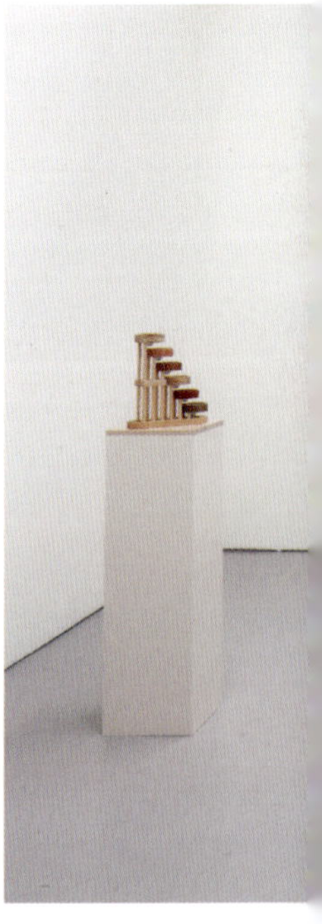

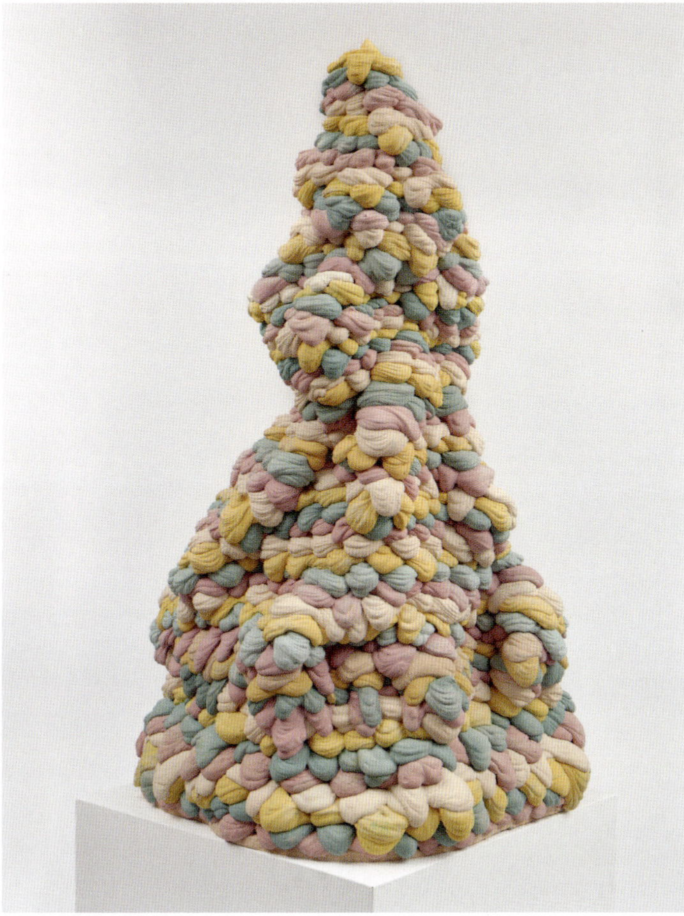

↖ *Dream Formation*, 2020, plaster and emulsion paint, 100 × 40 × 40 cm (39⅜ × 15¾ × 15¾ in.)
← *Anatomy of Melancholy (ii)*, 2023, plaster and emulsion paint, 105 × 55 × 55 cm (41⅜ × 21⅝ × 21⅝ in.)
↙ *Folly and Landscape*, 2013, installation view, Collective, Edinburgh, UK

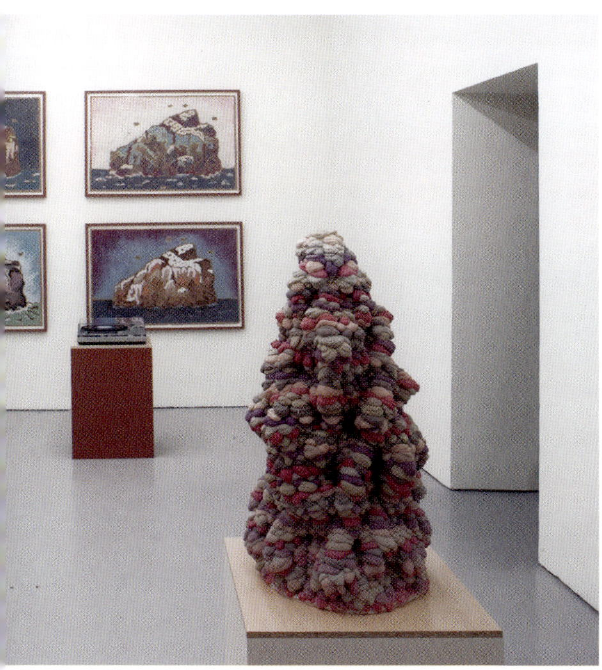

Described by Holden as 'part cake, part stalagmite, part pastel hangover',[1] the *Totems* and *Beerbottle Stalagmites* are created from dripped plaster and painted in colours based on interior design schemes from Homebase – the British home improvement and garden centre, which Holden worked for as a teenager. The sculptures are replete with associations, from caves to candy and more. However, despite their visual connections, Holden insists that each series 'requires a different set of interpretative approaches; you can't ask the same things of them, they ask to be read in completely different ways; one part aims to be the antithesis of another, even though both must exist together'.[2]

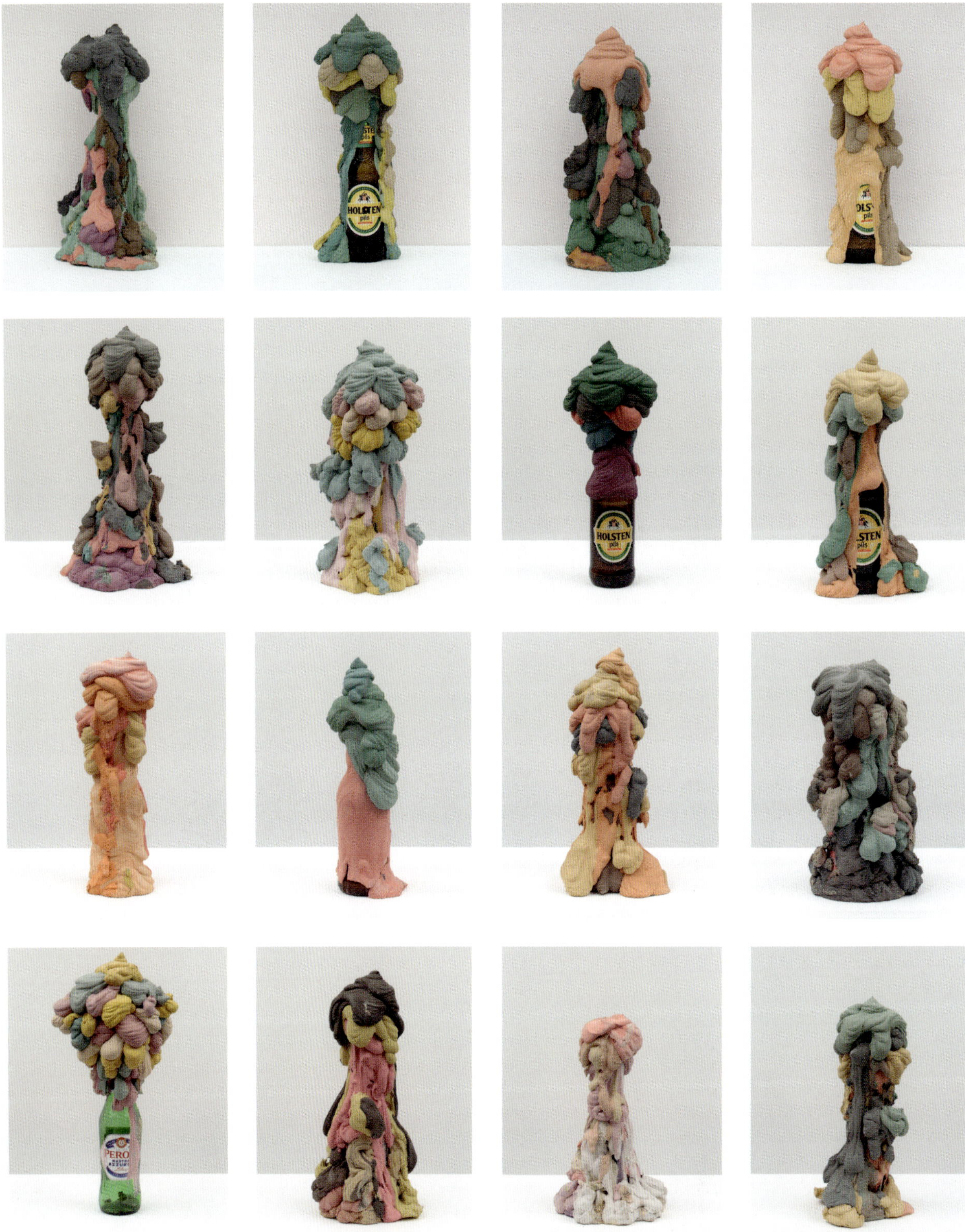

↑ *Beerbottle Stalagmites*, 2007–ongoing, plaster, emulsion paint and beer bottles, *c.* 25 × 12 × 12 cm (9 ⅞ × 4 ¾ × 4 ¾ in.)

↗ (From top to bottom) *Sales of Beerbottle Stalagmites* at Castor, London, 2024; Royal Society of Sculptors, London, 2025; Collective, Edinburgh, UK, 2013 (with Adam Jones); Seventeen, London, 2012 (with Jim Holden)

Since 2008, Holden has made something in the region of 2,000 *Beerbottle Stalagmites*. They are created from plaster leftover from the *Totems* which is then dripped onto the empty bottles – their contents consumed during long nights in the studio. None of the *Beerbottles* are numbered or signed. The artist aligns the cost of each sculpture to the cost of a round in a pub; they began at £20 and have, over the years, increased to between £40 and £70. Selling them on Instagram or pallets on the street outside private views where *Totems* were included, Holden views the fact that they're souvenirs of an exhibition as an echo of the *Pyramid Piece.* He says: 'They are deliberately unsigned and unlabelled and never counted – but in a way they don't need authenticating as in the moment of faking myself these are absolutely authentic.'[3]

Whereas the *Beerbottles* are small – not much larger than the bottles which form their support structure – the *Totems* range in size from under a metre to a couple of metres tall. In conversation with Dan Cox in 2011, Holden referred to the stalagmite form that is shared across both approaches. He described it as:

> A stupid compromise between control and gravity, gradually edging upwards like the Tower of Babel. But the further you go up, the wider the base you have to start with. It was initially a dripping down, but now it's pumped by hand through a funnel, which moved it away from the geological towards cake decorating, to stop it just being about time and give it other inclinations: a nod towards Minimalism, the abject or interior design.[4]

Holden likes to say that the sculptures 'reveal the time of their own construction' and that they were part of a 'wider framework whilst also being irrefutably autonomous'.[5] As with much of Holden's work, the *Totems* and the *Beerbottles* function on different levels. Both mass-produced and unique, they're at once insistently physical – blobby, colourful and oddly humorous – and, given the questions they prompt, metaphysical. For Holden, they're signifiers of a set of very particular memories.

1 https://artscouncilcollection.org.uk/artwork/totem-thingly-time-5 Accessed 2 Mar 2026
2 Andy Holden in conversation with Dan Cox, catalogue for 'Chewy Cosmos Thingly Time', Kettle's Yard, Cambridge, UK, 2011, p. 39.
3 Andy Holden, email to Jennifer Higgie, 5 November 2024.
4 Andy Holden in conversation with Dan Cox, catalogue for 'Chewy Cosmos Thingly Time', Kettle's Yard, Cambridge, UK, 2011, pp. 39, 43.
5 Andy Holden, email to Jennifer Higgie, 23 January 2025.

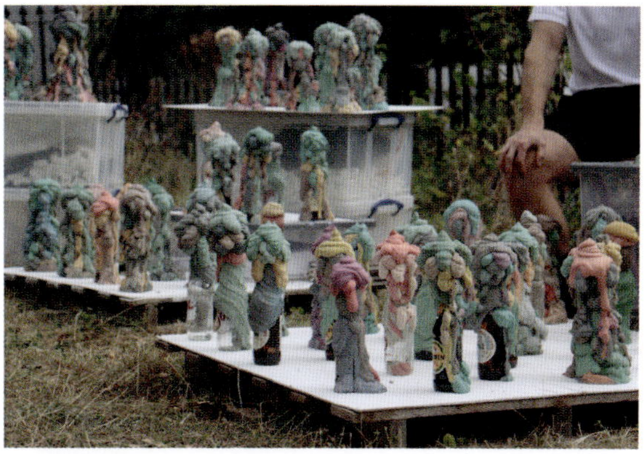

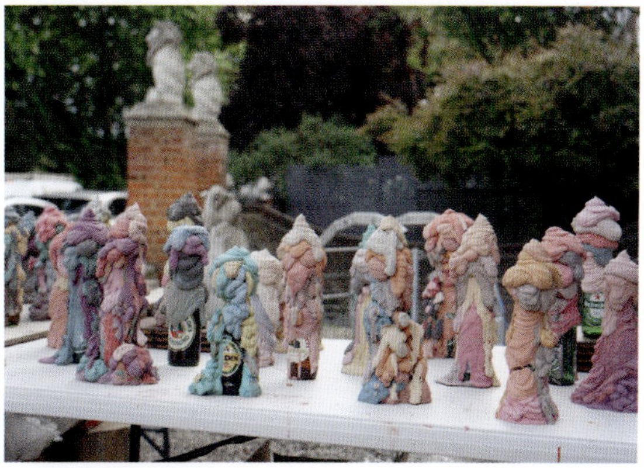

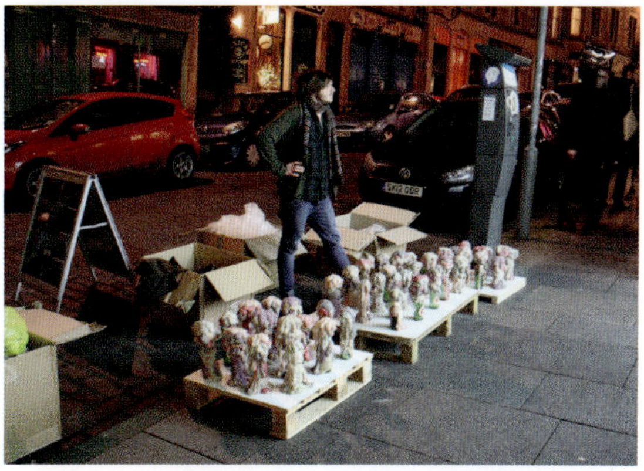

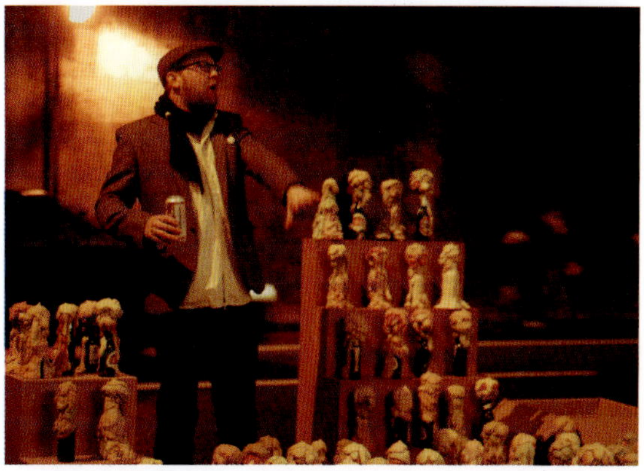

Song of Songs

2023

→ *Infinite Resignation (Unus Instar Omnium)*, 2023, collage on archival pigment print on cotton rag paper, framed, 152.6 × 102.9 cm (60 × 40½ in.)
↓ *Infinite Resignation (We Are the Size of What We See)*, 2023, collage on archival pigment print on cotton rag paper, framed, 152.6 × 102.9 cm (60 × 40½ in.)
↘ *Infinite Resignation (Time Is What Stops Everything Happening All at Once)*, 2023, collage on archival pigment print on cotton rag paper, framed, 152.6 × 102.9 cm (60 × 40½ in.). Private collection

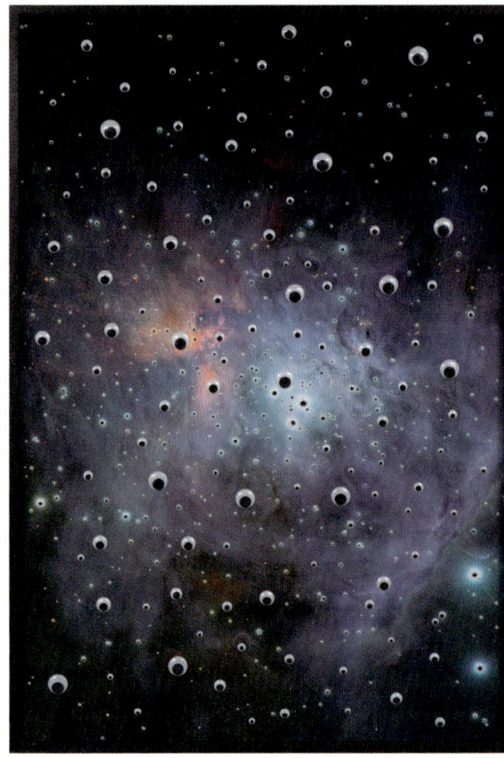

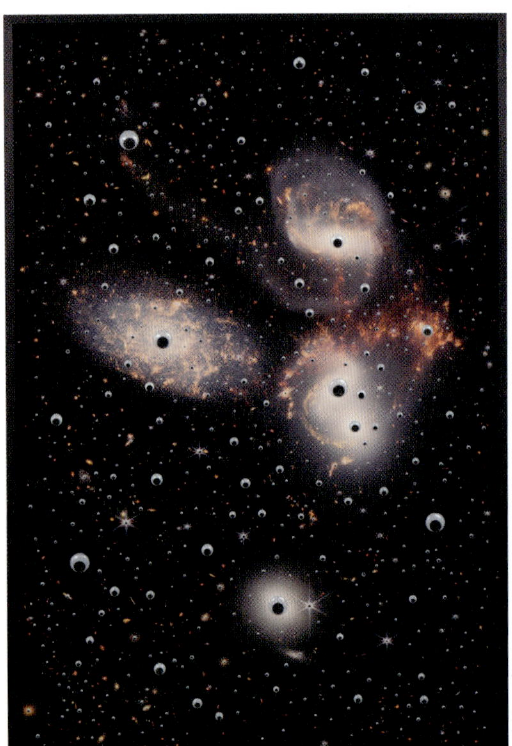

In Autumn 2023, Andy Holden staged a solo exhibition titled 'Song of Songs' at Seventeen gallery in East London. It was his first show in a commercial gallery in 15 years and comprised a new iteration of *The Dan Cox Library for the Unfinished Concept of Thingly Time* alongside installations that explore, from multiple angles, Holden's experiences of love and loss, grief and mourning. The exhibition's title is a reference to *just (after song of songs)*, a 13-minute, hypnotically beautiful song released in 2015 by American composer David Lang. Its foundational text is the *Song of Songs*, also known as the *Song of Solomon*, a collection of love poetry that can be found both in the Old Testament and the Tanakh: the Hebrew Bible. Lang's libretto is a list that builds into a threnody via the repetition of the word 'just'.

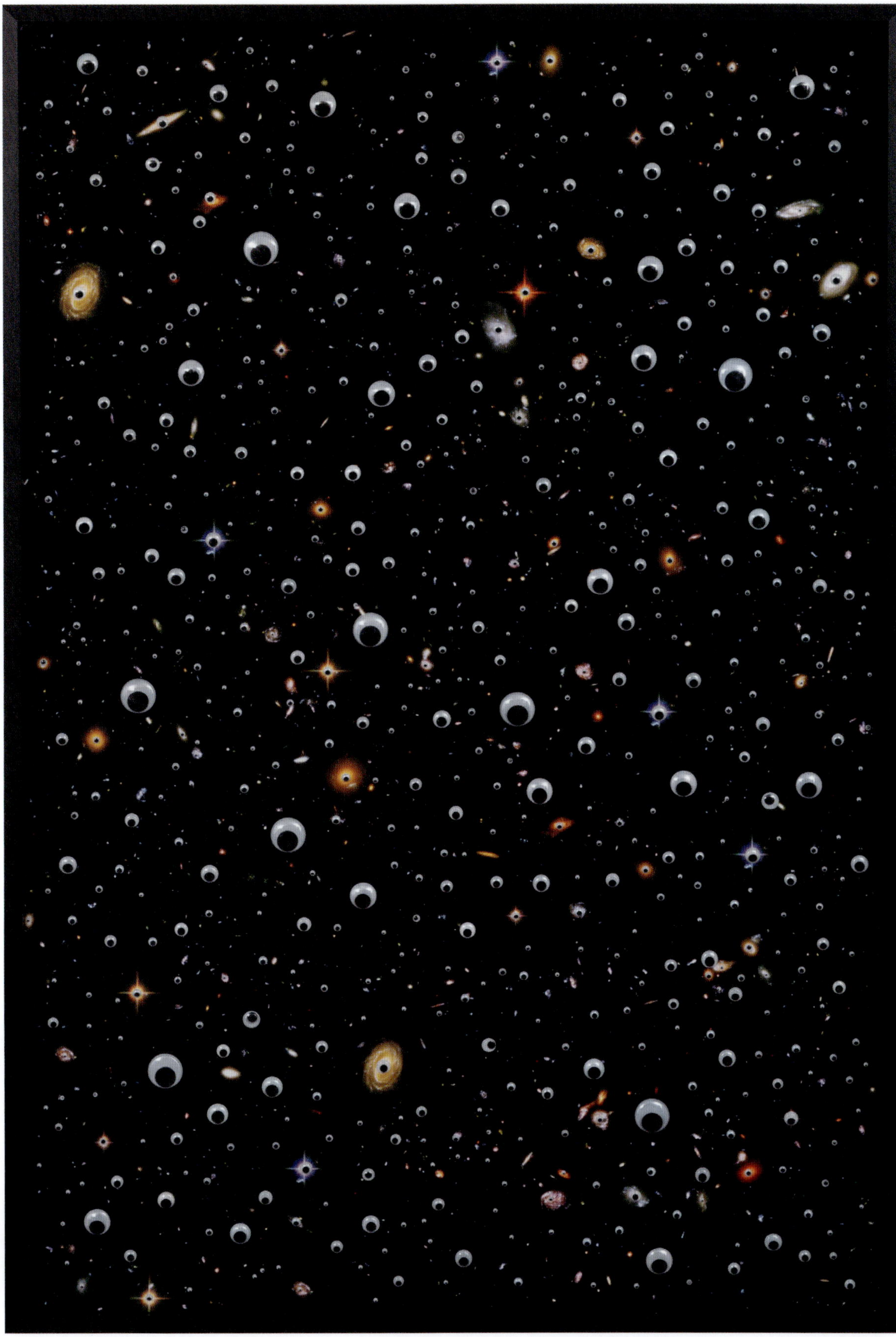

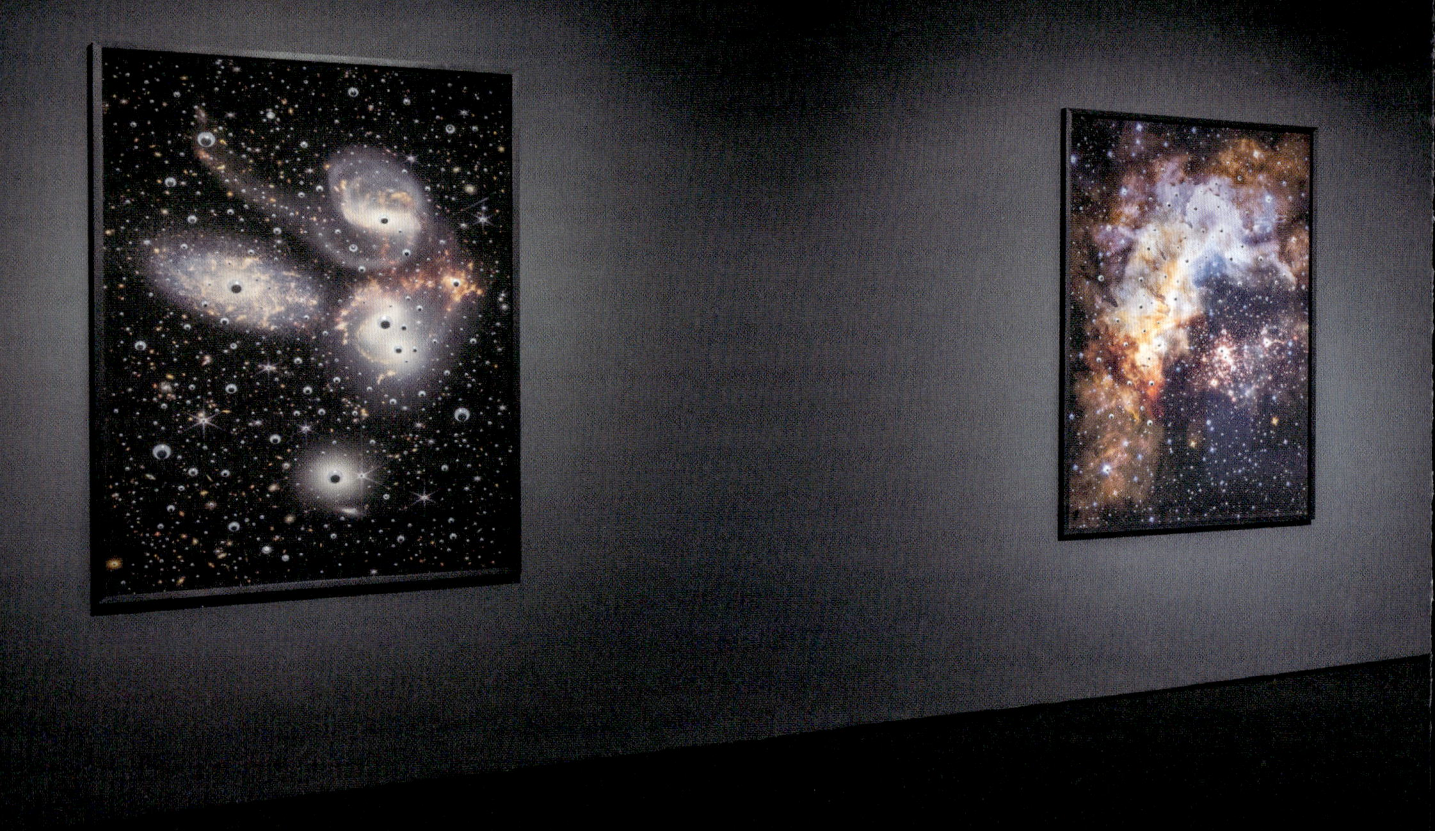

It opens with

just your mouth
just your love
just your anointing oils
just your name
just your chambers
just your love

Lang writes about his composition:

> One thing that has always interested me about the text is that the man and the woman in the *Song of Songs* have attributes, they notice things about each other, they own things, they have features that are desirable. In a love between people this would be no surprise. In a love between Man and God, however, that might mean that in this text are clues to the nature of God's own attributes, and a record of how they might attract us.[1]

The first room of the gallery was filled with sound: a 15-minute arrangement of *just (after song of songs)* performed by Holden and The Grubby Mitts and recorded in 16-channel spatialised sound. Holden's vocoded voice gradually builds with vocal harmonies and a soaring violin, a brass section, electronic loops, piano motifs and percussion. It's a haunting, heartbreaking piece of music, in which the words 'just' and 'and my beloved' thud like the intermingling of heartbeats.

Also in the first gallery were Holden's series of collages on archival pigment print on cotton rag paper.

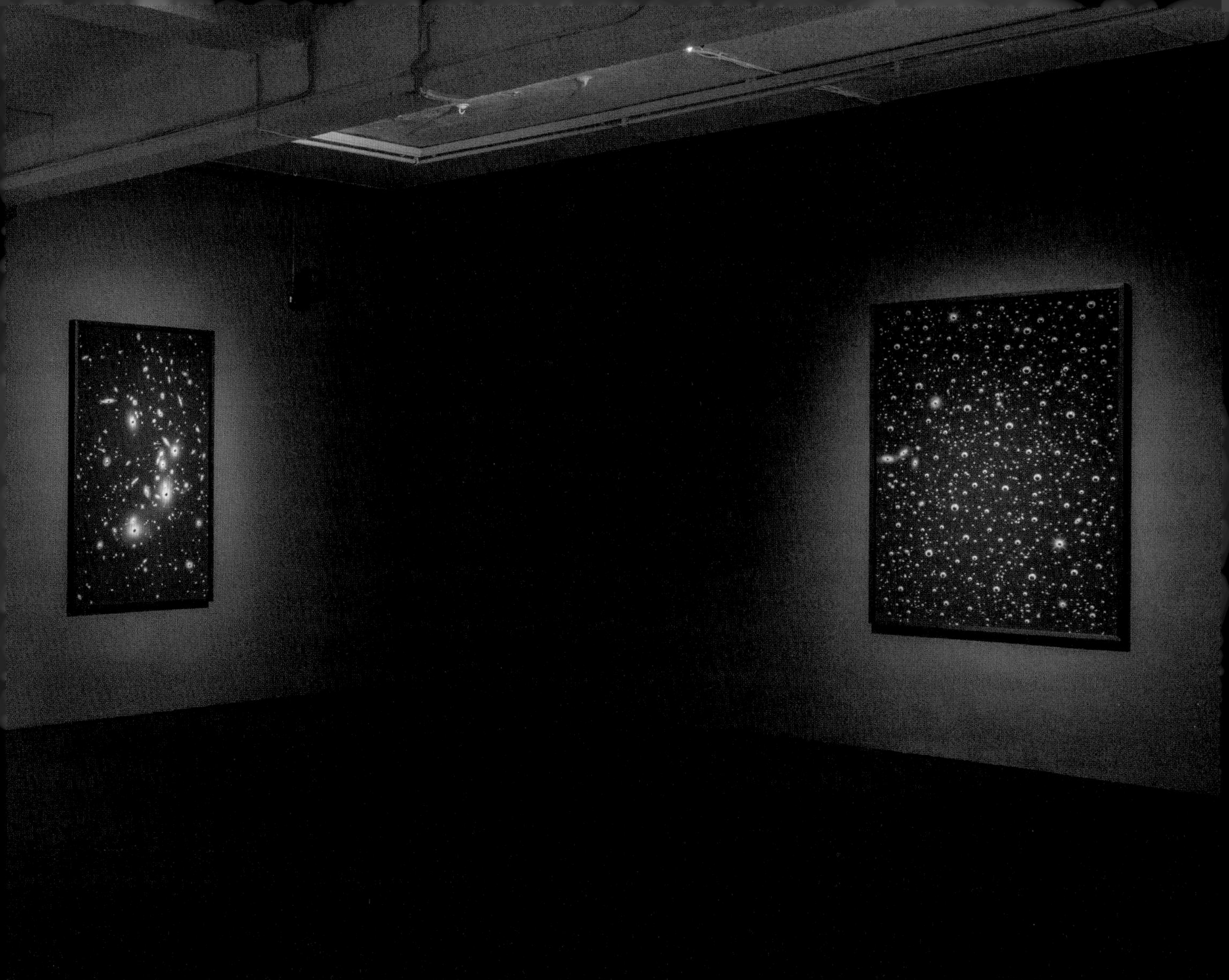

Song of Songs, 2023, installation view with 16-channel spatialised sound, Seventeen, London

Each work is titled *Infinite Resignation* with a parenthesis: *(Time Is What Stops Everything Happening All at Once)*, *(To Begin Again)* and so on. In 1843, the Danish philosopher Søren Kierkegaard published his book *Fear and Trembling*; in it, he posited the idea of 'infinite resignation' as the final step in the move towards faith – the paradox that one must lose everything to have it all. Holden's series is an idiosyncratic take on Kierkegaard's idea. Each image is the size of a large window and, at first glance, appears to be a view of the vastness of the dark universe glowing and speckled with cosmic dust. The photographs were taken by the James Webb Space Telescope which, according to NASA, 'has produced the deepest and sharpest infrared image of the distant universe to date' and allows us to look back in time 'to within a billion years after the Big Bang'.[2] Peer closely, however, and the stars and cosmic dust are, in fact, hundreds of plastic 'googly' eyes, something Holden has used in earlier works such as the *Untitled (Eyes in Space)* series (2011). Questions hover: is the sky watching us, or are the cartoon eyes a stand-in for humanity, always looking back as we move forwards? How, entrapped as we are in our vulnerable human bodies, can we possibly imagine the vast vagaries of time or visualise infinity? How can we find meaning in a universe that is essentially indifferent? Is anyone observing us? When you commit to loving someone forever, what does that entail? What does forever look like?

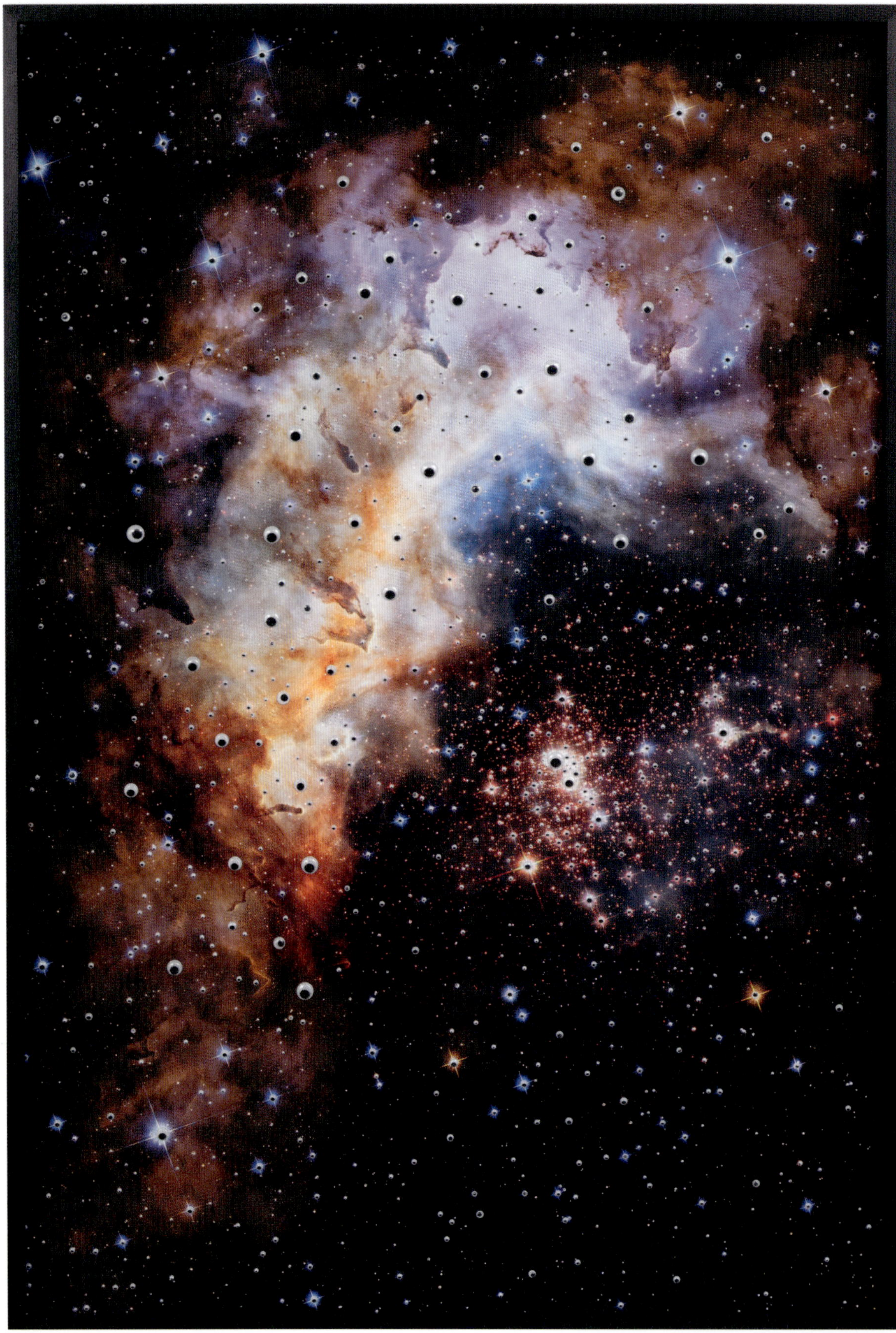

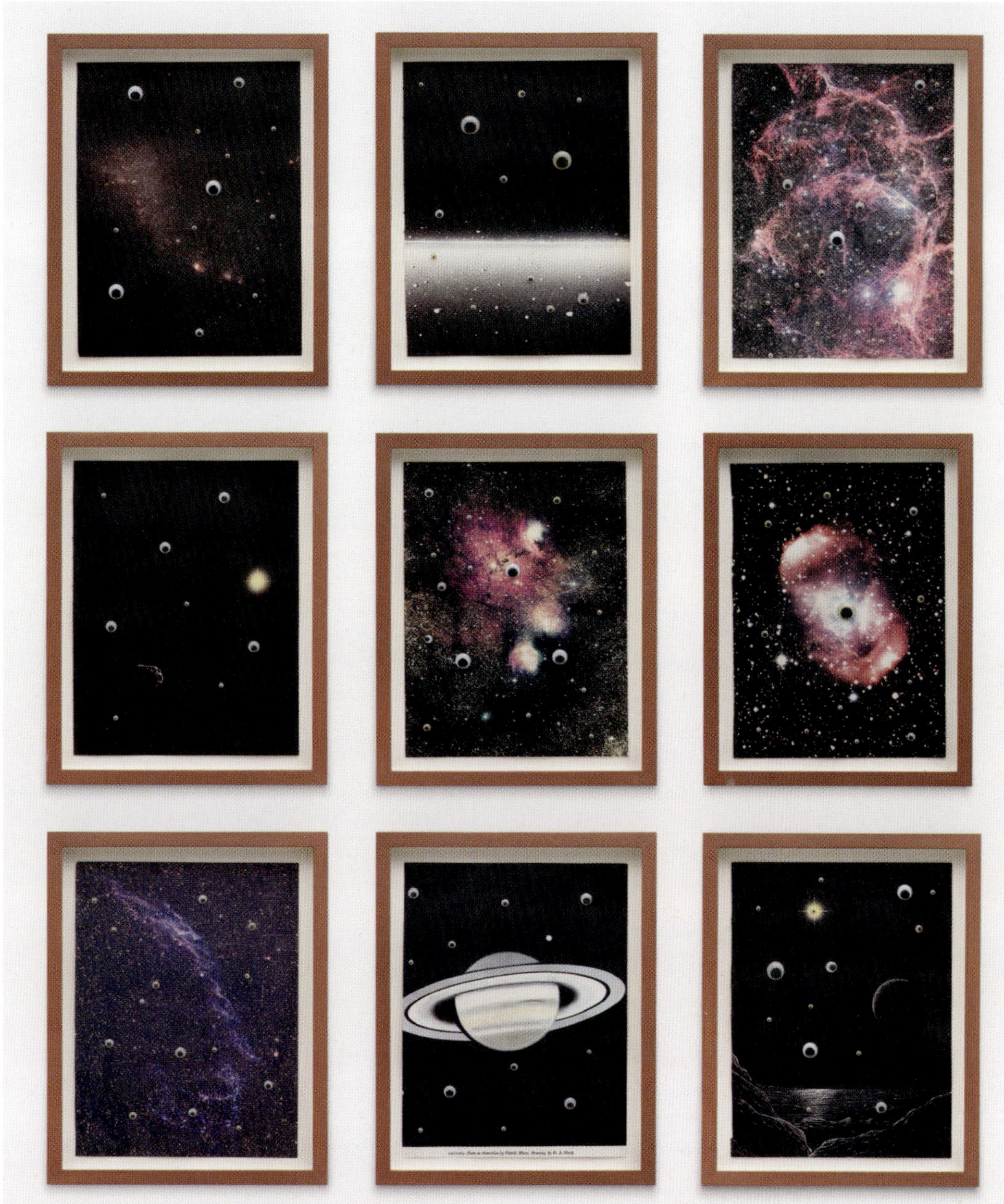

In the text for Holden's 2011 exhibition 'Chewy Cosmos, Thingly Time', the science fiction novelist Ursula K. Le Guin declares 'we are only at the beginning of our age of discovery. We must not become slaves to our own axioms. We have not yet lifted our eyes to the vaster horizons before us.'[3] It is a sentiment that was acutely visualised at Seventeen.

Infinite Resignation and *just (after song of songs)* evoke a slew of feelings prompted by the contrast between the unimaginable immensity of the universe and its inventory of details. Love, it intimates, is both immeasurable and unique, momentous and personal.

← *Infinite Resignation (Amor Fati)*, 2023, collage on archival pigment print on cotton rag paper, framed, 152.6 × 102.9 cm (60 × 40½ in.). Private collection

↑ *Firmaments*, 2011, collage on archival book plates, each: 24 × 14 cm (9½ × 5½ in.)

1 David Lang, programme note, *just (after song of songs)*, https://davidlangmusic.com/music/just-after-song-of-songs/. Accessed 2 Mar 2026.

2 'NASA's Webb Delivers Deepest Infrared Image of Universe Yet', NASA website, 12 July 2022, https://www.nasa.gov/image-article/nasas-webb-delivers-deepest-infrared-image-of-universe-yet. Accessed 2 Mar 2026.

3 Ursula K. Le Guin, '"The Author of the Acacia Seeds" and other Extracts from the Journal of the Association of Therolinguistics', in the catalogue published on the occasion of 'Chewy Cosmos Thingly Time', Kettle's Yard, Cambridge, UK, 14 May–10 July 2011, p. 15.

M!MS: Maximum Irony! Maximum Sincerity

1999–2003 and 2013

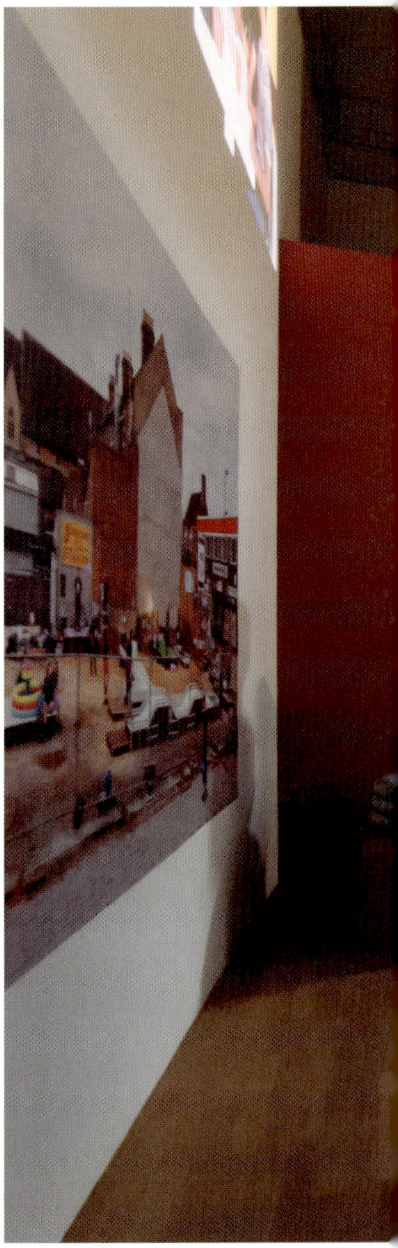

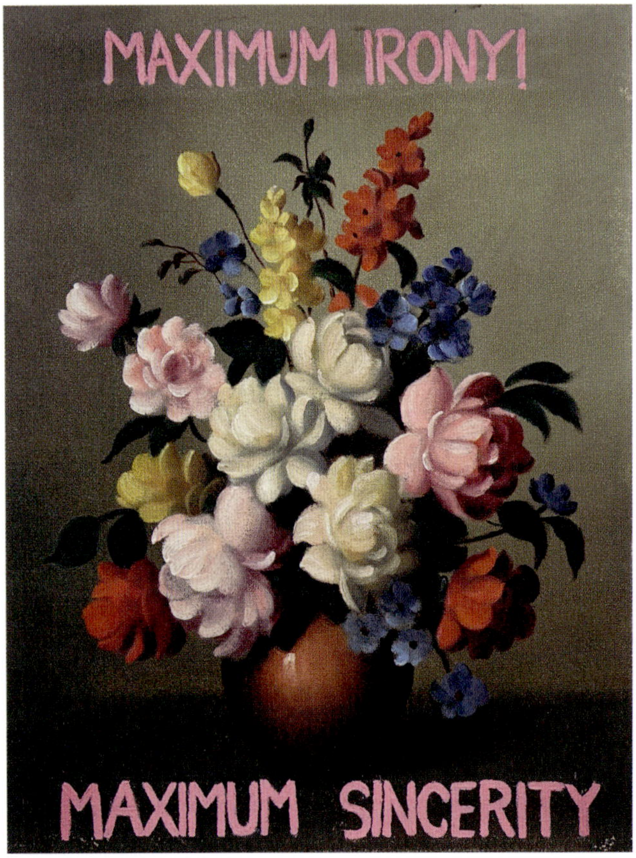

← *Maximum Irony! Maximum Sincerity*, 2013, acrylic on found canvas, 40.5 × 30.5 cm (15 ⅞ × 12 in.). Collection of Wayne Warren

↗ *Maximum Irony! Maximum Sincerity, 1999–2003: Towards a Unified Theory of M!MS*, 2013, variable dimensions, installation view, Kunsthalle Winterthur, Switzerland, 2015

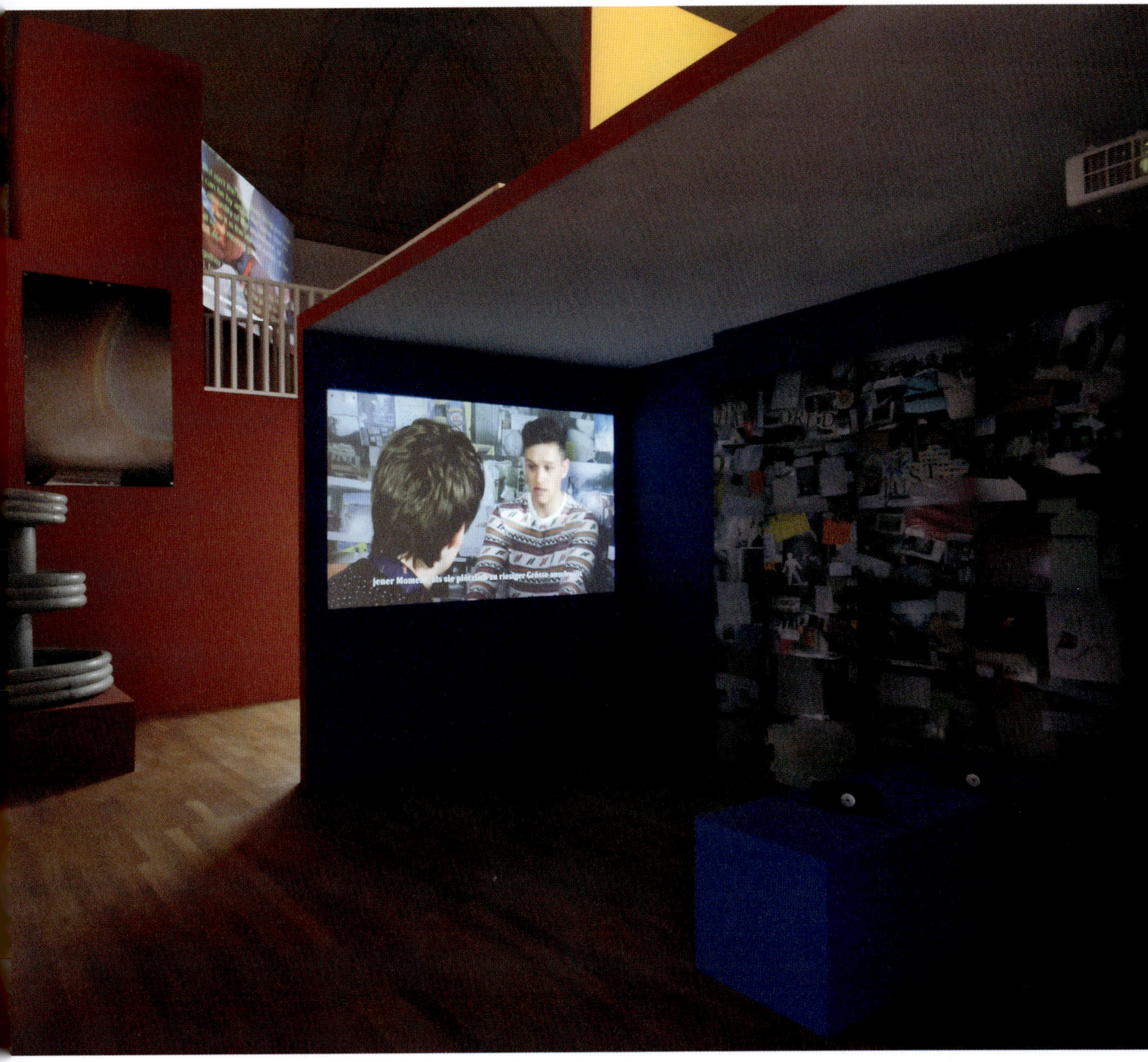

In Bedford, in July 2003, Holden, along with his childhood friends and fellow artists John Blamey, Roger Illingworth, James MacDowell and Johnny Parry, signed a manifesto titled: 'MI!MS: a Manifesto of Maximum Irony! Maximum Sincerity'. Its declarations included:

> We live in an age of irony *in mourning* for sincerity. Art reflects society and if society is to drown in the belly of the ironic whale that swims in the sea of postmodernism, so shall art...
>
> We live in an age of irony because of the sins of sincerity! The beautiful and sincere flowers are all too easily plucked and rearranged in the unflattering vase of mediocrity. The flower withers, leaving the vase empty.
>
> 'Maximum Irony! Maximum Sincerity' is an artistic movement for the sorrowful-yet-joyous, the disillusioned-yet-innocent, the ironic-yet-sincere!
>
> Let us not be ironic about our sincerity, let us be sincere about our irony. As Picasso said: 'We all know that art is not truth. Art is the lie that makes us realise the truth.'

What emerged from the Manifesto was multifarious: music, writing, artworks, films and performances that, over the following decades, have prompted new works. Many of the strands came together in 2013 at London's Zabludowicz Collection in the immersive exhibition 'Andy Holden: Maximum Irony! Maximum Sincerity 1999–2003: Towards a Unified Theory of M!MS'. The show was staged in rooms across various levels and was Holden's most ambitious to date. It was conceived to narrate the history of the Manifesto via a recreation of various important sites from Holden's youth, such as a friend's bedroom and the Poppins café in Bedford, which the young men 'ironically and sincerely'[1] adopted as their headquarters and where the MI!MS Manifesto was signed. It also included a feature-length film of seven chapters, shown on seven screens, narrating the history of the M!MS art movement, with teenage actors from Bedford standing in for the artist and his friends.

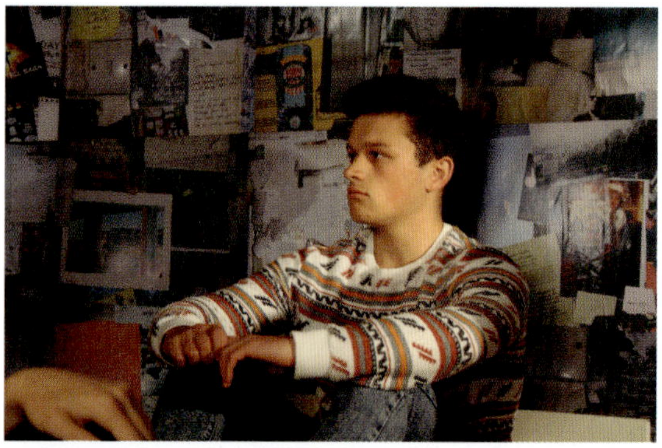

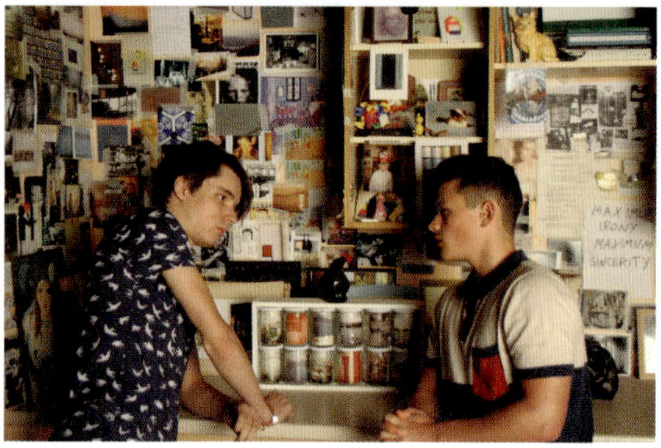

↗ (All images on this page) Documentation of the production of *Towards a Unified Theory of M!MS*, 2013

→ (Opposite and overleaf) *Maximum Irony! Maximum Sincerity, 1999–2003: Towards a Unified Theory of M!MS*, 2013, variable dimensions, installation view, Zabludowicz Collection, London, 2013

↠ (pp. 44–45) *MI!MS Manifesto*, 2003, photocopy on paper, 29.7 × 42 cm (11¾ × 16½ in.)

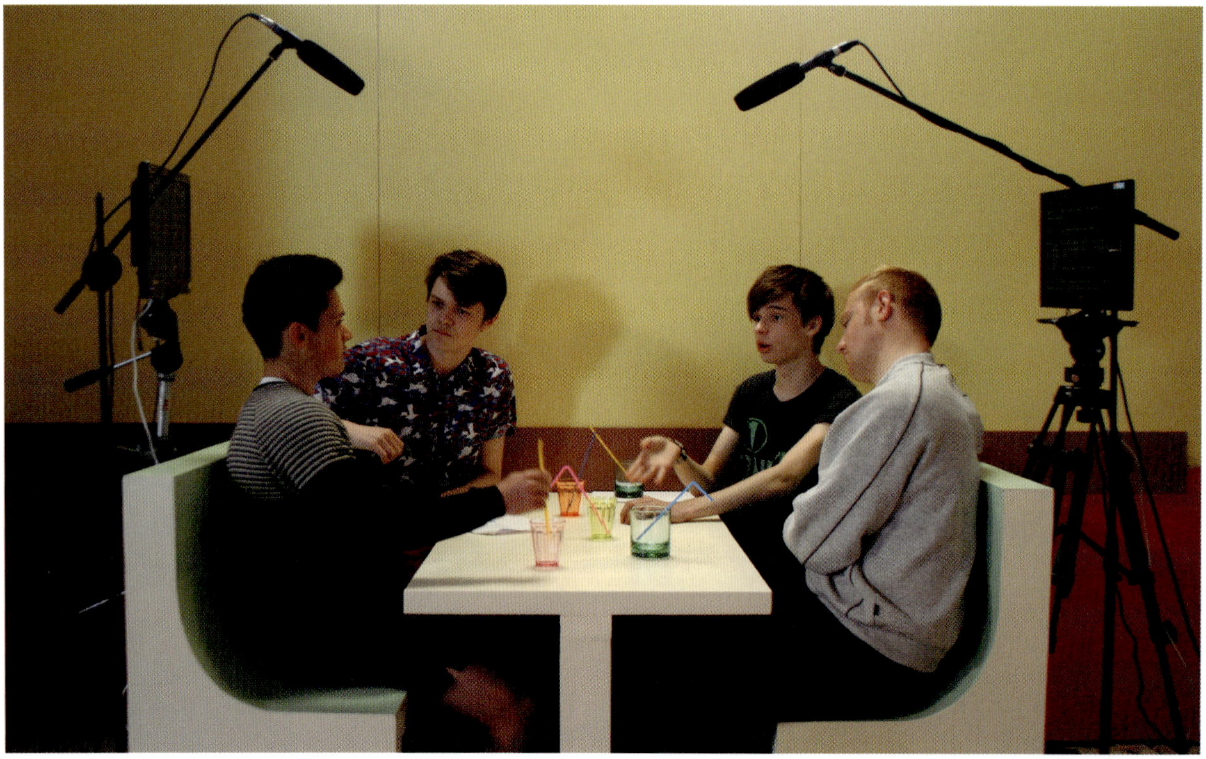

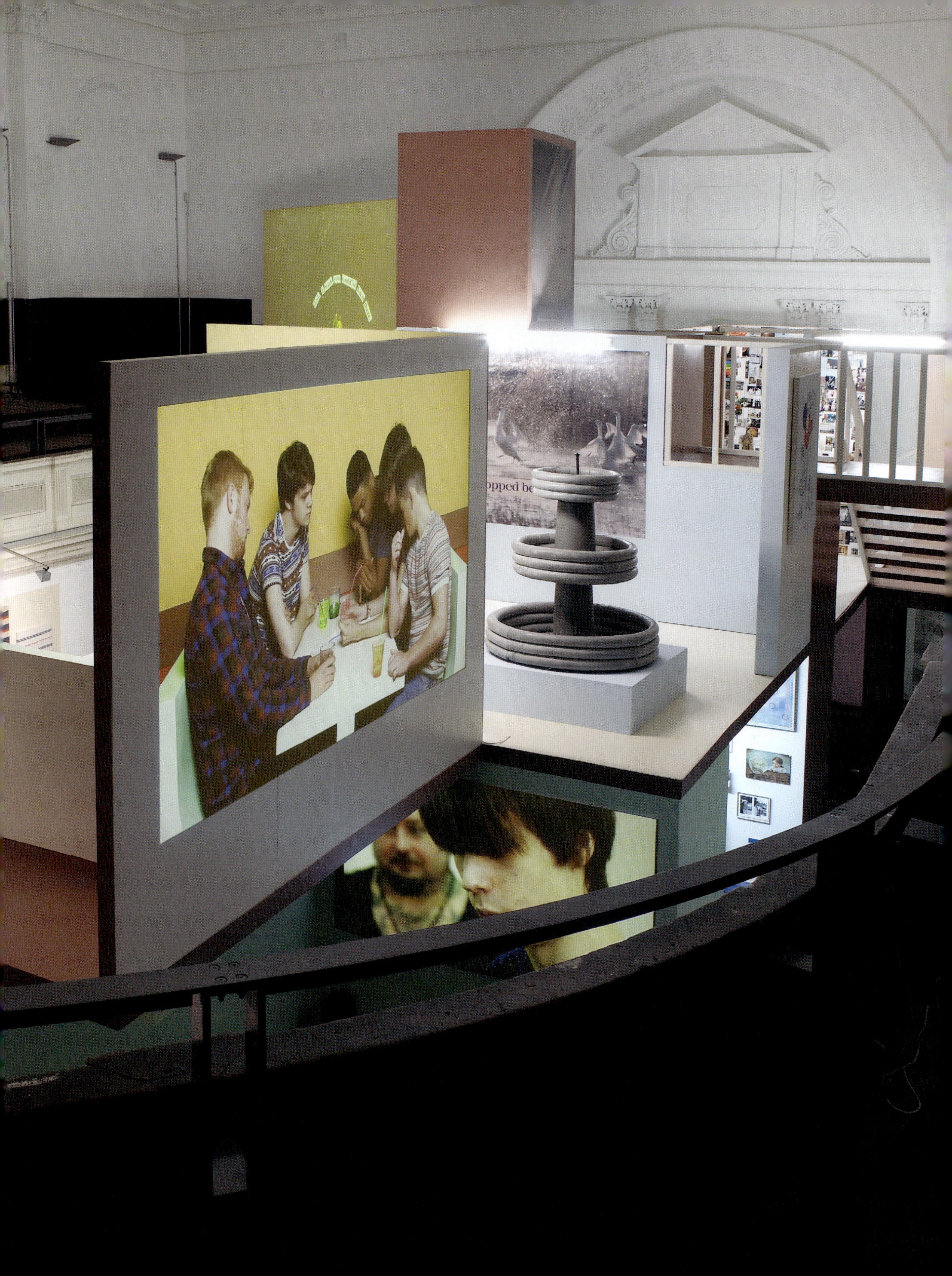

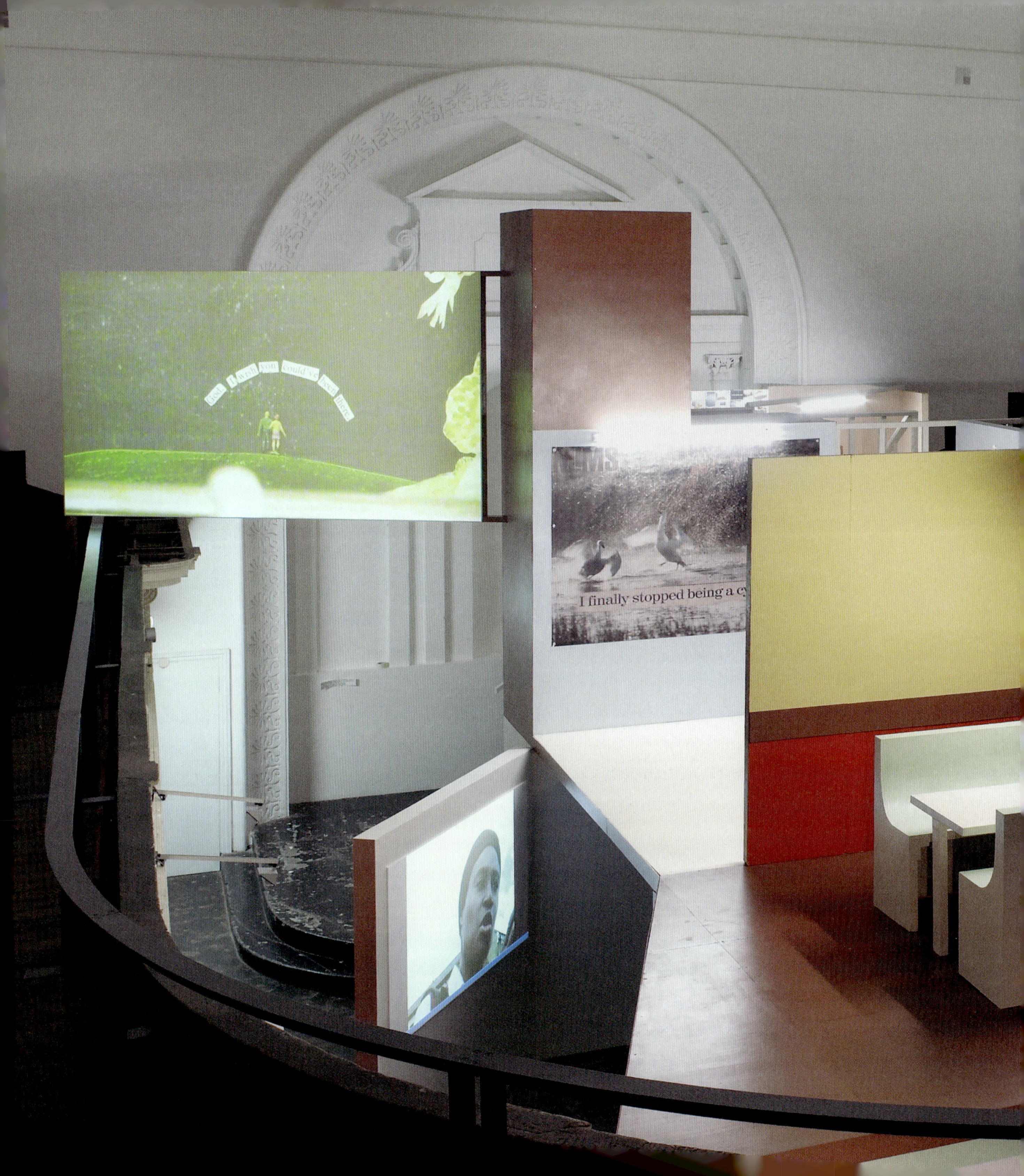
I wish you could've been there.
I finally stopped being a

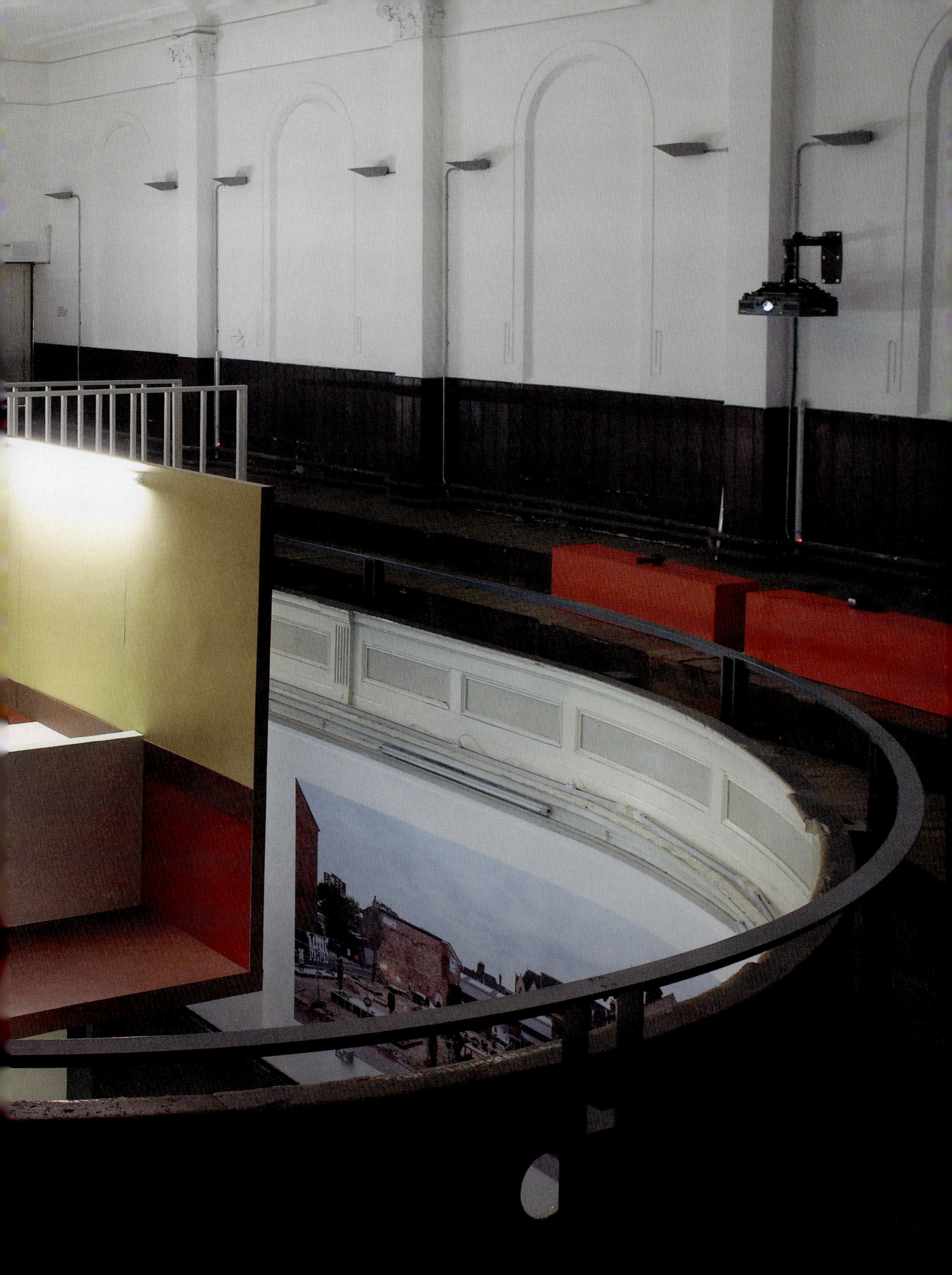

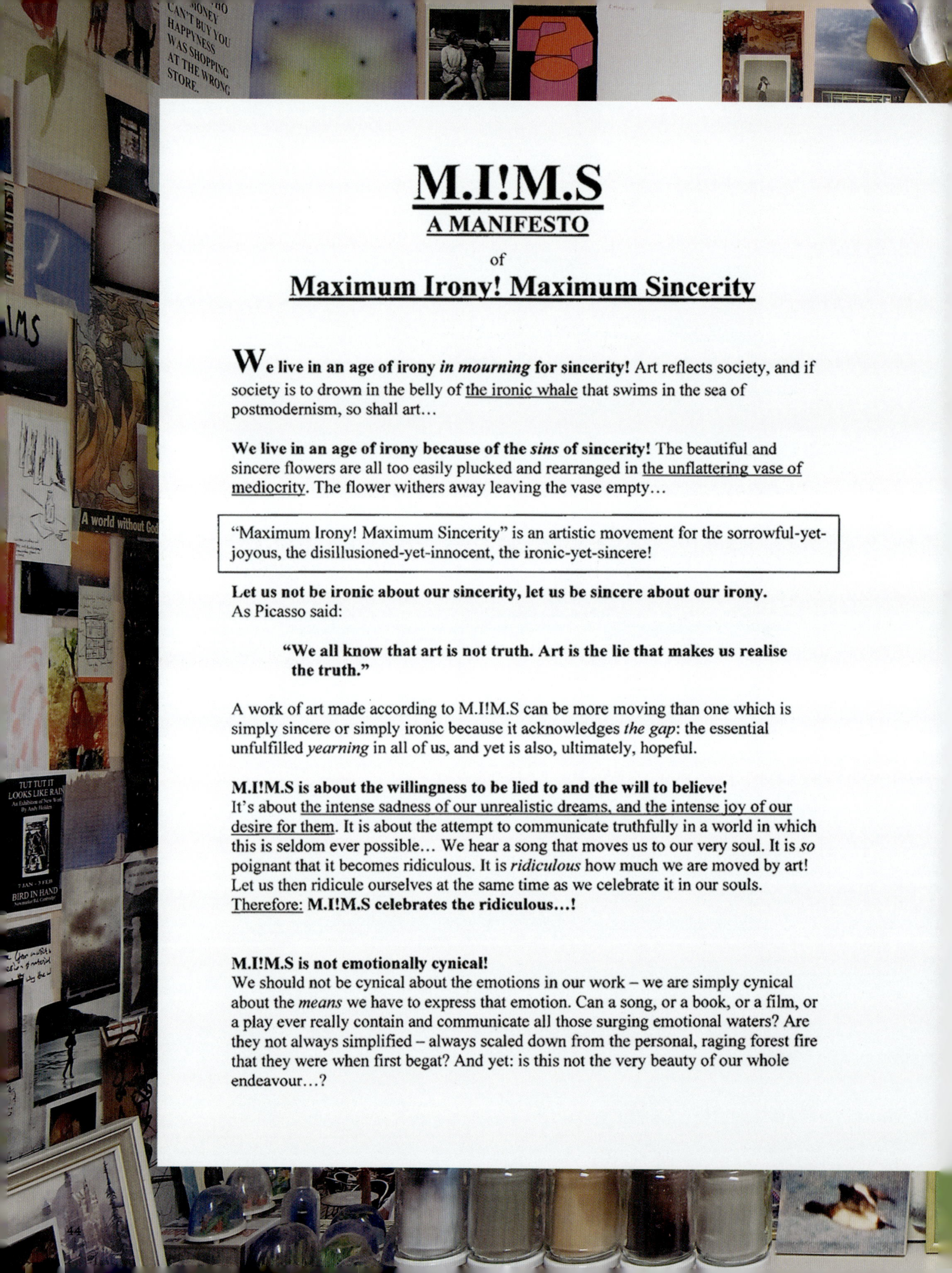

M.I!M.S

A MANIFESTO

of

Maximum Irony! Maximum Sincerity

We live in an age of irony *in mourning* for sincerity! Art reflects society, and if society is to drown in the belly of the ironic whale that swims in the sea of postmodernism, so shall art…

We live in an age of irony because of the *sins* of sincerity! The beautiful and sincere flowers are all too easily plucked and rearranged in the unflattering vase of mediocrity. The flower withers away leaving the vase empty…

"Maximum Irony! Maximum Sincerity" is an artistic movement for the sorrowful-yet-joyous, the disillusioned-yet-innocent, the ironic-yet-sincere!

Let us not be ironic about our sincerity, let us be sincere about our irony.
As Picasso said:

> **"We all know that art is not truth. Art is the lie that makes us realise the truth."**

A work of art made according to M.I!M.S can be more moving than one which is simply sincere or simply ironic because it acknowledges *the gap*: the essential unfulfilled *yearning* in all of us, and yet is also, ultimately, hopeful.

M.I!M.S is about the willingness to be lied to and the will to believe!
It's about the intense sadness of our unrealistic dreams, and the intense joy of our desire for them. It is about the attempt to communicate truthfully in a world in which this is seldom ever possible… We hear a song that moves us to our very soul. It is *so* poignant that it becomes ridiculous. It is *ridiculous* how much we are moved by art! Let us then ridicule ourselves at the same time as we celebrate it in our souls.
Therefore: **M.I!M.S celebrates the ridiculous…!**

M.I!M.S is not emotionally cynical!
We should not be cynical about the emotions in our work – we are simply cynical about the *means* we have to express that emotion. Can a song, or a book, or a film, or a play ever really contain and communicate all those surging emotional waters? Are they not always simplified – always scaled down from the personal, raging forest fire that they were when first begat? And yet: is this not the very beauty of our whole endeavour…?

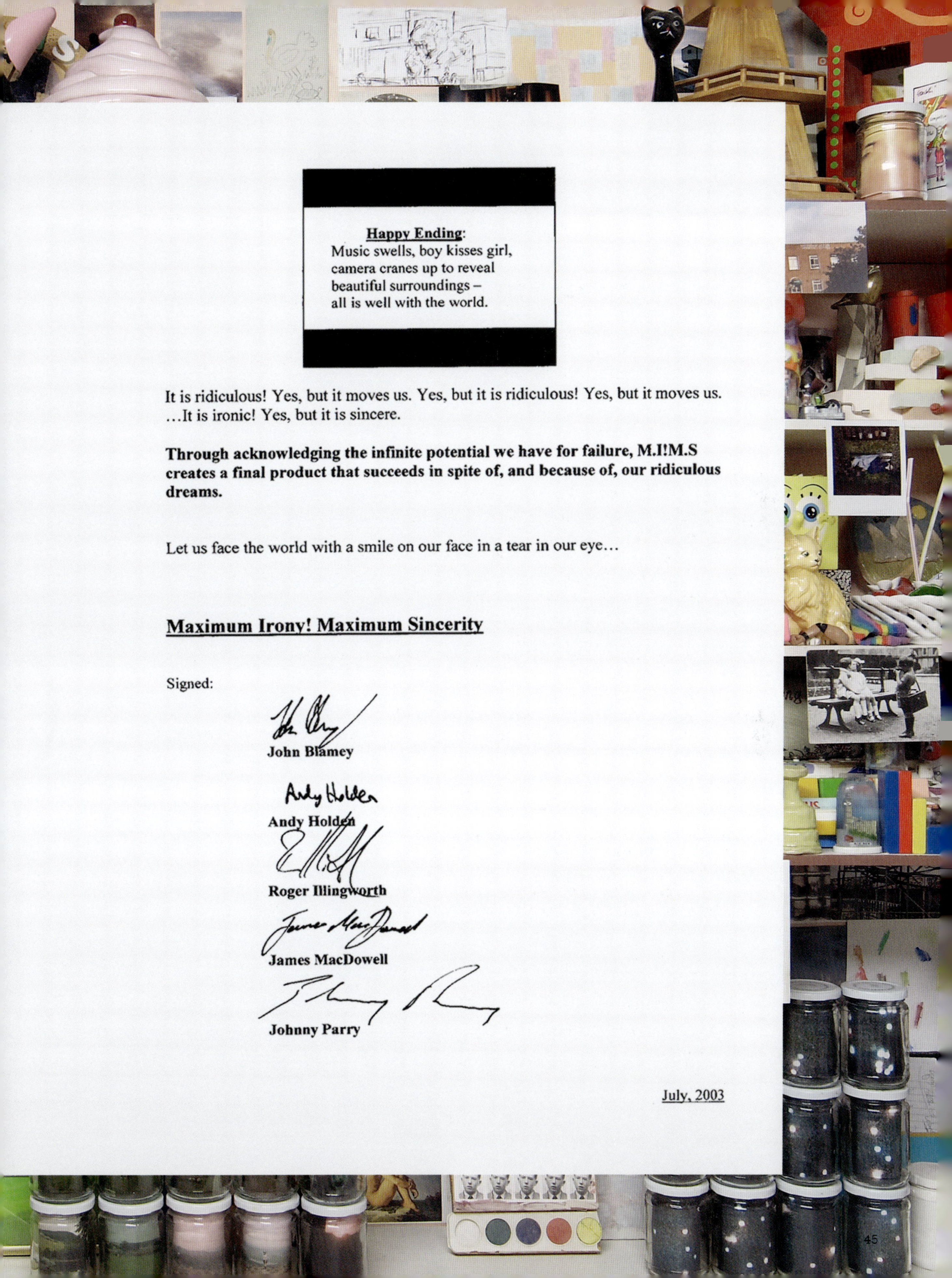

Happy Ending:
Music swells, boy kisses girl,
camera cranes up to reveal
beautiful surroundings –
all is well with the world.

It is ridiculous! Yes, but it moves us. Yes, but it is ridiculous! Yes, but it moves us. …It is ironic! Yes, but it is sincere.

Through acknowledging the infinite potential we have for failure, M.I!M.S creates a final product that succeeds in spite of, and because of, our ridiculous dreams.

Let us face the world with a smile on our face in a tear in our eye…

Maximum Irony! Maximum Sincerity

Signed:

John Blamey

Andy Holden

Roger Illingworth

James MacDowell

Johnny Parry

July, 2003

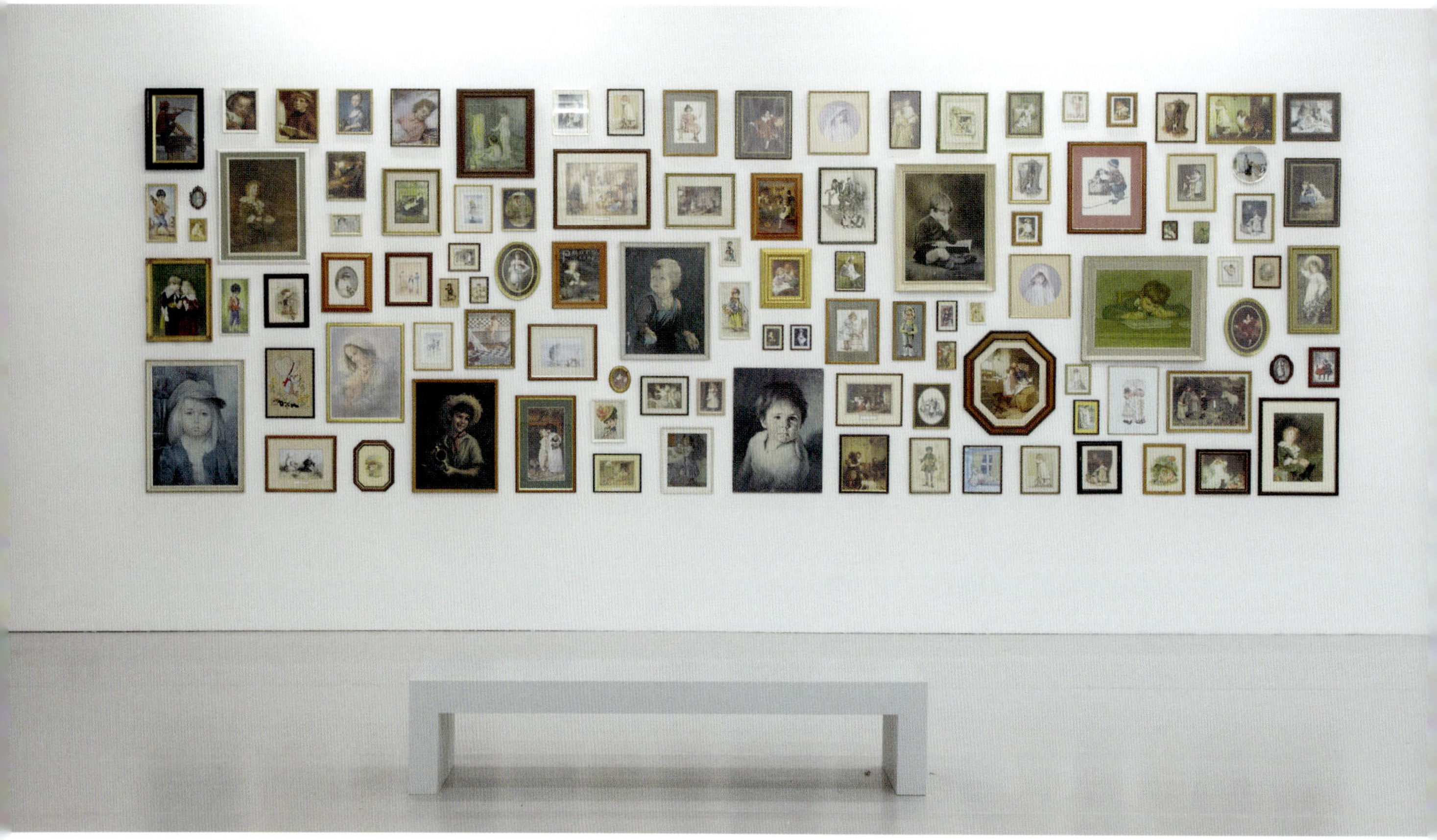

↑ *Last Stop for the Good Old Times*, 1999–2013, collected found images, variable dimensions, installation view, Spike Island, Bristol, UK

← *Unstuck Studio*, 2013, archival materials from the artist's teenage studio, variable dimensions, installation view, Spike Island, Bristol, UK. Zabludowicz Collection

↓ *Towards a Unified Theory of M!MS*, 12" vinyl, Lost Toys Records, 2015, 30 × 30 cm (12 × 12 in.), edition of 250

→ *Maximum Irony! Maximum Sincerity, 1999–2003: Towards a Unified Theory of M!MS*, 2013, variable dimensions, installation view, Zabludowicz Collection, London, 2013

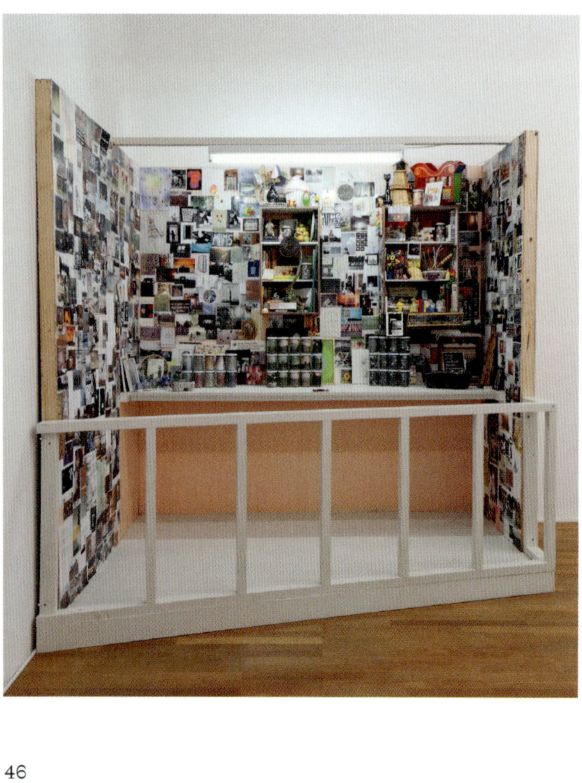

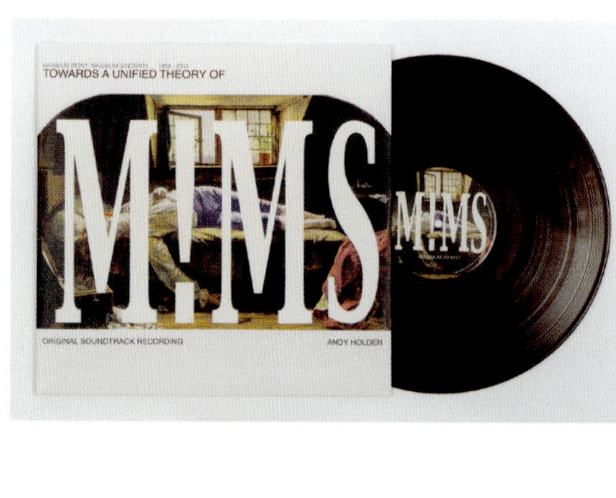

Music was central not only to the installation but to the foundational story of M!MS: all of the songs in the exhibition were written by the M!MS group. One film portrays a children's choir singing their love songs to a live audience. A recreated utility room (Holden's first studio) was filled with memorabilia from the artist's youth – stickers, snow globes, shoehorns and T-shirts wrapped around canvases – and with works of art made by the group, some in their original form and others entirely reimagined. These include photographs of people with dolls' arms attached to them, fridge magnets stuck together and a collection of bobbins wound with coloured thread. The idea was to make a work about the teenage Manifesto, according to its rules, as a way of travelling back in time.

The M!MS members had always wanted to build a mini-golf course but weren't able to, so ten years later, a lime green version was installed on a Bedford street and filmed. Another day-long performance by Holden, which involved the artist shaking the hands of random people in Bedford in 1999, was also recreated and filmed.

Also included in the exhibition was *Last Stop for Good Old Times (after The Age of Innocence)* (1999–2013), which comprises hundreds of paintings of idealised childhood sourced from local charity shops. Seen all together, its mix of saccharine sentiment and unfocused longing reveals a deep nostalgia for the Victorian period – a clear illustration of the MI!MS Manifesto point:

> It is ridiculous! Yes, but it moves us. Yes, but it is ridiculous. Yes, but it moves us... It is ironic. Yes, but it is sincere.

The exhibition was curated by Andy Holden's alter ego, Rudolf Schmidt, a sly nod to Holden Caulfield's alter ego in J.D. Salinger's novel *The Catcher in the Rye* (1951). Apart from the quiet joke of their shared names, Andy Holden felt that it 'seemed apt as the book contains a significant theme of nostalgia for childhood and I was amassing images of idealised childhood and starting to think of the collection as a work'.[2] He also liked the idea of being a fictional artist as a way of side-stepping biographical or psychoanalytical narratives being imposed upon the work.

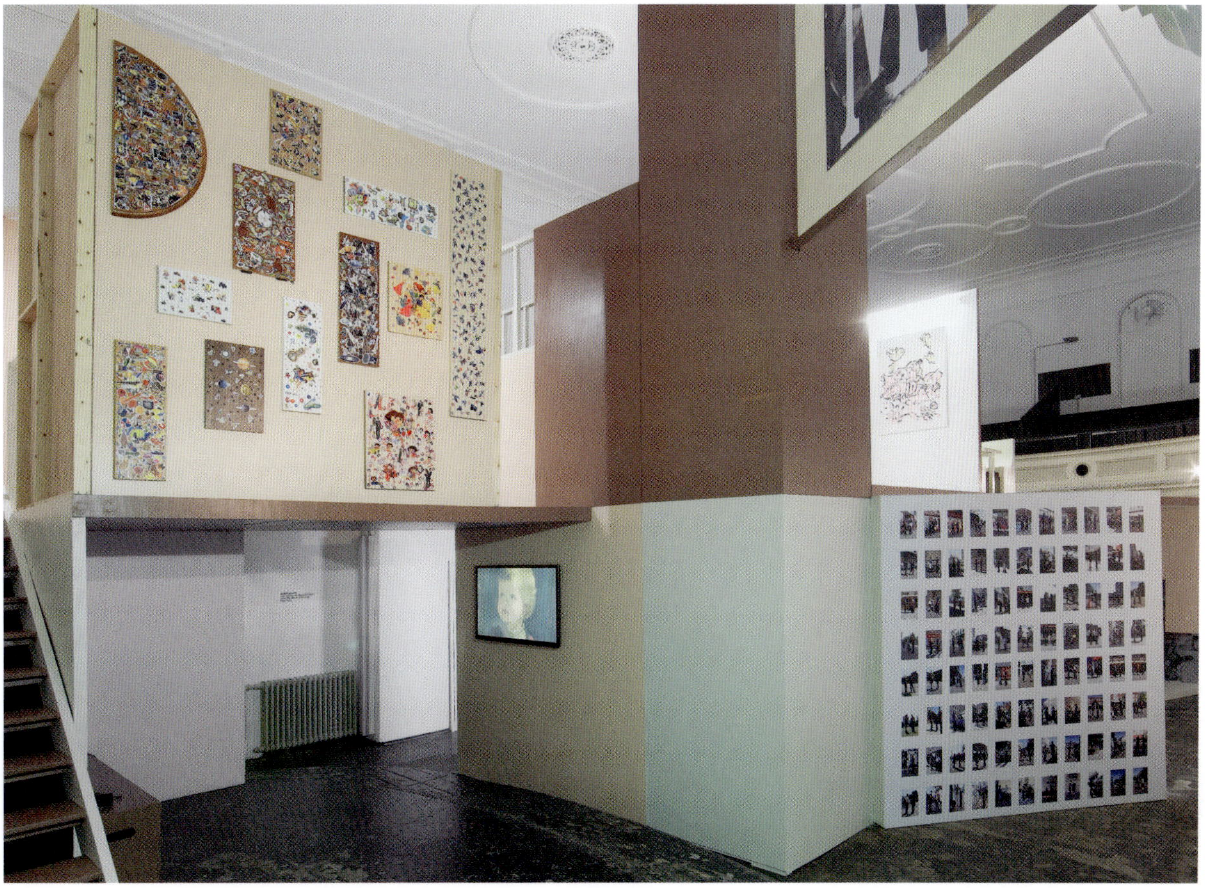

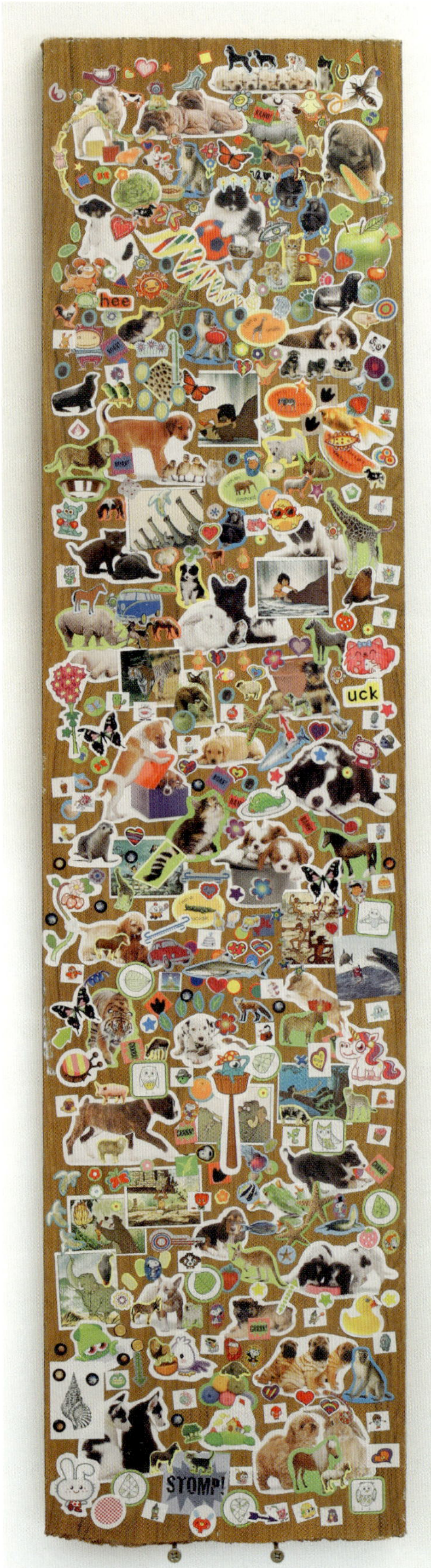

The Manifesto declares 'a willingness to be lied to and the will to believe! It's about the intense sadness of our unrealistic dreams, and the intense joy of our desire for them.' Holden said of the exhibition that he was looking 'at the idea of nostalgia as something that structures how we process the world. How we present the past to ourselves through the act of imagination.'[3]

To broadcast the idea of M!MS, ten years to the day after the Manifesto was written, Holden bought out the front and back pages of Bedford's local *Times & Citizen* free newspaper (circulation 90,000) and had the word M!MS, in large, bold text emblazoned on the cover. Inside, the Manifesto was published in full. The opening shot of the feature film shows the postman delivering the newspaper to homes and businesses across the city.

In 2014, 'Maximum Irony! Maximum Sincerity, 1999–2003: Towards a Unified Theory of M!MS' was restaged at Spike Island in Bristol. As in its earlier incarnation, the exhibition was both a record of a foundational period in the artist's life and also the embodiment of the MI!MS Manifesto: at once sincere and ironic, nostalgic and forwards-looking.

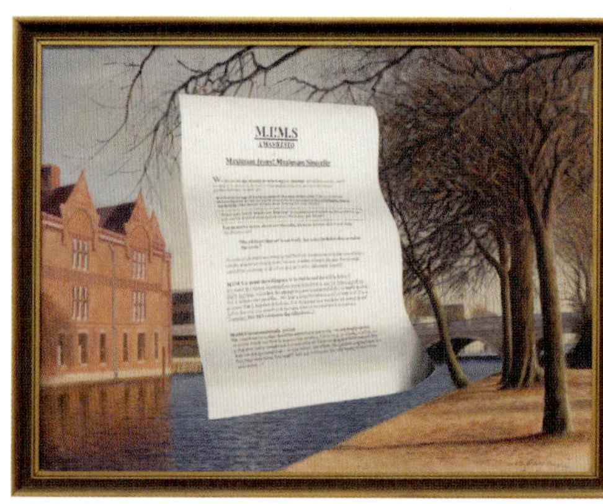

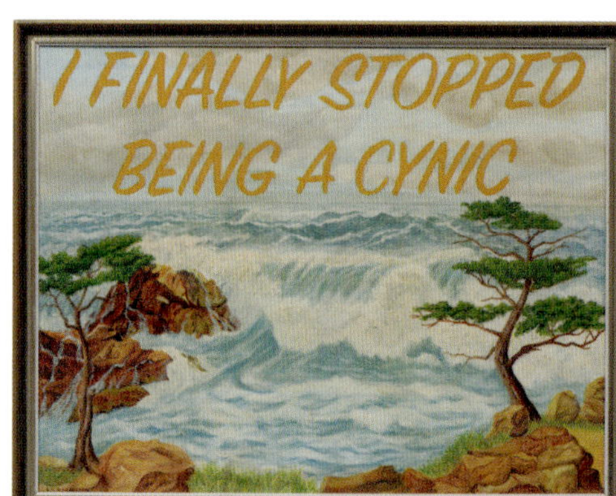

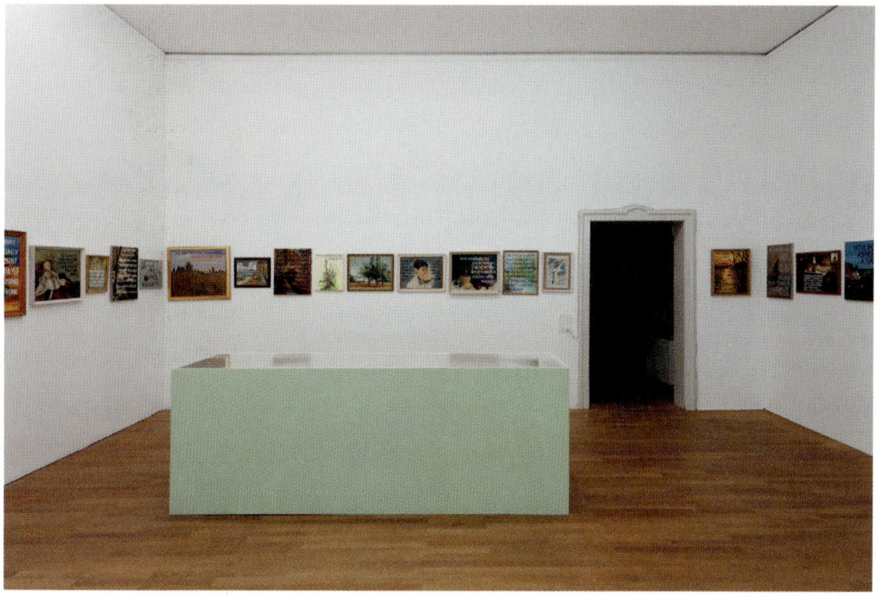

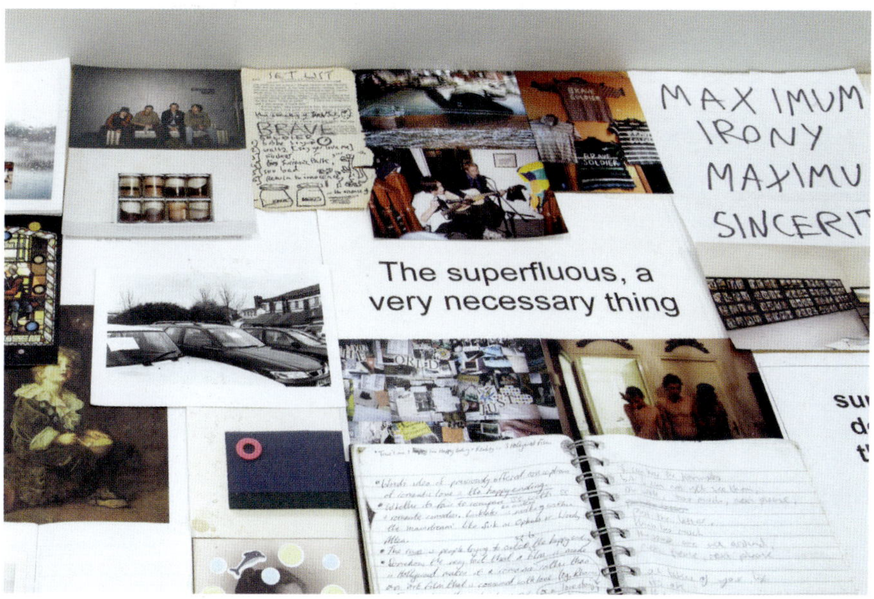

← *Maximum Irony! Maximum Sincerity, 1999–2003: Towards a Unified Theory of M!MS*, 2013, variable dimensions, installation view, Kunsthalle Winterthur, Switzerland, 2015
↙ *Maximum Irony! Maximum Sincerity, 1999–2003: Towards a Unified Theory of M!MS*, 2013, variable dimensions, installation view, Kunsthalle Winterthur, Switzerland, 2015
↓ *M!MS*, wrap-around cover for *Times & Citizen*, distributed in Bedford, UK, 2013

← *When the stars were the map of all possible paths*, 2013, stickers on laminated wood, 110 × 22 cm (43 ¼ × 8 ⅝ in.)
↖ *MI!MS Manifesto* (detail, part one of two-part painting), 2020, acrylic on found wood, 40 × 64 cm (15 ¾ × 25 ¼ in.)
← *I Finally Stopped Being a Cynic*, 2014, acrylic on board, 30 × 30 cm (12 × 12 in.)

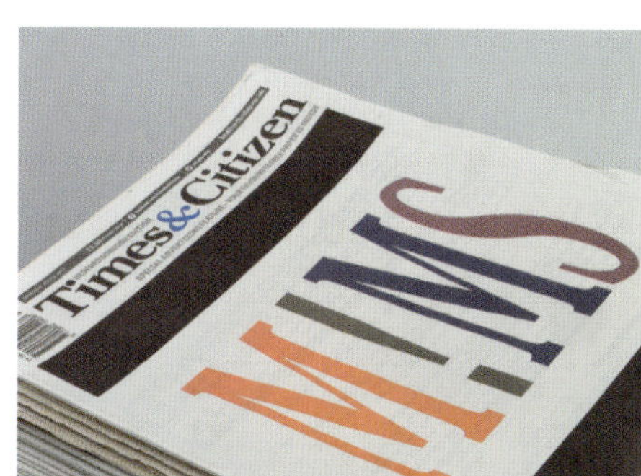

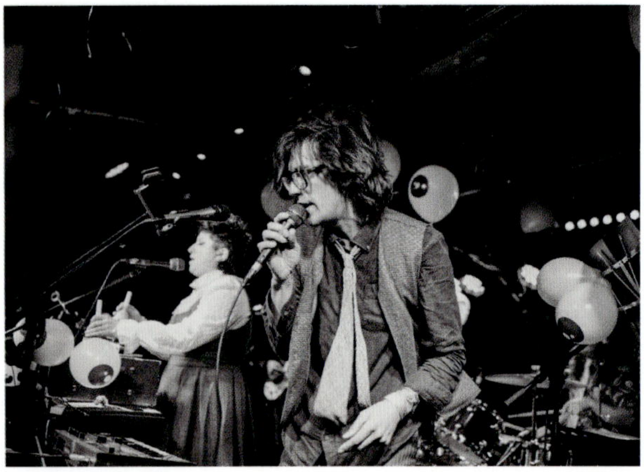

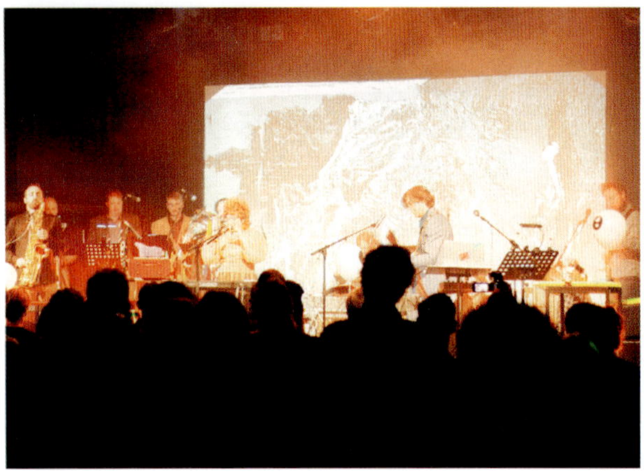

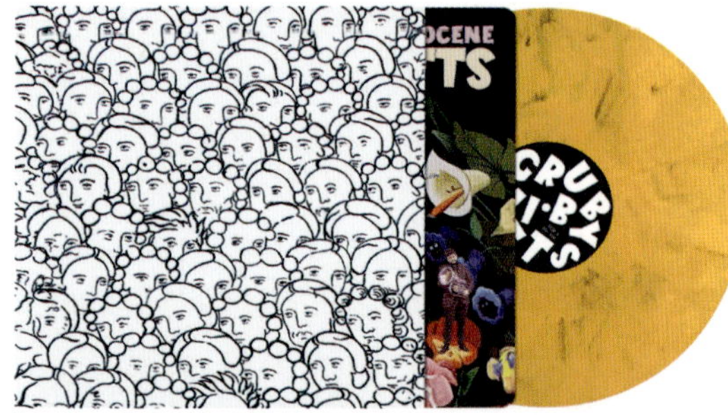

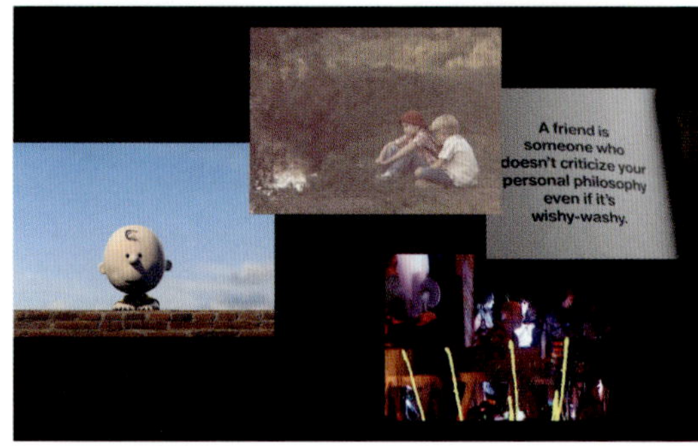

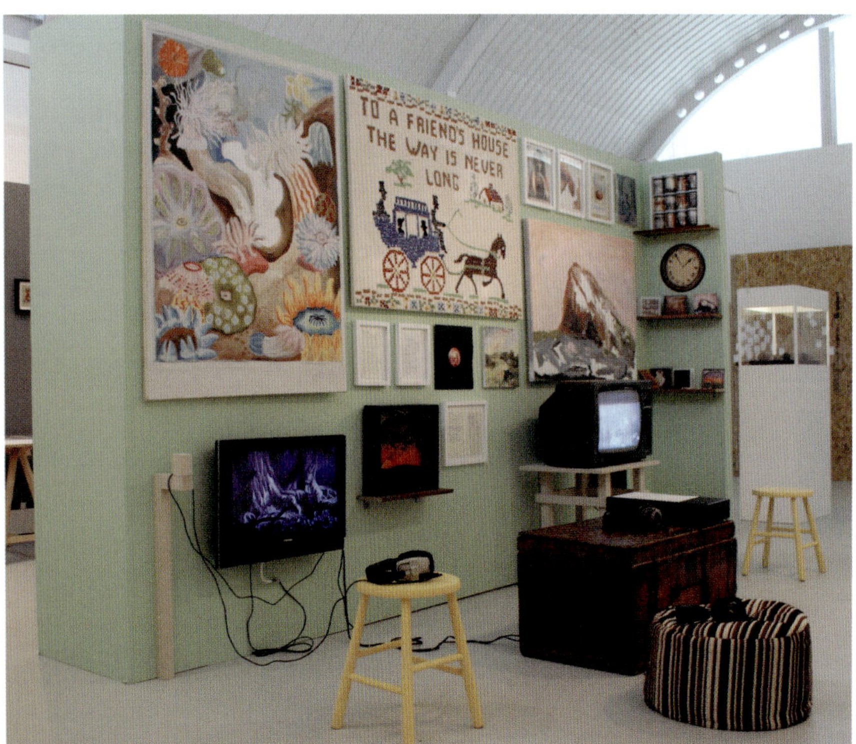

↖ The Grubby Mitts performing at Bedford Esquires, 2025
↖ The Grubby Mitts performing at ICA, London, 2025
↑ The Grubby Mitts, *Love in the Misanthropocene,* 2025, 12" vinyl, 30 × 30 cm (12 × 12 in.)
↑ *Oh! My Friends*, 2018, four-screen video projection, 40 mins., edition of 3, installation view, *Good Grief, Charlie Brown!*, Somerset House, London
← *Lost Toys Records: A Retrospective*, 2013, original paintings for record sleeves, installation view, *Performed*, Wysing Arts Centre, Cambridge, UK
↗ The Grubby Mitts, 2023
↠ (Overleaf) Andy Holden and The Grubby Mitts, 'Love in the Misanthropocene', installation view, Palmer Gallery, London, 2025

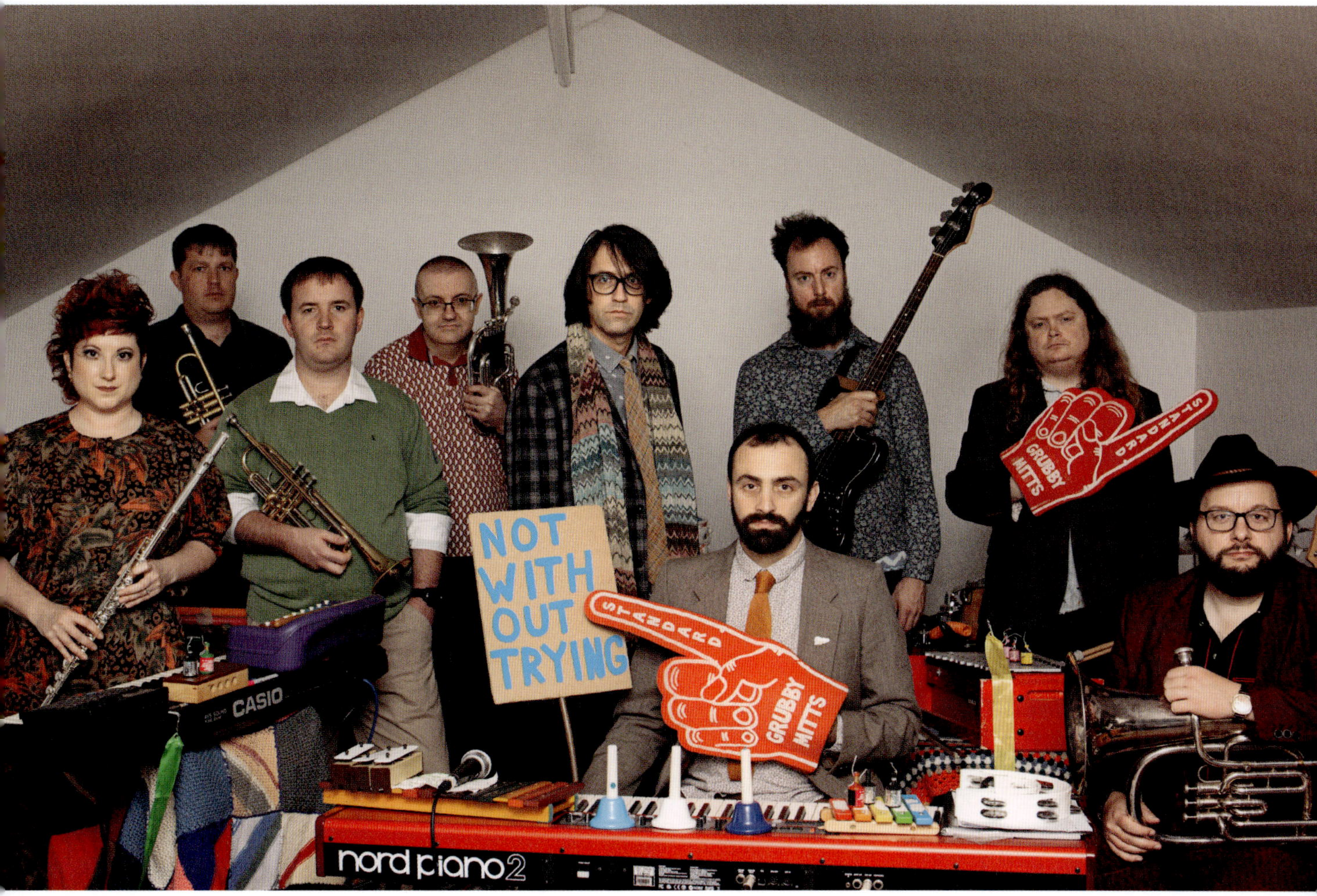

The influence of M!MS on Holden's creative output is ongoing. He still writes music with The Grubby Mitts, which in the original line up included all the signatories of the Manifesto, composing experimental pop songs according to the principles of M!MS. The music often has a conceptual framework that unearths, via repetition, a more emotive tone. The 2011 single, *To a Friend's House*, for example, comprises a single lyric line repeated over a string section that gradually builds towards a joyful, shouted finale; Holden's stage adaptation of David Foster Wallace's fictional study of alienation and absurdity, *Brief Interviews with Hideous Men* (1999), which premiered at London's Institute of Contemporary Arts (ICA) in 2012; and his film *Oh! My Friends* (2018) – a video essay exploring the role of creativity in friendship narrated over documentary footage of The Grubby Mitts on tour – were both also shaped by M!MS. The same logic of an oscillation between the seemingly antithetical poles of irony and sincerity returned again in *Laws of Motion in a Cartoon Landscape* (2011–17), embodied by the zig-zag wave form on Charlie Brown's T-shirt.

Although Holden's memories of his youthful formative years have been formalised in exhibitions, music and writing, their effect on him is not unusual: which of us could say that our teenage years meant nothing, had no impact? What is the past but a launching pad for a future we now inhabit?

1 Andy Holden in the short film made to introduce 'Andy Holden: Maximum Irony! Maximum Sincerity 1999–2003: Towards a Unified Theory of M!MS, 2013', Zabludowicz Collection, London, 2013.
2 Andy Holden, email to Jennifer Higgie, 3 February 2025.
3 Ibid.

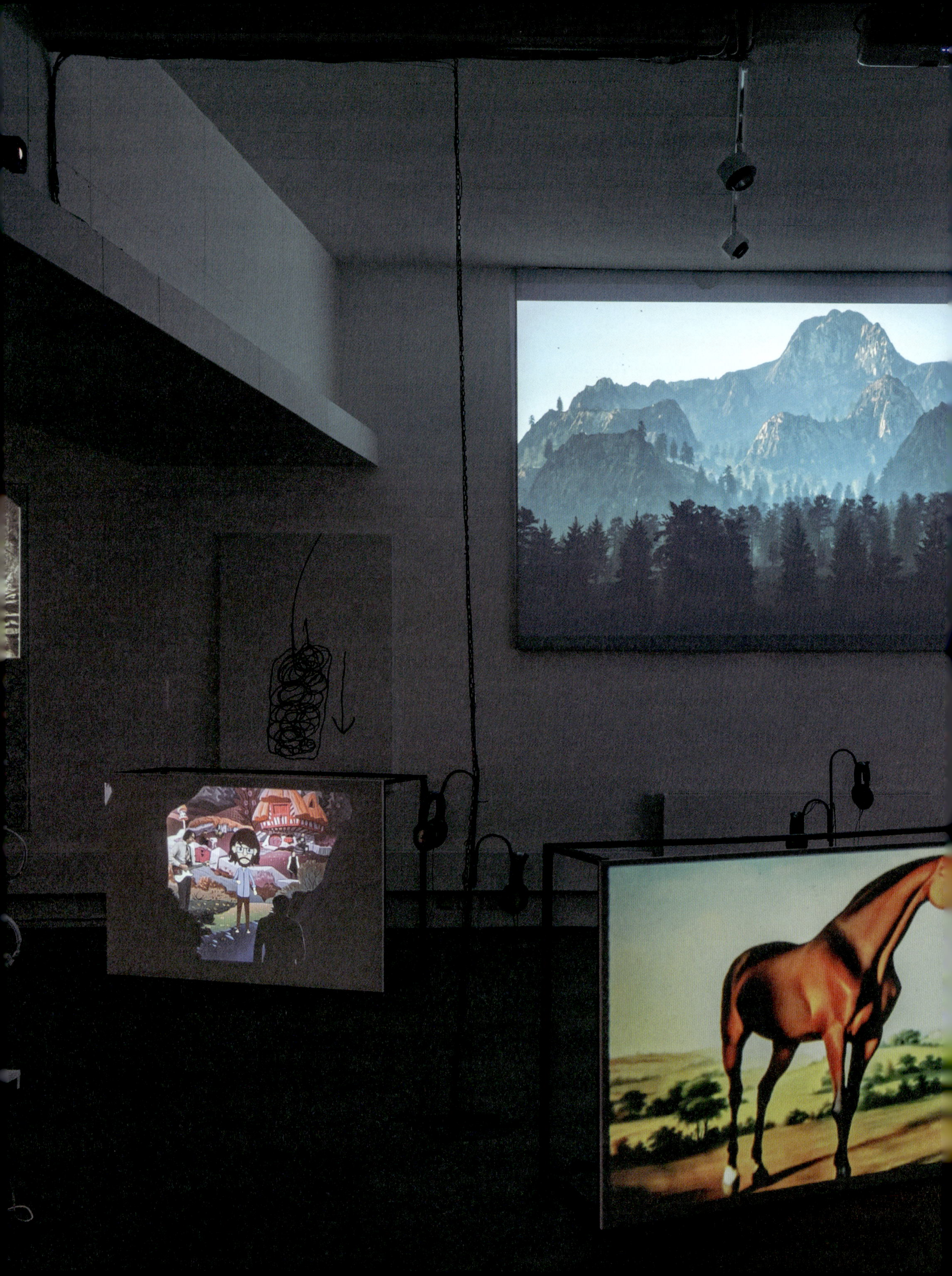

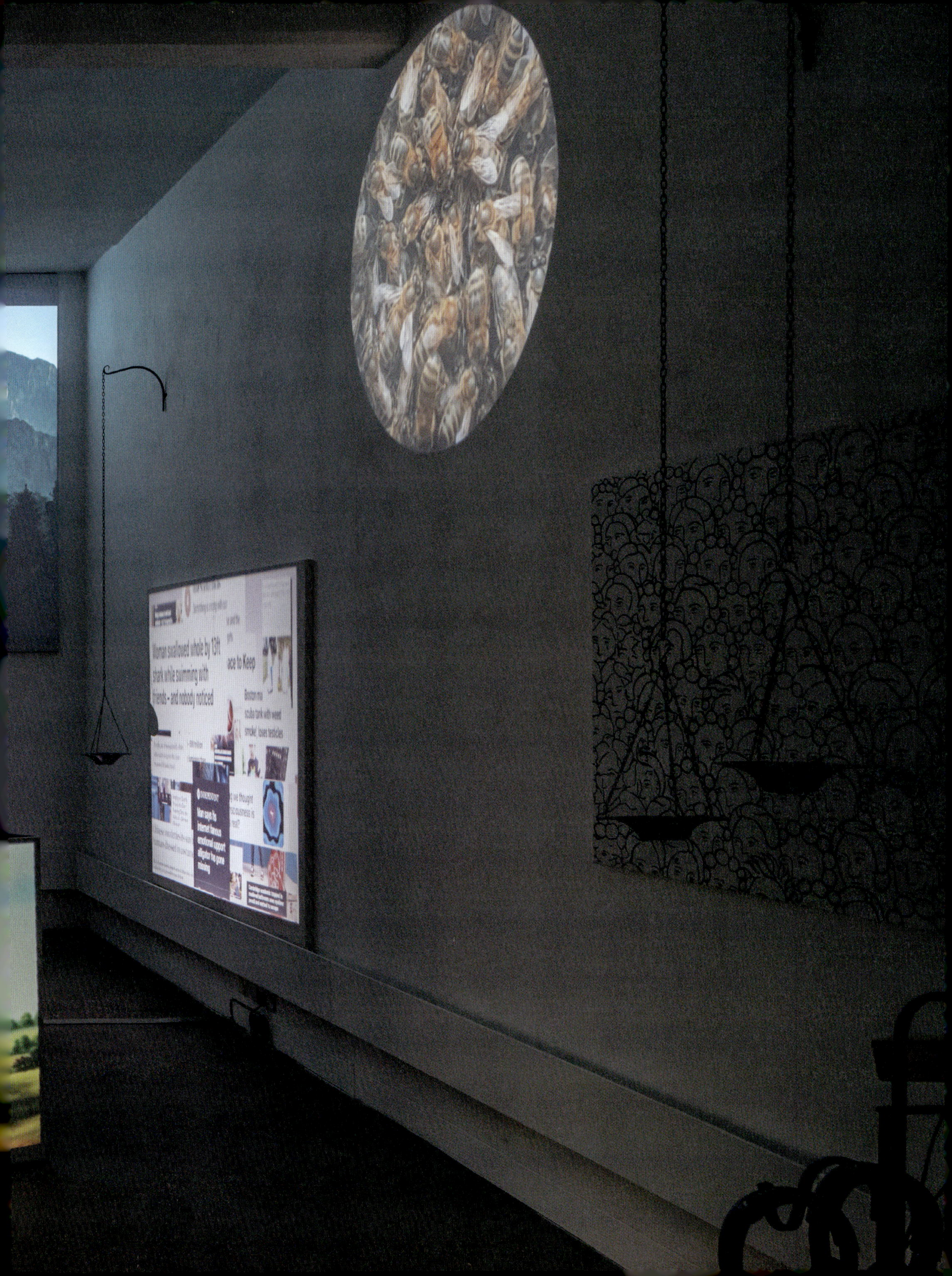
Woman swallowed whole by 13ft shark while swimming with friends – and nobody noticed
ace to Keep
scuba tank with weed smoke', loses testicles

Laws of Motion in a Cartoon Landscape

2011–17

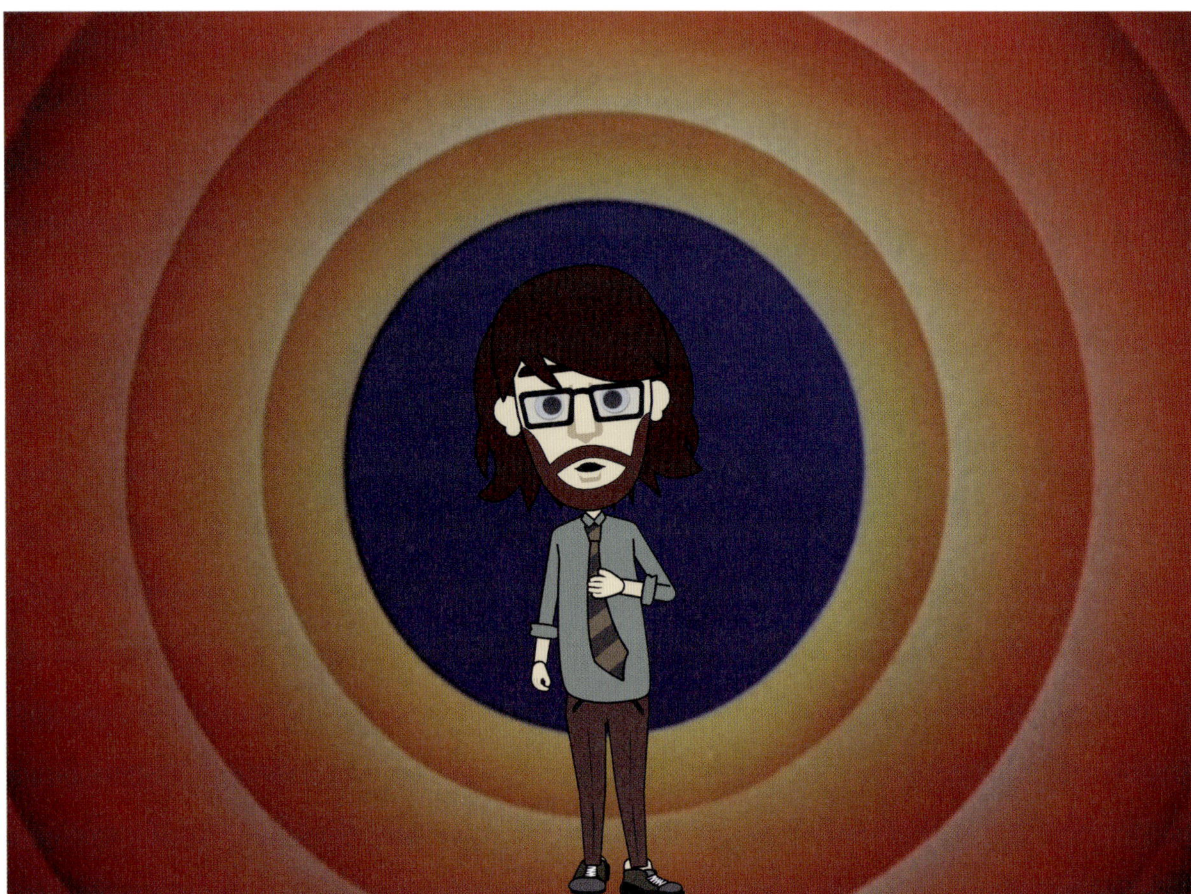

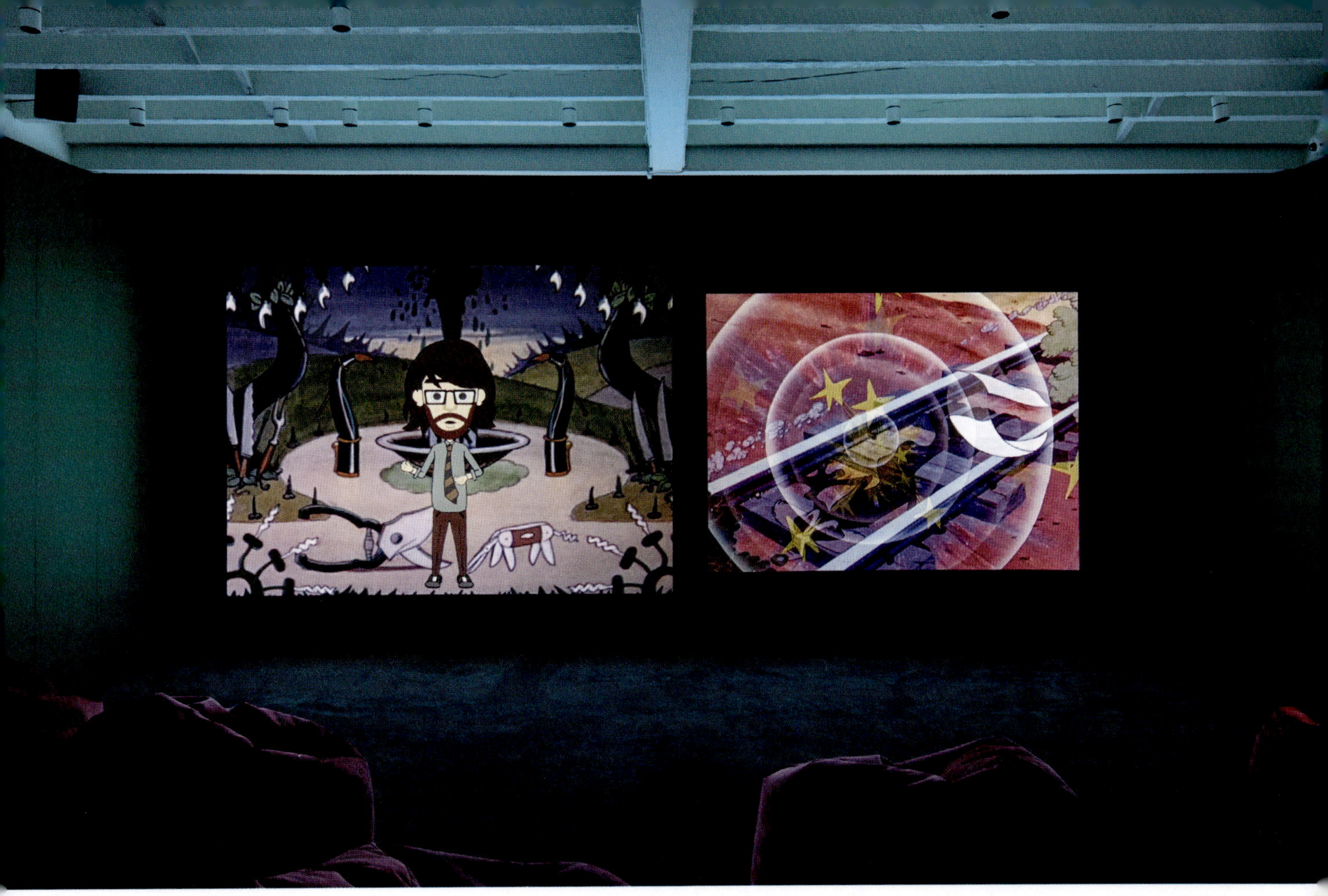

A mix of animation, narration and collaged video, *Laws of Motion in a Cartoon Landscape* (2011–17) is a two-channel, 57-minute cartoon which Holden describes as 'a manifesto for art after art history, based on the oscillating zig-zag wave form of Charlie Brown's jumper, the movement between knowing and not-knowing found in Bugs Bunny and the space of the plausible impossible'.[1] Moving at a cracking pace across the history of animation and art, Greek myth, cultural theory and physics, *Laws of Motion*... started out as a multimedia performance in which the artist presented his ideas in person alongside vintage video clips he had compiled as evidence of the case he was building. In 2016, the artist decided that, if the world was a cartoon, then he too must become an animated character. He inserted himself into the film using a second screen on which he appeared as an endearingly nerdy cartoon avatar, dressed in a khaki shirt and tie, wearing geometric glasses and sporting a lush beard.

In the work's opening moments, Holden's avatar ruminates against a background of what appear to be stars but which, on closer observation, are revealed to be eyeballs, spinning and sparkling in a grey expanse. He asks:

> If one took the entire mass of art history and piled it all up on top of itself to make a mountainous heap, how much would it all weigh? It would be very heavy. If an artist takes an object out of this dump, a steel girder, a piece of plywood, a glass Coke bottle, then an endless network of metonymical references unfolds. What is the weight of all these references? What is the weight of the imagination?

His answer is as allusive as it is elusive.

> The cartoon world exists in a gooey space-time. A multi-morphic space where categories are no longer ontologically distinct. Culture and nature have collapsed into a single, indivisible plane. A flat plane of protoplasmic, non-indifferent nature, populated by non-human subjects. History's come

← *Laws of Motion in a Cartoon Landscape* (detail, one of two screens), 2017, dual-screen animated film, 57 mins., edition of 7
↑ *Laws of Motion in a Cartoon Landscape*, 2017, dual-screen animated film, 57 mins., installation dimensions variable, edition of 7, installation view, The Perimeter, London, 2024

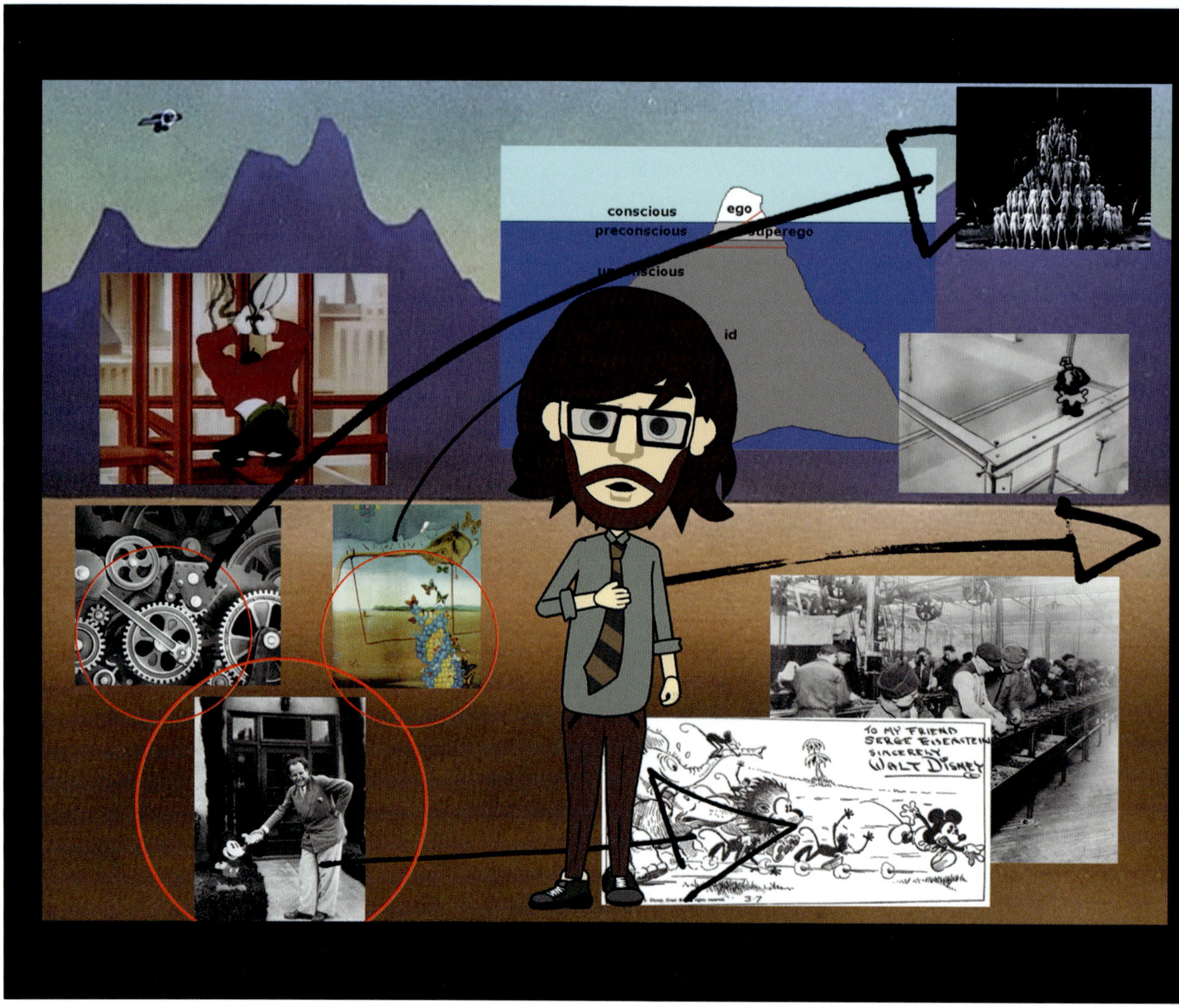

to an end. The world has come to resemble the cartoon landscape.

Laws of Motion... pivots on a theory that was first articulated by the cartoonist, screenwriter and novelist Mark O'Donnell, in a June 1980 *Esquire* magazine article titled 'O'Donnell's Laws of Cartoon Motion'. Written in blunt, faux-Newtonian language, the aim of the Laws is to make sense of, or give shape to, what is, essentially, a senseless world.

Holden builds on O'Donnell's Laws but further suggests that the golden age of animation – which ran from the 1920s to the 1950s and was driven, in the main, by the genius of Tex Avery, Chuck Jones, Max Fleischer and early Walt Disney – 'proved a prophetic, short-lived glimpse of the world we now find ourselves within'.[2] The first Law – 'Any body suspended in space will remain in space until made aware of its situation' – is illustrated by clips of Wile E. Coyote and Daffy Duck walking off cliff edges then remaining suspended in the air until they chance to look down; only when they become aware there is nothing below them do they fall. Holden's cartoon narrator informs us that this is because 'consciousness of the Laws makes conversion to the Laws inevitable'.[3] This first Law is both an explanation of the financial crash of 2008, as well as a metaphor for how an artist, if they are to survive the 'cartoon landscape', must not 'look down' when embarking on a new work.

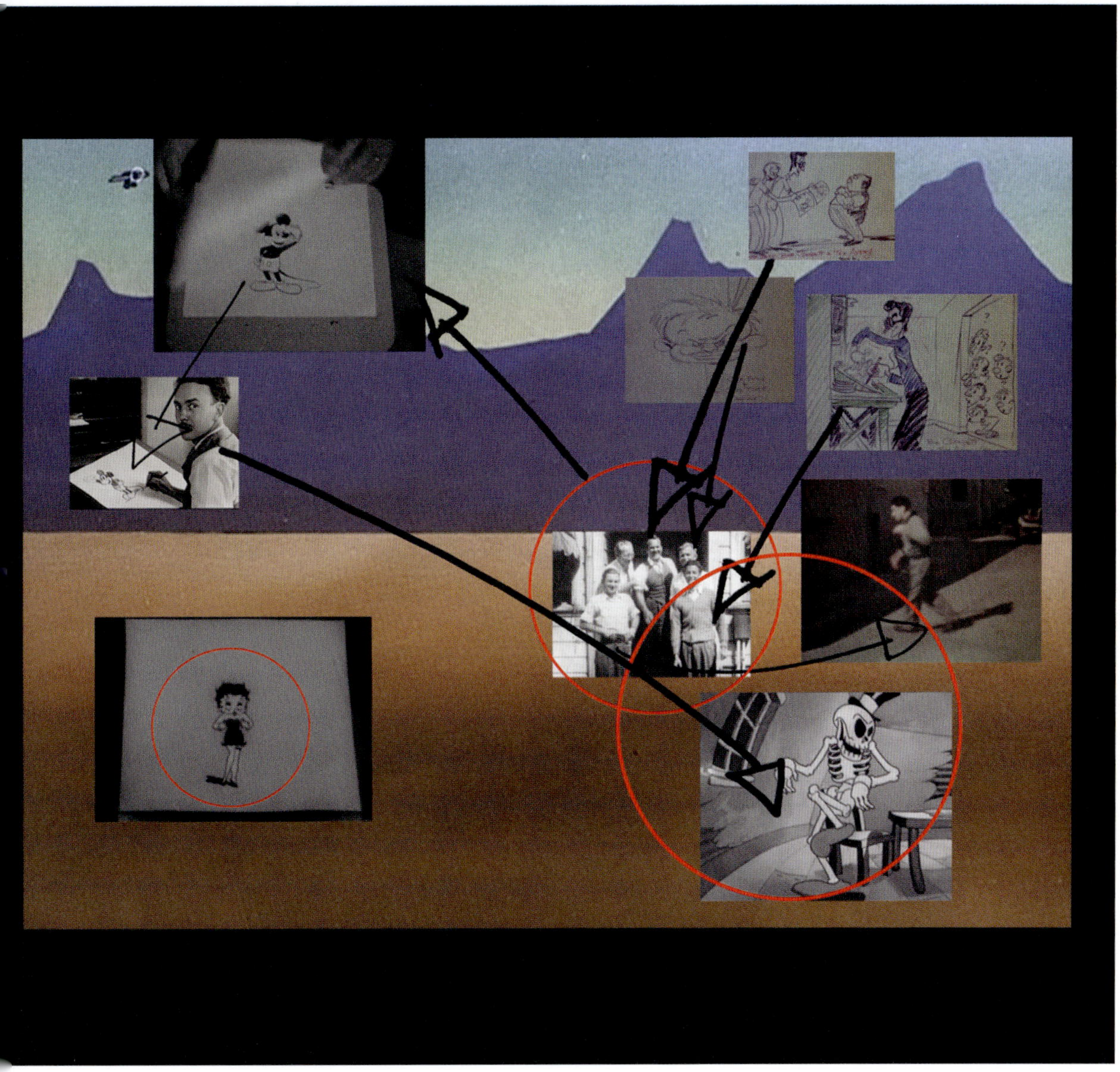

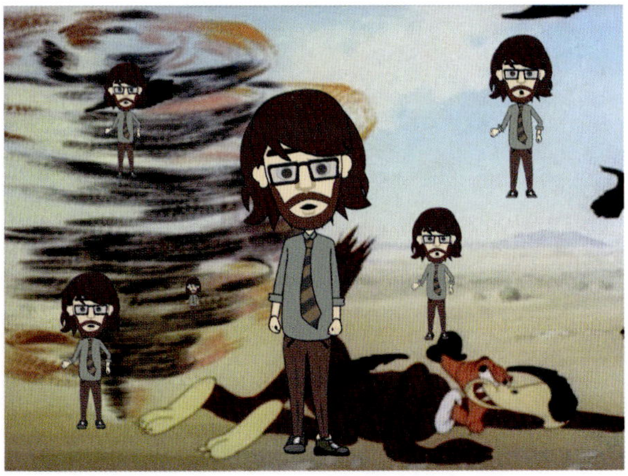

↖ *Laws of Motion in a Cartoon Landscape*, 2017, dual-screen animated film, 57 mins., installation dimensions variable, edition of 7. Tate collection (1); Arts Council Collection (2); Zabludowicz Collection (3); private collection (4)

← *Laws of Motion in a Cartoon Landscape (detail, one of two screens)*, 2017, dual-screen animated film, 57 mins.

At the end of his hour-long monologue, Holden's cartoon avatar looks down and, realising he is no longer on solid ground, drops out of the frame. The inversion of real-world physics in cartoons is gradually elaborated upon through analysis of moments in which characters collide with walls and temporarily become two-dimensional, or, when passing through walls, leave a 'cookie-cutter' shaped mark. In Law Five the observation that characters seem to be 'in several places at once' becomes a reflection on the speed of modern life and the current immersion in the online world, as well as ideas made theoretically possible by 'quantum superposition'.[4]

As the video progresses, Holden shifts the emphasis from cartoon physics to highlight the correlation between cartoons and contemporary politics – both, he notes, are driven by swift, reactive and unpredictable narratives fuelled by vengeance and reinvention. Following illustrations of numerous violent but temporary injuries to cartoon cats, in an attempt to explain why, in the cartoon landscape, 'any violent rearrangement of feline matter is impermanent',[5] Holden turns to more recent cartoons which depict 'the real world, animated'. He cites, 'Bart to the Future', the 17th episode of the 11th season of *The Simpsons*, which predicted Trump's presidency, and 'Die, Sweet Road Runner, Die', the 2010 episode of *Seth MacFarlane's Cavalcade of Cartoon Comedy*, in

↓ *Laws of Motion in a Cartoon Landscape* (detail, one of two screens), 2016, dual-screen animated film, 57 mins., edition of 7
→ *Laws of Motion in a Cartoon Landscape*, 2016, dual-screen animated film, 57 mins., installation dimensions variable, edition of 7, installation view, Glasgow International, Wasps Studios, Glasgow, UK, 2016

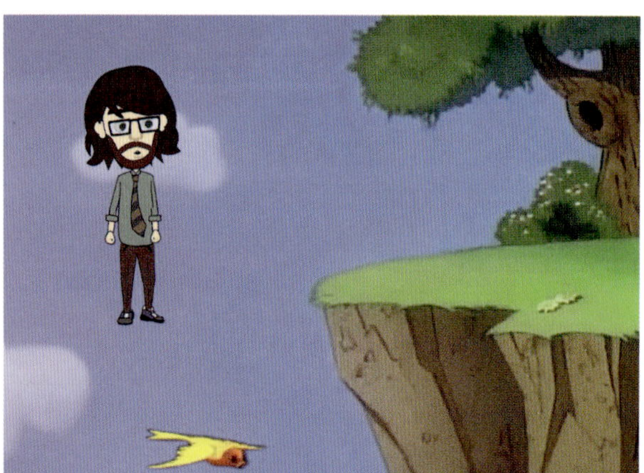

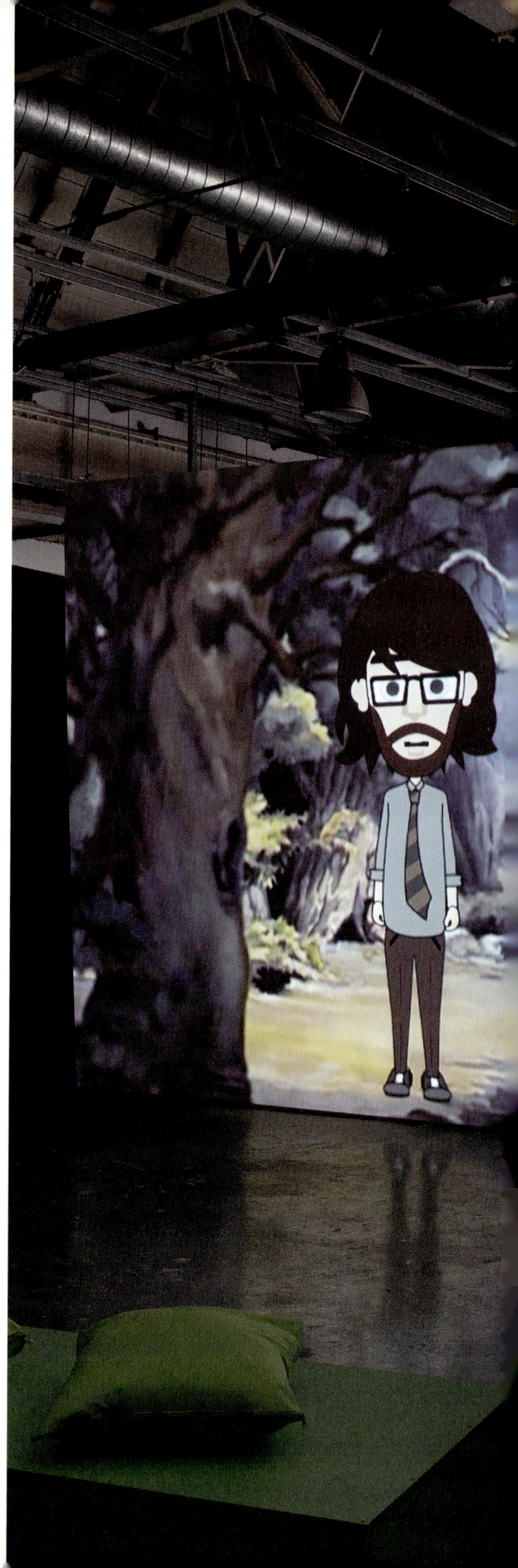

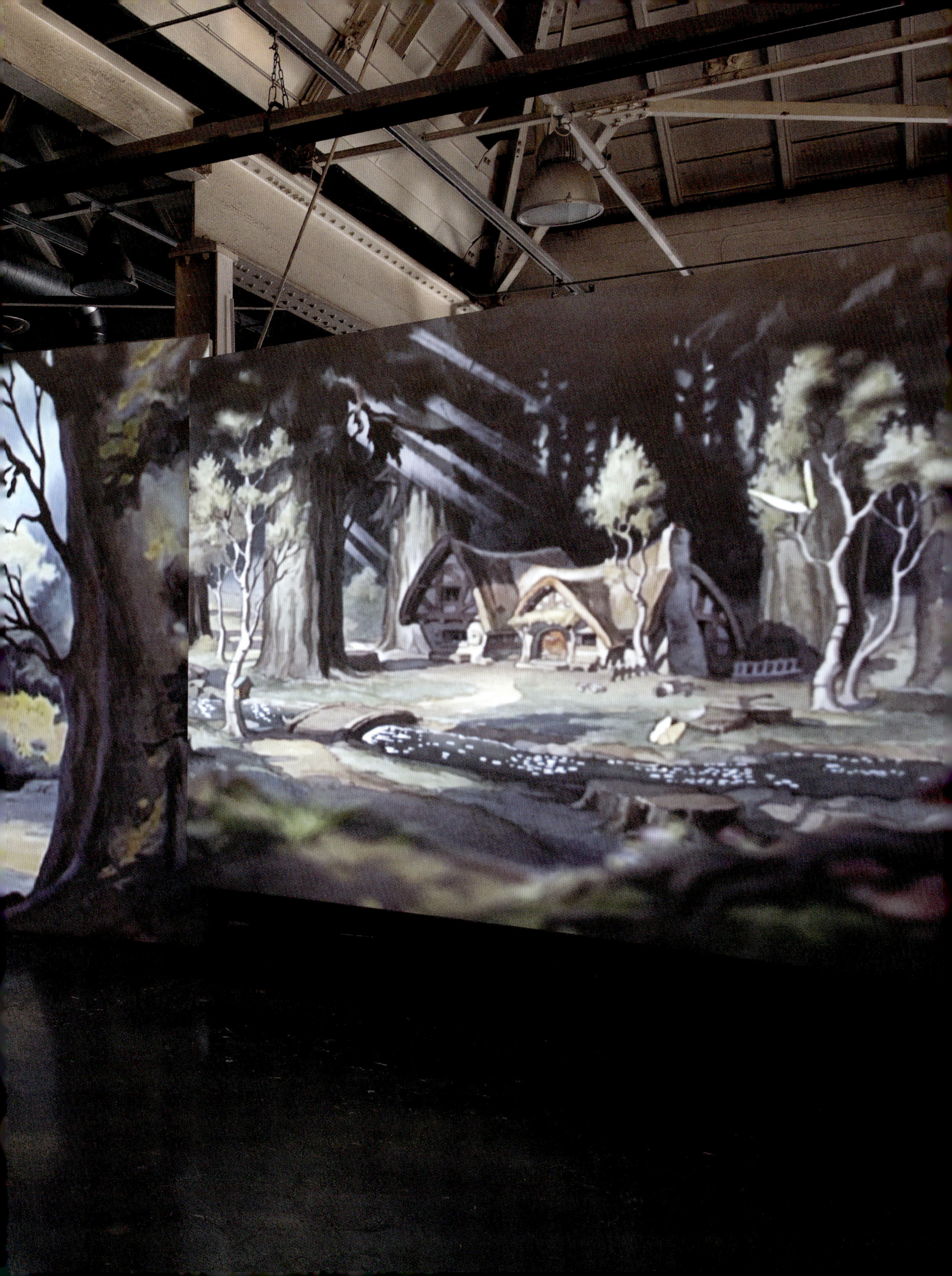

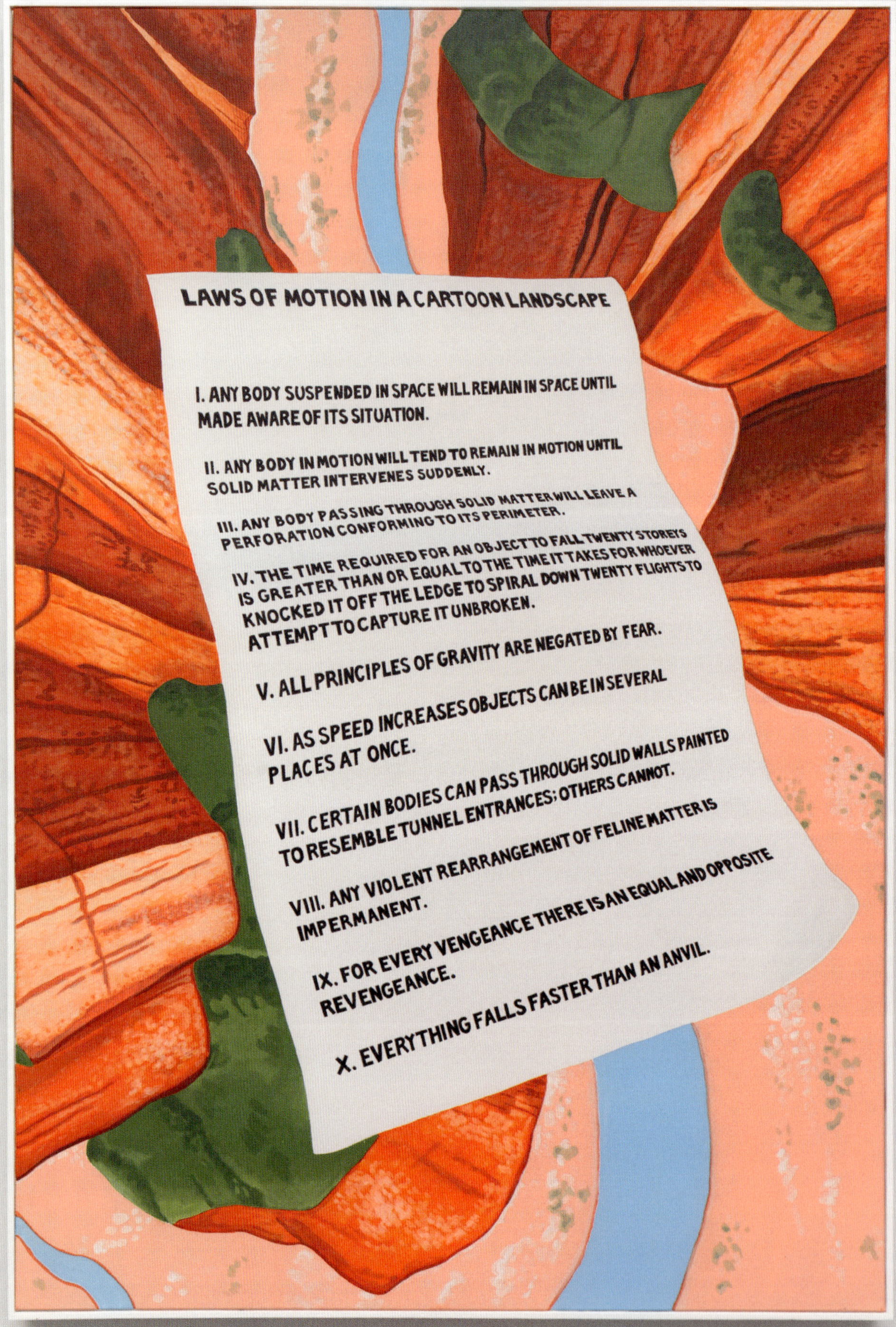
LAWS OF MOTION IN A CARTOON LANDSCAPE
I. ANY BODY SUSPENDED IN SPACE WILL REMAIN IN SPACE UNTIL MADE AWARE OF ITS SITUATION.
II. ANY BODY IN MOTION WILL TEND TO REMAIN IN MOTION UNTIL SOLID MATTER INTERVENES SUDDENLY.
III. ANY BODY PASSING THROUGH SOLID MATTER WILL LEAVE A PERFORATION CONFORMING TO ITS PERIMETER.
IV. THE TIME REQUIRED FOR AN OBJECT TO FALL TWENTY STOREYS IS GREATER THAN OR EQUAL TO THE TIME IT TAKES FOR WHOEVER KNOCKED IT OFF THE LEDGE TO SPIRAL DOWN TWENTY FLIGHTS TO ATTEMPT TO CAPTURE IT UNBROKEN.
V. ALL PRINCIPLES OF GRAVITY ARE NEGATED BY FEAR.
VI. AS SPEED INCREASES OBJECTS CAN BE IN SEVERAL PLACES AT ONCE.
VII. CERTAIN BODIES CAN PASS THROUGH SOLID WALLS PAINTED TO RESEMBLE TUNNEL ENTRANCES; OTHERS CANNOT.
VIII. ANY VIOLENT REARRANGEMENT OF FELINE MATTER IS IMPERMANENT.
IX. FOR EVERY VENGEANCE THERE IS AN EQUAL AND OPPOSITE REVENGEANCE.
X. EVERYTHING FALLS FASTER THAN AN ANVIL.

in which, after 60 years, Wile E. Coyote finally manages to kill the Road Runner. Rather than a celebration, this prompts a crisis of identity that results in Coyote finding God.

Asked by one interviewer to clarify what he was trying to communicate with *Laws of Motion…* Holden replied:

> At times the work feels close to the tone of a conspiracy theory video, and it should explain how a view of the world can be created and made plausible through the combination of otherwise unconnected elements and make us aware of how easy this can be. And how in a space where it seems anything can happen not anything can, rules, or laws, are always being created … it's very hard to say something about the work that the work doesn't already say.[6]

In 2021, Holden's passion for cartoons and comics led him to curate the exhibition 'Beano: The Art of Breaking the Rules' at Somerset House in London. *Beano*, which was launched in 1938 and is the longest running comic in the world, is known not only for its beloved characters – including Dennis the Menace, Minnie the Minx and The Bash Street Kids – but for its ongoing themes of rebellion, and specifically, since the 1950s, of kids against adults. Holden's starting point for the show was an examination of the ethics and moral laws embodied in the cartoons, and, like *Laws of Motion…*, it looks to the world of cartoons as a way of reinterpreting the rules that govern the world. He looked at *Beano*'s influence on the history of British culture through the lens of artists including Phyllida Barlow, Martin Creed, Gilbert & George, Sarah Lucas and Heather Phillipson; as well as Heath Robinson, claymation characters Wallace & Gromit, *Viz* magazine and punk music. Holden also included various stage sets he had designed, and conceived the catalogue as a comic book. Divisions between human existence and what humans have made to represent themselves dissolve.

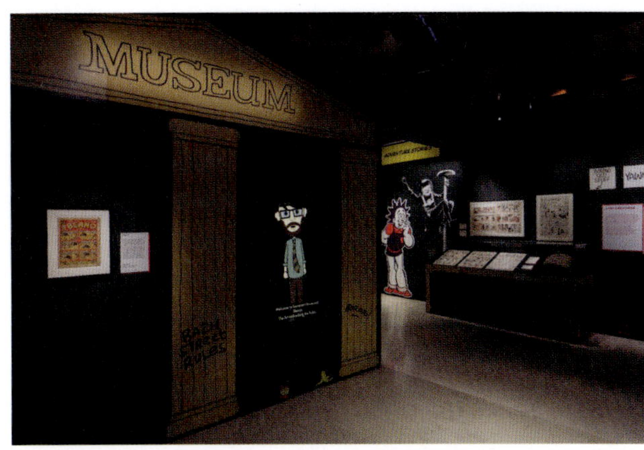

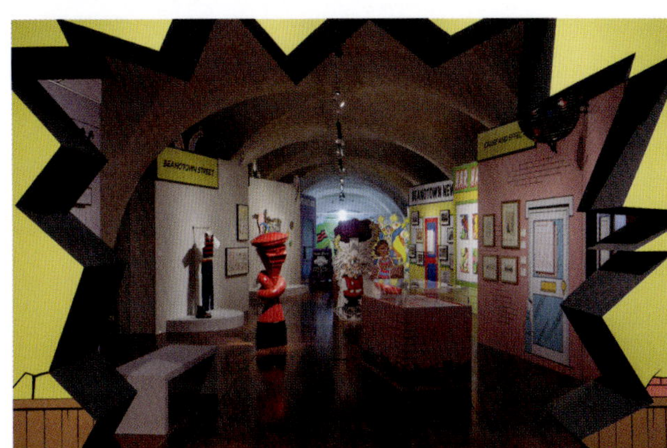

← *I Never Studied Law*, 2024, emulsion paint on canvas, 150 × 100 cm (59 ⅛ × 39 ⅜ in.)
→ 'Beano: Art of Breaking the Rules', curated by Andy Holden, installation views, Somerset House, London, 2020
↠ (Overleaf) *Laws of Motion in a Cartoon Landscape*, 2017, multi-layered print, 40 × 60 cm (15 ¾ × 23 ⅝ in.)

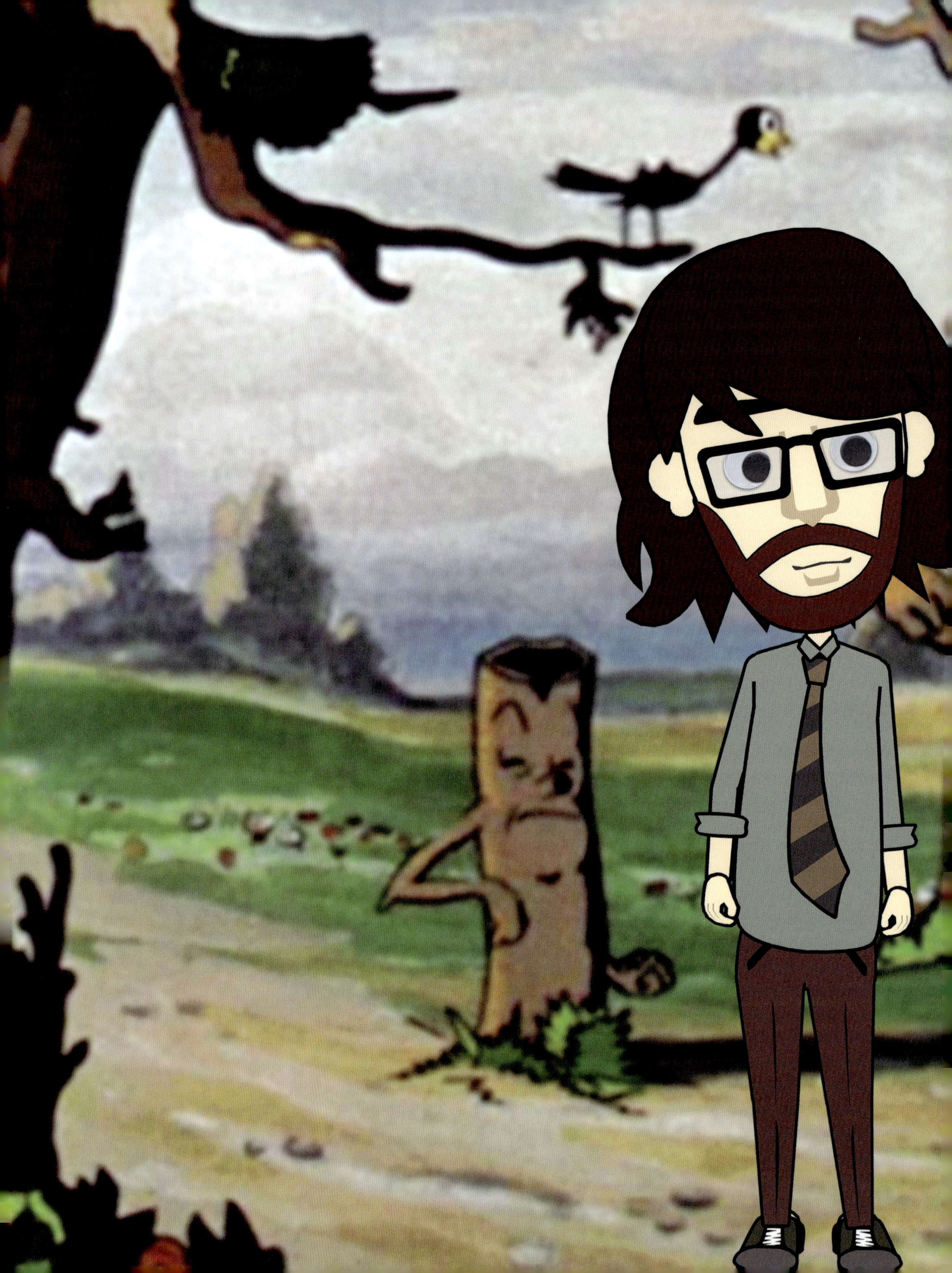

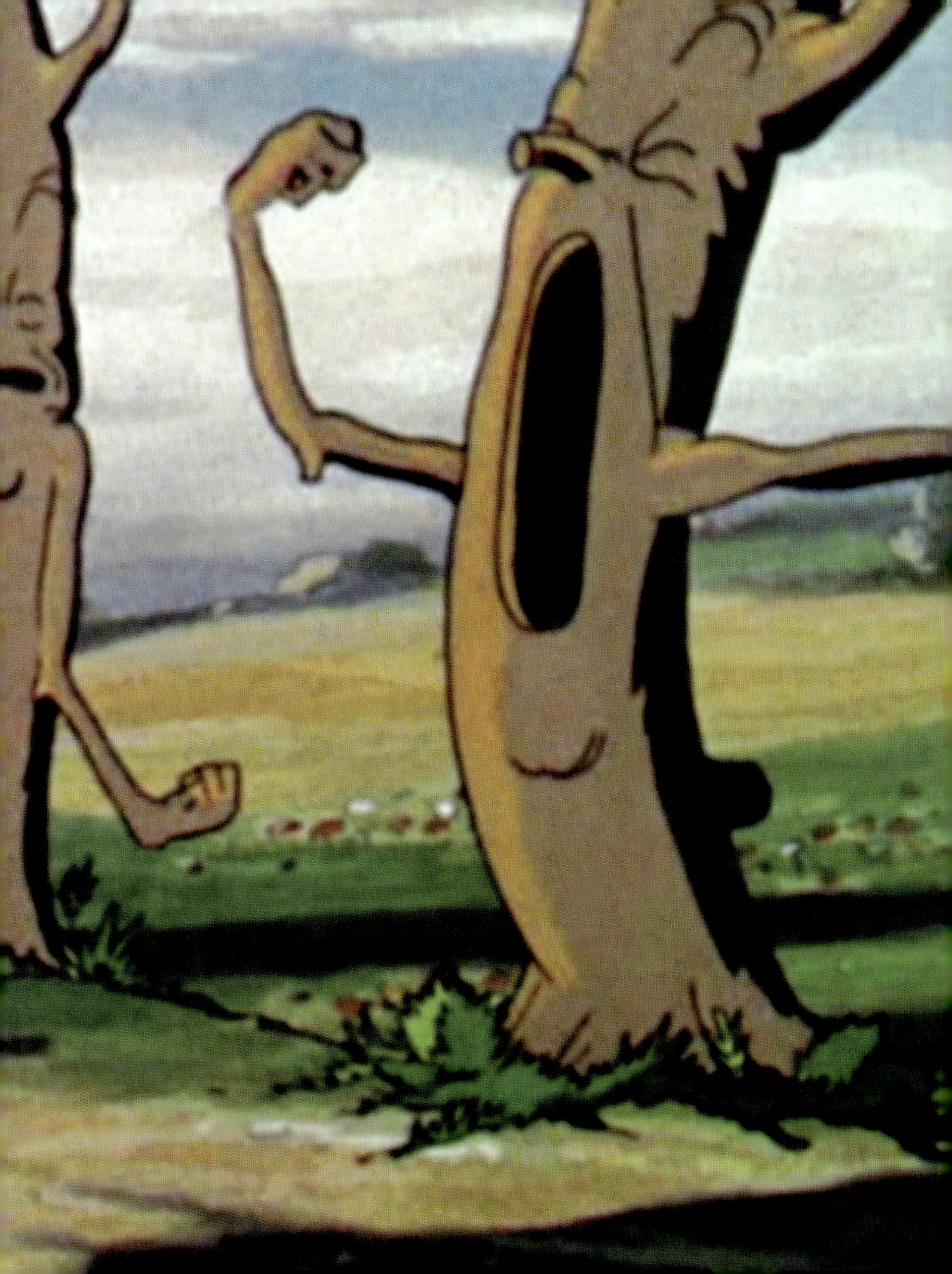

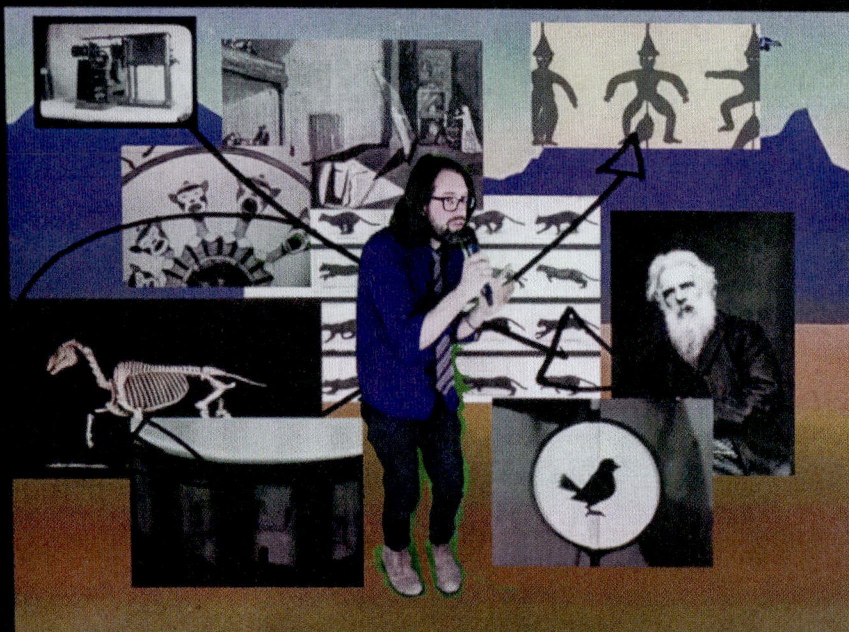

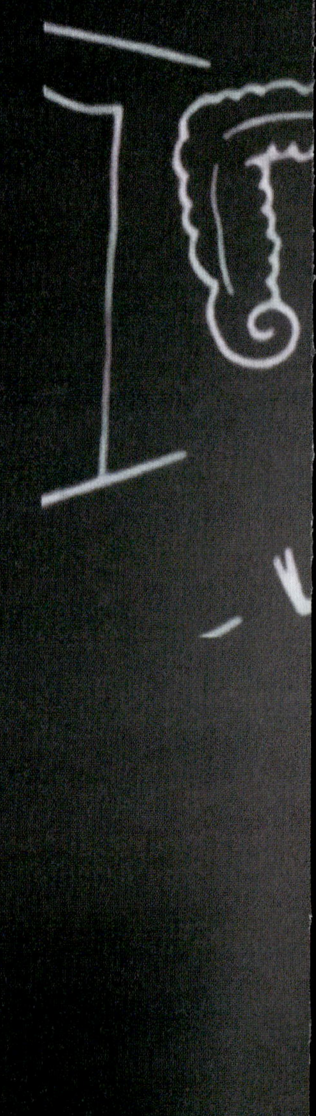

In the closing frames of *Laws of Motion...* Holden offers an insight into his thinking by giving the last word to Bugs Bunny, who, tied up with rope and suspended in the air, laughs maniacally and declares: 'I know this defies the law of gravity, but, uh, you see, I never studied law.' It's a funny scene that, like so much humour, reveals a deep truth: faced with the worst possible scenarios, our imaginations are, perhaps, our only saviour. In the blink of an eye, they can conjure a helping hand, a buoy, a safety net, a shelter.

1 Andy Holden quoted in the exhibition notes for 'Laws of Motion in a Cartoon Landscape' at The Perimeter, London, 2024, https://www.theperimeter.co.uk/pages/laws-of-motion-in-a-cartoon-landscape. Accessed 2 Mar 2026.
2 Andy Holden, narration in *Laws of Motion in a Cartoon Landscape* (2011–17).
3 Ibid.
4 Ibid.
5 Ibid.
6 Andy Holden interviewed by Richard Bright, *Interalia Magazine*, July 2019, https://www.interaliamag.org/interviews/andy-holden. Accessed 2 Mar 2026.

→ *Laws of Motion in a Cartoon Landscape, Live Performance*, 2018, performance for *Groundwork*, Academy of Music and Theatre Arts, Falmouth University, Cornwall, UK

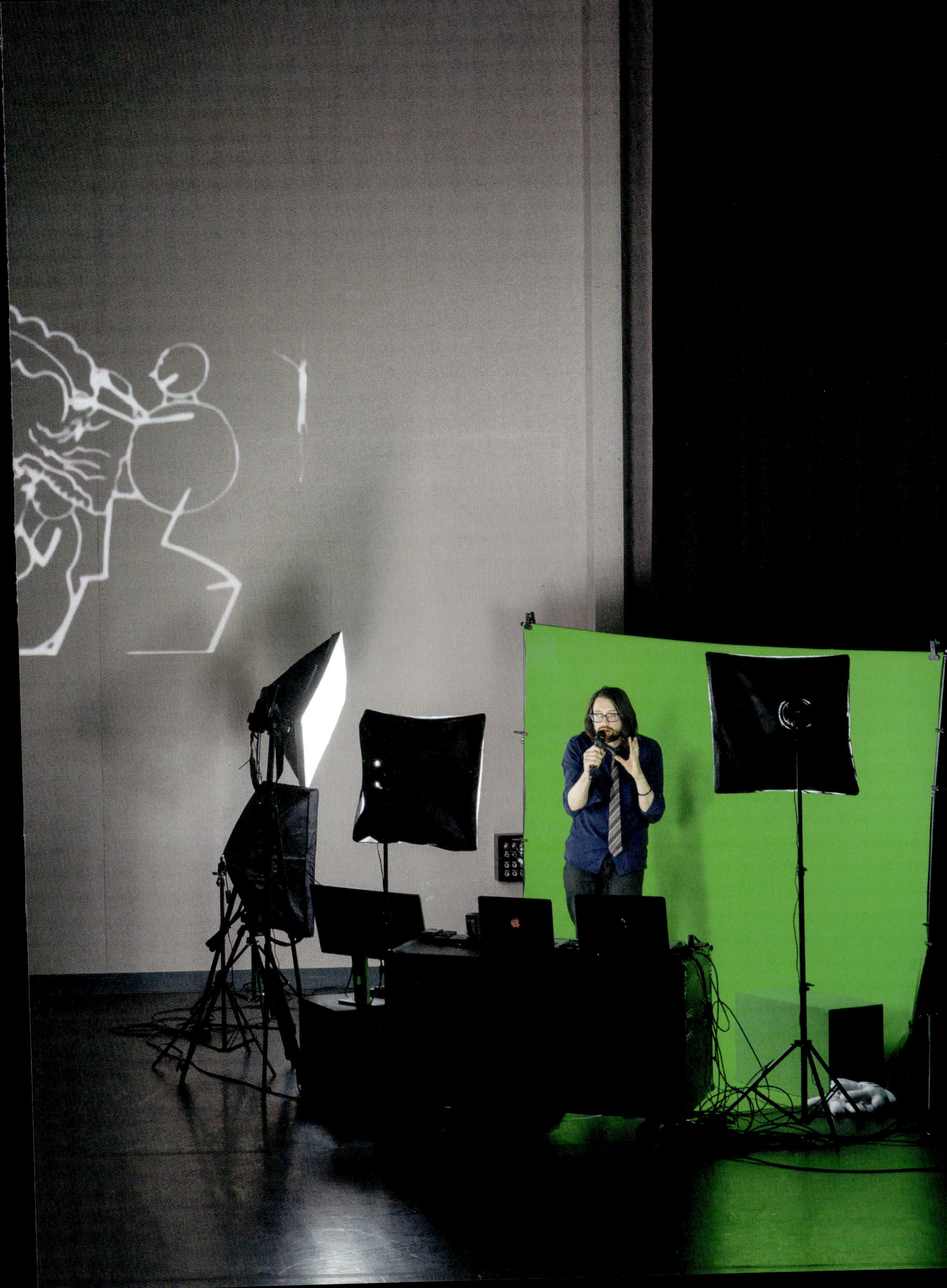

Structure of Feeling

2020

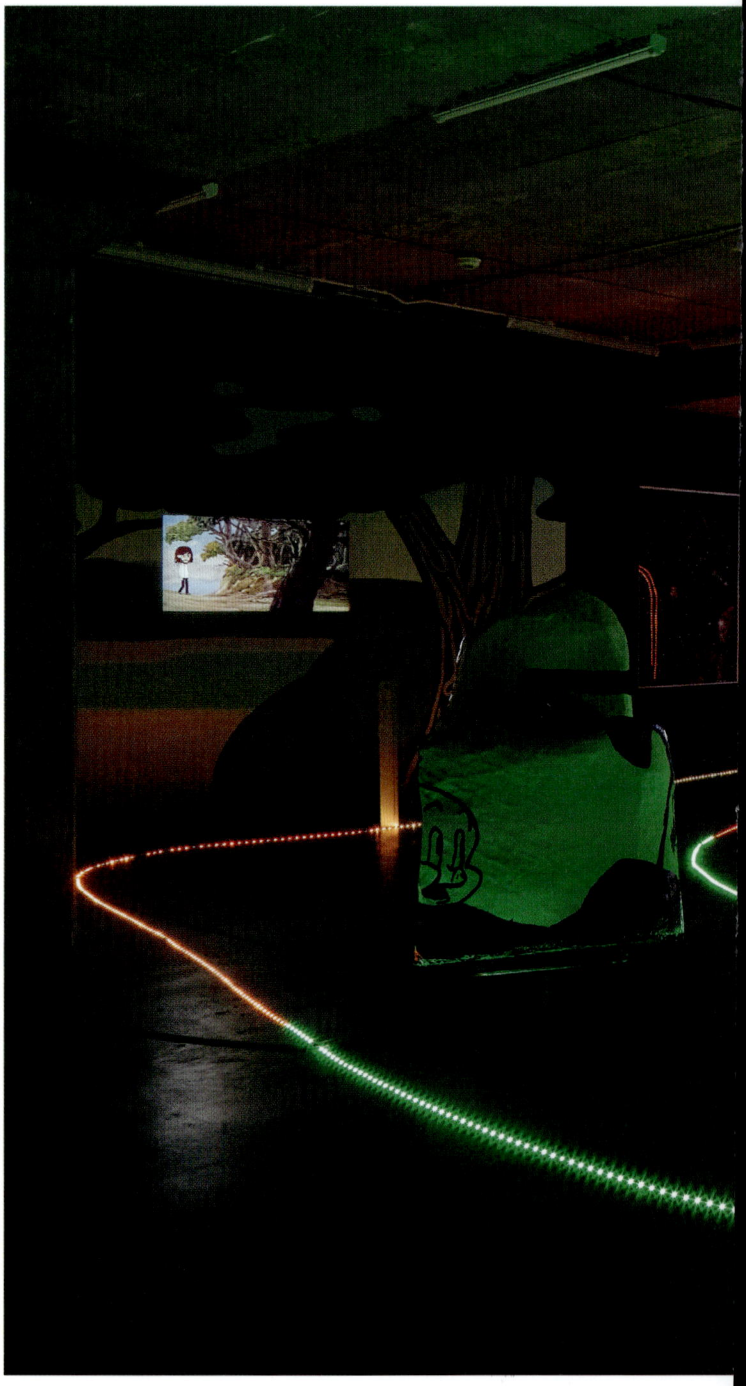

Structure of Feeling (2020) is a theme-park sequel to *Laws of Motion in a Cartoon Landscape*. Its title is a reference to the concept of the same name coined by Raymond Williams in his 1954 book *Preface to Film*. Holden's use of the term, though, is specific and idiosyncratic. He explains:

> It is a way of understanding through many interconnected media, or literature and culture in general, which for Williams, probably badly paraphrased, is a sensibility that is not yet dominant but can be observed in the process of emerging. It's not defined yet in any one artefact but is perceptible in the way component parts interact to reveal a tone or worldview...[1]

Holden's intention with *Structure of Feeling* was to expand on Williams's ideas in order to 'explore the outer edges of the cartoon landscape, to use psychoanalysis to examine the hidden depths of the cartoon world which seems very close to our own'.[2] He did this via a group of 3D printed sculptures, four short animations that feature Holden's avatar and a set of painted self-portraits showing the artist in various comic and tragic situations – crying next to a crying emoji, dressed as a crocodile, asking 'why?' next to an elephant and so on. First presented in September 2020 at Block 336, an artist-run project space in South London, a psychedelically painted and lit backdrop evoked a desolate cartoon landscape. Each of the four films marked a different 'chapter' in the installation, which, because of the Covid-19 pandemic, could only be viewed from a socially distanced ghost train: a fleet of sculptural motorised carts, made from converted mobility scooters reworked in fibreglass to replicate a theme-park ride.

↓ *Structure of Feeling*, 2020, installation view, Block 336, London

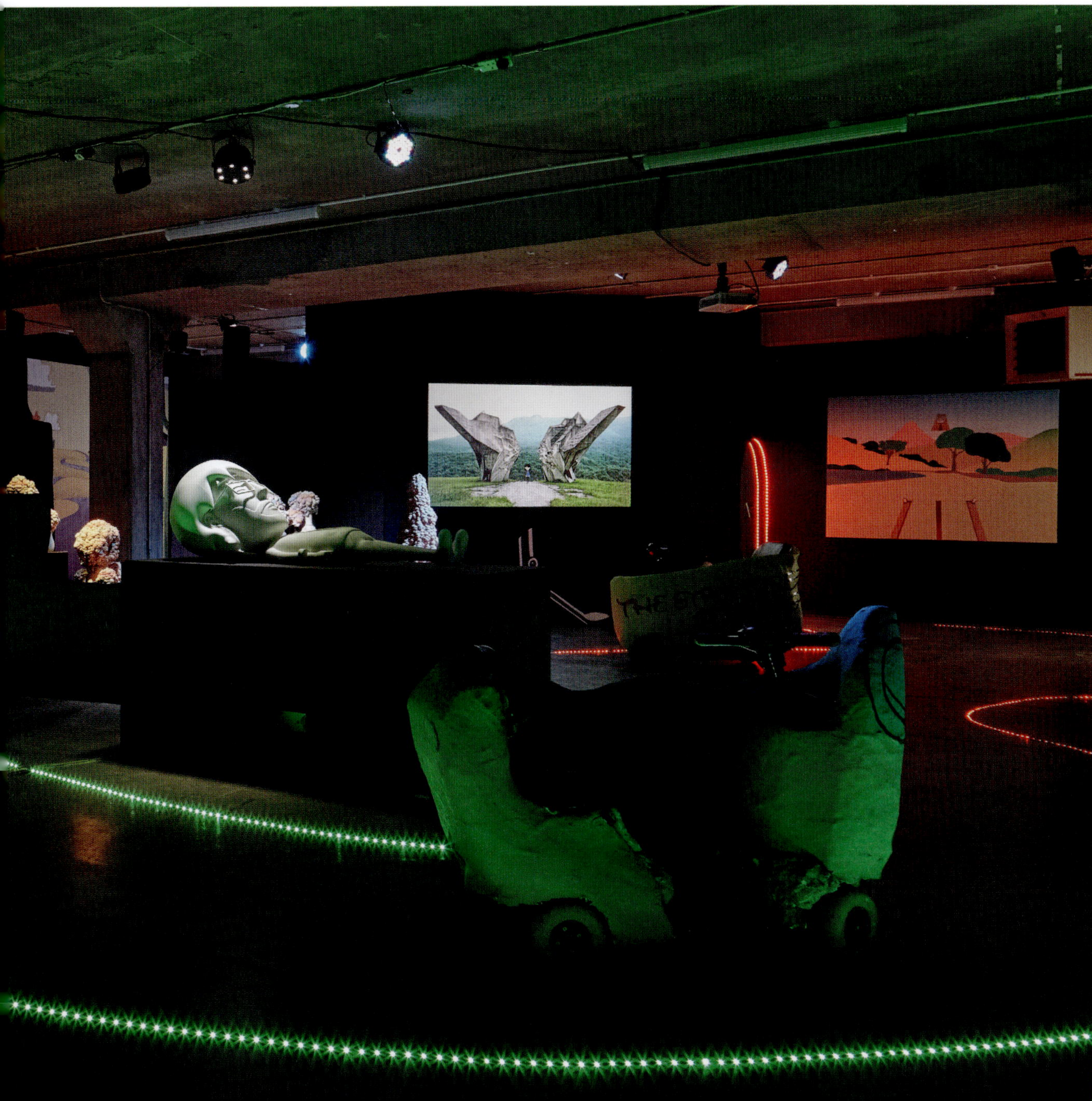

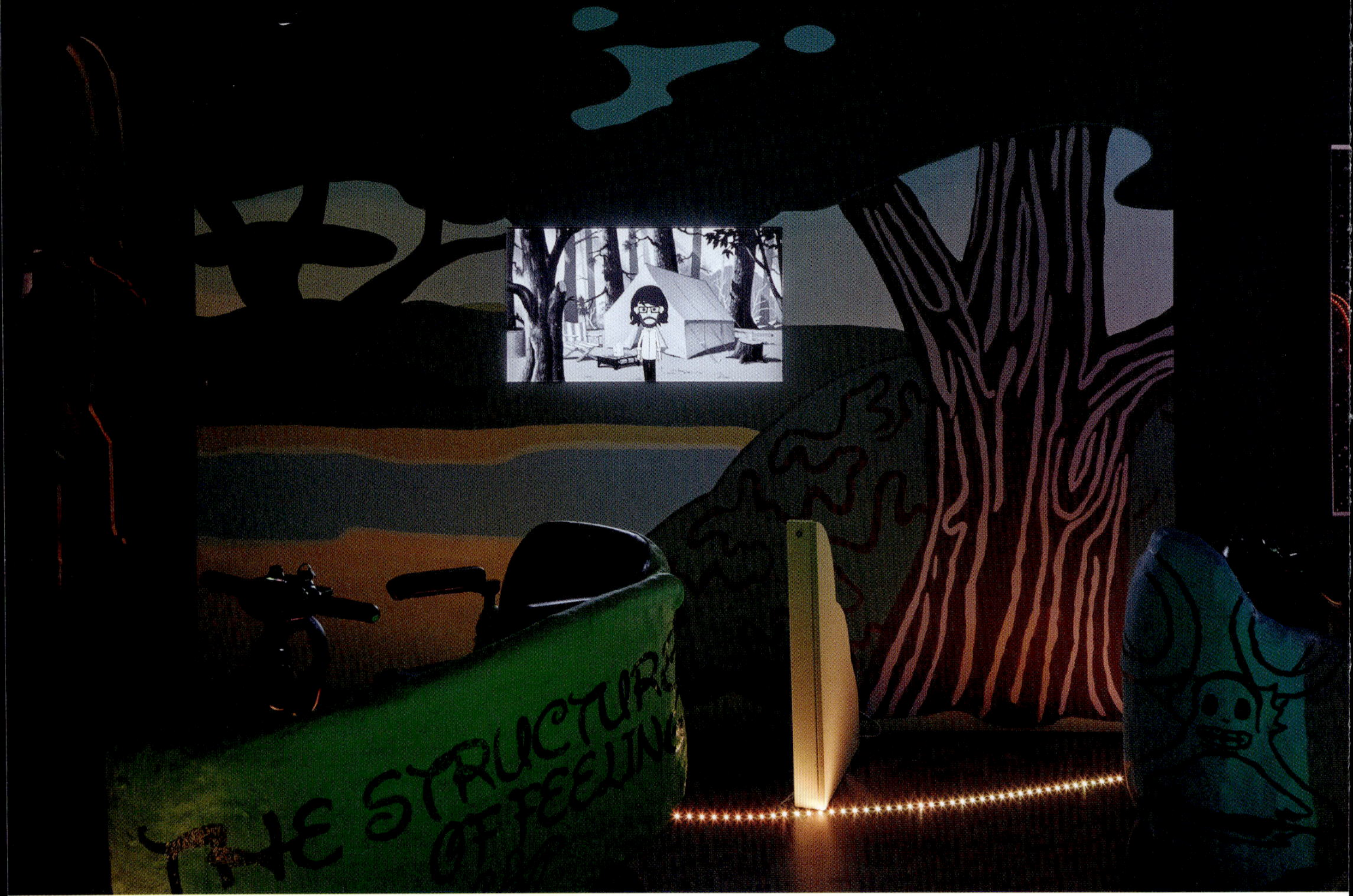

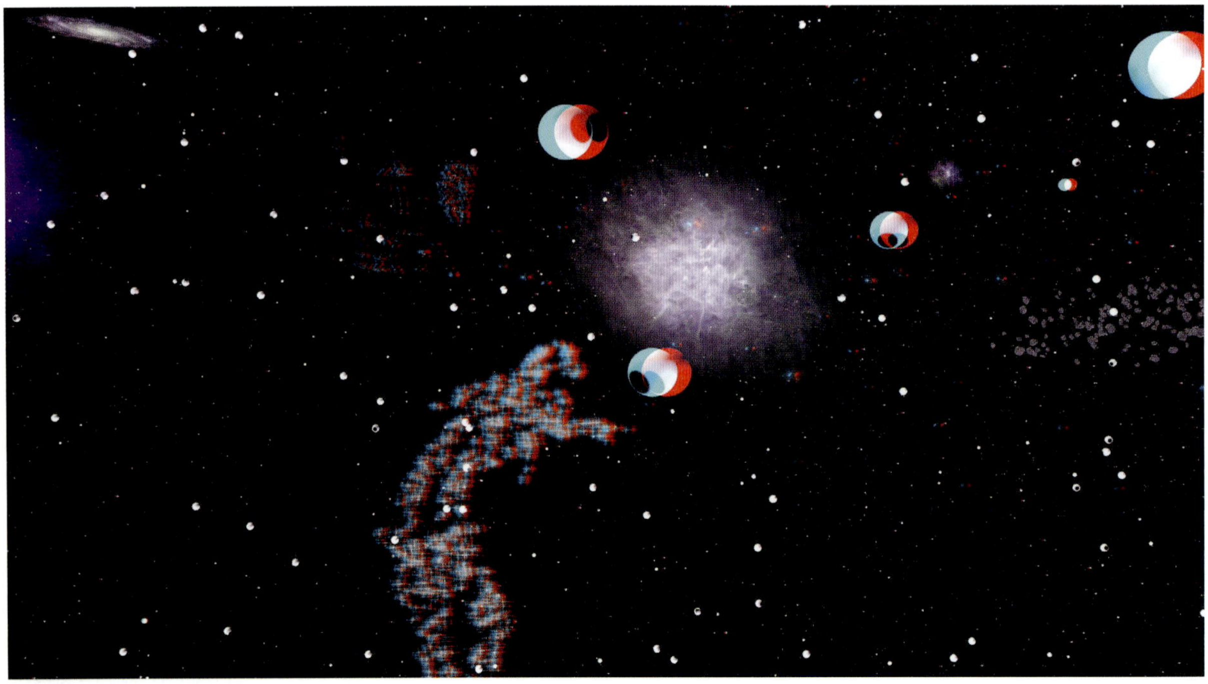

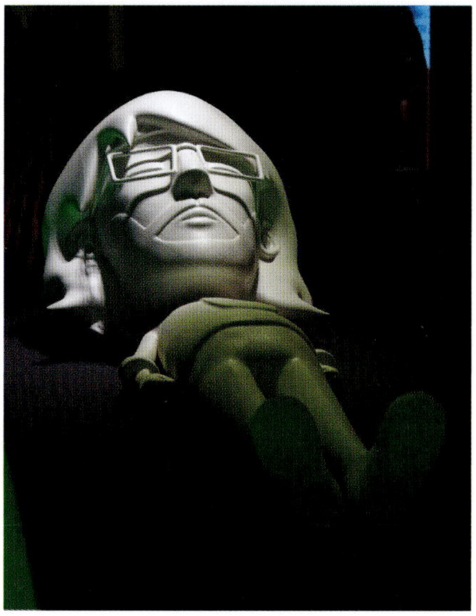

On a 40-minute journey, viewers moved from the desert, through the woods, past a sepulchre, a haunted library and an uninhabited city. Every ten minutes the gallery was plunged into darkness, then illuminated by a large 3D film of the cosmos, populated by floating eyeballs and cartoon constellations. In the gallery's centre, like a fallen knight, Holden's gleaming white, life-sized avatar lay stretched out on a tomb. References abounded: churches and nightmares and fairytales and planetariums; of the sinister thrill of fairgrounds at night and a vague longing for enchantment. As the artist Ed Atkins reflected in an essay that accompanied the exhibition: 'I thought about Holbein's *The Body of the Dead Christ in the Tomb* (1520–22); I thought about the gun in Roger Rabbit.'[3]

The first film, *Prelude* (2016), opens with Holden's avatar – whom he has described as 'part tourist, part last-man fantasy'[4] – walking through a desert landscape, along perilous mountain roads, railways tracks and an empty road, scenes culled from *Wile E. Coyote and the Road Runner* which the artist uses as stand-ins for the Lake District after a climate collapse. As he walks, he recites lines from William Wordsworth's 1850 autobiographical poem *The Prelude or, Growth of a Poet's Mind*. Holden sees Wordsworth's poem – a melancholic response to the landscape he visited and loved so well as a child – as a distant echo of his own changing relationship to his hometown of Bedford, a way of processing the past in order to better understand the present.

As he trudges through a landscape – inspired, in parts, by the desolation of Wim Wenders's 1984 film *Paris, Texas* (1984) and J. G. Ballard's 1965 novel *The Drought* – Holden's avatar comes across billboards emblazoned with various statements that, in their concision and incongruity, read like social-media clickbait: 'The 31 most beautiful punctuation marks last summer'; and 'Ten things you have been doing wrong this whole time'. He recites further lines from *The Prelude*, whilst avoiding traps left by Wile E. Coyote – a teetering boulder, a flimsy bridge, giant mousetraps. He intones:

> Even the loose stones that cover the highway, I gave a moral life / I saw them feel / Or linked them to some feeling. / The great mass lay bedded in a quickening soul / and all that I beheld respired with inwards meaning.

In the film's final minute, Holden's avatar collapses on the road, no longer able to inhabit the cartoon landscape as a cartoon character, as the Laws of cartoon motion proposed. In the next frame, he's resurrected against a black background; his final words are 'of my own heart'.

↖ *Structure of Feeling*, 2020, installation view, Block 336, London
↙ *Even Darker Matter*, 2019, animated 3D video, 6 mins., edition of 3
↑ *Death of a Hipster*, 2020, CNC cut high density foam, painted, 60 × 200 × 60 cm (23⅝ × 78¾ × 23⅝ in.), installation view, Block 336, London
↓ *Prelude*, 2016, animated video, 7 mins., edition of 5

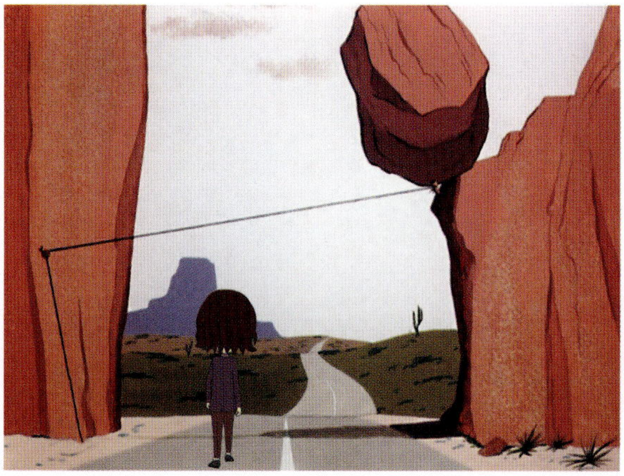

The second film, *Sticky Vapours* (2020), is an equally trippy meditation on the nature of reality and the perils of communication, loosely based on a short story the artist wrote as a teenager under the influence of psychedelics. The text, which he found several years later, gradually morphs into *Confessions of an English Opium-Eater* (1821) by Thomas De Quincey. Holden put the text through early beta-version AI tools that generated and scrambled it, which adds to the hallucinatory atmosphere of the work. It opens as a sinuous mist dances across a black-and-white cartoon windmill and then travels to a lake and a forest. (Each background was culled from the artist's vast archive of cartoon stills of forests and pastoral scenes, which he then reworked and reanimated with light touches of cinematic effects.) A sign asks, 'Quiet, isn't it?'

The soundtrack is by The Grubby Mitts; the musical motifs are recreations of birdsong made on tuned percussion. Holden's avatar walks from a campsite into a field, telling anecdotes about living in the countryside, collecting berries, being a child. At times, his statements – for example, 'I went to the shop to buy some vegetables / I shopped for vegetables' – become fractured and repetitive as computer-generated text intervenes. Suddenly, the artist himself, no longer an avatar, enters the frame, which features a squirrel with a baseball bat. He ignores it, reads a piece of paper, is scrutinised by a cartoon duck. He stretches up and pulls a black-and-white landscape down, which he then paints over to reveal, in full colour, his avatar. He holds up a sign that asks: 'Silly, isn't it?' The film ends with an exploratory dive into a throat – a place where words can stick. The artist, talking incoherently, steps into an idyll, a reworking of Walt Disney's 1940 *Fantasia*. He disappears.

The film works on numerous levels: as a fantastical, dream-like meditation on the complicated, digital/human mash-up that constitutes contemporary current reality; as well as a coded set of references to Holden's earlier works, especially *Chewy Cosmos Thingly Time*; to earlier artists, such as the Dadaist Tristan Tzara's famous nonsensical maxim 'thought is made in the mouth'; and to the first Law of cartoon motion: 'Any body suspended in space will remain in space until made aware of its situation'.

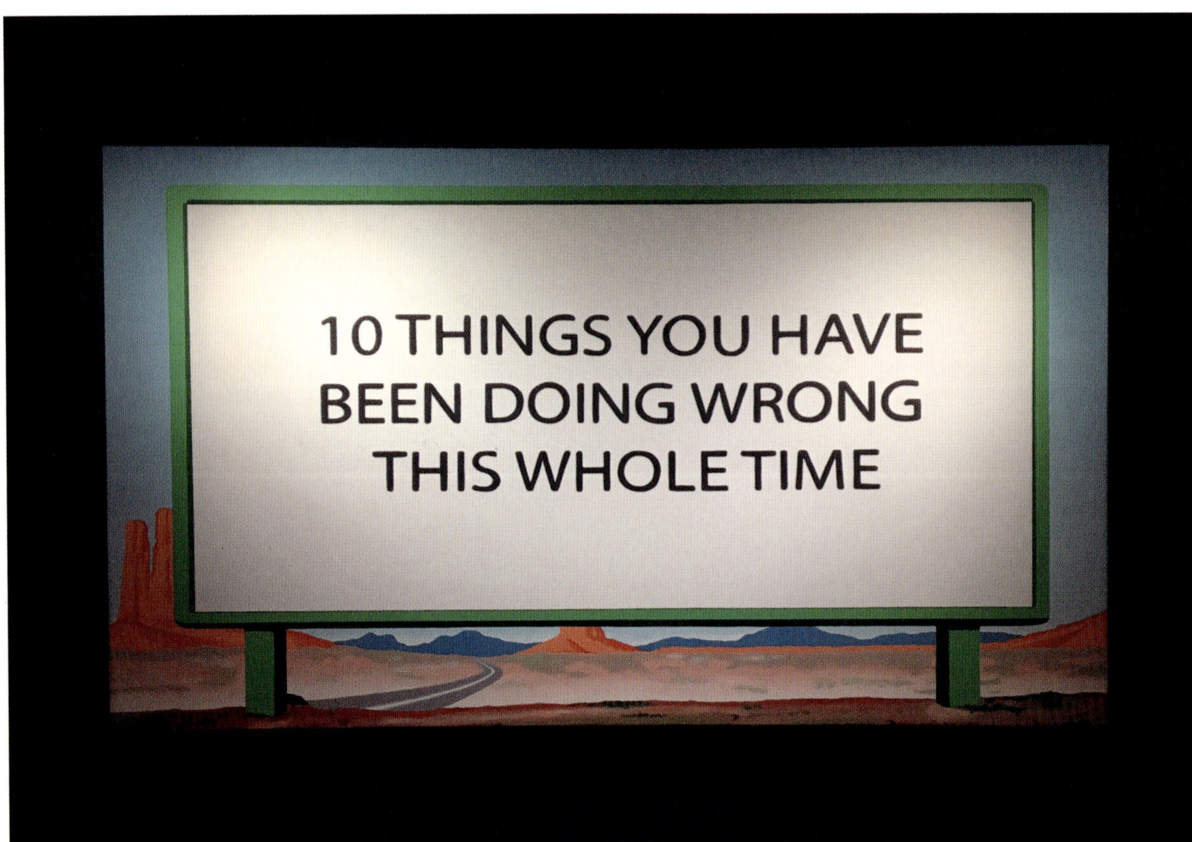

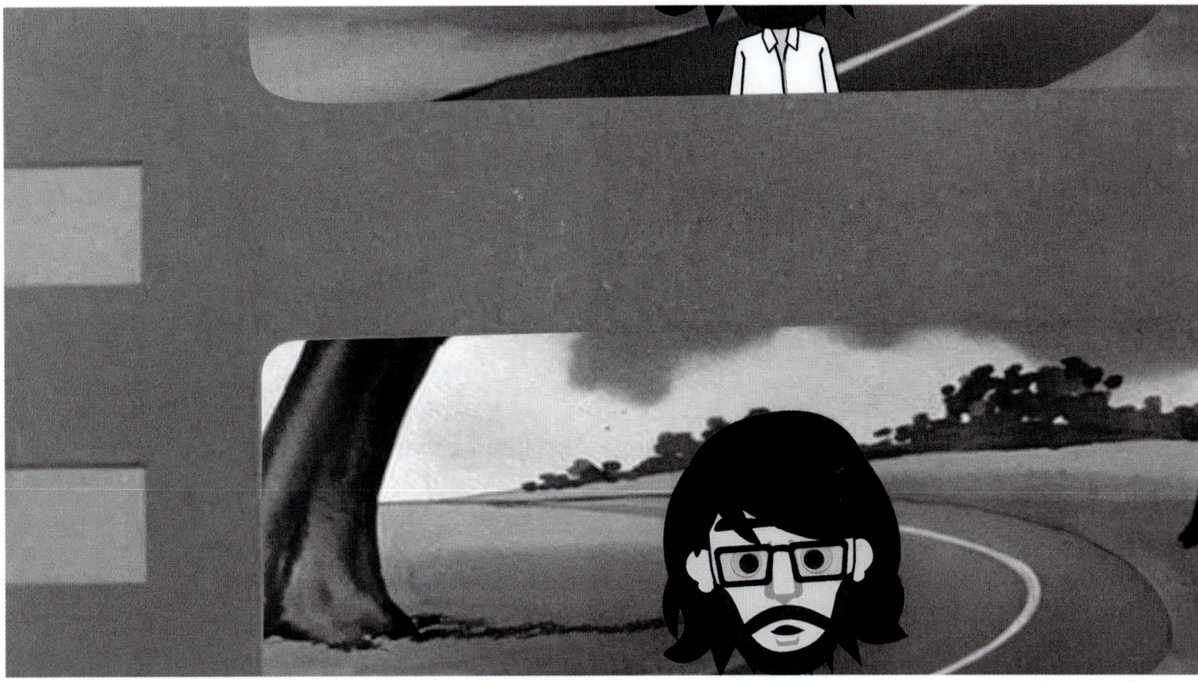

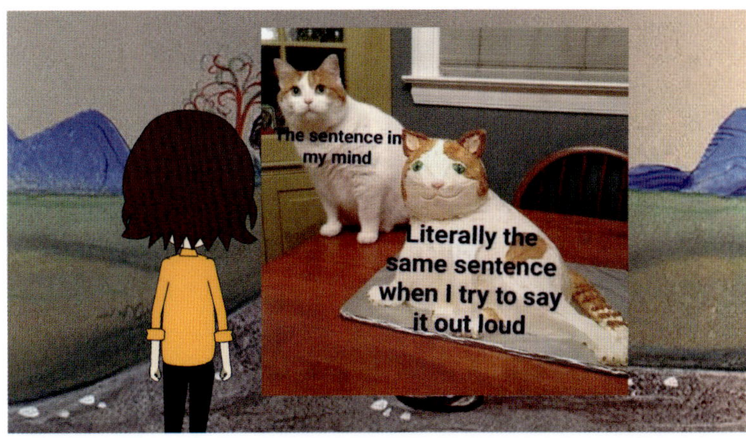

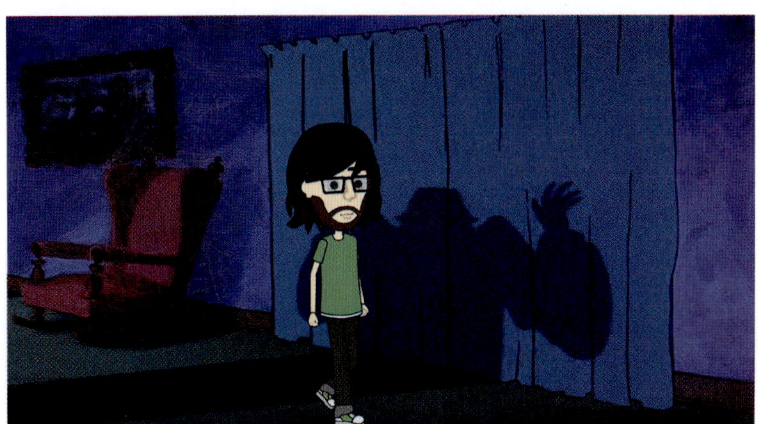

← *10 Things You Have Been Doing Wrong This Whole Time*, 2017, emulsion paint on canvas, 280 × 160 cm (110 ¼ × 63 in.), installation view, Block 336, London, 2020
↑ *Sticky Vapours*, 2020, animated video, 7 mins.
↗ *Enigma of Capital*, 2020, animated video, 7 mins.
→ *I Wouldn't Dream of It*, 2017, animated video, 7 mins.

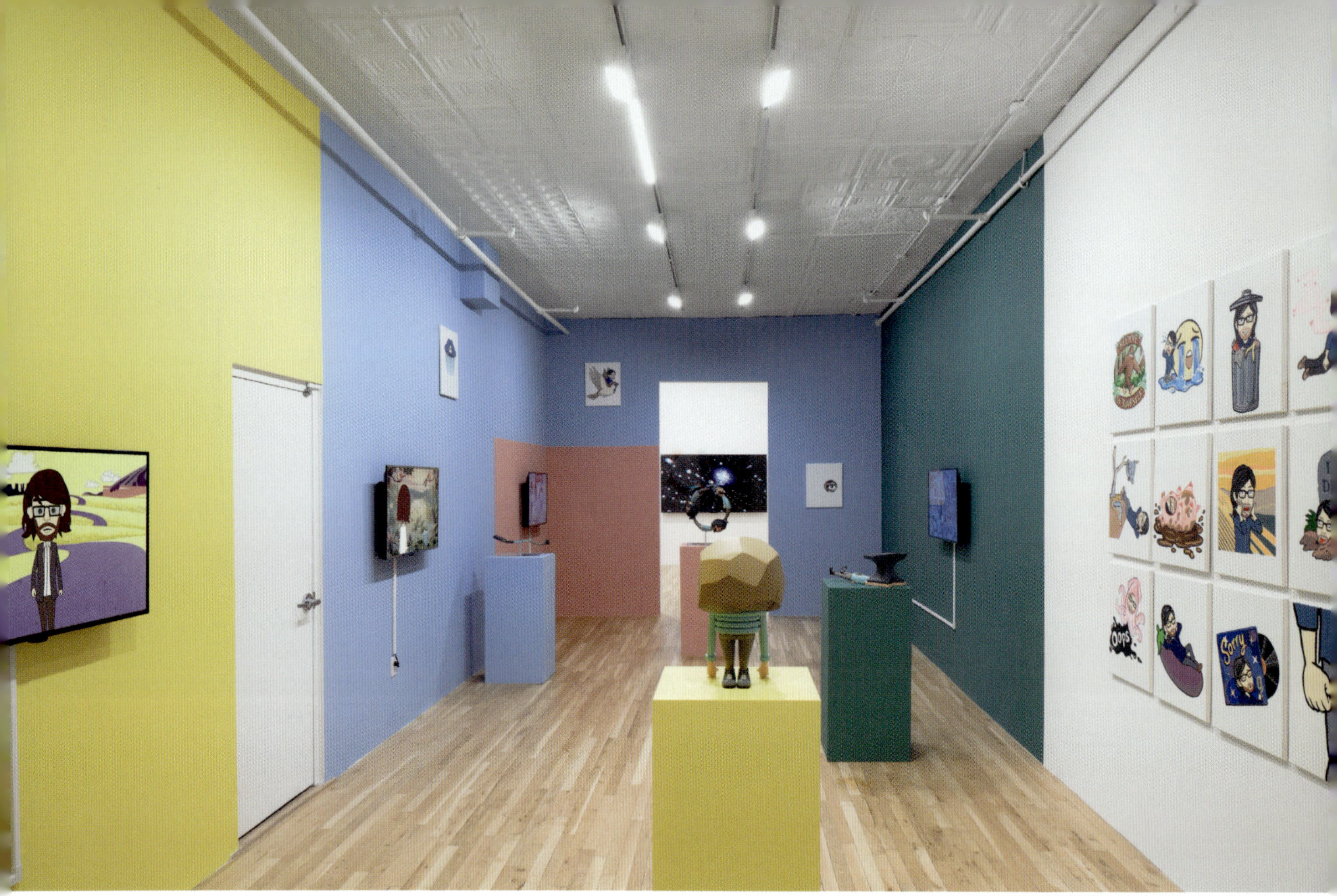
Oops
Sorry

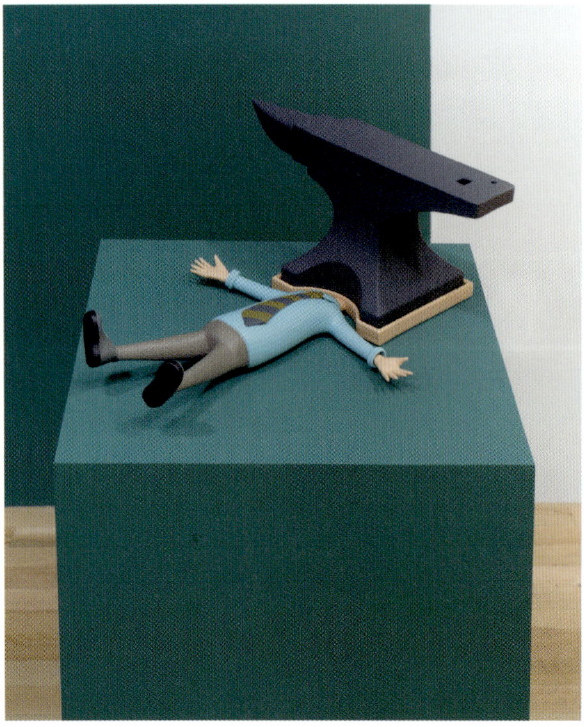

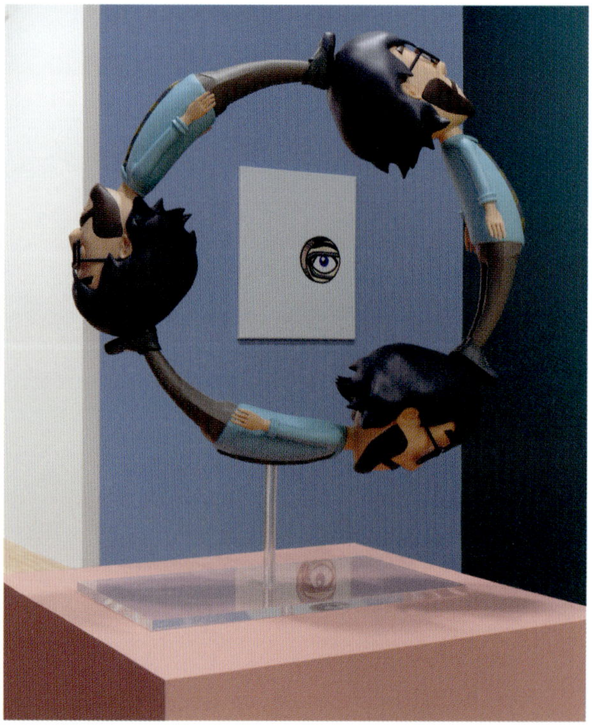

In the opening moments of the third film, *I Wouldn't Dream of It* (2017), to a soundtrack of murmured conversation, Holden walks beneath a golden moon, sinister trees and an empty road. Each background frame is taken from episodes of *Scooby Doo* when no characters are present, an act of collage that creates a disjointed, defamiliarised landscape. The narration draws heavily from Sigmund Freud's 1899 book *The Interpretation of Dreams*, which Holden describes as 'the first attempt to place a logical, analytical structure on the space of the unconscious, a space previously deemed mythological or illogical'.[5] He says that: 'It was in this tradition that *Laws of Motion in a Cartoon Landscape* hoped to operate.'[6]

In the film, Holden's avatar declares: 'There is a reason we say "I wouldn't even dream of it...". Every dream reveals itself as a psychological structure.' Dislocation reigns. Over the following seven minutes, Holden's avatar delivers a lecture about the nature of dreams. The cartoon version of Holden queries their necessity, their illogic, their unpleasantness and, using dream logic, attempts to understand the cartoon he has found himself inhabiting. 'Why', he asks, 'can't dreams say exactly what they mean?' The dream and the ghost story become interchangeable. The most potent hauntings are, it would seem, the ones we inflict upon ourselves.

Overall, *Structure of Feeling* is imbued with a sense of something both incomplete and finite – a sense that is embodied with the avatar's tomb in the middle of the installation. But, like wandering through a penny arcade, the over-stimulation prompts, conversely, a mood of longing for something just out of reach. Holden described the installation as:

> A number of pieces trying to articulate something that is not yet accessible to me, which is the end of the cartoon landscape. *Laws of Motion...* thrashed out a thesis of the world as a cartoon, and *Structure of Feeling* is still within the cartoon landscape, but at the point where it feels something else is about to emerge. A new way to make sense of the world, for me, might be required.[7]

It is perhaps apt that the first iteration of *Structure of Feeling* was postponed because of the Covid-19 pandemic. Holden's lonely figure wandering through a barren landscape was something of an eerie premonition of the collective isolation that was to come – and the cultural reckoning that followed it.

1 *Andy Holden, Collected Free Labour: Blog Interviews, 2010–2021,* Slimvolume, 2021, p. 103.
2 Andy Holden, email to Jennifer Higgie, 25 January 2025.
3 Ed Atkins, 'The Structure of Feeling (A Ghost Train Ride)', commissioned by Block 336, London, September 2020, in conjunction with Andy Holden's exhibition.
4 Andy Holden, email to Jennifer Higgie, 3 February 2025.
5 Andy Holden, email to Jennifer Higgie, 25 January 2025.
6 Ibid.
7 *Andy Holden, Collected Free Labour: Blog Interviews, 2010–2021,* Slimvolume, 2021, p. 103.

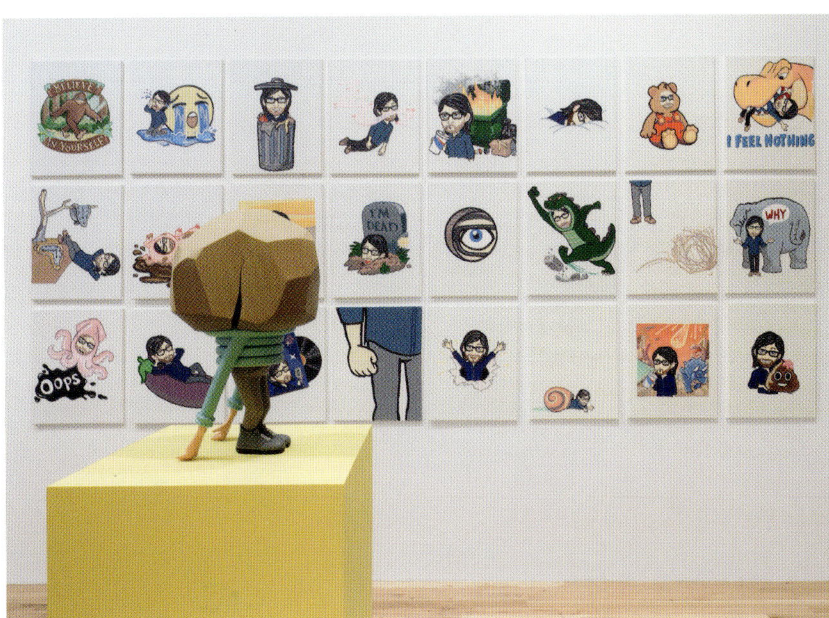

↖ Installation view, 'What I Was for What I Am Becoming', Charles Moffett, New York, 2024
← *Uchronian Self-Portrait – Anvil,* 2024, handpainted 3D-printed sculpture, 18.4 × 33 × 45.7 cm (7 ¼ × 13 × 18 in.), installation view, Charles Moffett, New York
← *Uchronian Self-Portrait – Eternal,* 2024, handpainted 3D-printed sculpture, 57.1 × 19.1 × 45.7 cm (22 ½ × 7 ½ × 18 in.), installation view, Charles Moffett, New York
→ *General Principles of the Emotions* with *Uchronian Self-Portrait – Rock* (foreground), 2024, emulsion paint on canvas (rear) and handpainted 3D-printed sculpture, installation view, Charles Moffett, New York
↠ (Overleaf) *Structure of Feeling,* 2020, installation view, Block 336, London

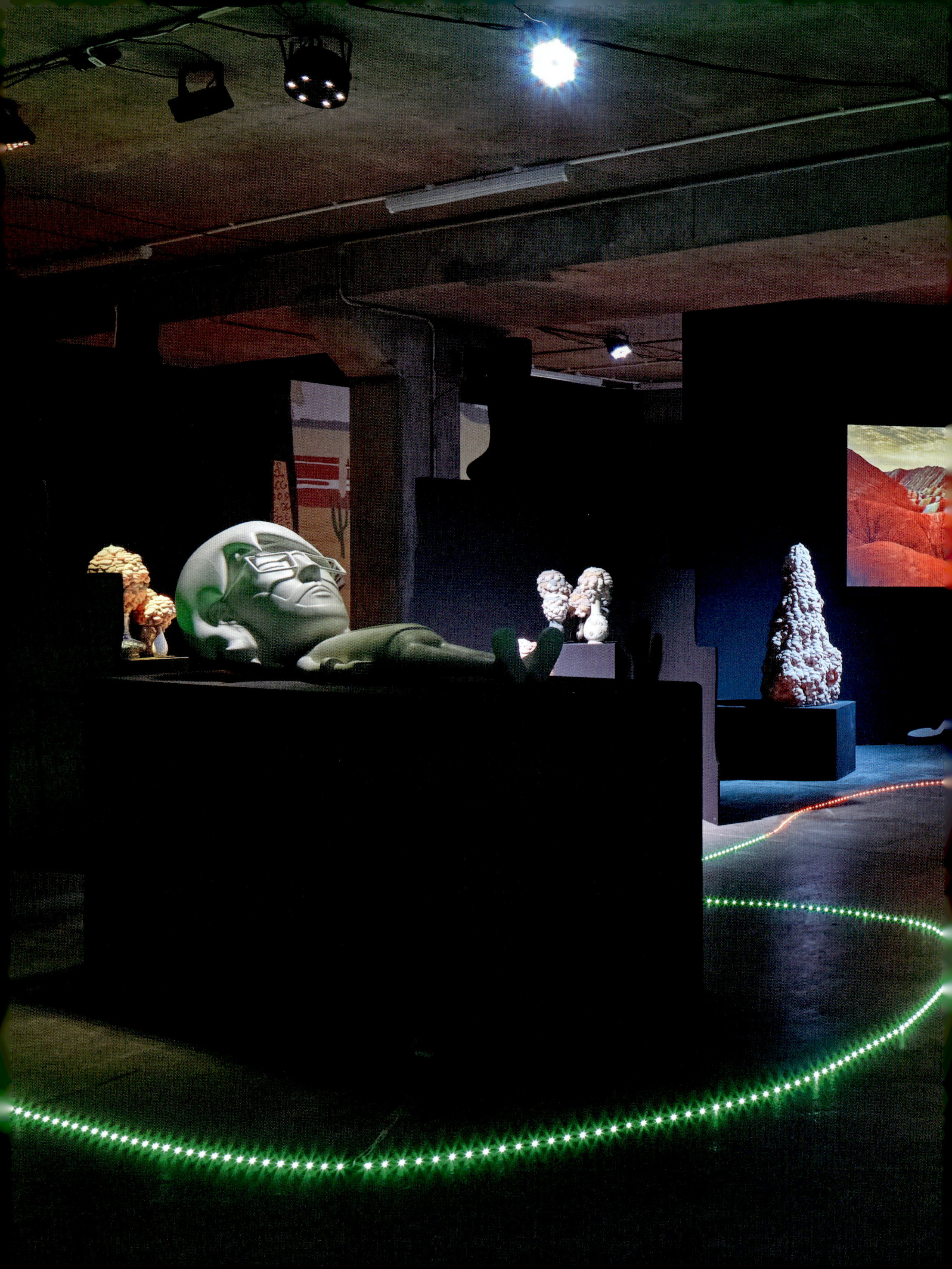

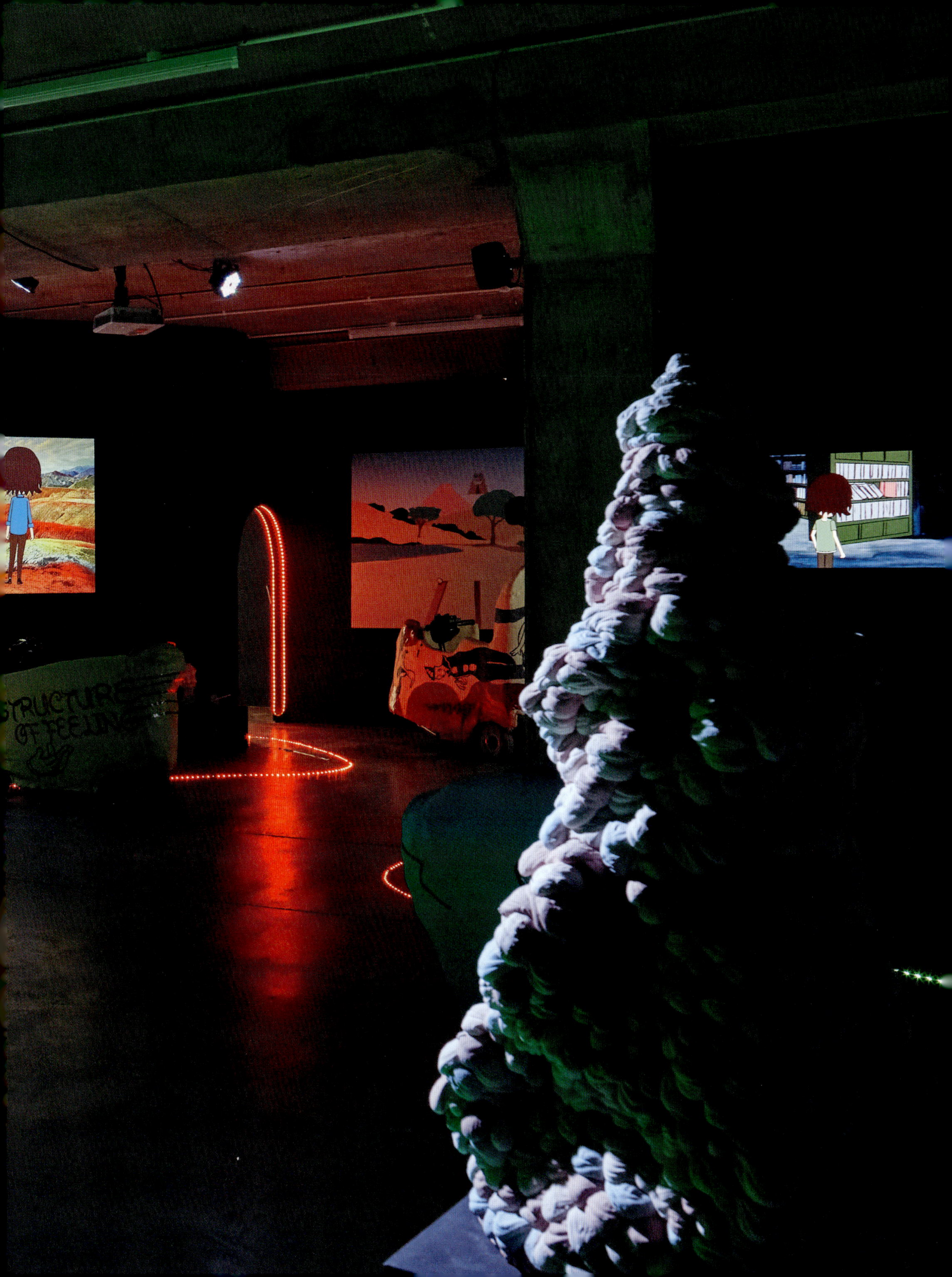

Folly

2004–14

Rocks, boulders and stones are a recurring motif in Holden's work. He has, over the years, created numerous, large-scale wooden sculptures, mostly titled with a variation of 'Folly', which he has placed in various incongruous locations. Resembling large, roughly constructed boulders, they have appeared, for example, elevated in an East London garden (*Guston's Boulder, Mile End*, 2004), on a roof in south London (*Black Boulder Monochrome Folly, Deptford*, 2006), in a field (*Third Attempt, Vijfhuizen, Netherlands*, 2008) and on a hilltop (*Folly (Sand Hills), Bedfordshire*, 2014). Each work, although appearing like a full boulder, is only partial, a semi-spherical shape with the back exposed to reveal the structure. The works in the series were by necessity temporary, with some staying in place for only a few days, seen by just a handful of people and existing primarily as documentation. Later iterations

→ *Folly (Sand Hills) Bedfordshire*, 2014, plywood, timber and paint, 4.8 × 2.5 × 4.8 m (15 ¾ × 8 ¼ × 15 ¾ ft.), installation view, Sandy, Bedfordshire, UK

» (Overleaf) *The Third Attempt, Vijfhuizen, Netherlands,* 2008, plywood, timber and paint, 4.8 × 2.5 × 4.8 m (15 ¾ × 8 ¼ × 15 ¾ ft.), installation view, Kunstfort Vijfhuizen, Netherlands

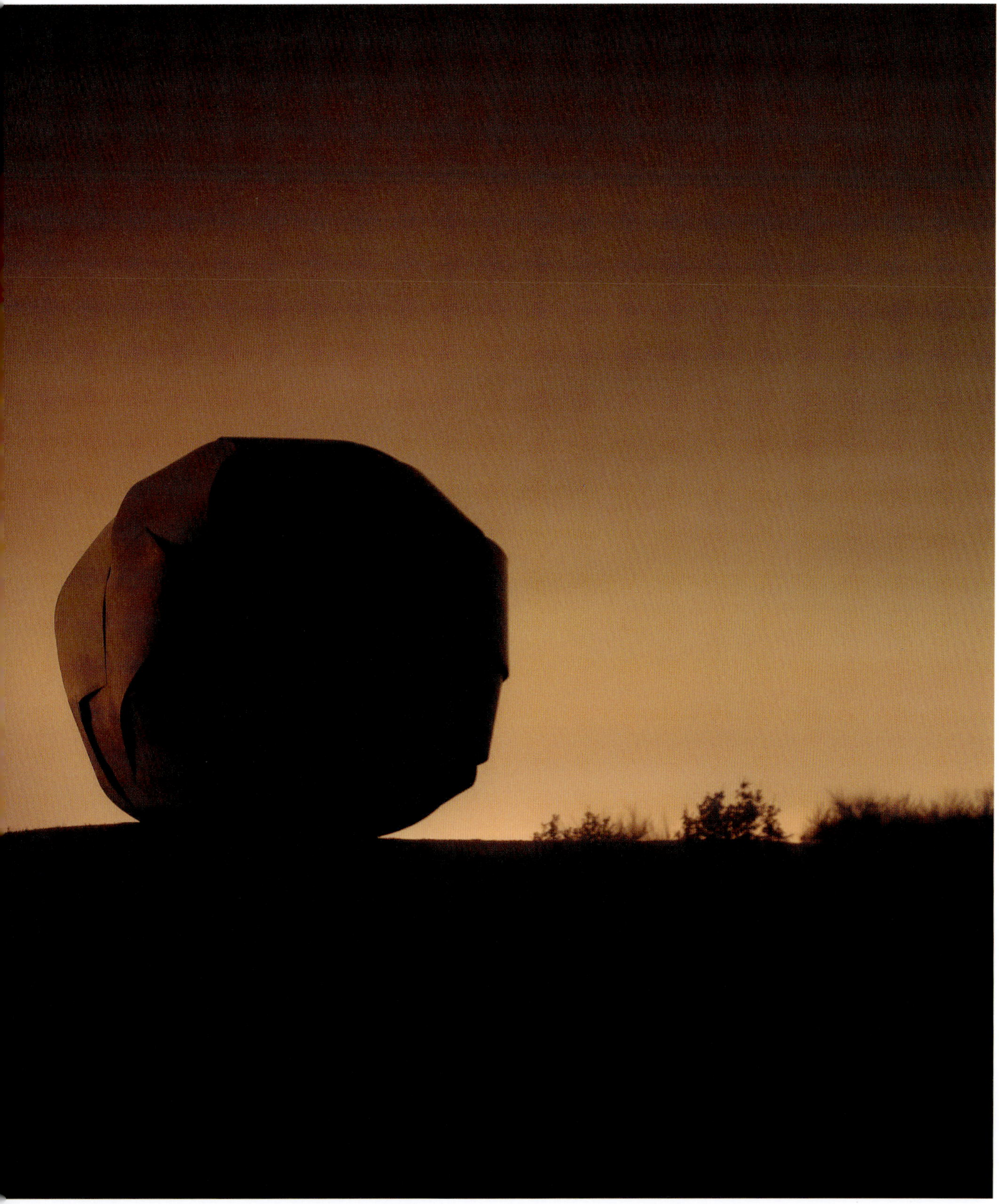

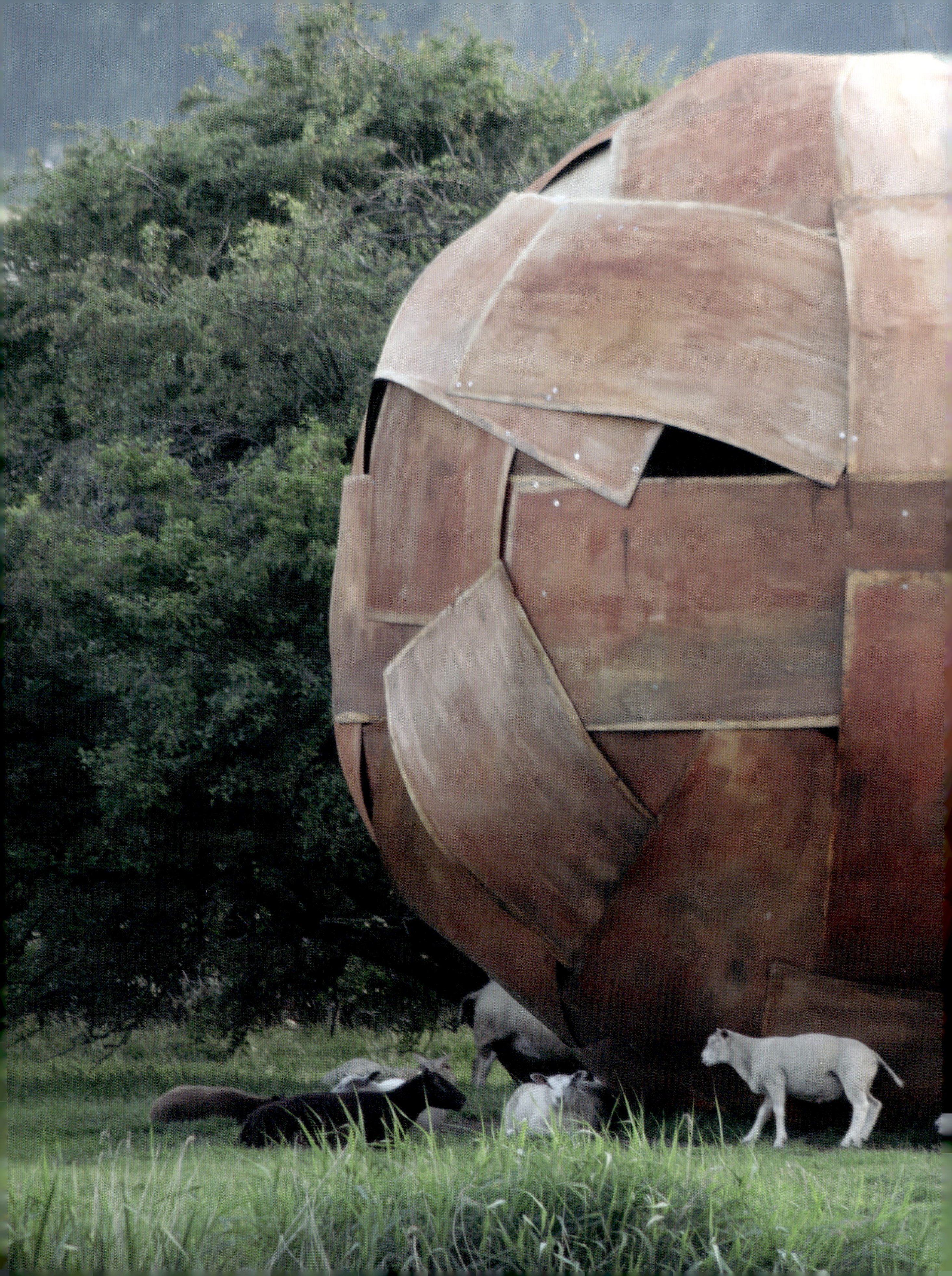

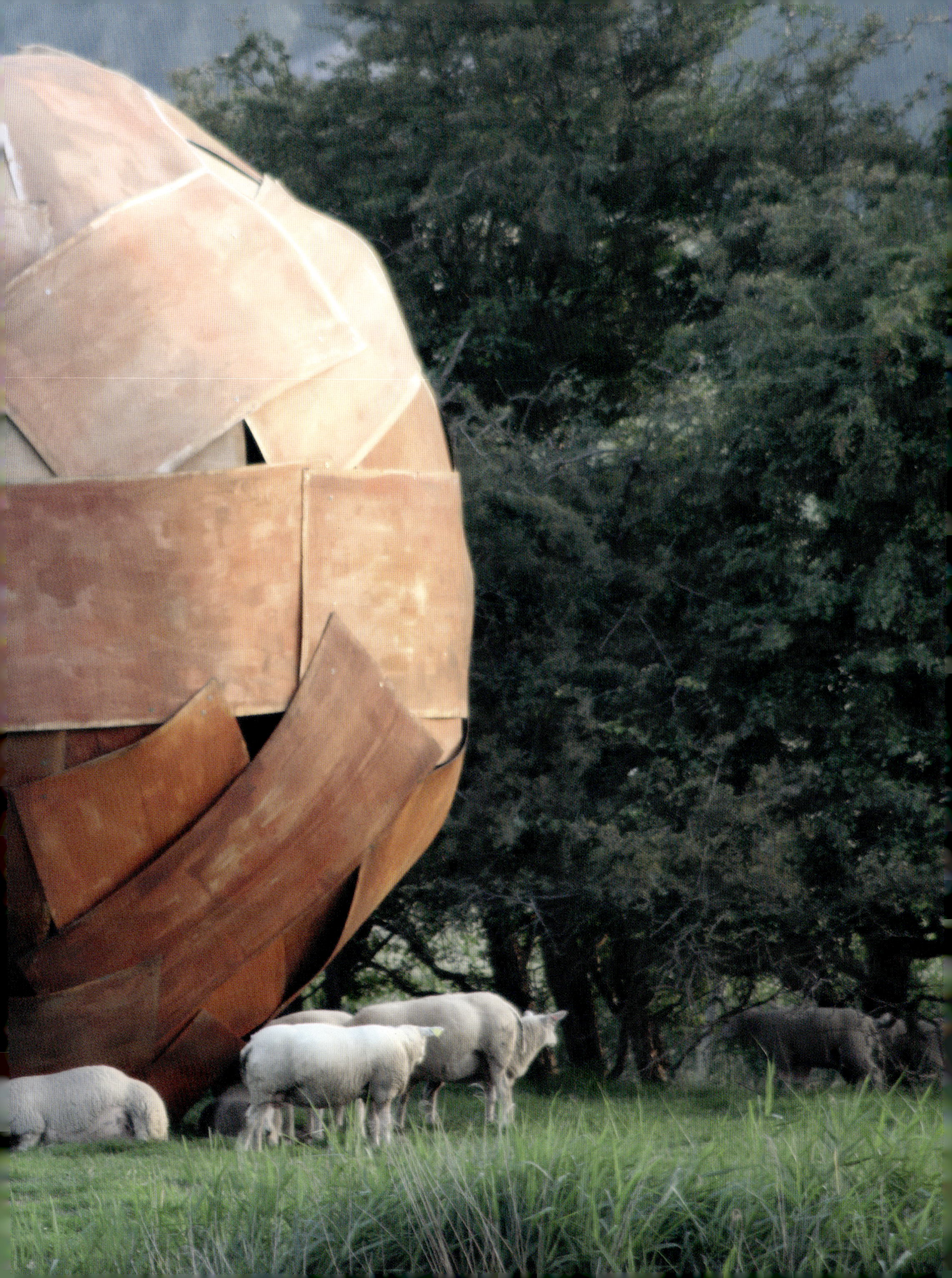

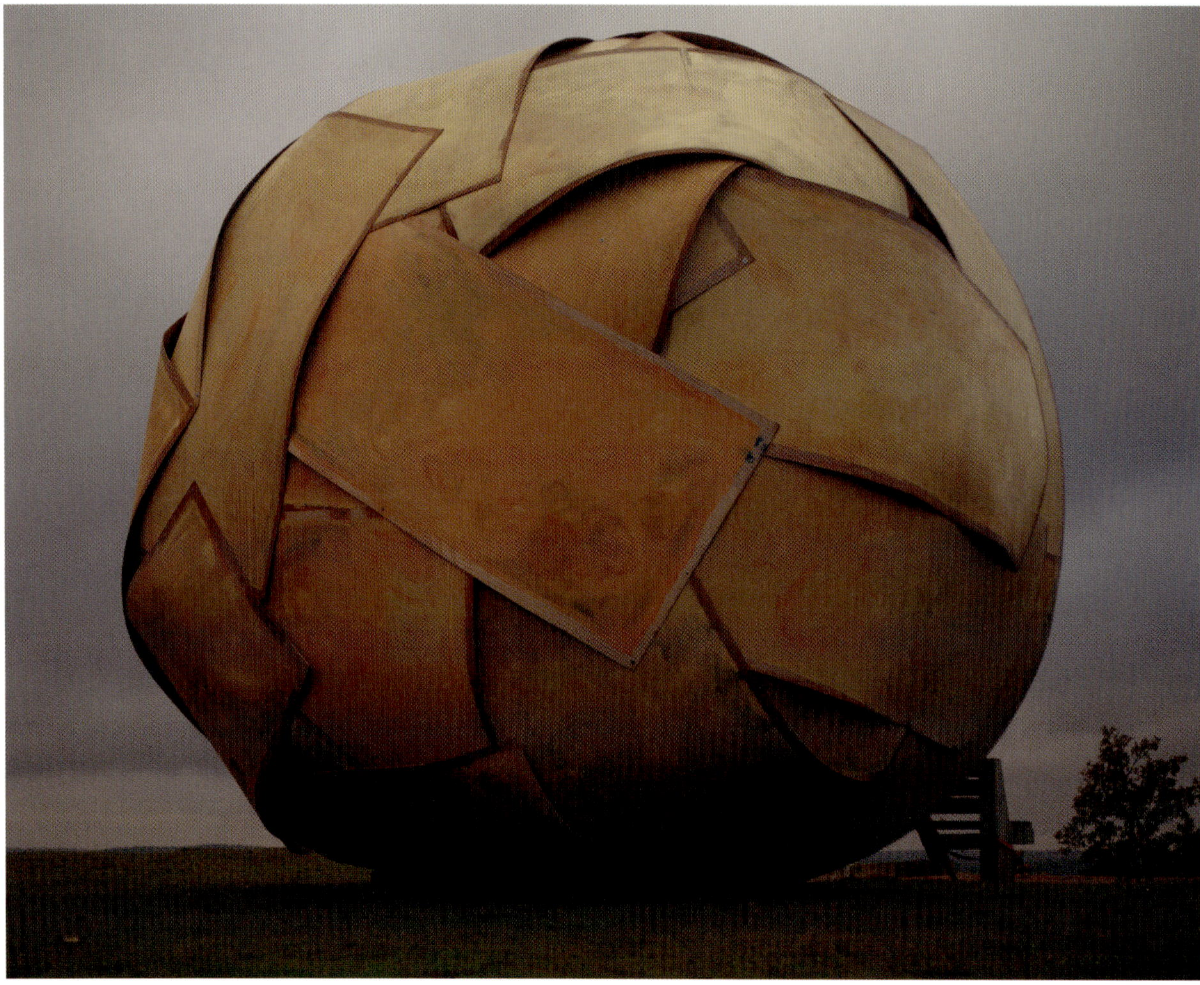

such as *In Praise of Folly* (2021), located on the roof of Peckham Library in London and visible through a telescope from the roof of Bold Tendencies, lasted a little longer, staying in place for a few months.

The word 'folly' can mean many things: a kind of stupidity or a deceptive construction – for example, the facade of a hut built to look decrepit in order to evoke an imaginary past. Holden's manifestation of the folly as a boulder form conjures numerous associations: the large rock frequently pushed off a cliff by Wile E. Coyote in order to crush Road Runner but that, thanks to a reversal of gravity, usually ends up crushing the coyote instead; ideas of oneness and coherence; comets and meteorites, numinous stones; and the creation of meaning through accident. 'Although,' he says, 'explicitly, they came from walking in Turkey whilst on holiday and admiring the boulders.'[1] Holden also sees them as a signifier of Albert Camus's 1942 philosophical essay *The Myth of Sisyphus,* in which

↑↓ *Folly (Sand Hills) Bedfordshire*, 2014, plywood, timber and paint, 4.8 × 2.5 × 4.8 m (15¾ × 8¼ × 15¾ ft.), installation view, Sandy, Bedfordshire, UK

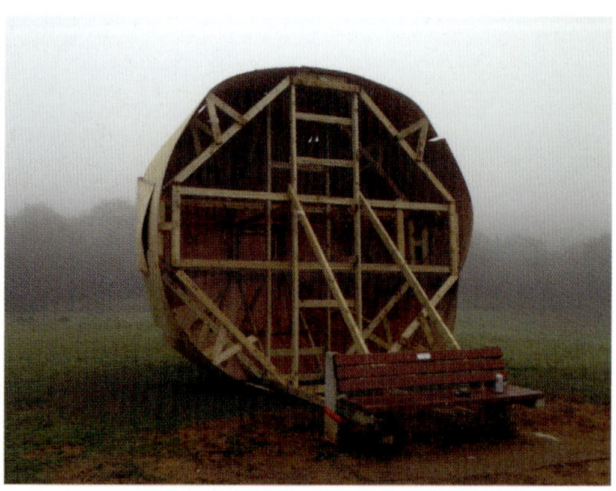

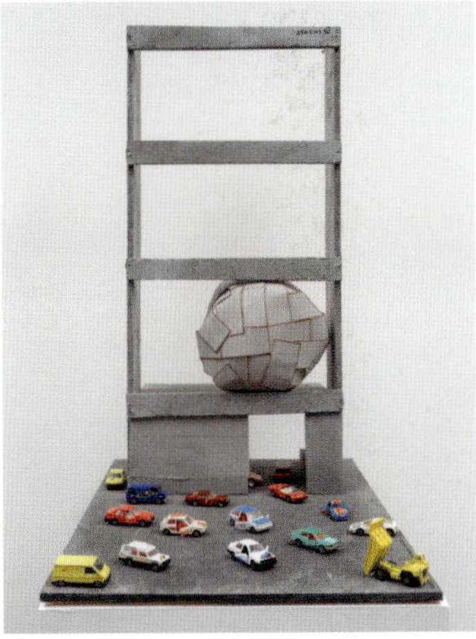

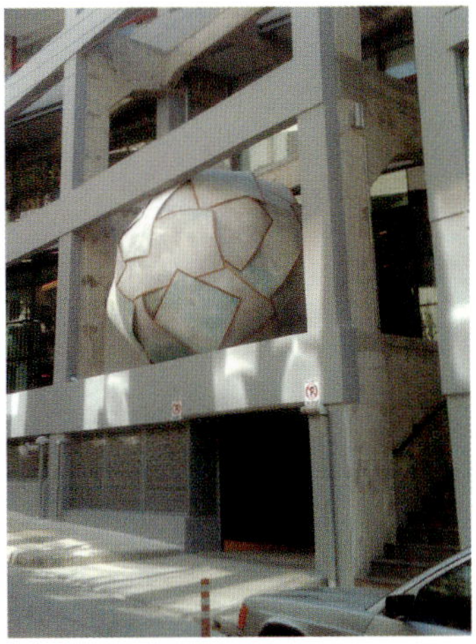

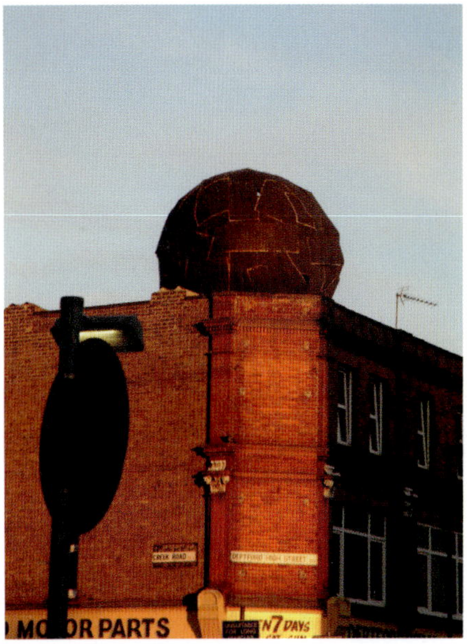

↑ *Model for Folly IV (Athens)*, 2010, wood and paint with toy cars, 40× 40 × 90 cm (15 ¾ × 15 ¾ × 35 ⅜ in.)
↗ *Folly IV (Athens)*, 2010, plywood, timber and paint, 4.8 × 2.5 × 4.8 m (15 ¾ × 8 ¼ × 15 ¾ ft.), installation view, Athens
→ *Black Boulder Monochrome Folly, Deptford,* 2006, 4.8 × 2.5 × 4.8 m (15 ¾ × 8 ¼ × 15 ¾ ft.), installation view, Deptford, London
↓ *The Naturist (Folly V, Jaywick)*, 2011, plywood, timber and paint, 4.8 × 2.5 × 4.8 m (15 ¾ × 8 ¼ × 15 ¾ ft.), installation view, Jaywick, Essex, UK

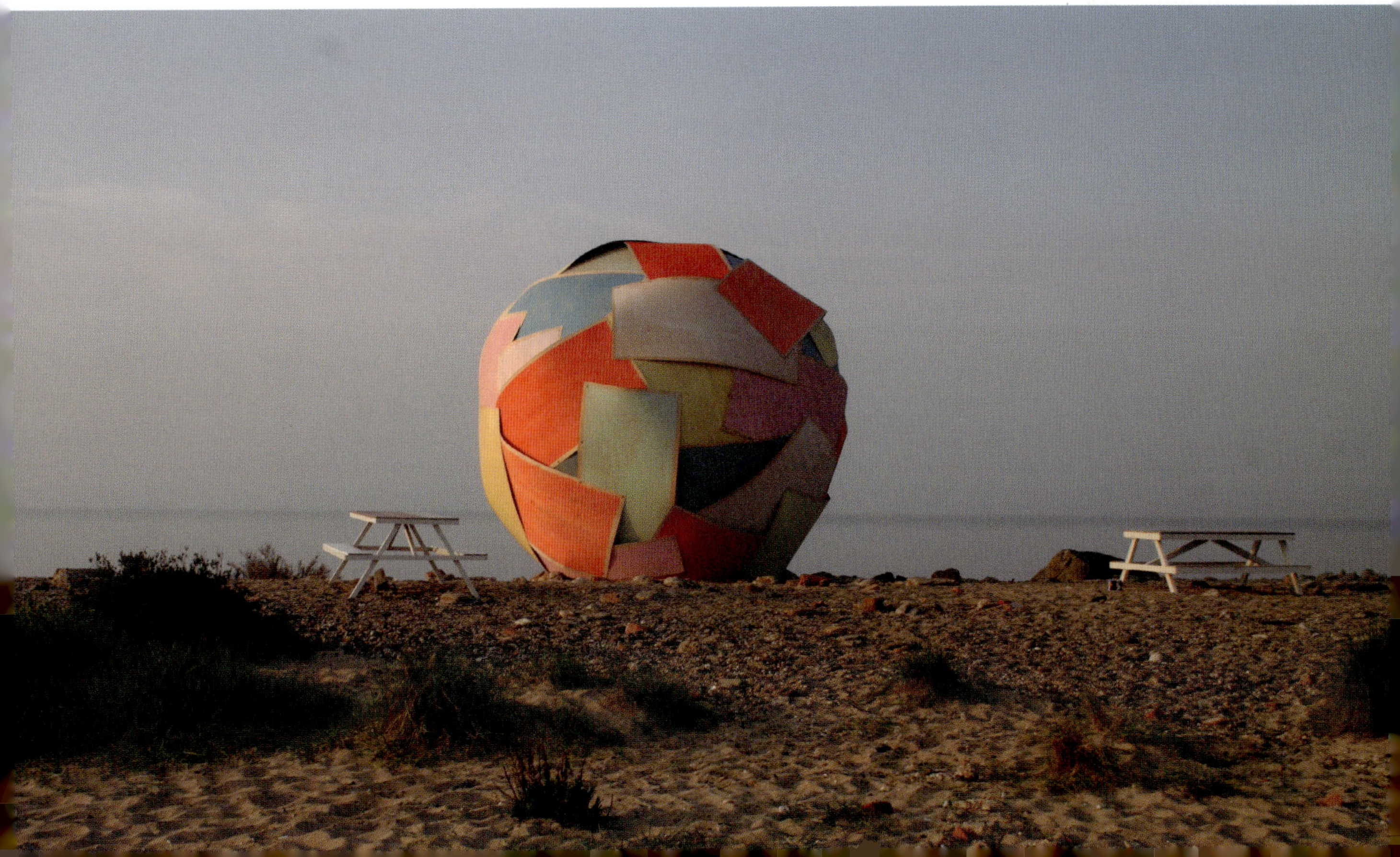

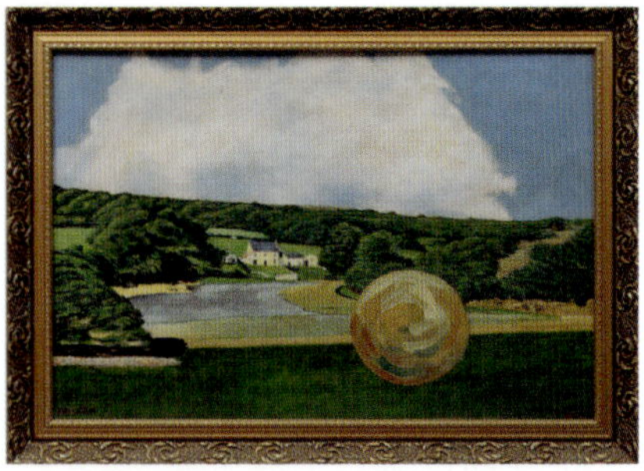

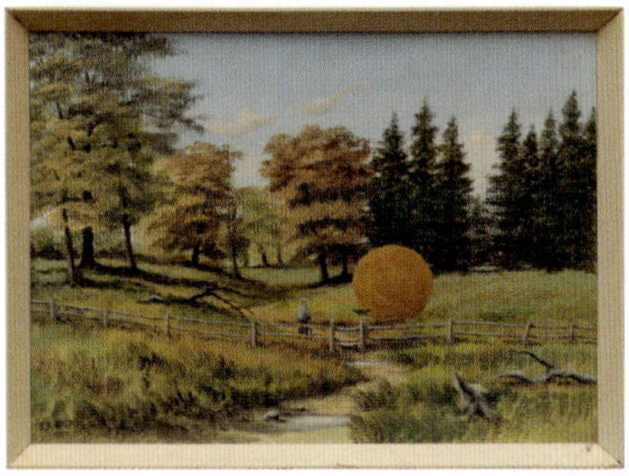

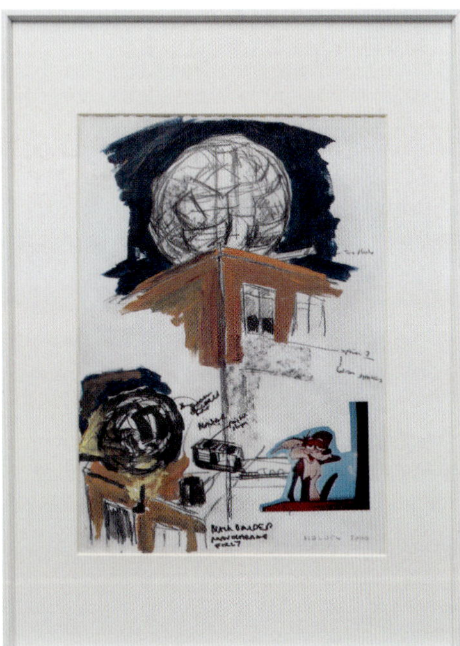

the French writer compares the absurdity of human existence with that of the Greek mythological figure who was condemned to push a boulder up a mountain only to see it roll down again as he reaches the top. Holden sees a parallel between the myth and the repetitious construction of artworks that, conversely, can animate familiar landscapes.

Cookham Erratics (2011) are six knitted enlarged replicas of stones and pebbles taken from the grounds of the Holy Trinity Church in Cookham in England, where the British artist Stanley Spencer set his painting *The Resurrection, Cookham* (1924–27). As with so many of Holden's projects, the work combines a personal anecdote with historical fact: the artist's great uncle lived next to Spencer and, as a child, threw stones at the artist over the garden wall. Holden took the story and ran with it. He composed a narrative that ranges across geological, autobiographical and art-historical accounts, which he then split into six parts for six sculptures. First installed in the Benaki Museum in Athens amongst the museum's ancient sculptures, each of Holden's sculptures simultaneously broadcasted the various narratives. These ranged from the anecdote about Stanley Spencer to musings on small-scale market gardening; the 17th-century poet John Donne and the film director George Romero; the fact that an 'erratic' is a rock deposited as the glacier that has been carrying it begins to melt; a story by Virginia Woolf; the origins of Spider-Man, and several more. The ensuing cacophony was a kind of personal archaeology, an accrual of memory and history, both cultural and personal, that is both specific to Holden and, more generally, familiar to all humans. As Holden noted in one interview: 'Often truth is only visible in moments of interruption, in breaks in the causal chain'.[2]

1 *Andy Holden, Collected Free Labour: Blog Interviews, 2010–2021*, Slimvolume, 2021, p. 107.
2 Ibid., p. 28

↖ *Untitled*, 2014, paint on found canvas, 50 × 70 cm (19¾ × 27½ in.)
↖ *Untitled*, 2014, paint on found canvas, 50 × 70 cm (19¾ × 27½ in.)
↖ *Study for Folly II*, 2006, pencil and paint on paper, 42 × 29 cm (16½ × 11⅜ in.)

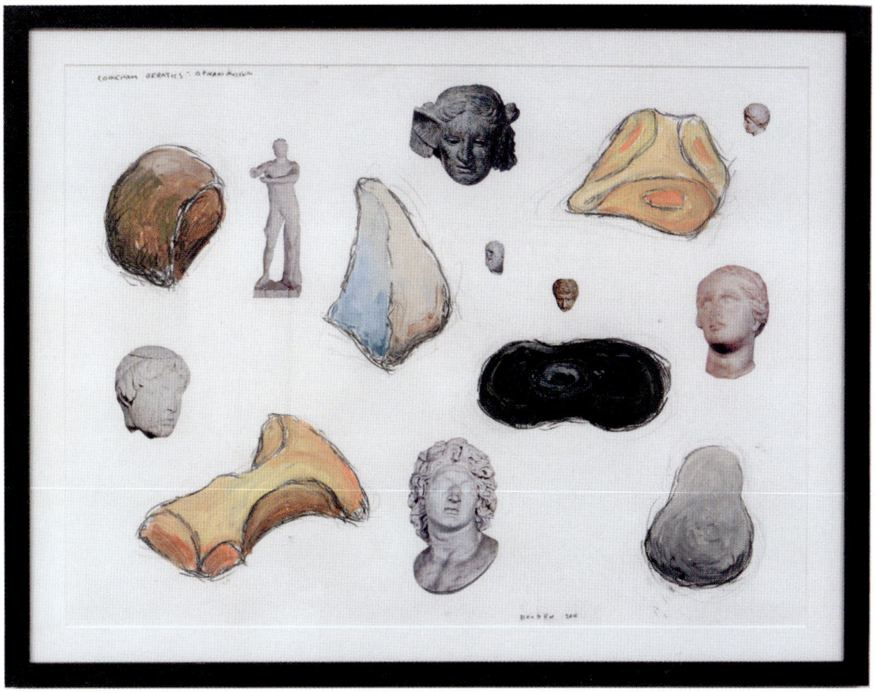

→ *Study for Cookham Erratics,* 2011, pencil and paint on paper, 42 × 60 cm (16 ½ × 23 ⅝ in.)

↓ *Cookham Erratics,* 2011, knitted yarn, foam, steel and speakers, variable dimensions, installation view, Benaki Museum, Athens

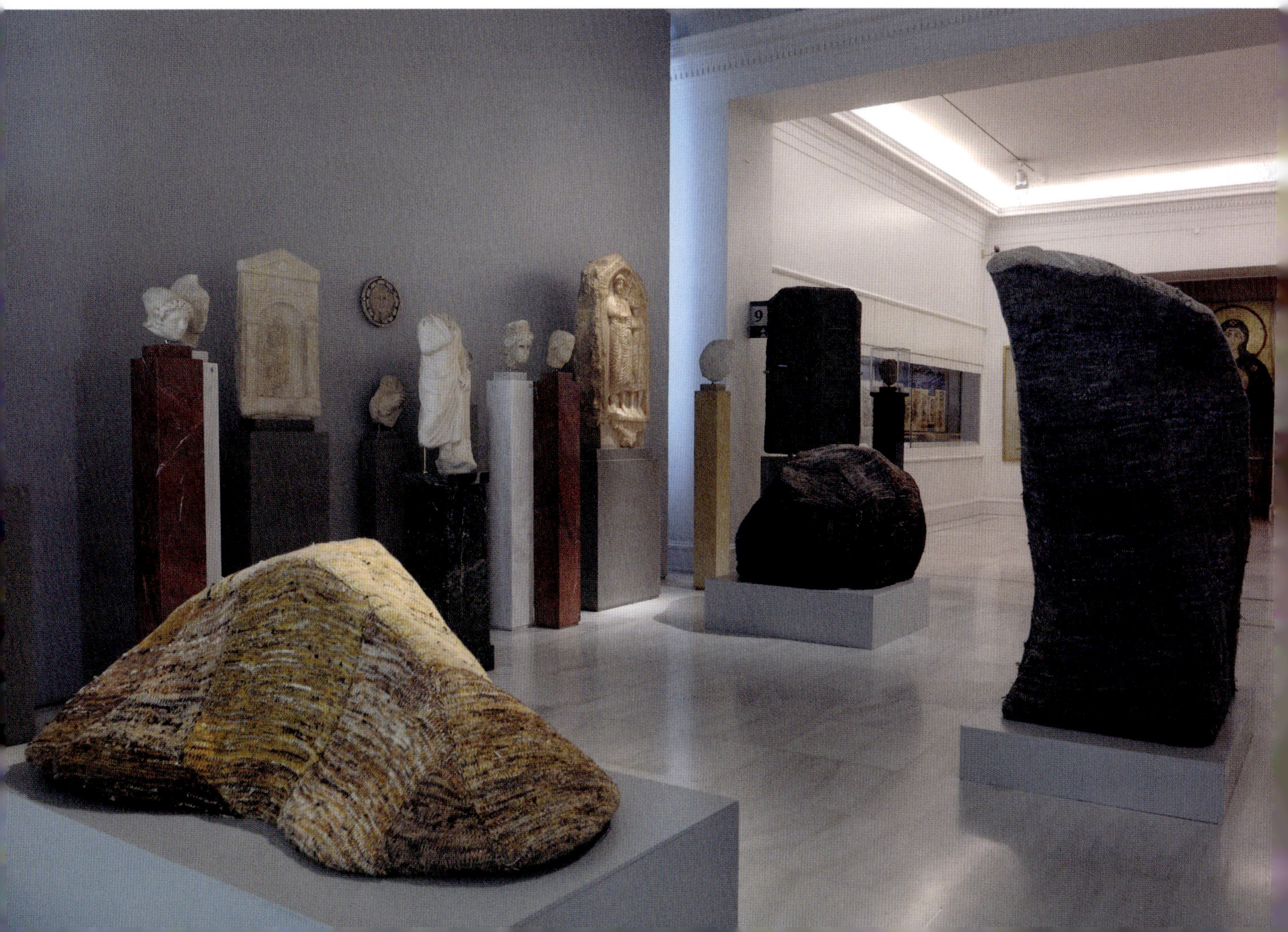

Natural Selection

2017

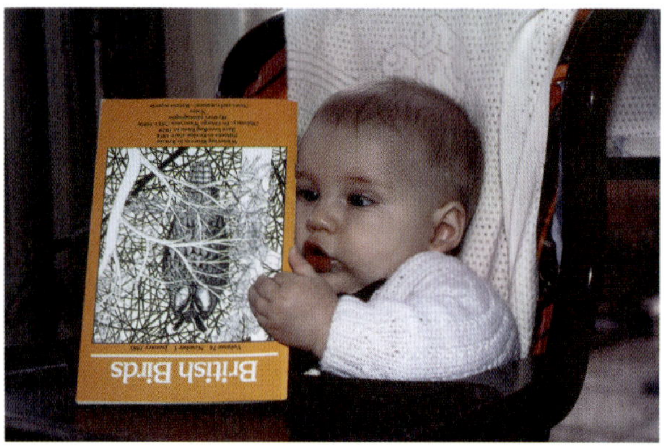

← *Andy Holden by Peter Holden (1982)*, 2017, digital print from transparent slide, 40 × 60 cm (15 ¾ × 23 ⅝ in.)
↓ *Lecture on Nesting Poster*, 2010, screenprint on paper, 51 × 39 cm (20 ⅛ × 15 ⅜ in.), edition of *c.*25. Tate collection

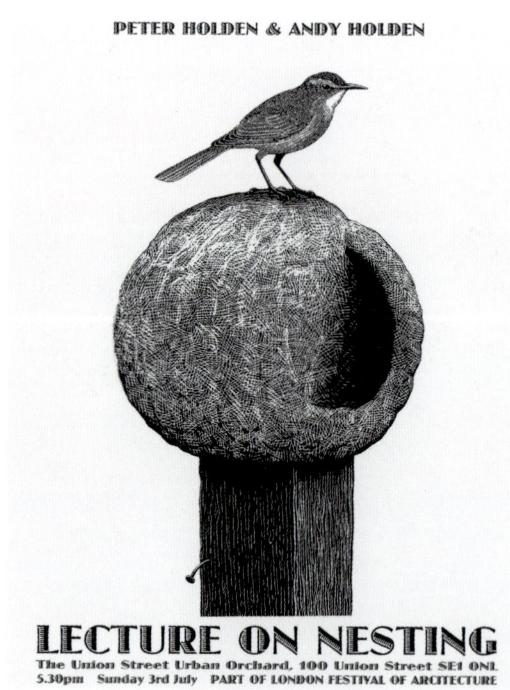

Andy Holden's father Peter is an ornithologist who has written a number of books on birds, worked for the Royal Society for the Protection of Birds (RSPB) for 40 years and founded the Big Garden Birdwatch, the world's largest garden wildlife survey. He also talked about birds on the BBC children's TV programme *Blue Peter* in the 1970s and 80s, and presented the BBC1 series *Bird in the Nest* in the 1990s. As a child, Andy had no interest in his father's passion. In 2010, however, the artist was invited to talk at the London Festival of Architecture and something shifted. He had moved back home and on long walks in the surrounding countryside he began to notice birds' nests and realised they were a potential subject for his upcoming talk. As he explains:

> It was a project that I began around the time of first reading Bruno Latour, and thinking about objects as actors, the bird's nest is an interesting object in that it makes clear a network of relations between site, material and design.[1]

The artist consulted with his father and they ended up co-presenting an image-led talk about nest-building. It was the beginning of a rich collaboration that resulted in live lectures performed from 2010 to 2015. They also worked, and continue to work, on *Lecture on Bird Song* (2011–ongoing), which sees them presenting audio clips, photographs, videos and musical instruments in an exploration of how humankind has drawn inspiration from birdsong.

In 2018, the duo were commissioned by the British art agency Artangel whose byline is 'extraordinary art, unexpected places' to stage a two-part UK exhibition. 'Natural Selection' consisted of two halves, 'A Natural History of Nest Building' and 'A Social History of Egg Collecting', and travelled to eight venues across England and Scotland. It comprised multi-screen films, a vast willow sculpture, a collection of nests and a floor-based installation of porcelain eggs.

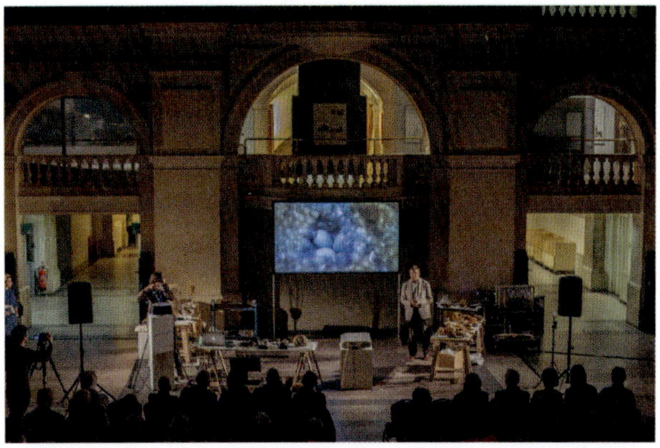

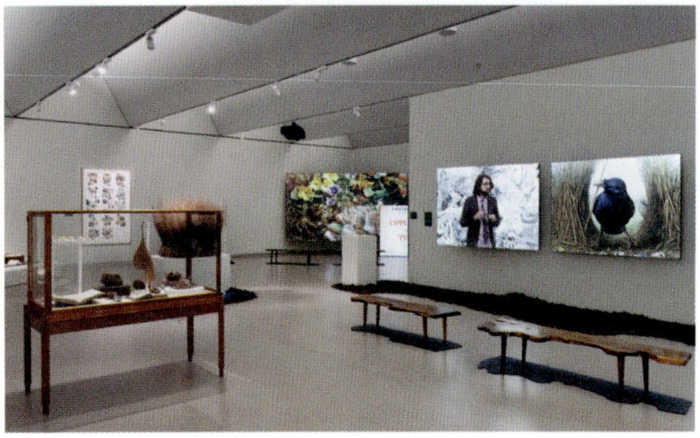

↗ *Lecture on Nesting*, 2010–15, live performance, Bristol Museum & Art Gallery, UK, 2015
→ *Natural Selection*, 2017, installation view, Kröller-Müller Museum, Netherlands, 2024
↓ *Natural Selection*, 2017, installation view, Leeds Museum and Art Gallery, UK, 2018

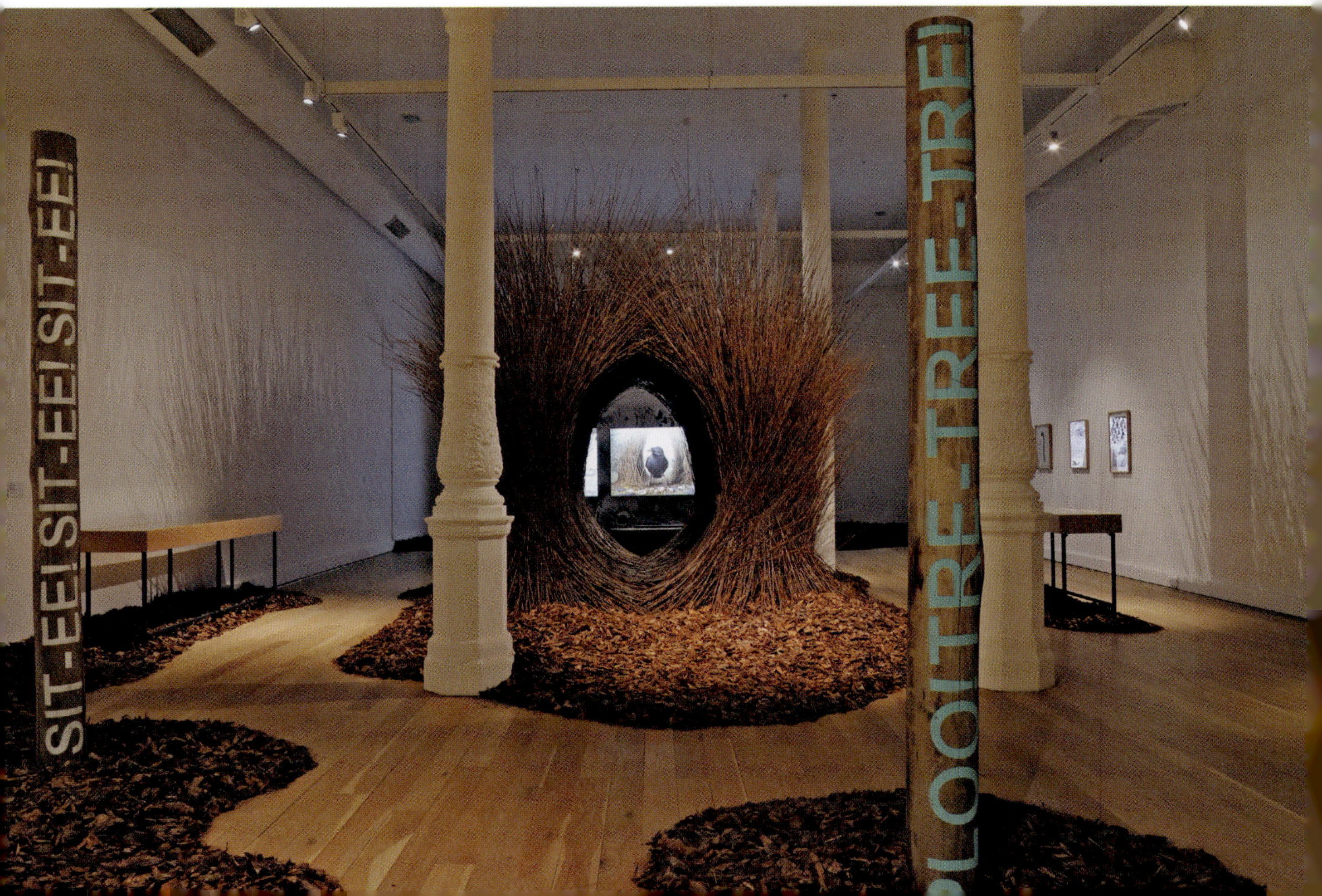

'A Natural History of Nest Building' comprised a display of nests – some collected by the artist and some recreated in straw and clay – and a three-screen, 30-minute film version of the father and son's lecture that was organised across three chapters, 'Nest Type', 'Nest Site' and 'Material'. The film opens with a blackbird's nest and concludes with a meditation on the bowerbird, the only living non-human creature that regularly creates structures for display. In between, the pair discuss cuckoos, weaver birds, mute swans that work together in pairs, chaffinches, rooks, tailorbirds and more.

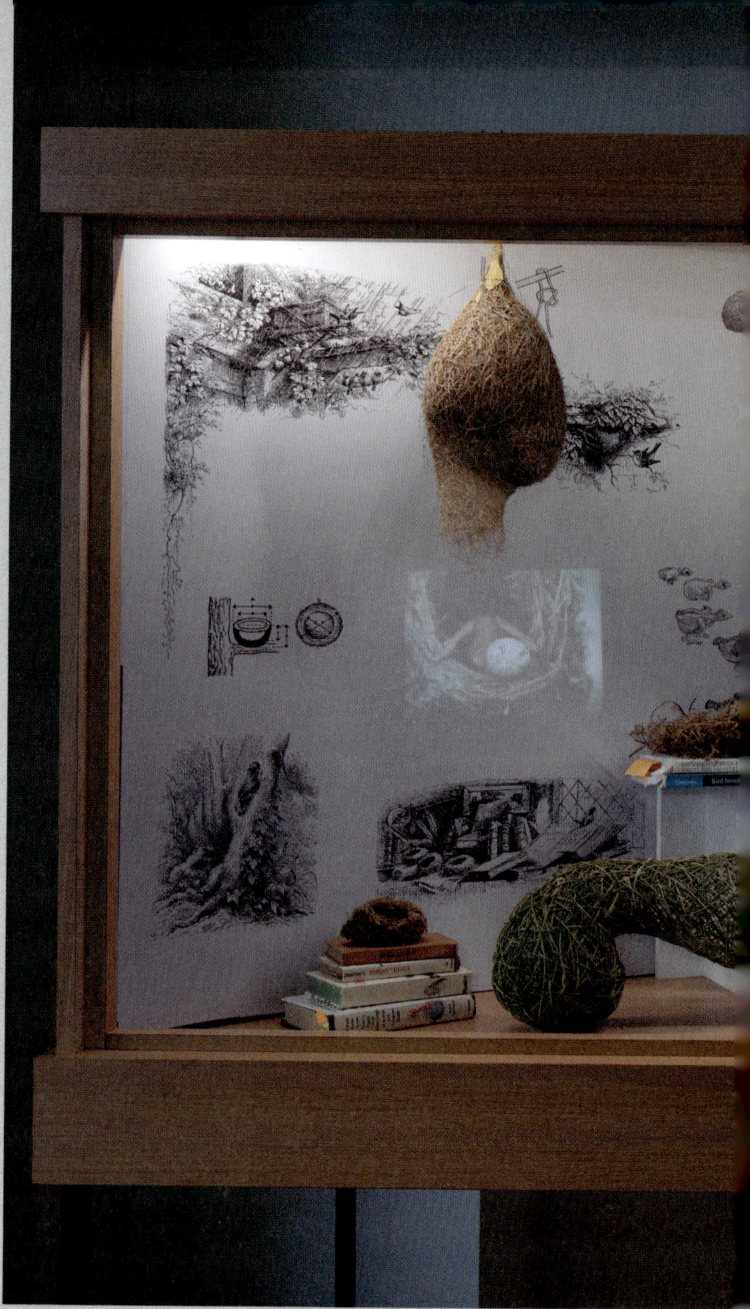

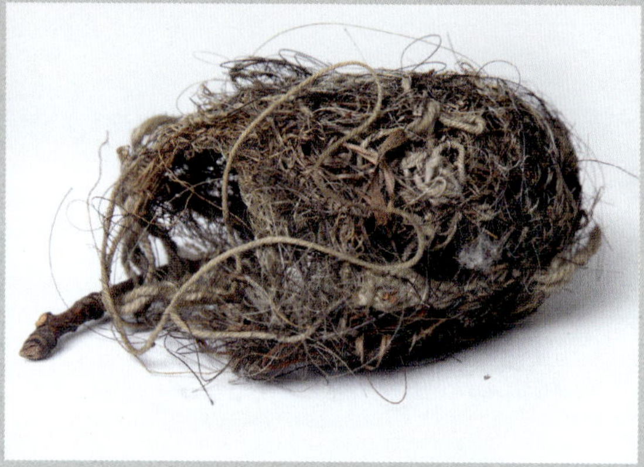

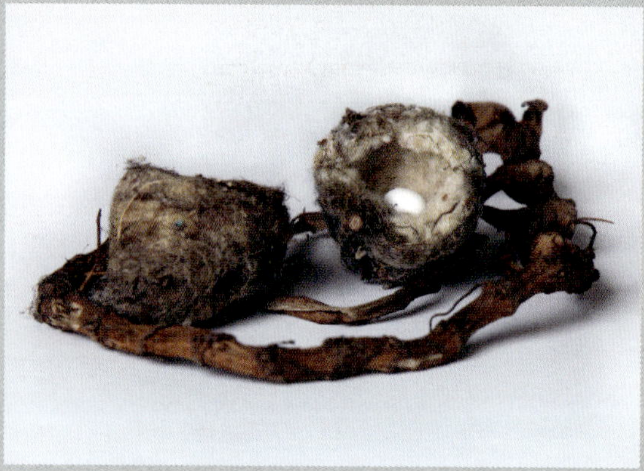

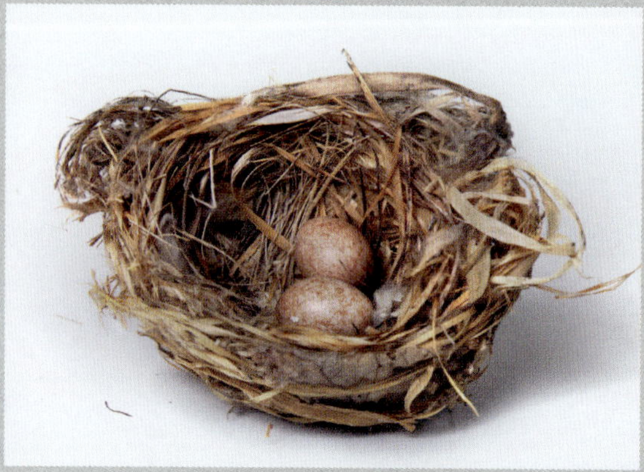

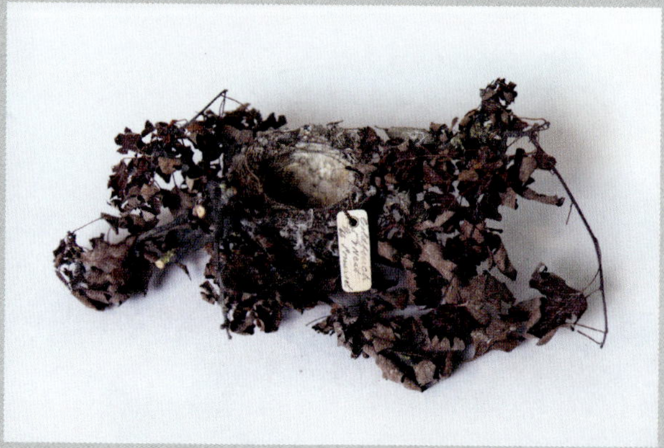

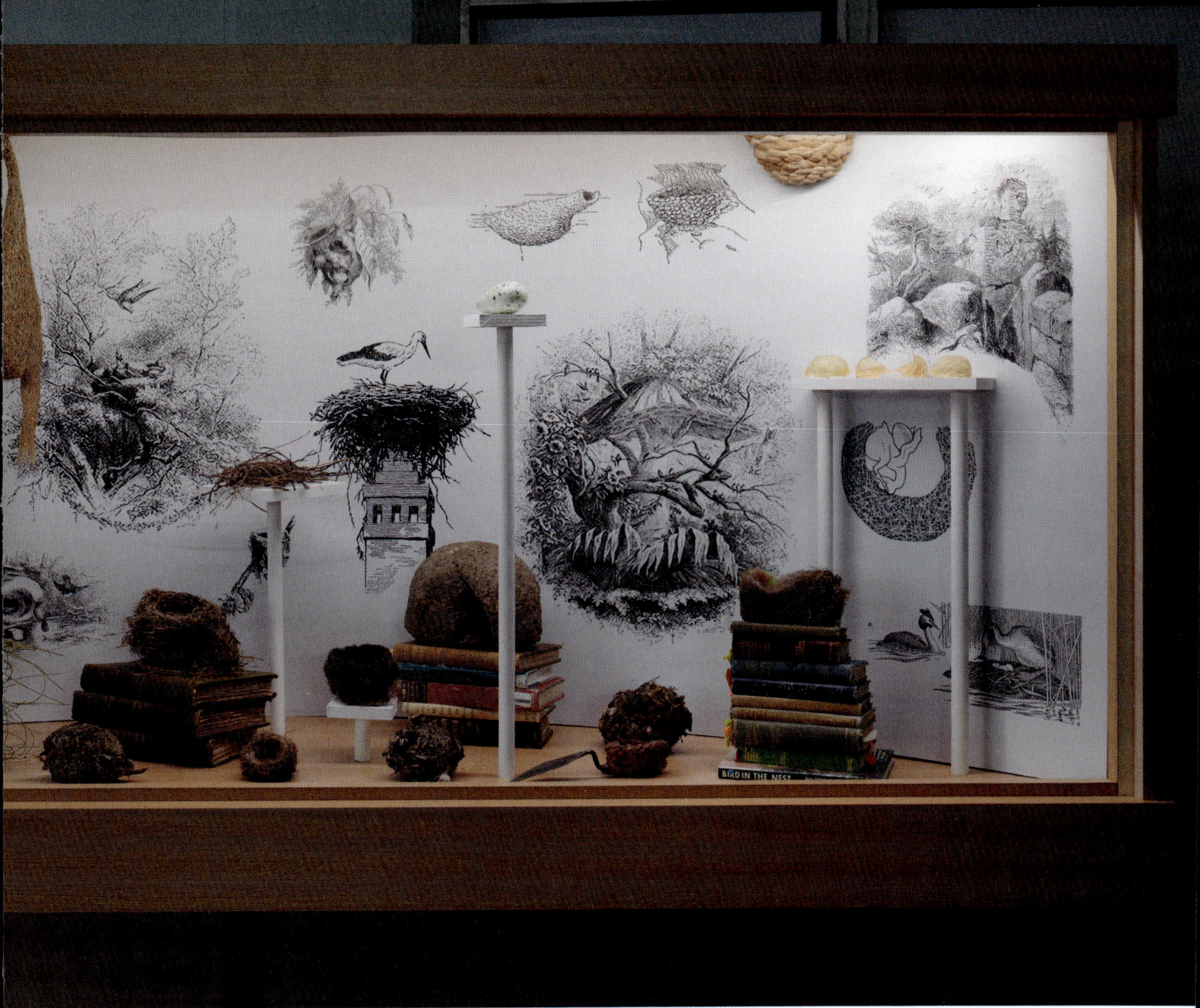

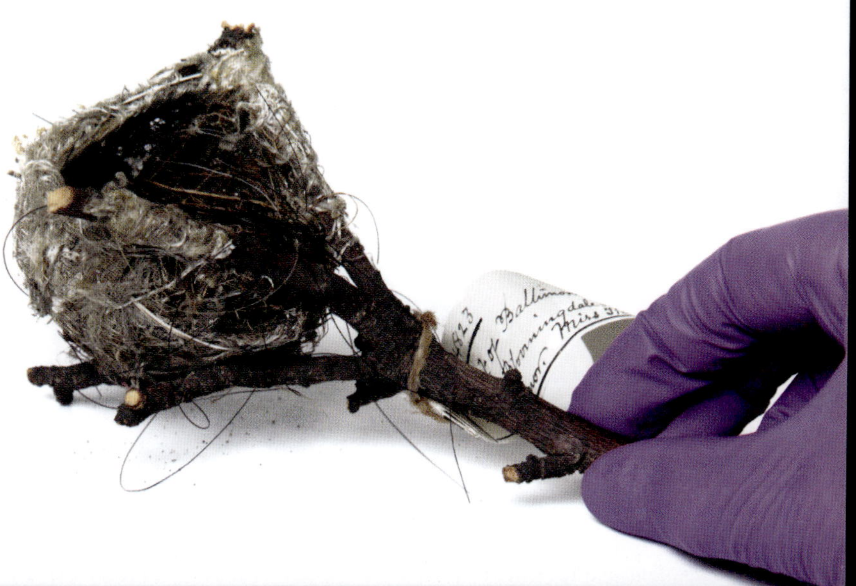

↑ *Natural History of Nest Building (Collection of Andy Holden)*, 2017, found birds nests, wood, books, clay and natural materials with printed backdrop and projection, 100 × 260 × 60 cm (39⅜ × 102⅜ × 15¾ in.)

← (All other images) *Natural History of Nest Building* (details), 2017, three-channel projection with four-channel sound, 30 mins.

The duo's various approaches to the subject are nuanced and idiosyncratic. Andy, full of wonder, discusses nests as inventive sculptural objects and birds as creative beings, while Peter espouses Charles Darwin's theory of evolution and ideas of natural selection, outlining the genetically inherited behaviours that might lead to a nest's particular design. Their discussions are both informed and intimate, an expression not only of their shared interests but of their familial bond. Although the springboard for the film is nests, as it develops, it becomes clear that it's also a study of how interests are formed and how the idea of free will, in a family structure, is a complex one. The psychoanalyst, Darian Leader, was commissioned to write a text for the show. He observed that:

> As his father explained nests as the result of evolutionary imperatives, to generate innate mechanisms of construction which could subsequently be ignored, the son saw something else. Just as Freud had challenged the idea of dreams as contingent and secondary by-products of the psyche, so Andy Holden sensed that more was at stake here. And just as the nest had been more or less written out of ornithology as a subject worthy of study in itself, he wanted to bring it back. The nest, Holden says, was like the unconscious of ornithology.[2]

The soundtrack to the film was inspired by the blackbird section of Olivier Messiaen's composition for solo piano, *Catalogue d'oiseaux* (catalogue of birds), which he wrote between 1956 and 1958. Holden explains:

> As the film starts with a blackbird nest I decided to take Messiaen's transcription of the blackbird and use extracts throughout, as song is a way of defending the territory. It links with another collaboration with my father, *Lecture on Birdsong*, a live work which I'm slowly adapting into a film (by slowly I mean I've recorded a bit every spring for about ten years) which is also indebted to the work of Messiaen, who was both ornithologist and composer.[3]

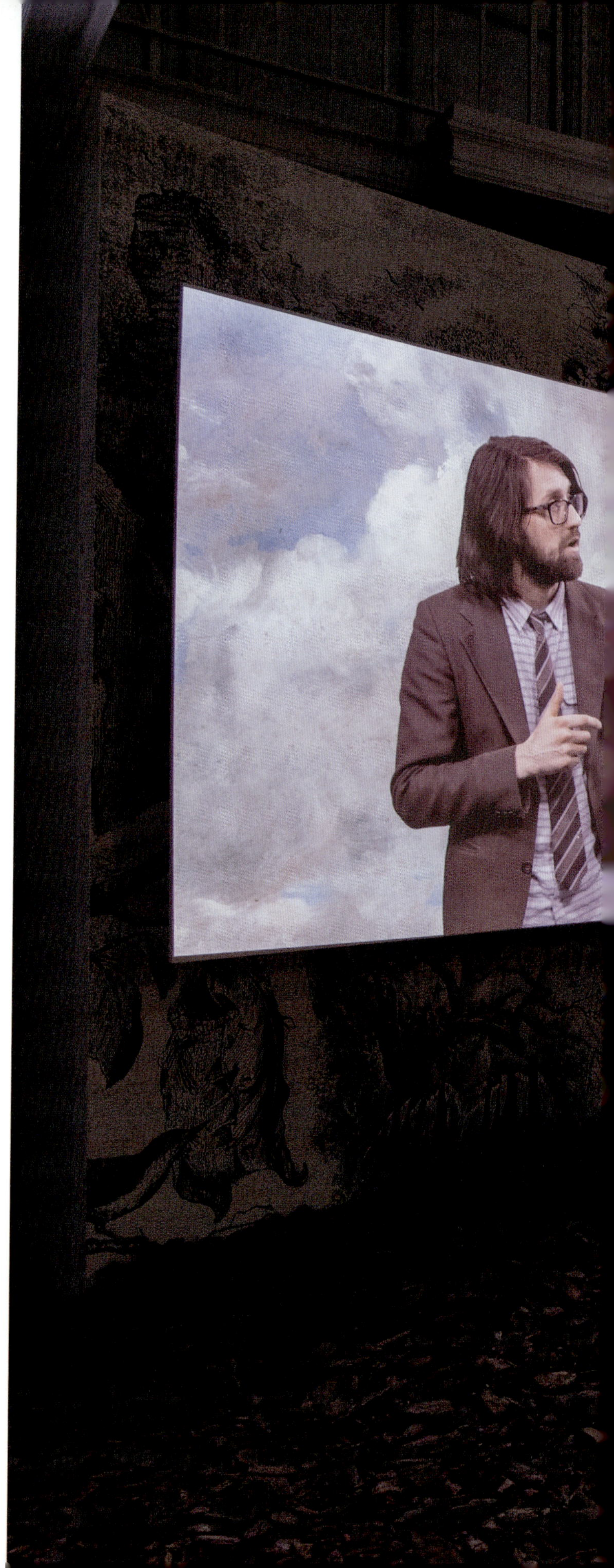

→ *Natural History of Nest Building*, 2017, three-channel projection with four-channel sound, 30 mins., installation dimensions variable, installation view, former Newington Library, London, commissioned by Artangel. Tate collection

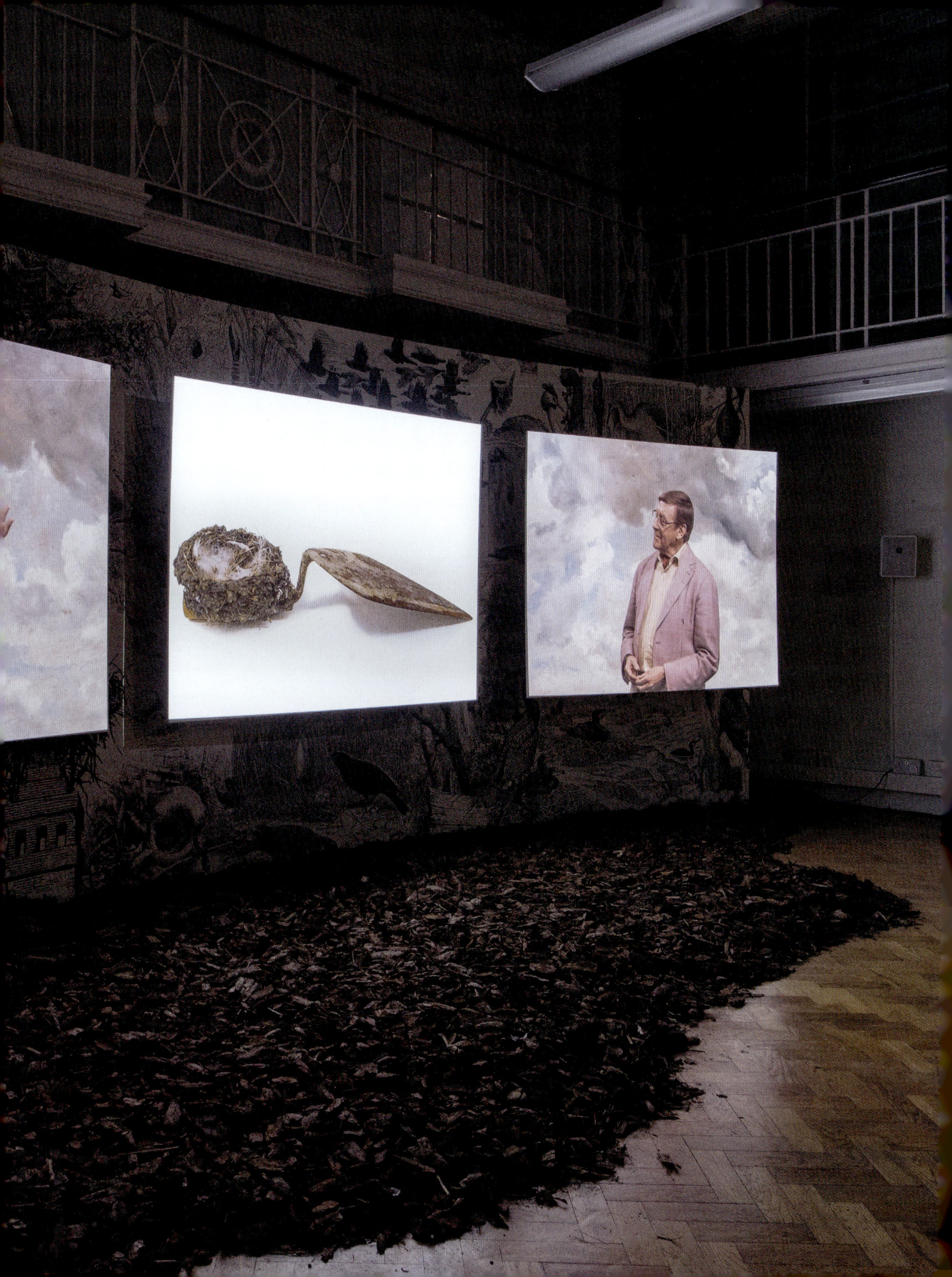

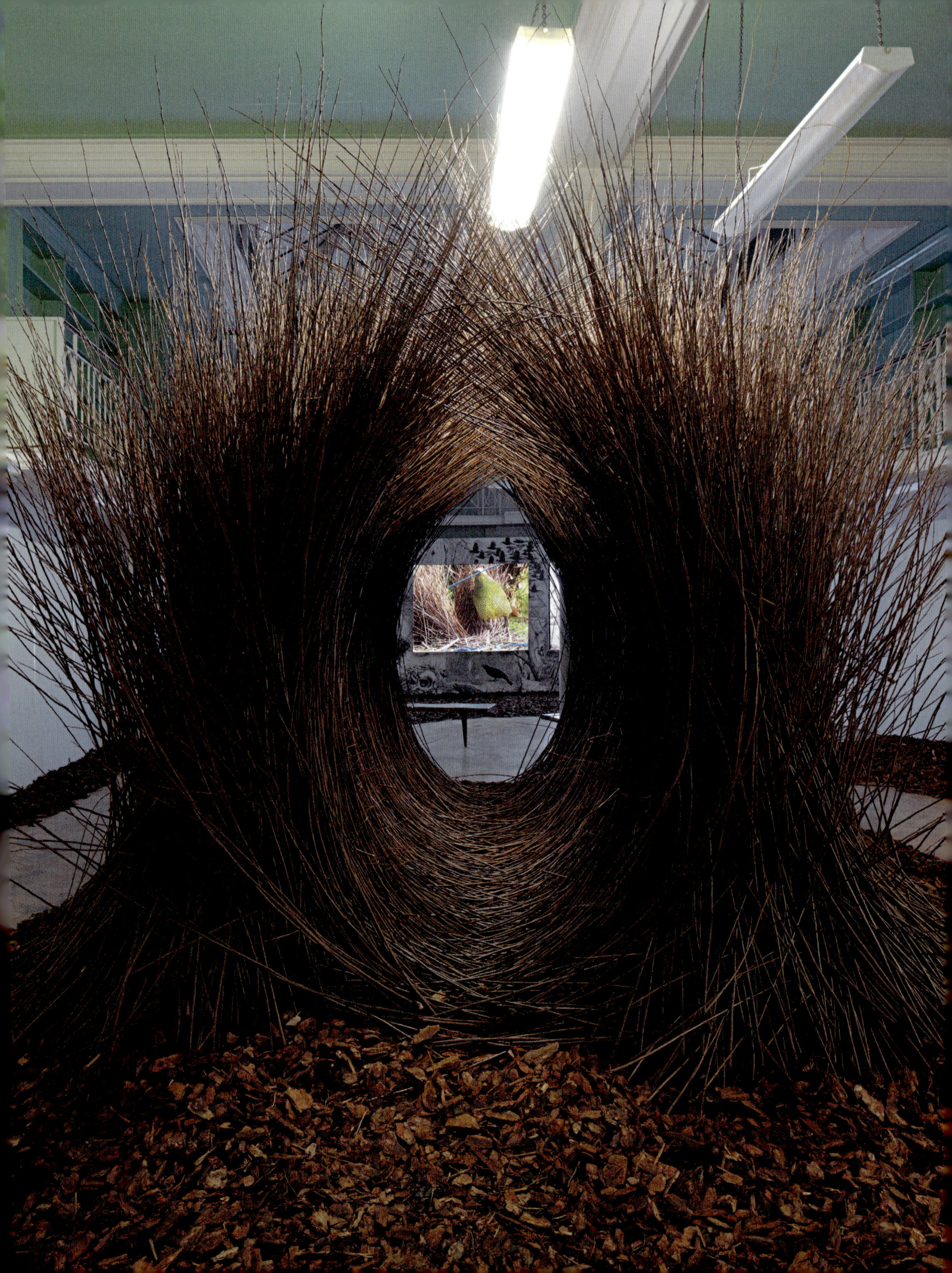

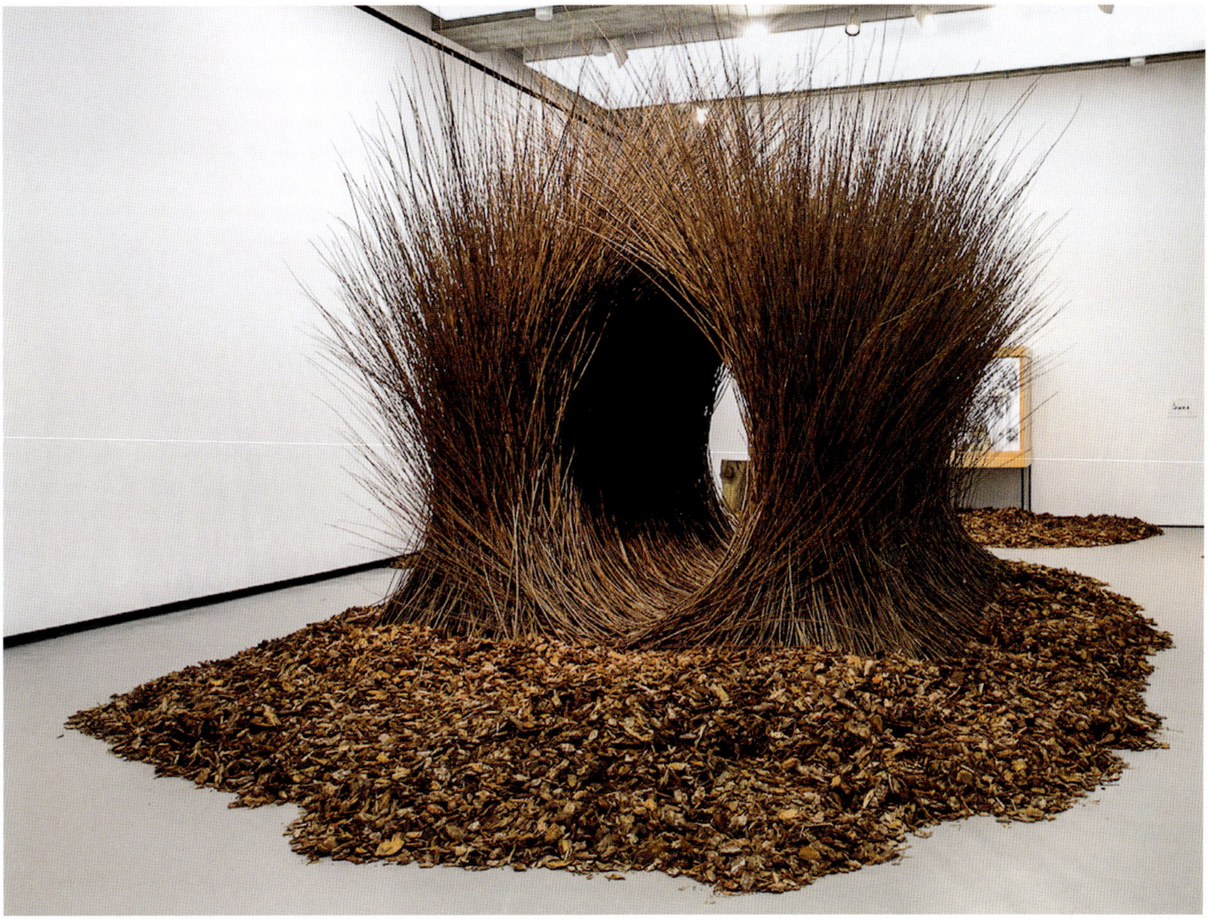

← *Origin of the Work of Art (Bower)*, 2017, kiln-dried willow, steel and bark, 3.5 × 3.5 × 3 m (11½ × 11½ × 9¾ ft.), installation view, former Newington Library, London, commissioned by Artangel. Private collection
↑ *Origin of the Work of Art (Bower)*, 2018, kiln-dried willow, steel and bark, 3 × 3 × 3 m (9¾ × 9¾ × 9¾ ft.), installation view, Towner Eastbourne, UK. Private collection

The centre of the exhibition was dominated by *Origin of the Work of Art (Bower)* (2017), a large recreation in willow of the kind of structure bowerbirds build in order to attract a mate. Elegant, curved and minimal, it recalls works by major modernist artists such as Richard Serra. Holden's homage to the bird's creativity can also be read as an evocation of the mysterious impulses to create art which is tempered by his questioning of the traditionally human-centred nature of our discourse around it.

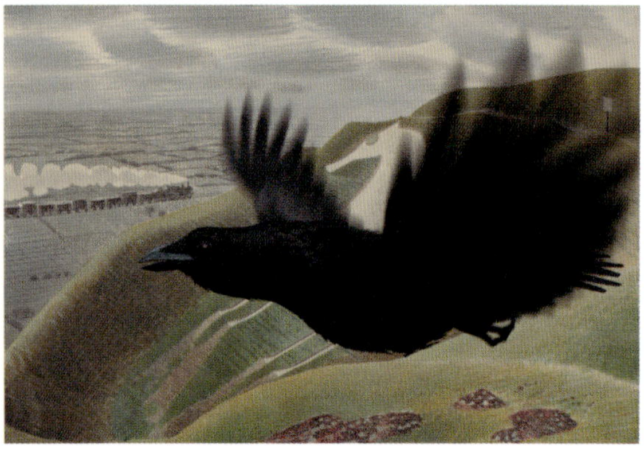

The exhibition's second section, 'A Social History of Egg Collecting', featured the three-screen video *Opposite of Time* (2017), which is narrated by an animated crow (voiced by Holden) flying across a series of well-known, chronologically presented British landscape paintings, beginning with John Constable and moving through works by artists including J. M. W. Turner and David Hockney. The film documents how egg collecting, or oology, developed from a serious, science-based practice in the 19th century that formed the basis of museum collections, through to a popular hobby for working-class men in the early 20th century. After a change in the law in 1954 to protect endangered species, it became an outlawed activity, only undertaken by egg addicts, a strange case of enthusiasts actively destroying the very thing they love. The film charts fluctuating attitudes in Britain towards both class and the natural world. Holden writes: 'The way we experience nature is something constantly socially negotiated, part of our own natural selection and evolutionary struggle, as we are not, as it were, outside of nature, but part of it.'[4]

↑ *Opposite of Time: A Social History of Egg Collecting* (detail, one of three screens), 2017, three-channel animated film, 30 mins., edition of 5. Artangel Collection (1); Bristol Museum & Art Gallery and Leeds Art Gallery (2)
↓ *Social History of Egg Collecting*, 2017, three- channel animated film, 30 mins., installation view, former Newington Library, London, commissioned by Artangel
→ *Natural Selection*, 2017, installation view, Kröller-Müller Museum, Netherlands, 2024
↘ *Oologists Record*, 2019, handpainted porcelain eggs and found materials, 137 × 190.5 × 129.5 cm (54 × 75 × 51 in.), edition of 2, installation view, Kröller-Müller Museum, Netherlands, 2024

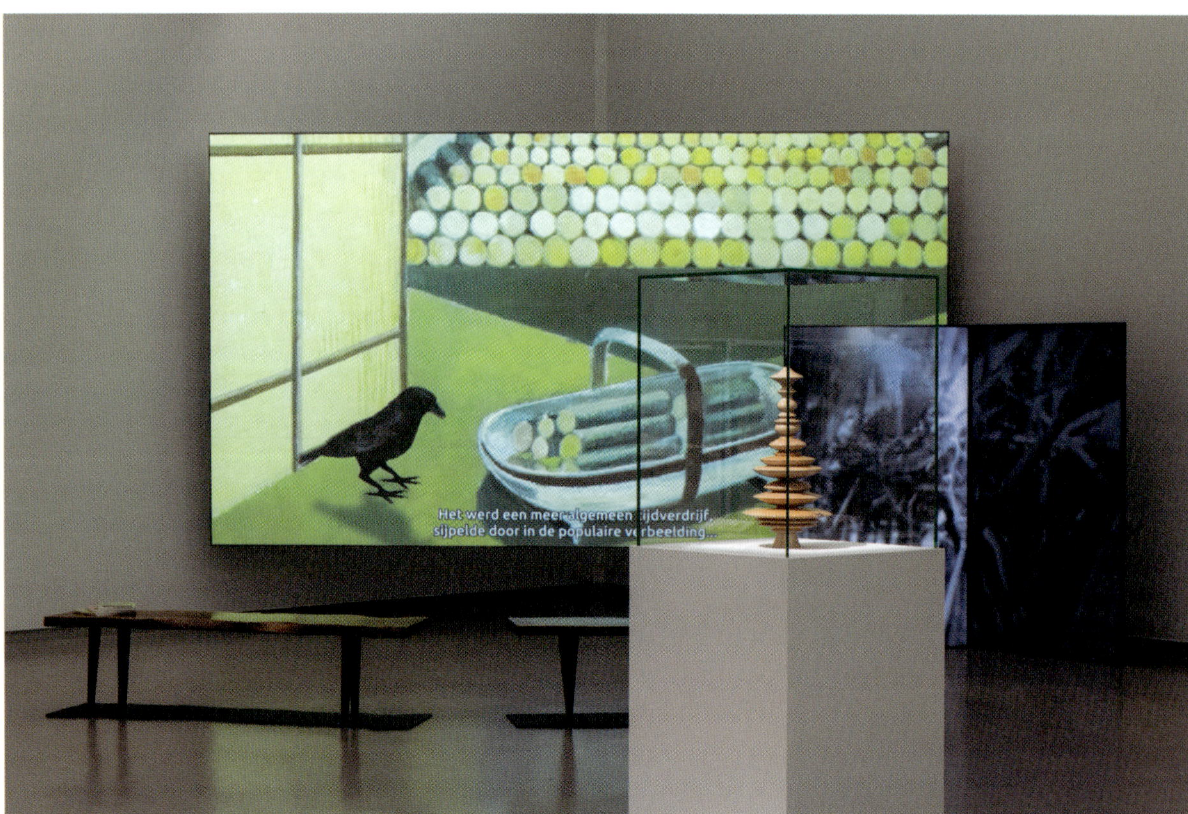

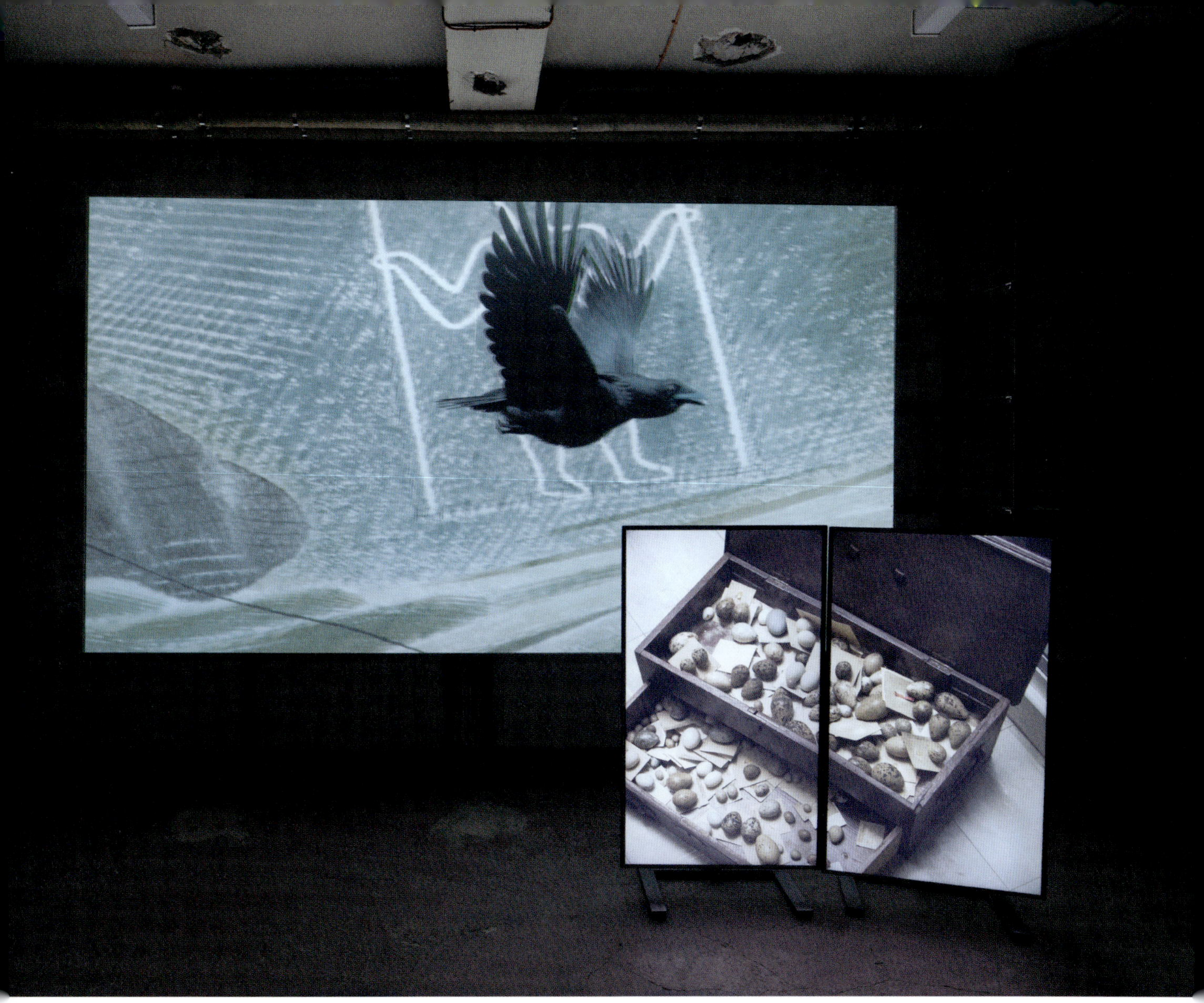

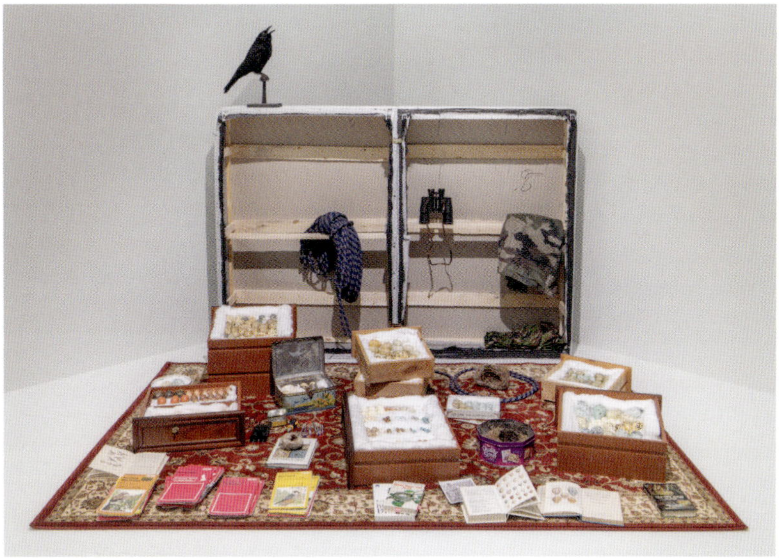

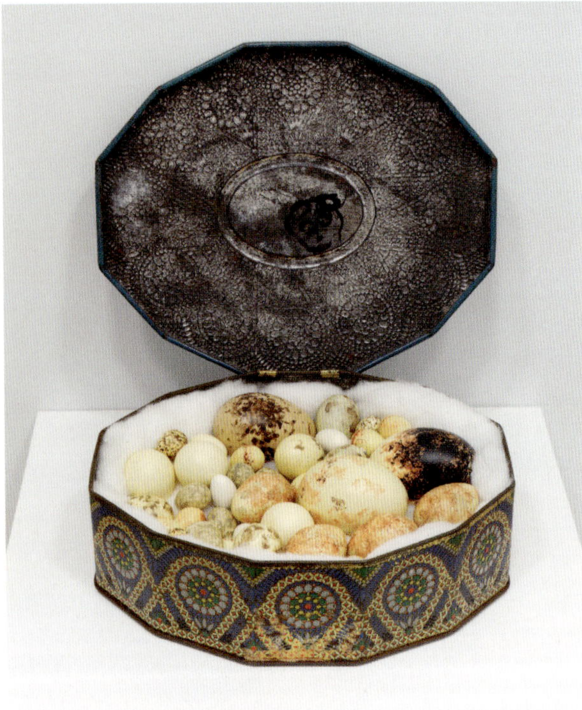

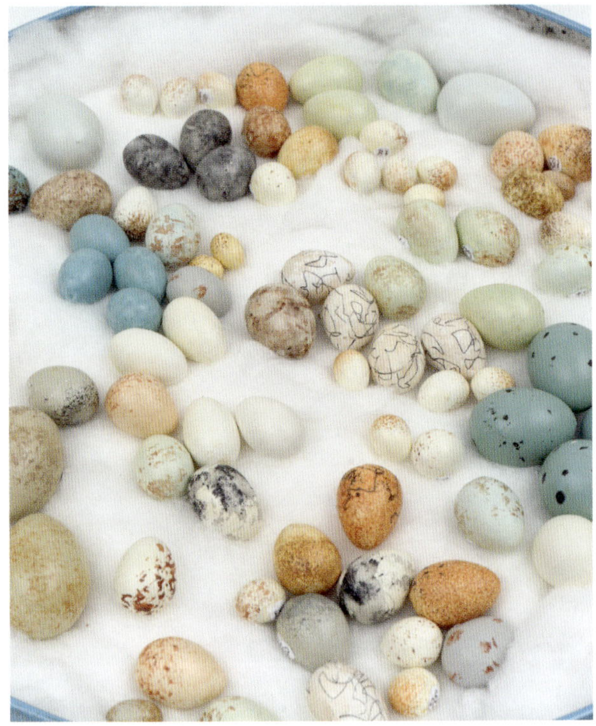

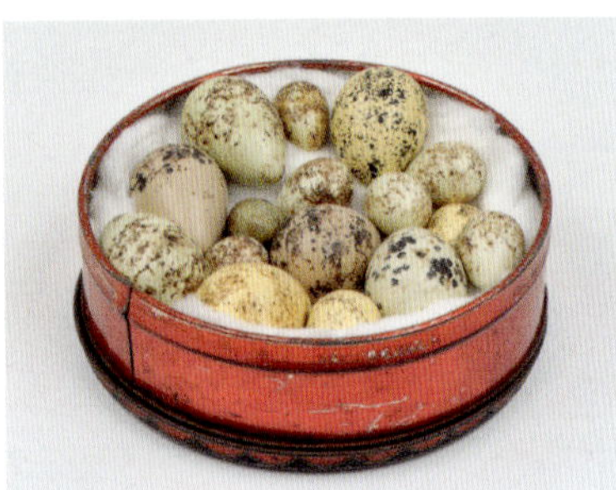

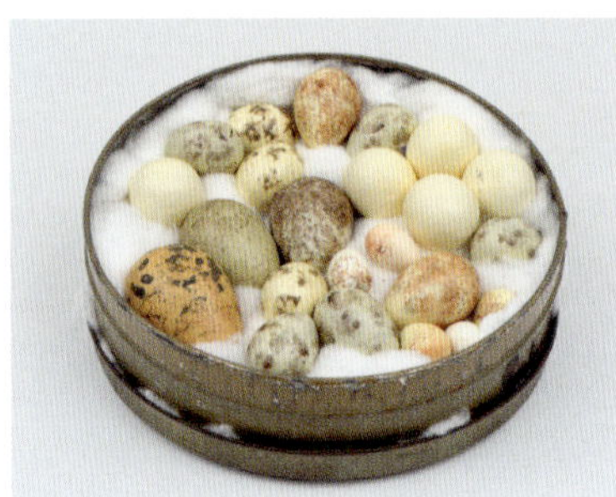

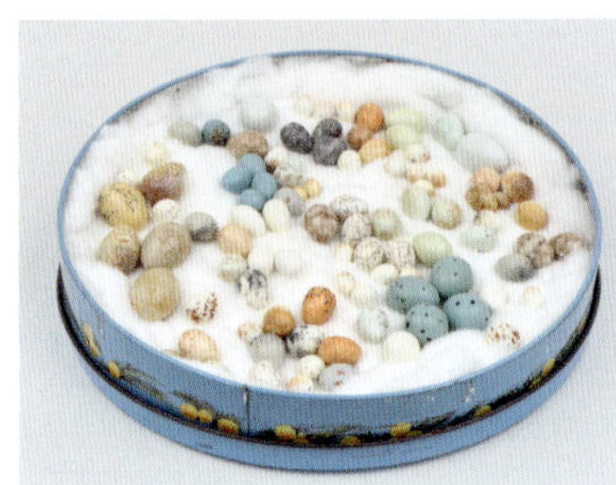

The film was placed next to the large floor-based sculpture *How the Artist Was Led to the Study of Nature* (2017). To create it, Holden commissioned a retired gamekeeper-turned-craftsman to carve several thousand eggs in porcelain, which he then displayed, like stolen goods, in biscuit tins and fish crates. The installation was a recreation of a police photograph that documented the largest illegally accrued collection of wild birds' eggs ever uncovered. Although the collection would have been of great scientific value, since the eggs were collected illegally, they were destroyed by the RSPB in 2007 as a deterrent to other collectors.

↑ *How the Artist Was Led to the Study of Nature,* 2017, handpainted porcelain eggs and tins, tins: 16 to 30 cm (6 ⅝ to 12 in.) in diameter

→ *How the Artist was Led to the Study of Nature,* 2017, handpainted porcelain eggs and tins, variable dimensions, installation view, former Newington Library, London, commissioned by Artangel. Collection of Bristol Museum & Art Gallery and Leeds Art Gallery

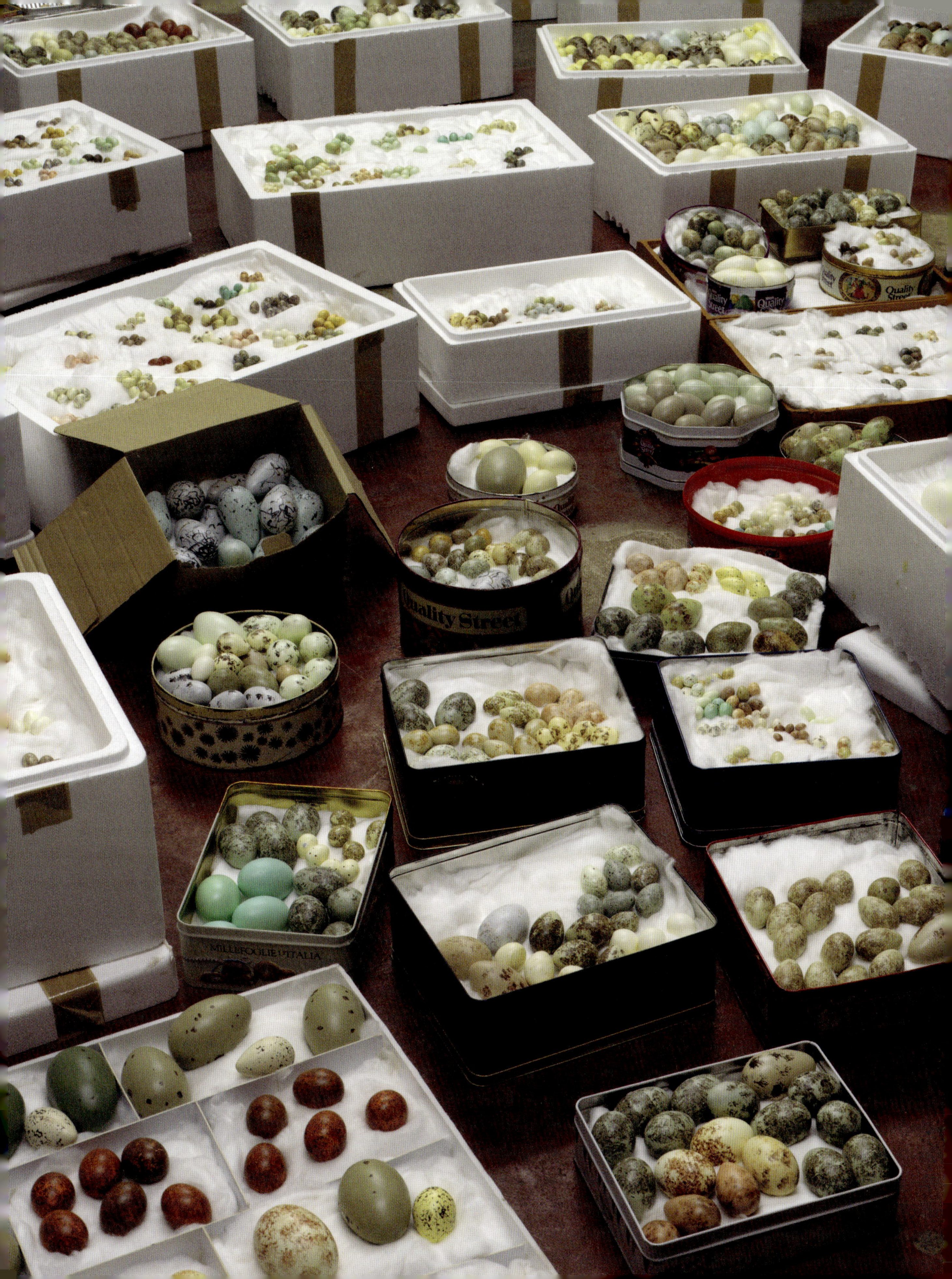
Quality Street
MILLEFOGLIE D'ITALIA

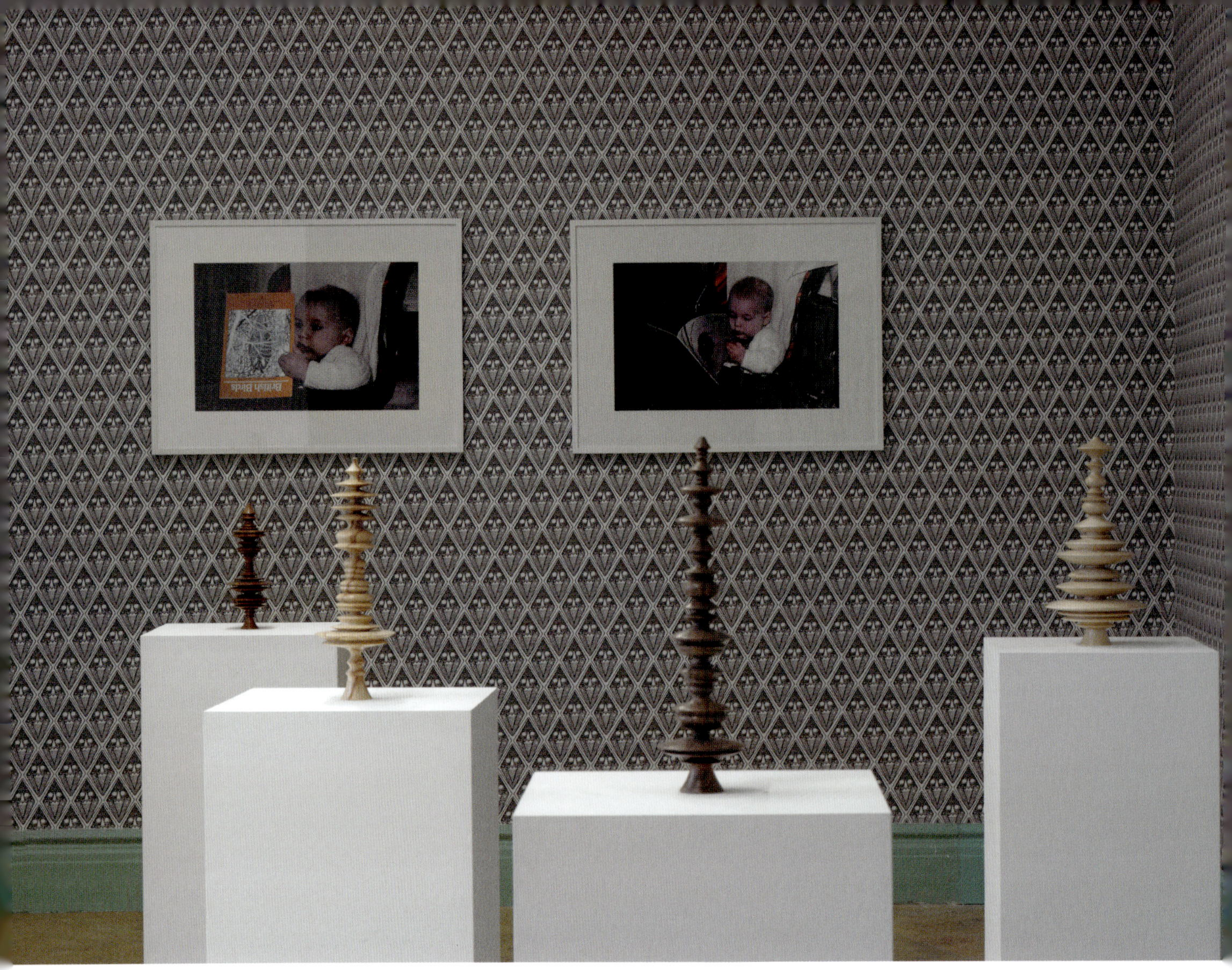

Themes of loss were also evoked in *Silent Spring* (2017), a series of sculptures created by transposing electronically visualised sound waves of birdsong into carvings made from wood sourced from the trees in which the birds nest. (Holden commissioned the wood-turner Geoffrey Leeson to carve them.) The title is a reference to Rachel Carson's 1962 book of the same name, in which she identifies the decline of birdsong as a symptom of the harmful effects of pesticides, which proved a catalyst for the environmental movement.

Holden later expanded this idea in a series of sculptures, *Auguries (Last Calls)* (2023). To create them, he again transformed wave forms of birdsongs, but this time shaped them into vertical bronze totems. Each one depicts a bird native to the British Isles that is in decline, such as the yellowhammer, the swift and the mistle thrush. The title *Auguries* refers to the ancient Roman tradition of using birds to divine the future. Holden chose bronze as it will, more than likely, outlive the species represented by the song, what the artist describes as 'a melancholy record of a vanishing sound'.[5]

↑ *Songs of Common Garden Birds* (foreground), *Andy Holden by Peter Holden* (wall), *Superstimulus (Cuckoo Mouth)* (wallpaper), all 2017, wood turnings, framed prints and wallpaper, variable dimensions, installation view, former Newington Library, London, commissioned by Artangel

1 *Andy Holden, Collected Free Labour: Blog Interviews, 2010–2021*, Slimvolume, 2021, p. 94.
2 Darian Leader, 'On Eggs and Nests', Artangel, https//www.artangel.org.uk/natural-selection/on-eggs-and-nests. Accessed 2 Mar 2026.
3 Andy Holden, email to Jennifer Higgie, 9 December 2024.
4 Andy Holden, email to Jennifer Higgie, 17 January 2023.
5 Andy Holden, email to Jennifer Higgie, 17 January 2025.

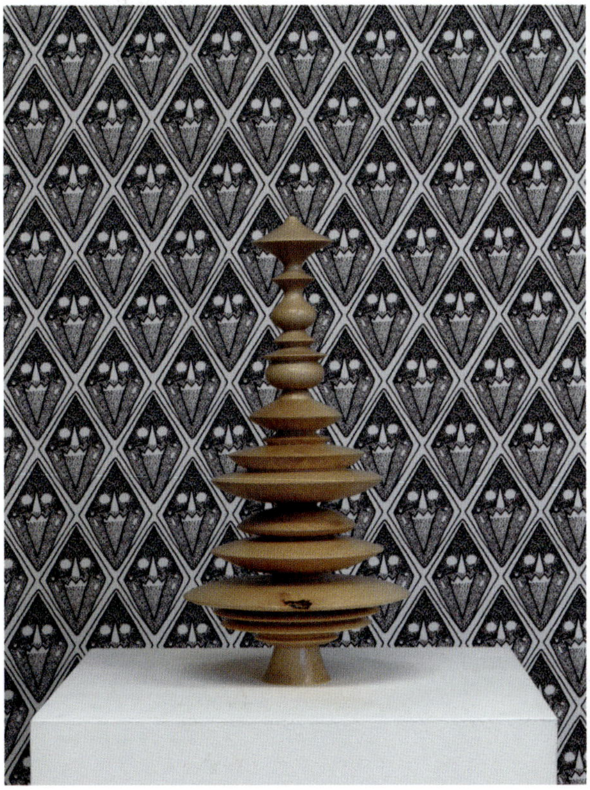

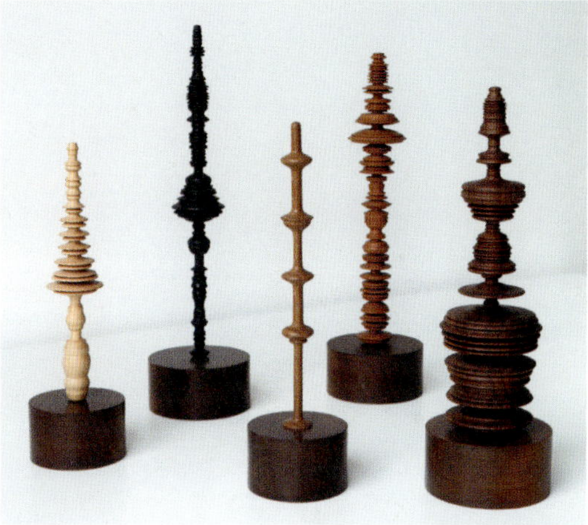

← *Blackbird*, with *Superstimulus (Cuckoo Mouth)* wallpaper in the background, 2017, turned wood, sculpture: h. 24 × diam. 12 cm (9 ½ × 4 ¾ in.), installation view, former Newington Library, London, commissioned by Artangel. Private collection

↑ *Auguries (Last Calls)*, 2023, turned wood, h: 28 cm (11 in.). Private collection

↓ *Auguries (Last Calls)*, 2024, patinated bronze and concrete, 50 × 50 × 210 cm (19 ¾ × 19 ¾ × 82 ⅝ in.), installation view and collection Kröller-Müller Museum, Netherlands

» (Overleaf) *Auguries (Lament)*, 2025, bronze with patina in three parts with reclaimed telegraph pole, variable dimensions, installation view, 'In the Shadows: Frieze Sculpture', Regent's Park, London. Private collection

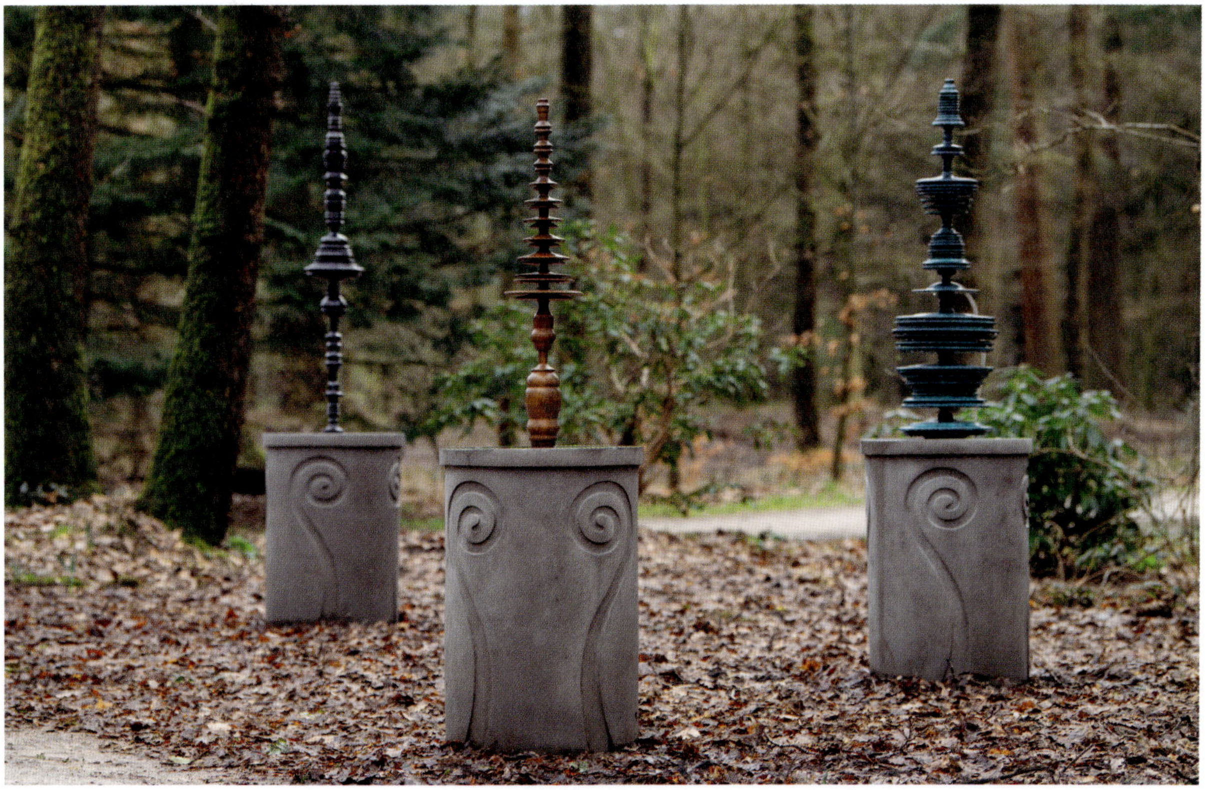

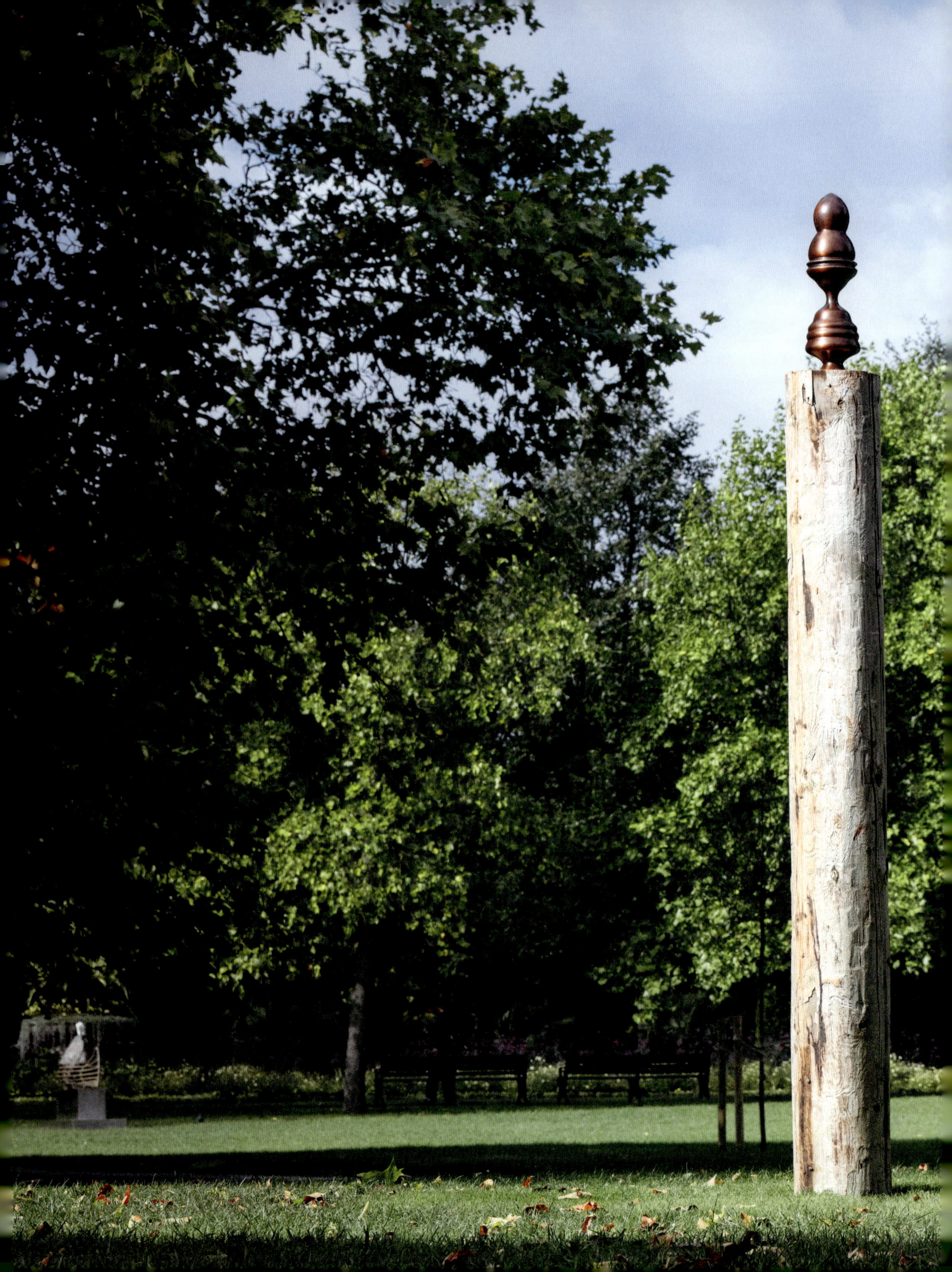

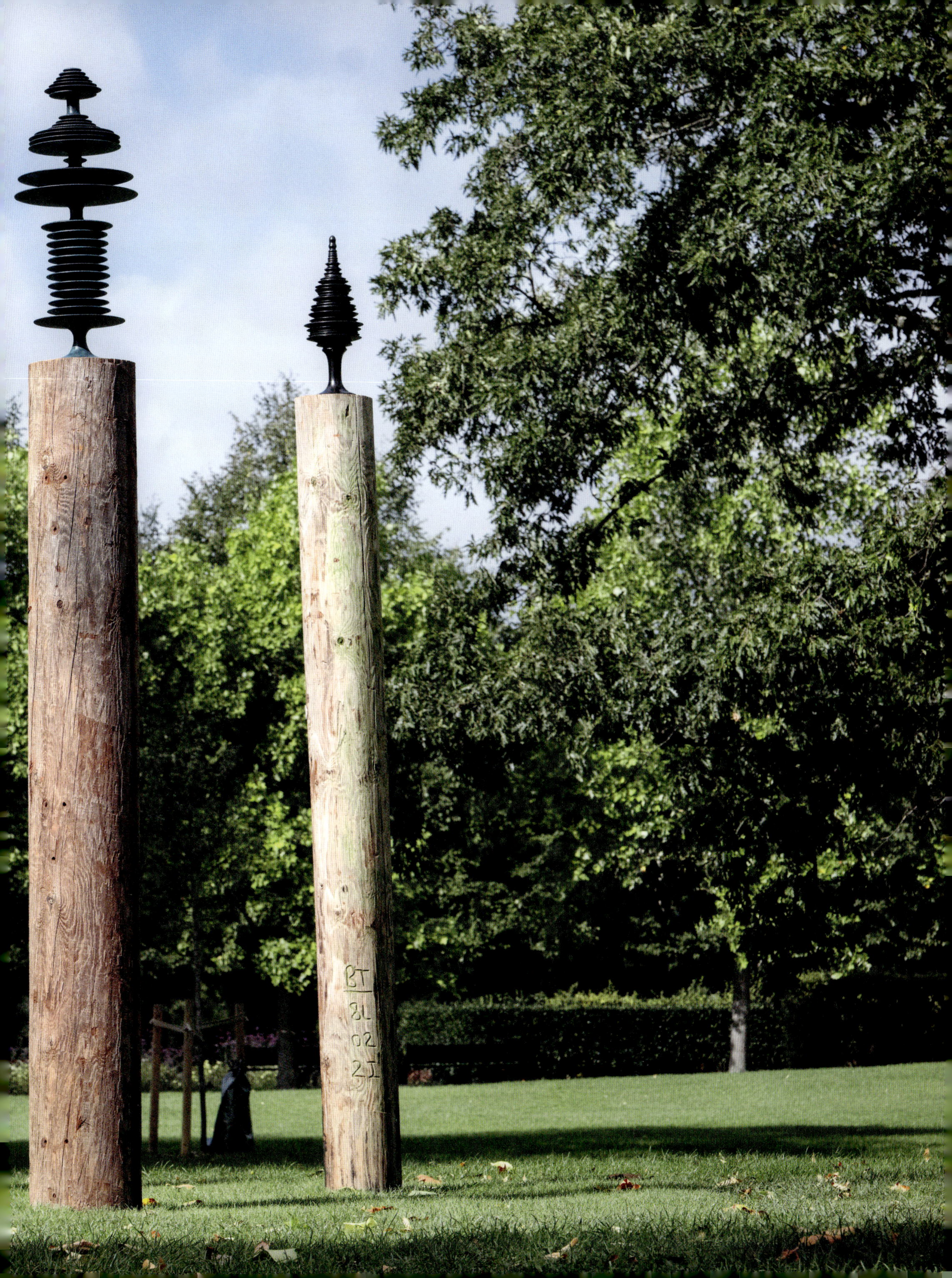
BT

Full of Days / Hermione: Kingdom of the Sick

2021–23

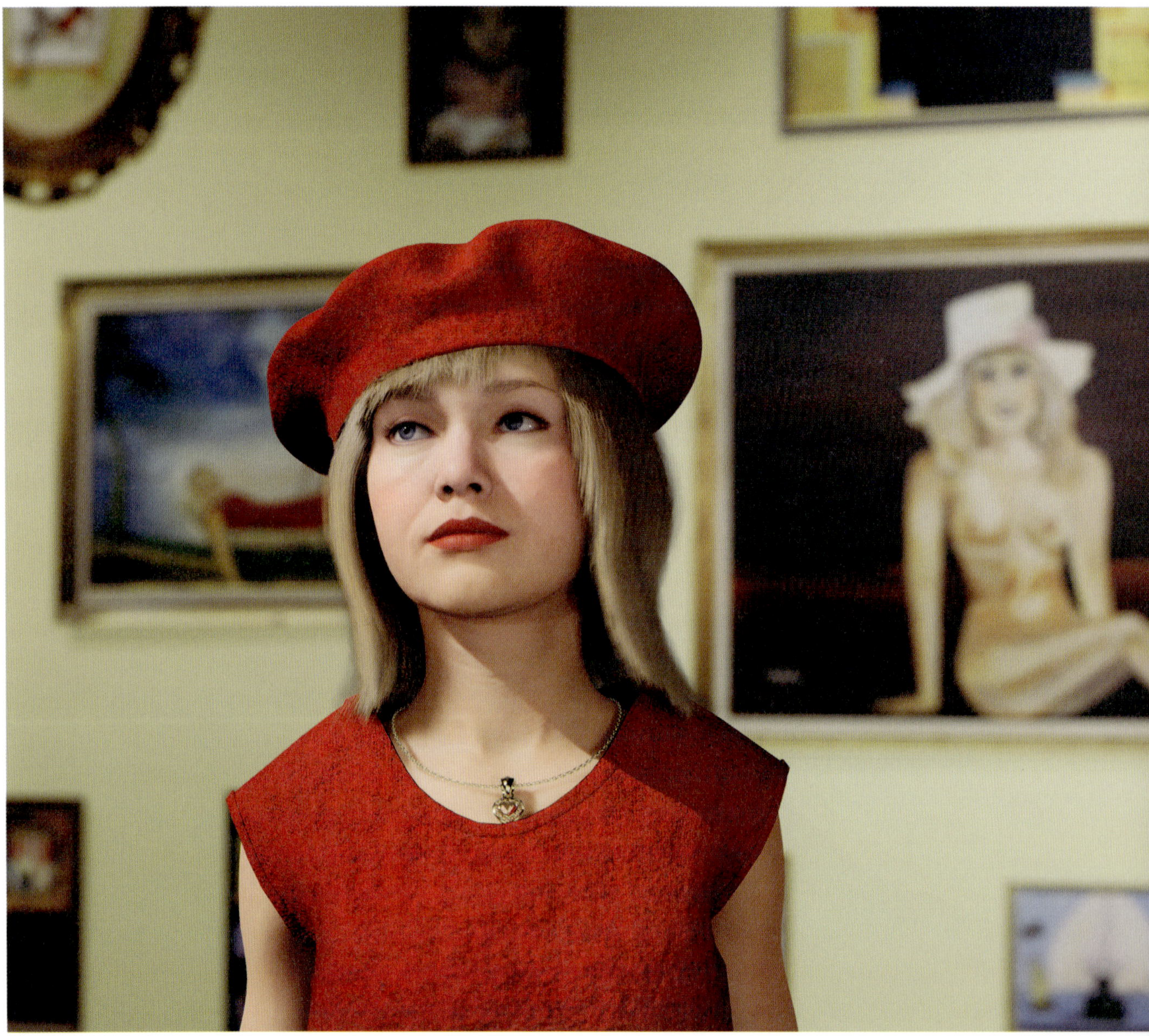

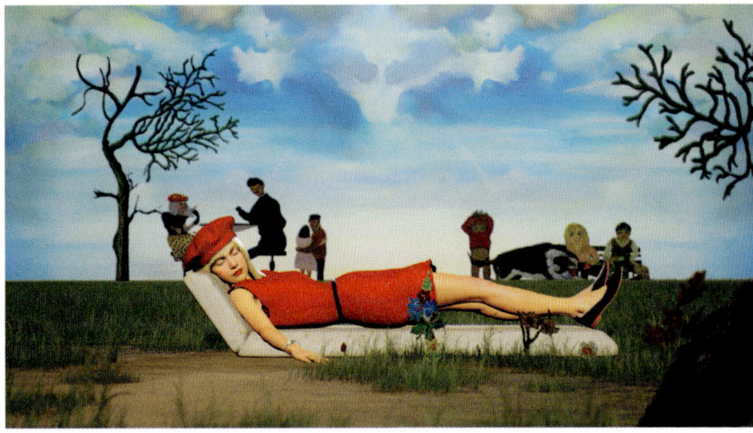

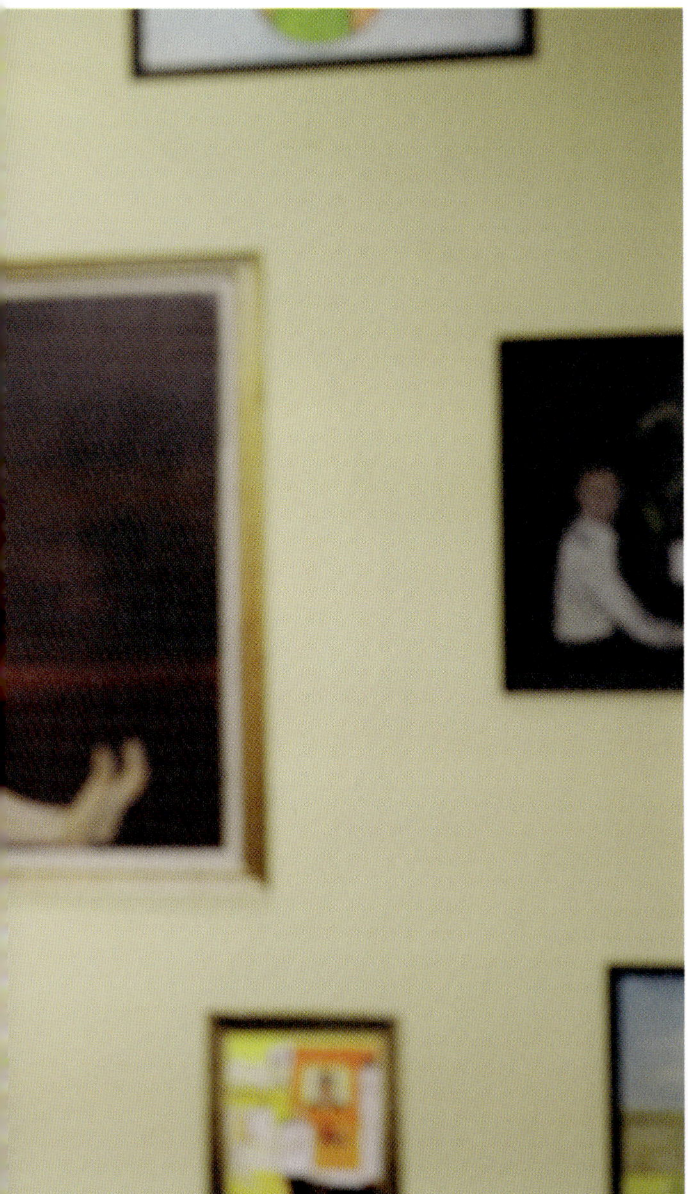

In 2017, Andy Holden visited a charity shop and came across a group of curious figurative paintings signed 'HERMIONE'. He also discovered a self-published booklet: *Hermione Burton: A Journey through the Paintings*. Holden bought the lot.

Over the following year, Holden learned more about the artist: Hermione Burton was a Bedford-based, self-taught painter who was born in 1925 with rheumatic heart disease. She married three times and had a beloved daughter, Jacqui, who also became an artist, but who predeceased her in her early 30s from the same heart condition as her mother. Hermione died in 2007. Her work was only exhibited once.

Holden eventually managed to acquire 20 more of Hermione's paintings. Her subjects range from land- and seascapes to interiors and various portraits, including a man with a beard and a pipe and another, smiling, playing the piano; as well as paintings of her daughter Jacqui – whose resemblance to her mother is uncanny – dozing in a garden beneath a barren tree and, in another, dressed as a bride. Hermione was also an avid painter of self-portraits; she pictures herself naked and smiling in a large white hat; in bed in hospital, her golden hair a halo; dressed in riding gear with her eyes closed; and unconscious at the bottom of the stairs after a fall, a cat by her side, Cubist paintings on the wall. In two paintings titled *Phoenix Rising from the Ashes*, Hermione pictures herself as a disembodied head, surrounded by a hearth, a globe, a tiny still life of flowers. One work, *Hermione's Retrospective*, depicts a room crowded with 17 paintings – flower studies, a cowboy boot,

← *Hermione: Kingdom of the Sick*, 2022, animated film and documentary footage, 40 mins., edition of 3

↑ *Time of the Sick (II)*, 2023, digital print on Somerset paper with acetate overlays, 22 × 40 cm (8¾ × 15¾ in.), edition of 10 portraits of a fox and a smiling woman, landscapes, and more – some of which are identifiable, while others might be lost or fictitious. Holden sees Hermione's employment of skewed perspective and distortion as a form of realism. In his voice-over narration of the film *Hermione: Kingdom of the Sick* (2022), which he created as a homage to Burton, Holden remarks:

> She paints to tell others of the story. Time happens all at once and is laid out on a flat plane.... In the time of the sick, experiences are unassailable fragments that refuse to become past, instead haunting the present. Things do not proceed according to the conventions of perspective. Scale is ordered not by where the figures are in the picture plane, but for significance or emphasis. Figures in the foreground or background are the same. Animals can be very large. Children are very large. Those of secondary narrative importance are scaled accordingly.

In 2018, 'The Estate of Hermione' was the inaugural exhibition at Ex-Baldessarre, the project space Holden runs from his Bedford studio; it was accompanied by mixtapes of tracks by musician Jarvis Cocker and artist-poet Heather Phillipson, plus a text by artist-writer Tessa Norton, who wrote:

> In Susan Sontag's framing, 'everyone who is born holds dual citizenship, in the kingdom of the well and in the kingdom of the sick' and Hermione's citizenship can't fail to inform her gaze. The prosaic and limited interiors of her sick bed (light switches, chinoiserie motifs, husbands, doctors) become abstracted and mobilised to explain her place in the world.[1]

Five years later, in 2023, at the Gallery of Everything – London's first commercial space dedicated to self-taught artists or those who made work outside the cultural mainstream – Holden staged another exhibition devoted to Hermione's life and work. Its title 'Full of Days: Hermione Burton and Andy Holden' is a reference to a Biblical line, Job 42:17 – 'So Job died, being old and full of days', (after having been tested with immense suffering). It is both a celebration of Hermione's art and a heartfelt lament to Holden's partner, Mira Calix, who provided the draft voice over to the film, but who tragically took her own life in 2022 whilst the project was still in development.

The exhibition included 32 of Hermione's paintings and the 40-minute film, *Hermione: Kingdom of the Sick*, titled after Sontag's quote. Against a dreamy, upbeat electronic soundtrack by the band Saint Etienne, appears a line, stark against a black background, from Sylvia Plath's 1962 poem 'Tulips': 'And comes from a country far away as health.'

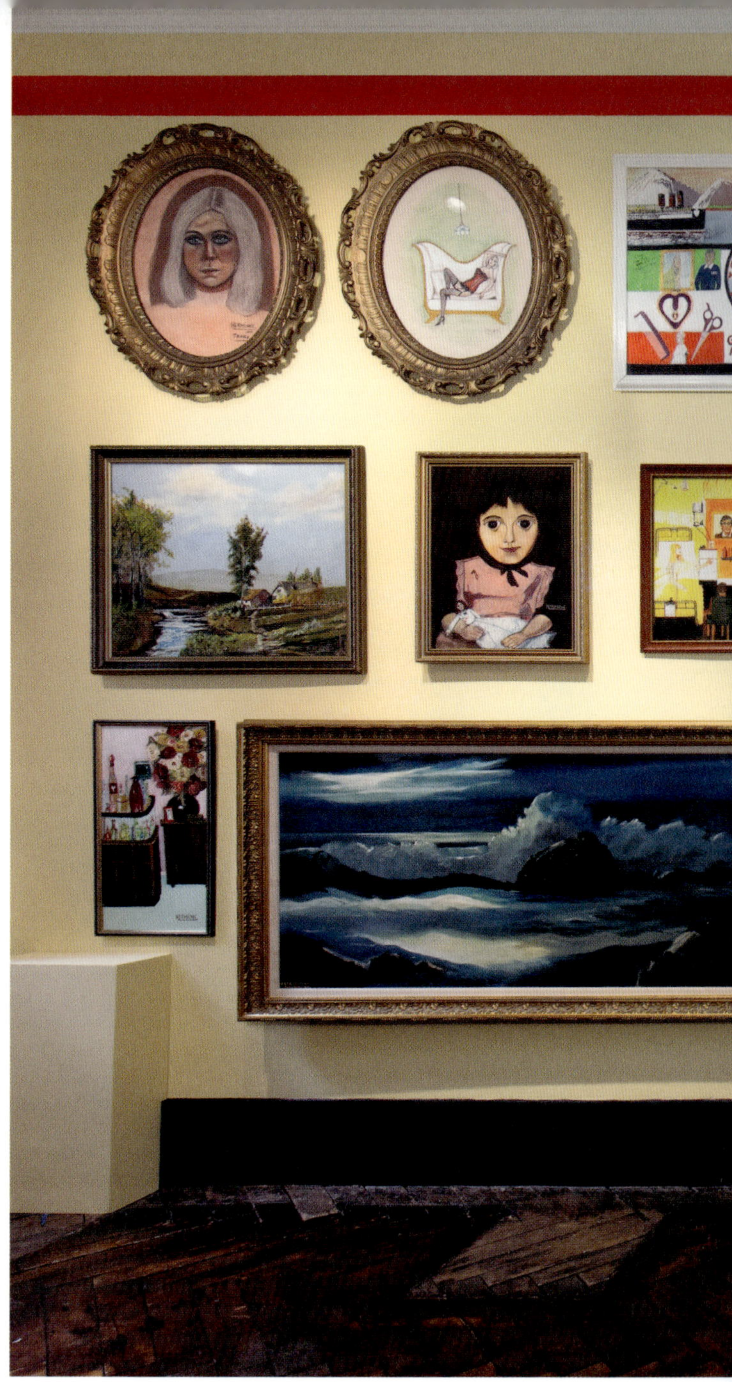

↑ *Full of Days*, 2023, collected paintings of Hermione Burton and HD video, variable dimensions, installation view, Gallery of Everything, London

→ *Hermione: Pleasant Thoughts*, 2023, handpainted 3D print, 10 × 30 cm (4 × 11 ¾ in.). Private collection

→ *Full of Days*, 2023, gallery exterior, Chilton Street, London

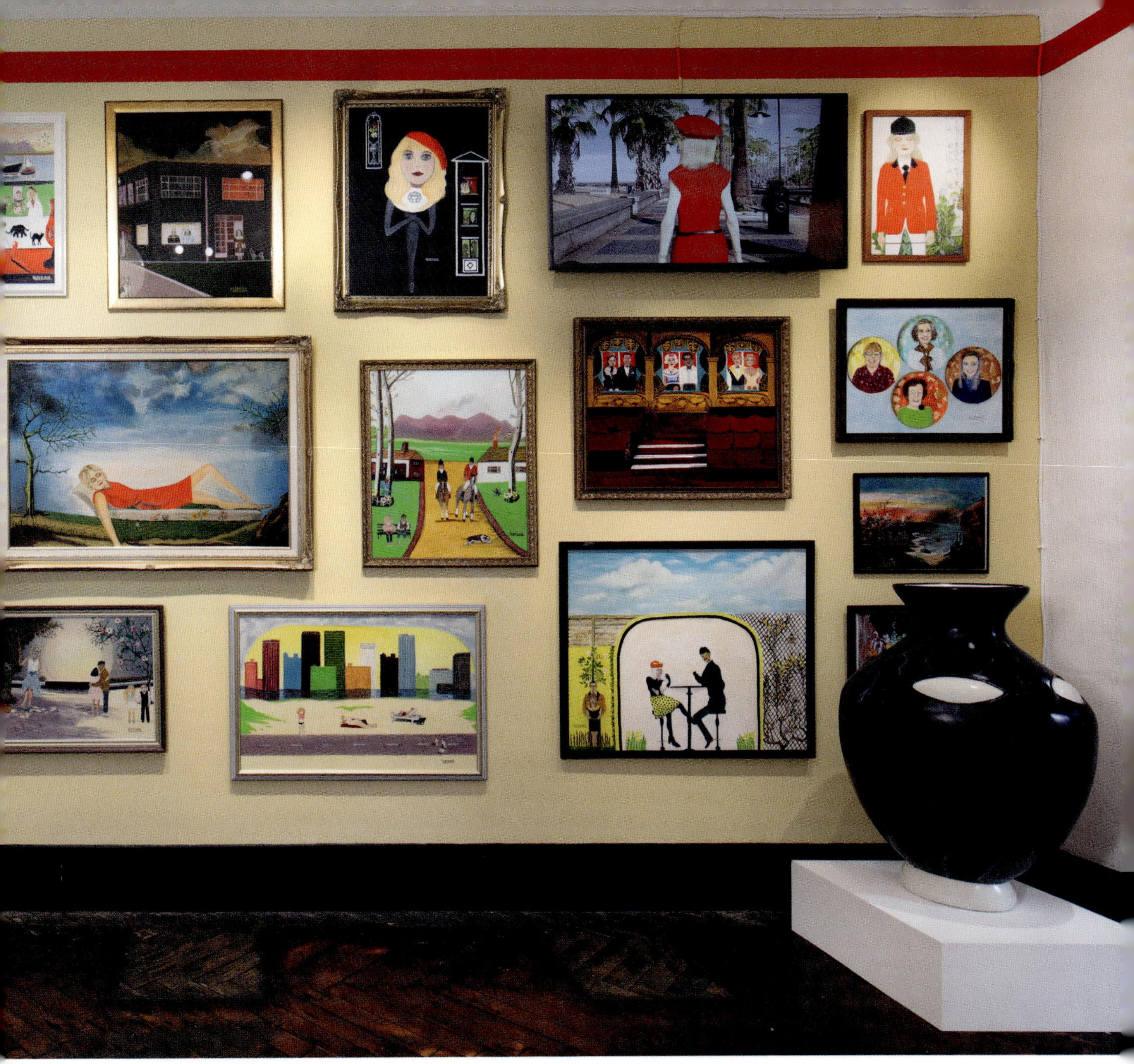

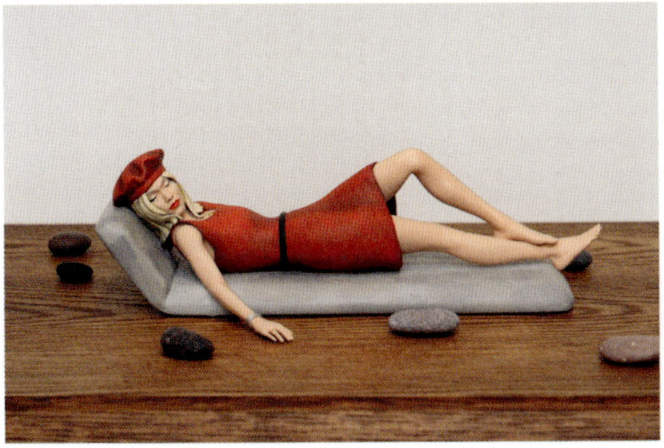

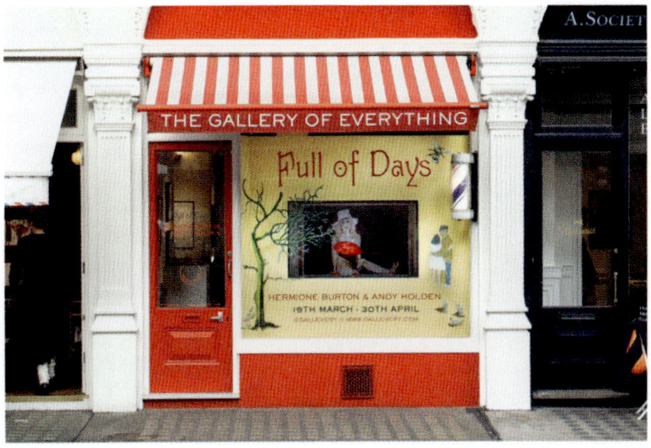
A.SOCIET
THE GALLERY OF EVERYTHING
Full of Days
HERMIONE BURTON & ANDY HOLDEN
19TH MARCH - 30TH APRIL

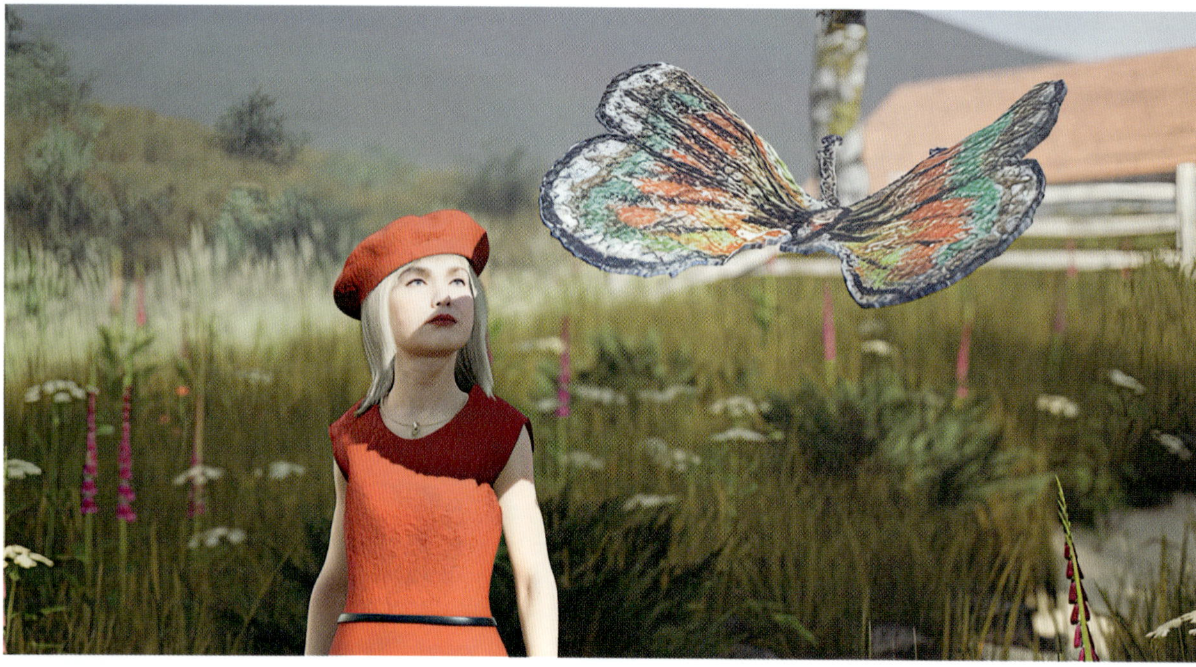

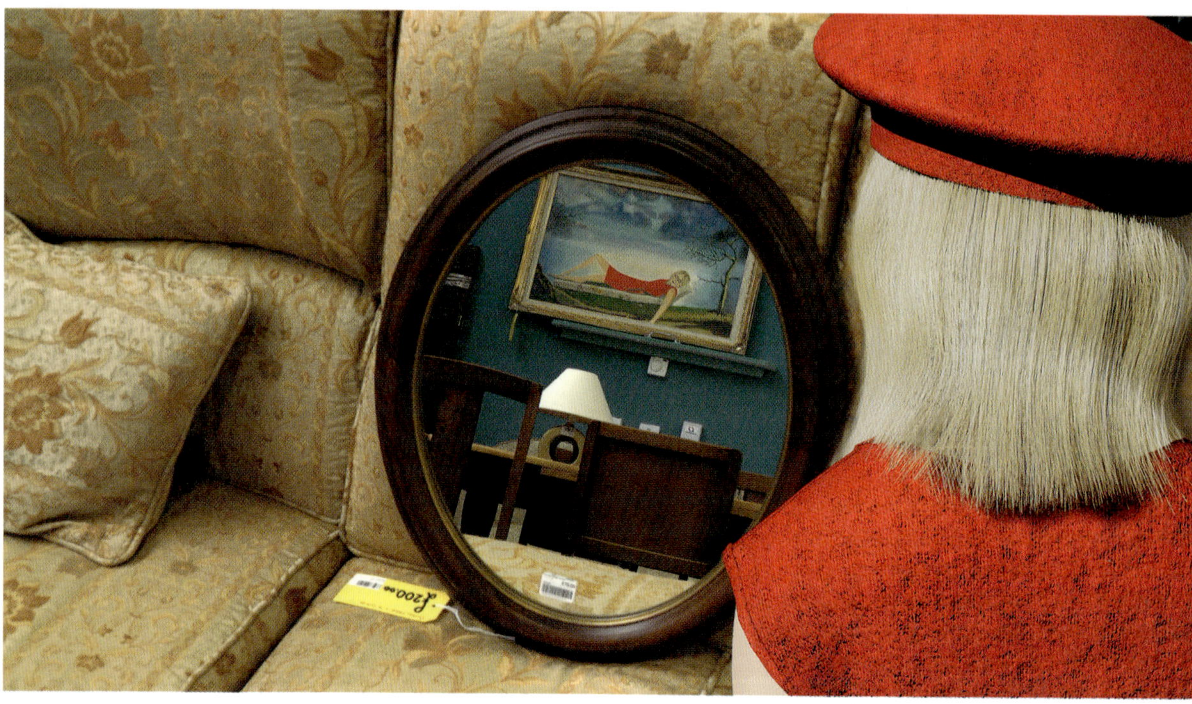

↑ *Time of the Sick (3 + 8)*, 2023, Somerset paper with acetate overlays, each: 22 × 40 cm (8 ¾ × 15 ¾ in.), edition of 10

→ Hermione Burton, *Hermione's Art Exhibition*, u.d., oil on canvas, 40 × 60 cm (15 ¾ × 23 ⅝ in.)

→ *Kingdom of the Sick*, 2022, collected paintings of Hermione Burton and HD video, installation view, *British Art Show 9*, The Whitworth, Manchester, UK (organised by Hayward Gallery Touring)

Hermione's avatar, in a red beret and short red dress, is the star; voiced by Sarah Cracknell, the singer of Saint Etienne, she tells us her life story. Her manner is stilted, slightly out of synch, sincere, as if the story of a life can never truly be told, however well-intentioned the narrator. As Holden notes, reflecting on the slim biography Hermione left behind: 'But what about the gaps between the paragraphs?... There is no such thing as a false personal account. Her evasion is also her truth.' He asks: 'Do we trust the painted image, or the biographical facts?' After Hermione recounts the story of her open-heart surgery, Holden asks: 'Can we finally give in to the metaphor that this film is tugging at us to acknowledge and say that Hermione's paintings are like open-heart surgery? We see inside and we see what the facets of her external life can't tell us.'

Five minutes into the film, another quote, by the sociologist Arthur W. Frank, appears: 'To tell one's own story a person needs others' stories.' This is apt. Holden made *Kingdom of the Sick* at a time of great personal sorrow, and the issues that haunt him – artistic agency, vulnerability, illness and healing, the efficacy of art to help a troubled mind and body – inflect the film. Two more quotes appear at intervals: Rainer Maria Rilke's famous call to action, 'You must change your life', and Virginia Woolf's 'Illness is the great confessional, a childish outspokenness in illness; things are said, truths blurted out, which the cautious respectability of health conceals' – a line from her 1925 essay 'On Being Ill', which she wrote as she was recovering from a breakdown. Her suggestion that people reveal truths when they're unwell, applies to both Hermione, whose paintings are a form of confessional, and to Holden, whose raw grief at the loss of his partner led him to examine, and to articulate, the complexities of his feelings.

Hermione's story is interspersed with accounts from people who knew her, including several members of the Bedford Art Club; John Black, Director of The Gallery, which he ran from his home in Wellingborough, and who gave Hermione and Jacqui a dual exhibition in the 1980s; and the portrait painter James Lynch. Everyone is united in their praise of Hermione's glamour and kindness. It also becomes clear that her talent as an artist, despite her pride in what she had achieved, was, in the main, unappreciated in her lifetime. Holden challenges simplistic readings of her work, asking: 'What is outsider art? It consists of subcategories of yet more definitions, so all-inclusive that it is close to becoming meaningless.... It is often associated with some form of illness or a subsequent recuperation process. This is certainly true for Hermione.'

Also included in the exhibition were small works by Holden, including posters and a 3D printed sculpture of Hermione's avatar surrounded by visitation stones – the Jewish tradition of remembrance, a quiet homage by the artist to both Hermione and Mira Calix. Art, here, is presented as a paradoxical form of communication, a way of expressing the inexpressible. As Holden remarks: 'Illness can provide a crisis in the self, because there becomes an uncertainty that one's own self is still there.... Hermione's paintings tell stories as a form of resistance.'

1 Tessa Norton, text for 'The Estate of Hermione', Ex-Baldessarre, Bedford, 2018, https://andyholdenartist.com/the-estate-of-hermione. Accessed 2 Mar 2026.

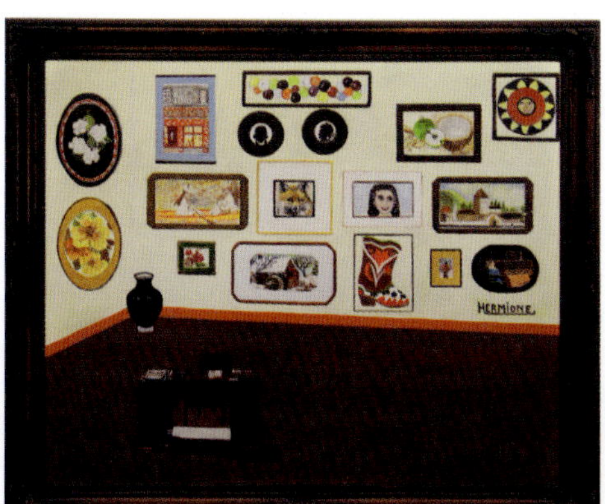

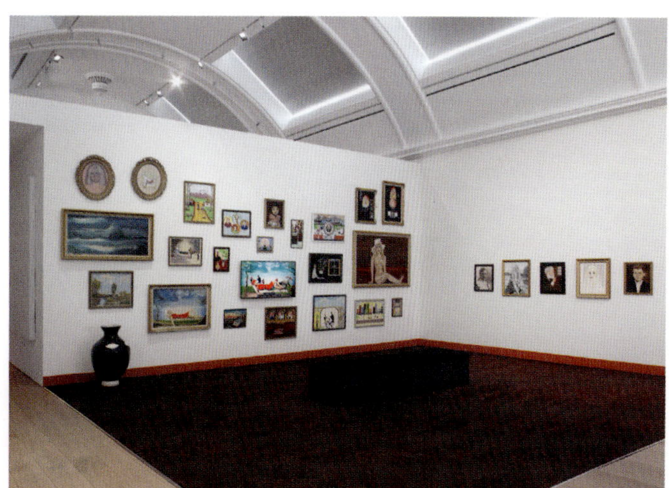

Cat-tharsis

2016–22

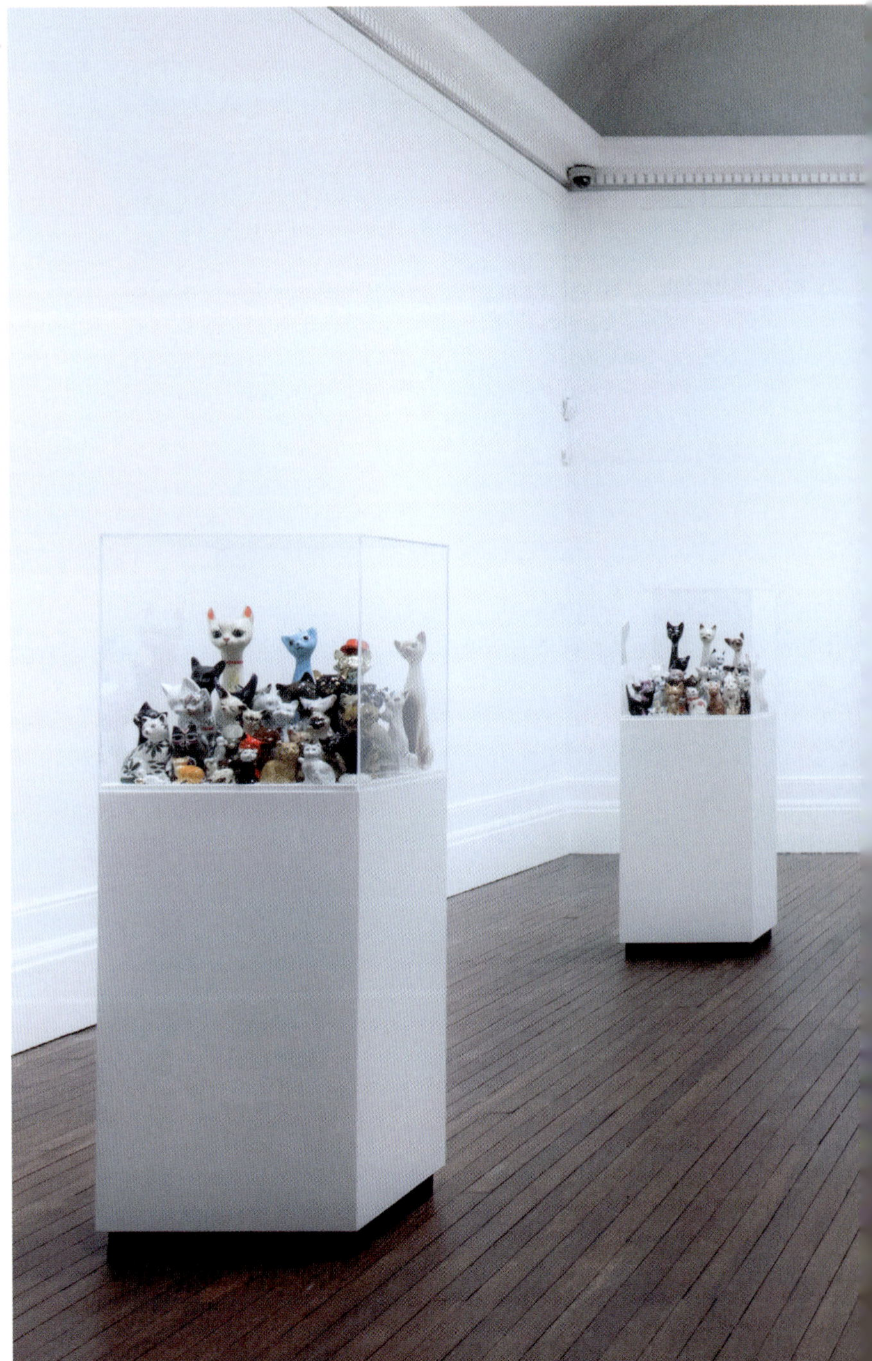

→ *Cat-tharsis*, 2022, 280 ceramic cat figurines and HD video with music by The Grubby Mitts, 17 mins., installation view, Grundy Art Gallery, Blackpool, UK
↠ (Overleaf) *Cat-tharsis* (detail), 2022

When Andy Holden's grandmother died, she left him her collection of over 200 ceramic cats. They are giddy in their range: thin, fat, psychedelic, cute, realistic, tiny, tall, sad, smiling. Some have hats or wear neckerchiefs; their eyes are closed or open, with long lashes or none; their eyes twinkle or stare into nothingness.

Holden's response to his inheritance was typically questioning, multifaceted, sincere and light-hearted. Collectively titled *Cat-tharsis,* it became a live improvised comedy performance, an exhibition of the figurines and a 17-minute video with music composed by The Grubby Mitts. The collection became a springboard for him to not only pay homage to his grandmother, but to think about the cultural impulses that shape collecting, the role of cats in social history and the nature of obsession. In the video, Holden narrates

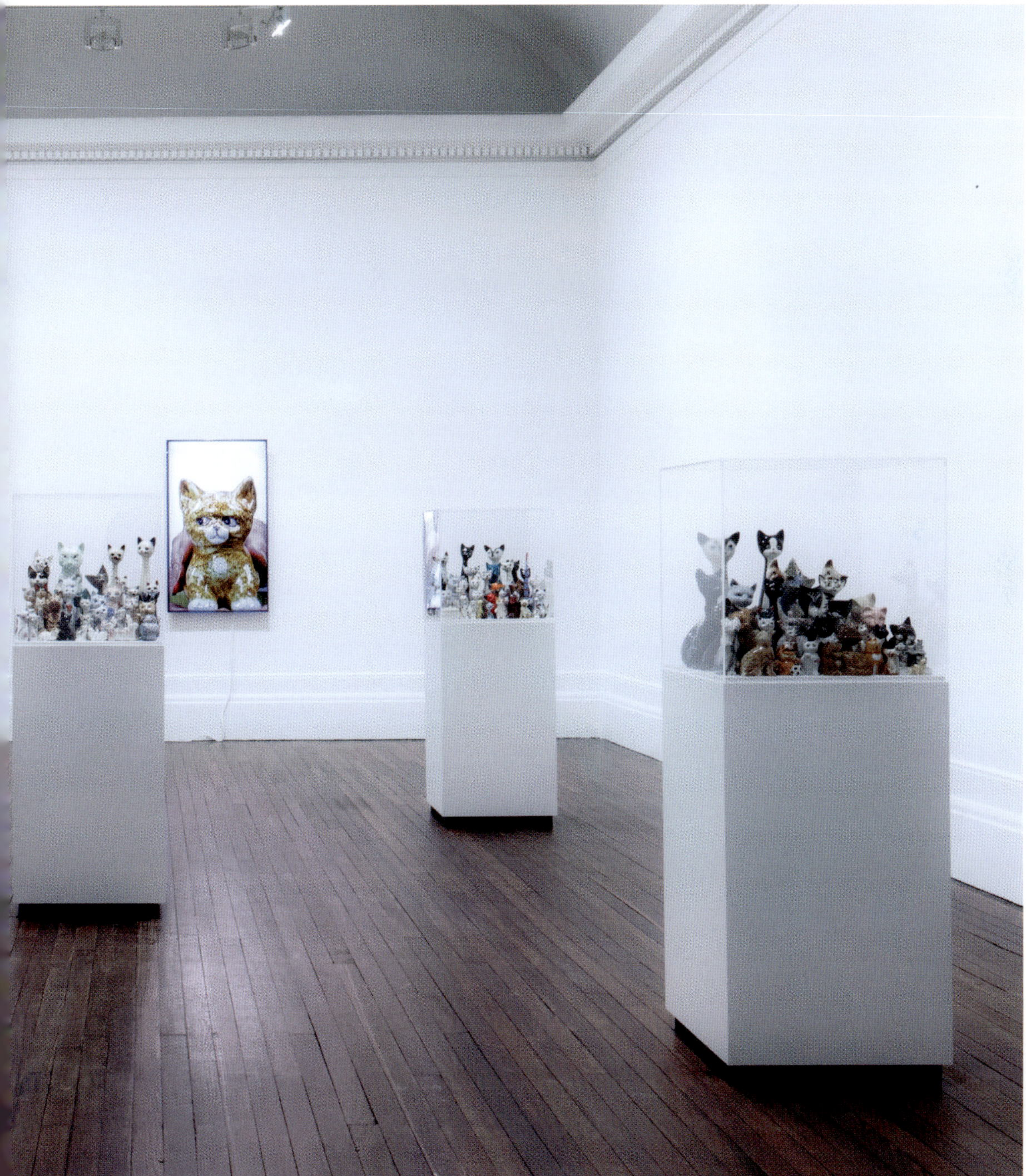

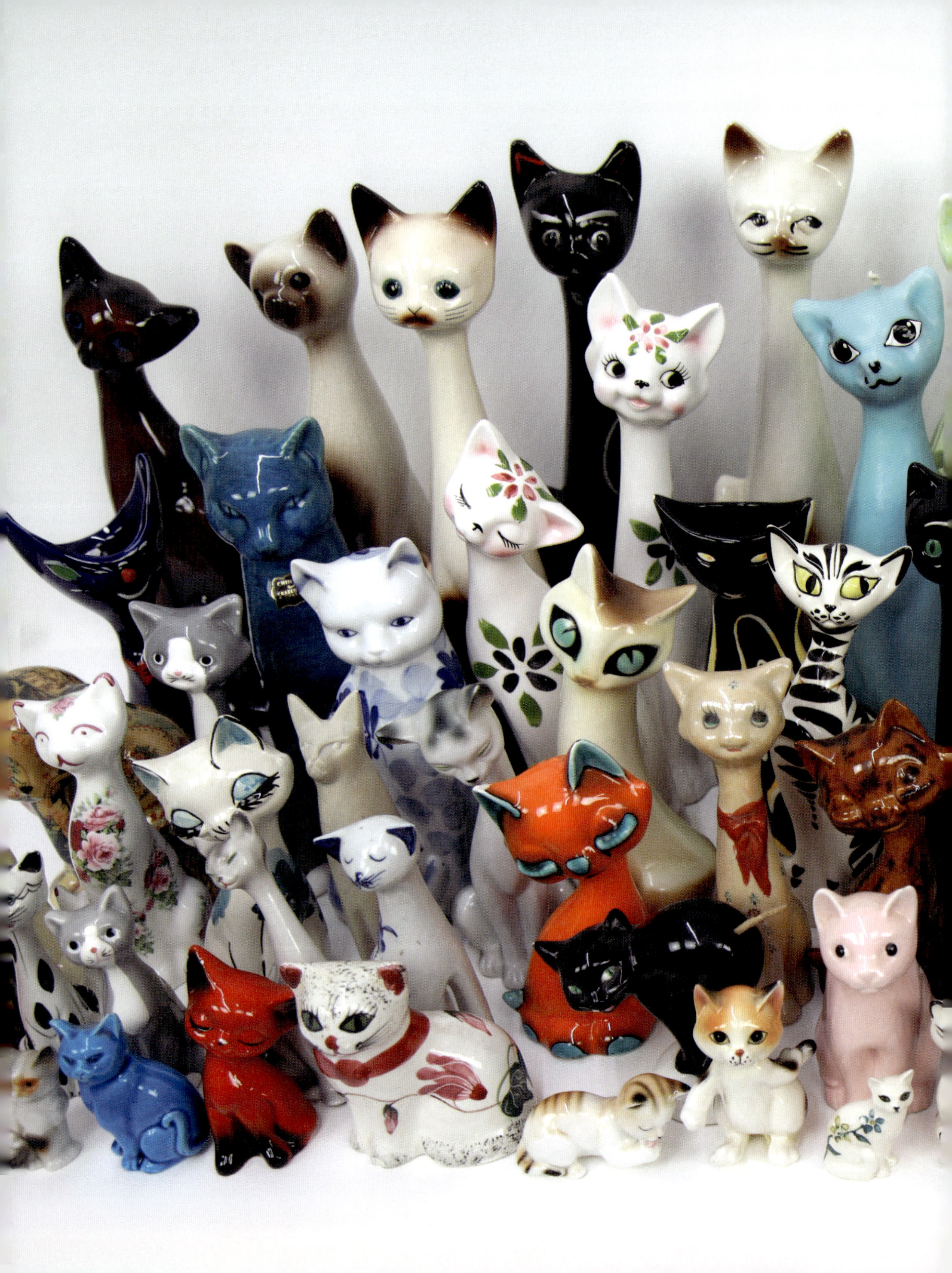

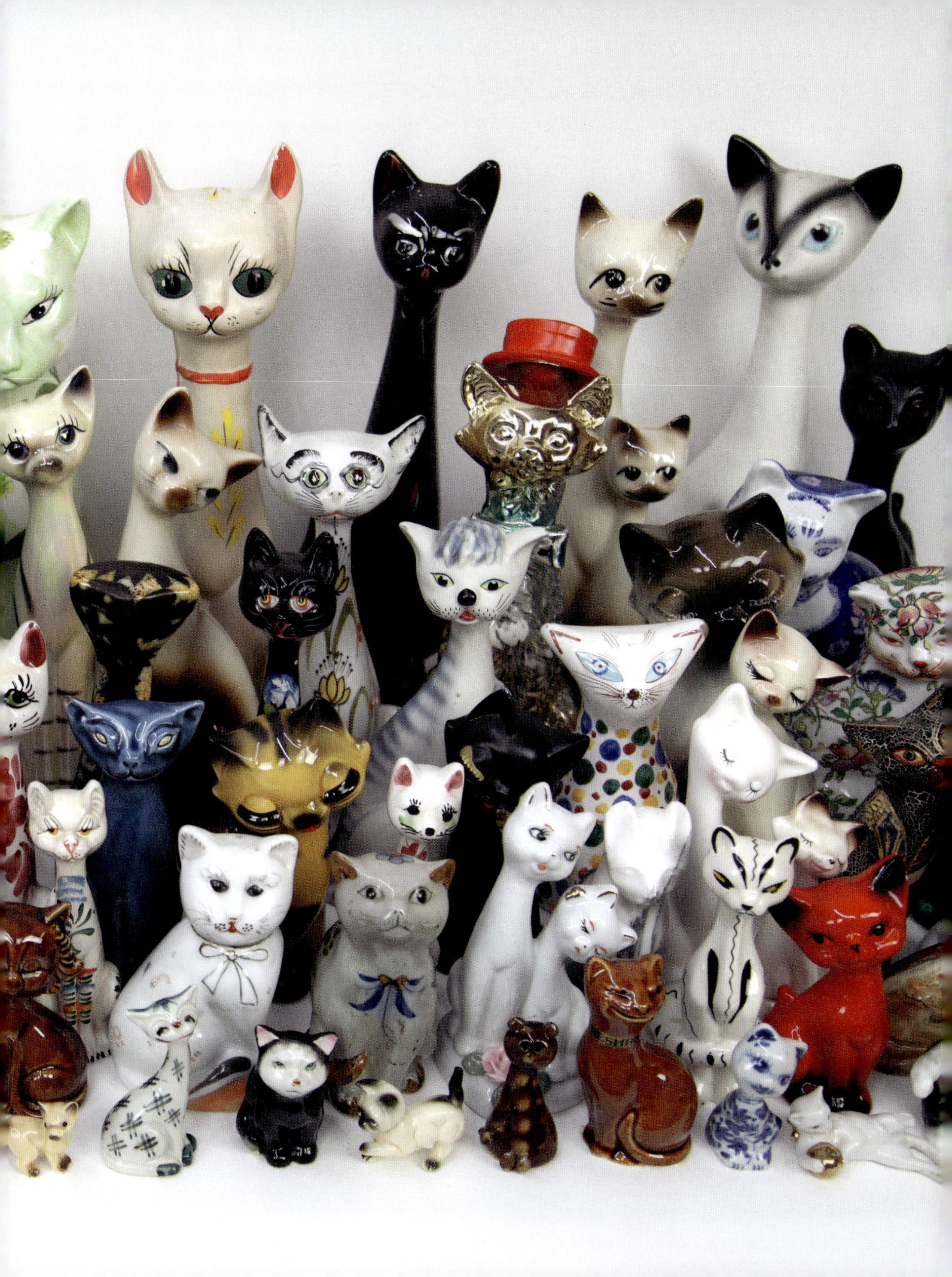

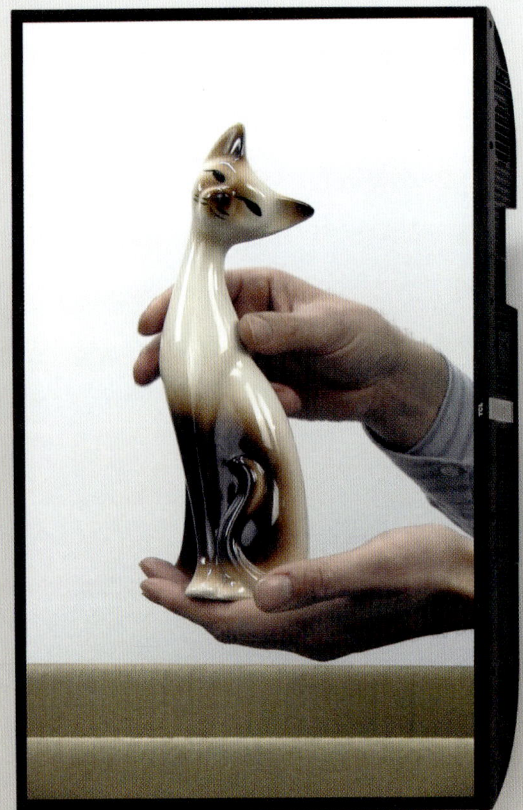

→ *Cat-tharsis,* 2022, 280 ceramic cat figurines and HD video with music by The Grubby Mitts, 17 mins., installation view, Charles Moffett, New York
↓ *Cat-tharsis,* 2022, video stills

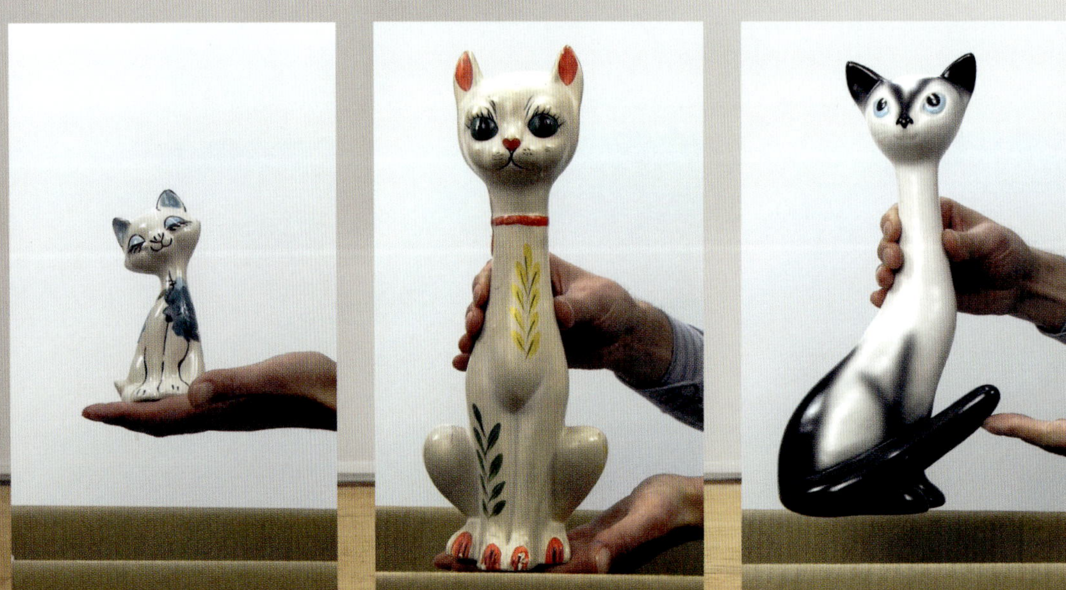

his thoughts as his hands are shown opening the eight cardboard boxes and unwrapping each of the cats, which were carefully packed in sheets of the *Daily Mail* – his grandmother's favourite newspaper.

As he reveals the cats, the artist narrates a stream of consciousness, wondering first why, despite her obsession, his grandmother never owned a cat, before realising that he hasn't either, because he's allergic to them. He goes on to remember that the first time he had an erection was when Catwoman appeared in *Batman Returns* (1991) and then relates curious facts, such as Isaac Newton being credited with having invented the cat flap. He discusses his fondness for kitsch and notes that these figurines are often souvenirs of foreign travel, yet his grandmother never left the UK. He gives a potted history of charity shops and the role of cats in ancient Egypt and China. He briefly outlines the psychoanalytic theory of collecting and describes it as an 'old echo from the behaviour of our ancestors, implanted deep in the human psyche, while the need to collect nuts and berries for survival still lingered', that it satisfies the need for 'psychological security' and is a response to our distress, our inability to control our bodily expulsions, and the trauma caused by the loss of shit and flow from us. In Freud's hypothesis, therefore, the collector is 'trying to gain back control of their bowels, as well as their possessions, which were long flushed down the toilet'.

Holden then ponders the connection between collecting and control, especially given that his

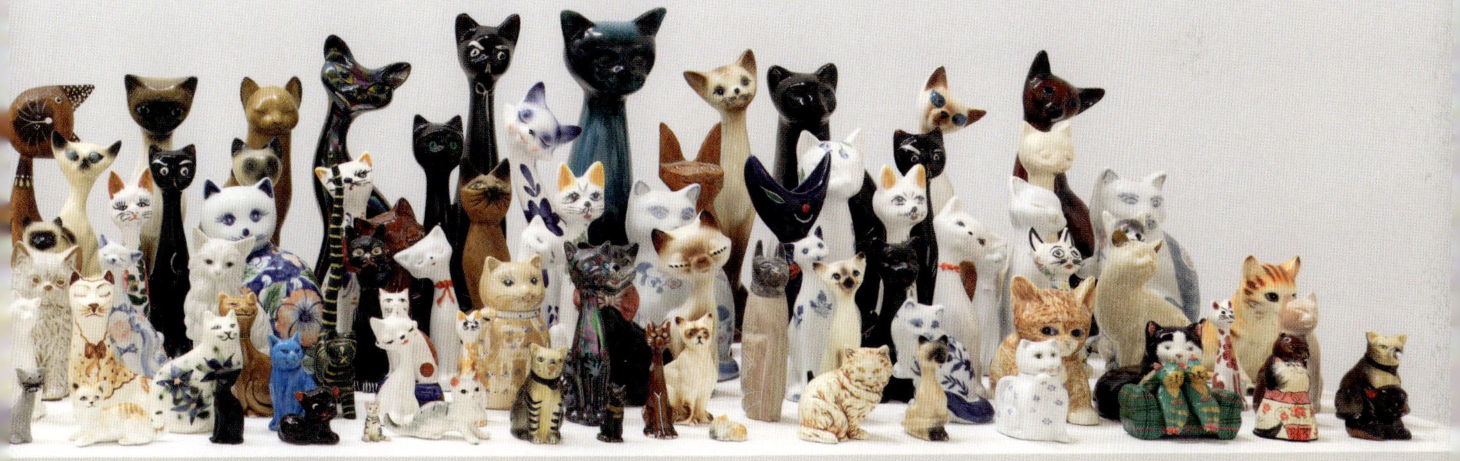

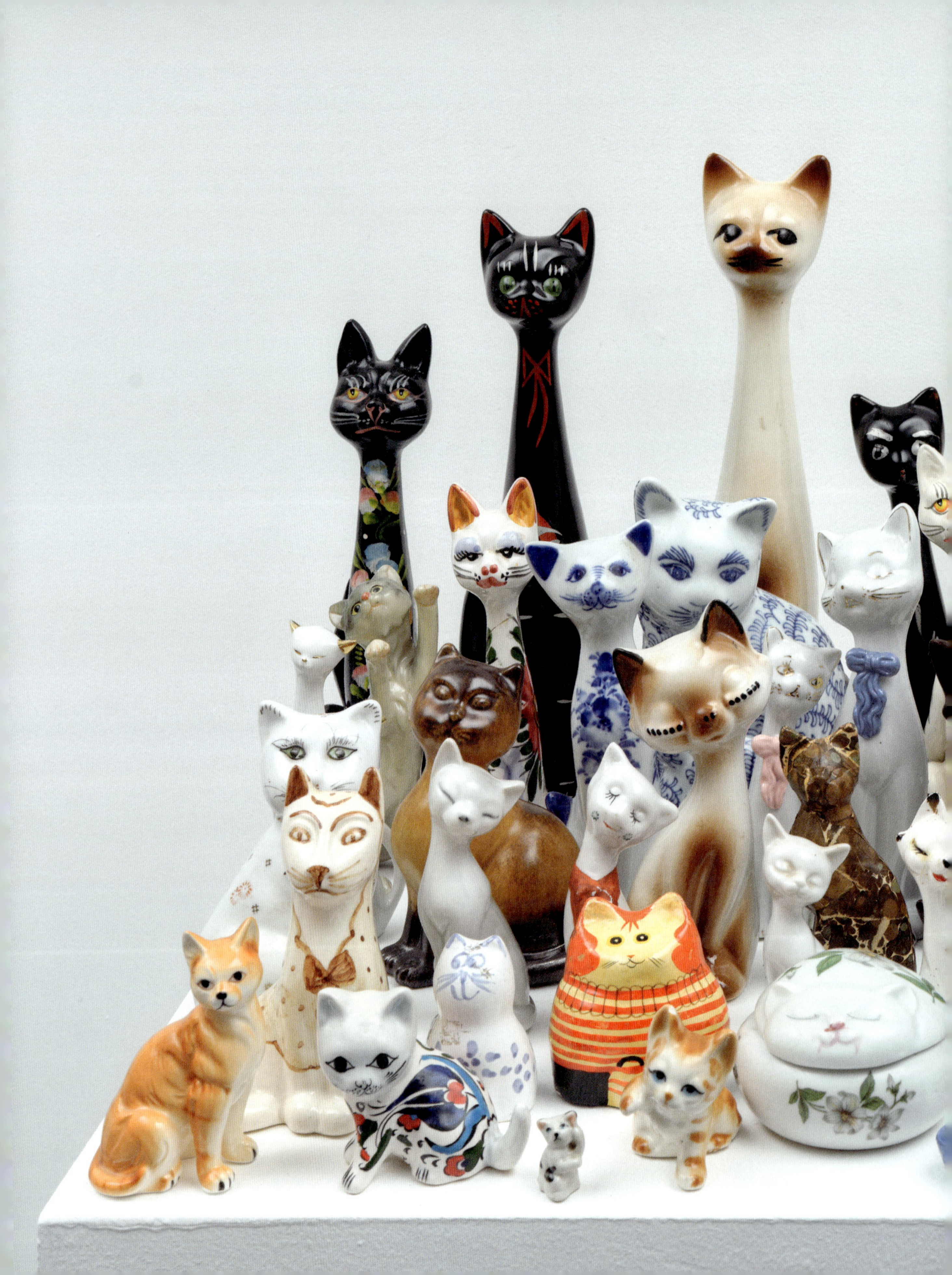

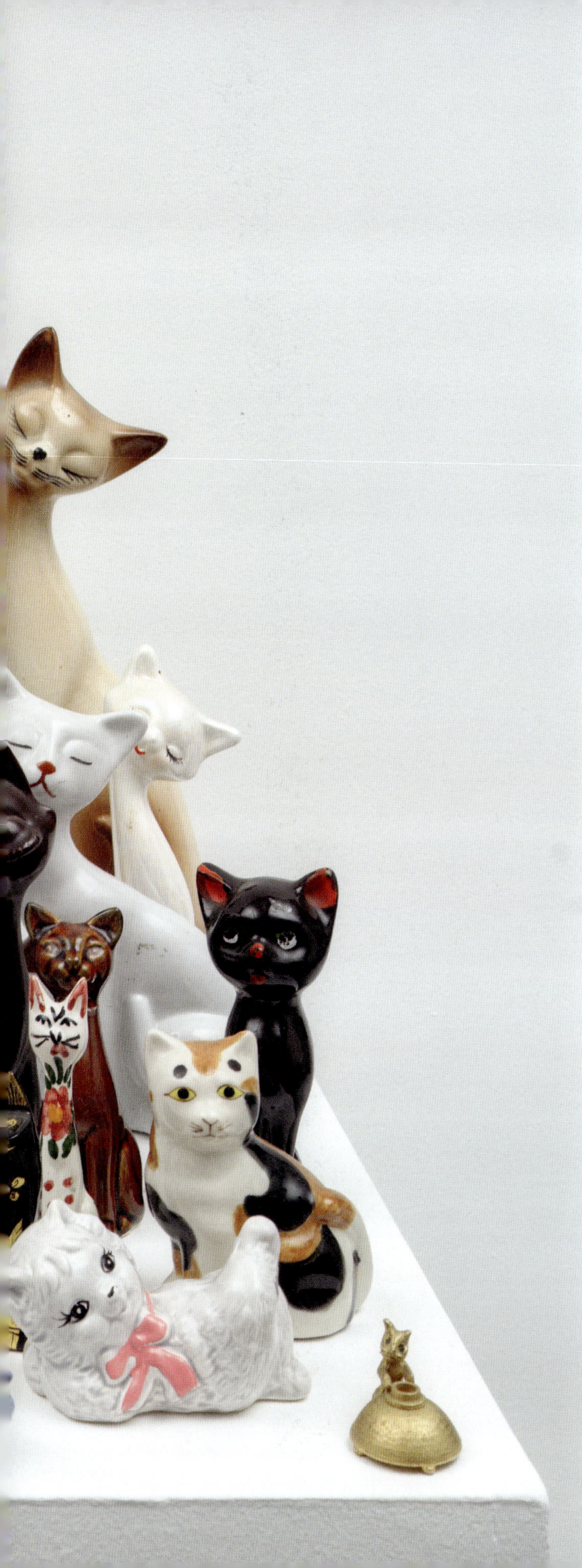

grandmother began collecting the cats around the time her husband was diagnosed with Early-onset Alzheimer's. He says, in a passage of the film that could equally apply to the desire to collect birds' eggs: 'To complete a collection is basically to signify death. A collection of course will always outlive you. When experienced as a whole, the collection does something to time. The organisation of the collection replaces time. Time is no longer something to be returned to its origin.'

The artist then wonders about the proliferation of cat images on the internet and asks if it's 'something to do with the unselfconsciousness of the cat'. The facts are blunt: there are an estimated 6.5 billion cat pictures online and two million cat videos on YouTube, each watched an average of 12,000 times. He's aware, though, that this is a Western-centric reading. He muses that:

> If you are online in Uganda, you'd be much more likely to share an image of a goat. Chinese internet users predominantly share images of the river crab, in Mexico it is pictures of lamas. It's possible if my grandma was Mexican, these would have been ceramic lamas.

The video finishes with someone, off camera, asking: 'Andy? How did it feel?' The artist replies with a joke: 'It felt cat-thartic.' As with so many of his projects, *Cat-tharsis* operates on various registers: an act of love that, in its intimacy and idiosyncrasy, also reveals something more generally about the power of objects and the solace of collecting – whatever shape or form they, or it, might take.

← *Cat-tharsis (Travelling Edition)*, 2022, 53 ceramic cat figurines and HD video, 17 mins.

Collected Domestic Conceptualism

2021

In 2021, Andy Holden staged an exhibition called 'Collected Domestic Conceptualism' at Pitt Studio, Worcester, UK. Three floors of a townhouse were crowded with studies, models, books, photographs, nests, sculptures, paintings and drawings. The exhibition architecture became a work in itself: plinths and walls were created from cardboard and packing boxes, all of which suggested that someone was either moving in or moving out – a nod to the idea, perhaps, that both art history and the stories we tell ourselves are works in progress. Visitors were given three options – a virtual tour, to visit in person or to have an online guided tour – and the five rooms and corridors were 3D scanned and available to view online. Given the viewing restrictions of the Covid-19 pandemic, the exhibition was conceived so that the digital render was the primary means of viewing it.

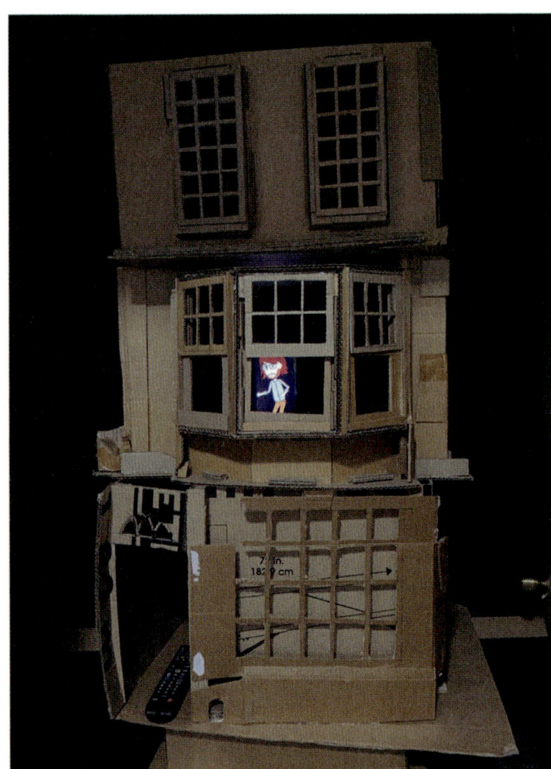

→ (Both images and overleaf) *Collected Domestic Conceptualism* (details), 2021, various works, cardboard and video with sound, 10 mins., variable dimensions, installation view, Pitt Studio, Worcester, UK

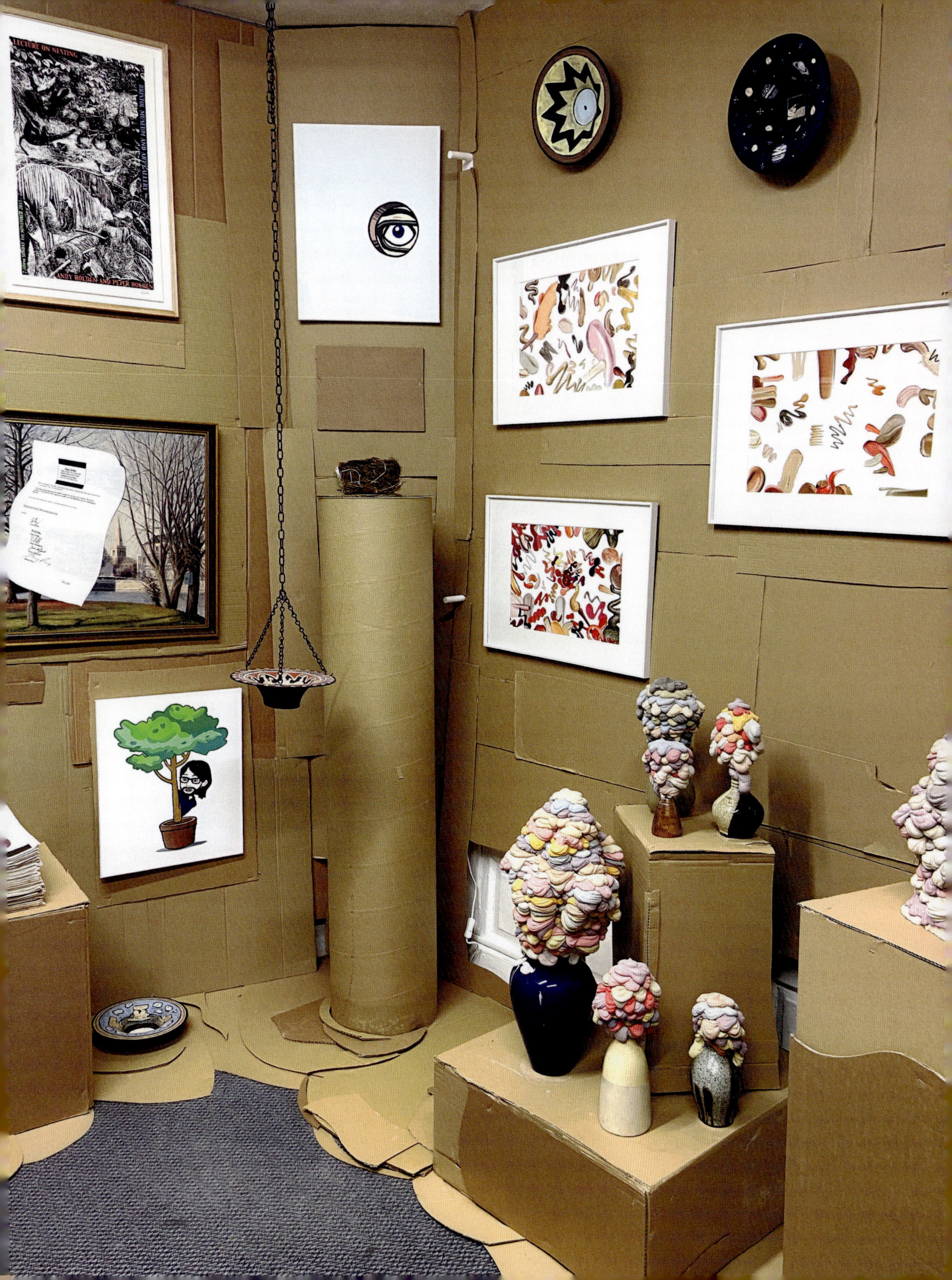
LECTURE ON NESTING
ANDY HOLDEN AND PETER HOLDEN

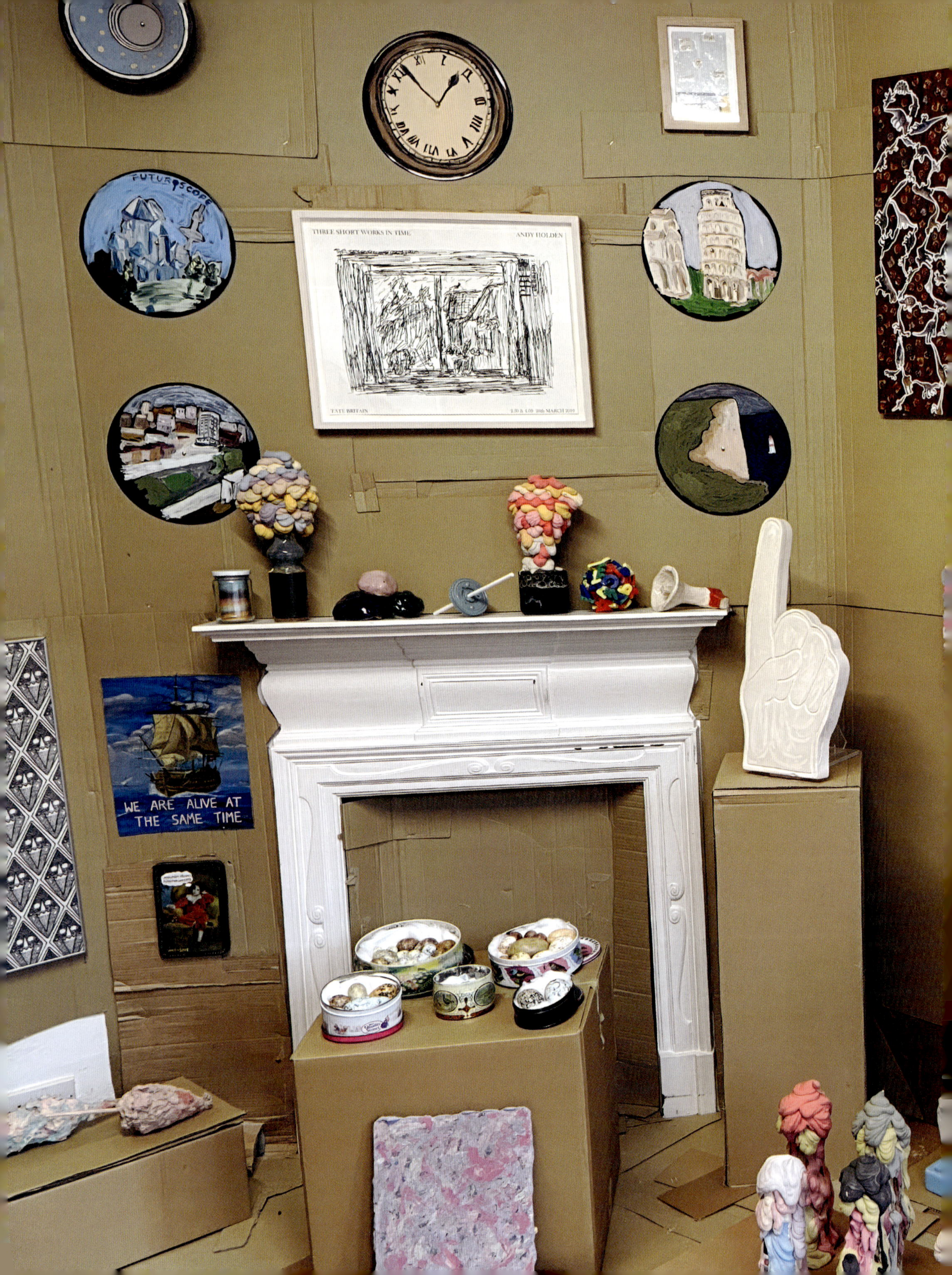
FUTUROSCOPE
THREE SHORT WORKS IN TIME
ANDY HOLDEN
TATE BRITAIN
WE ARE ALIVE AT
THE SAME TIME

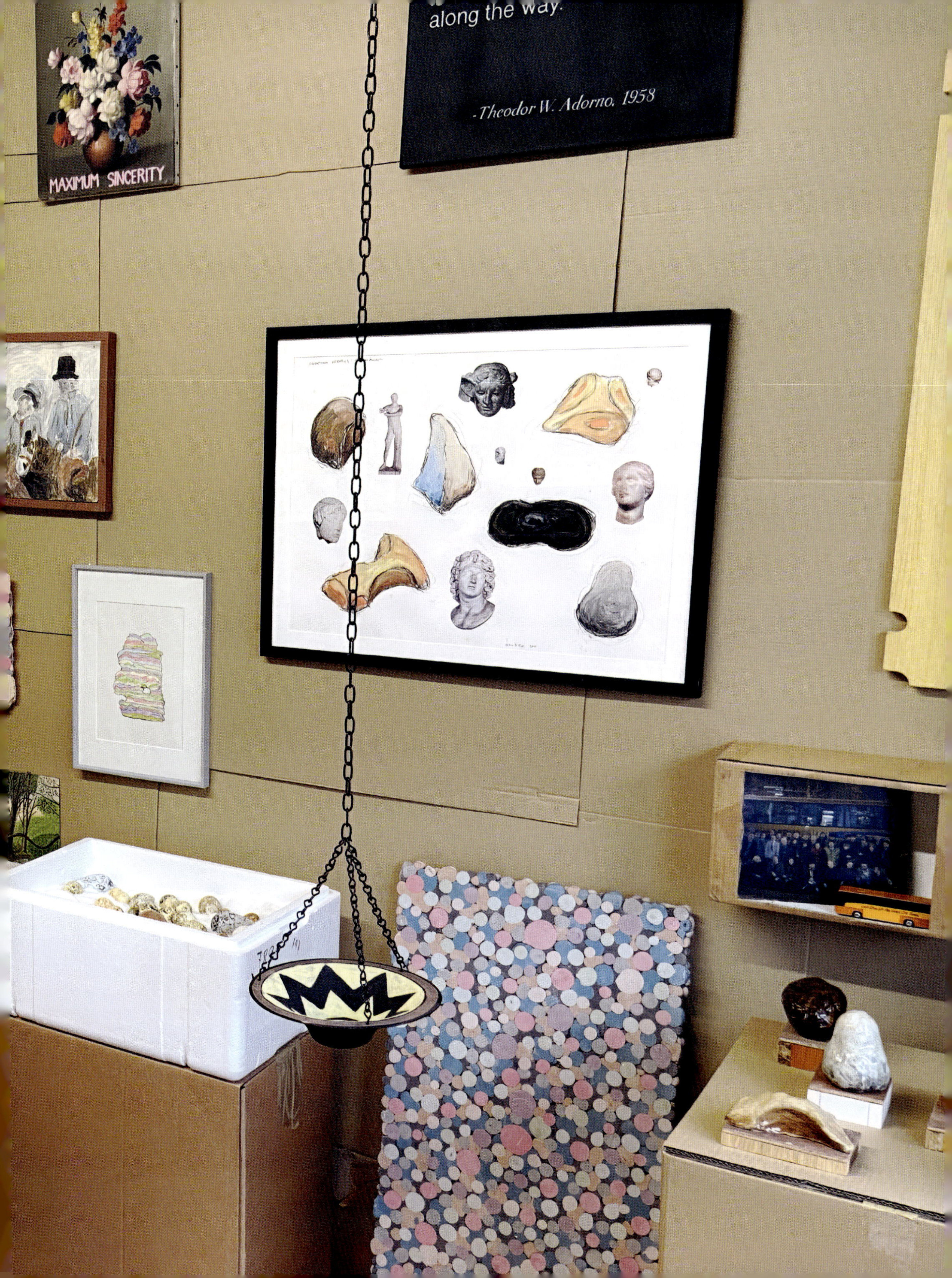
along the way.
-Theodor W. Adorno, 1958
MAXIMUM SINCERITY

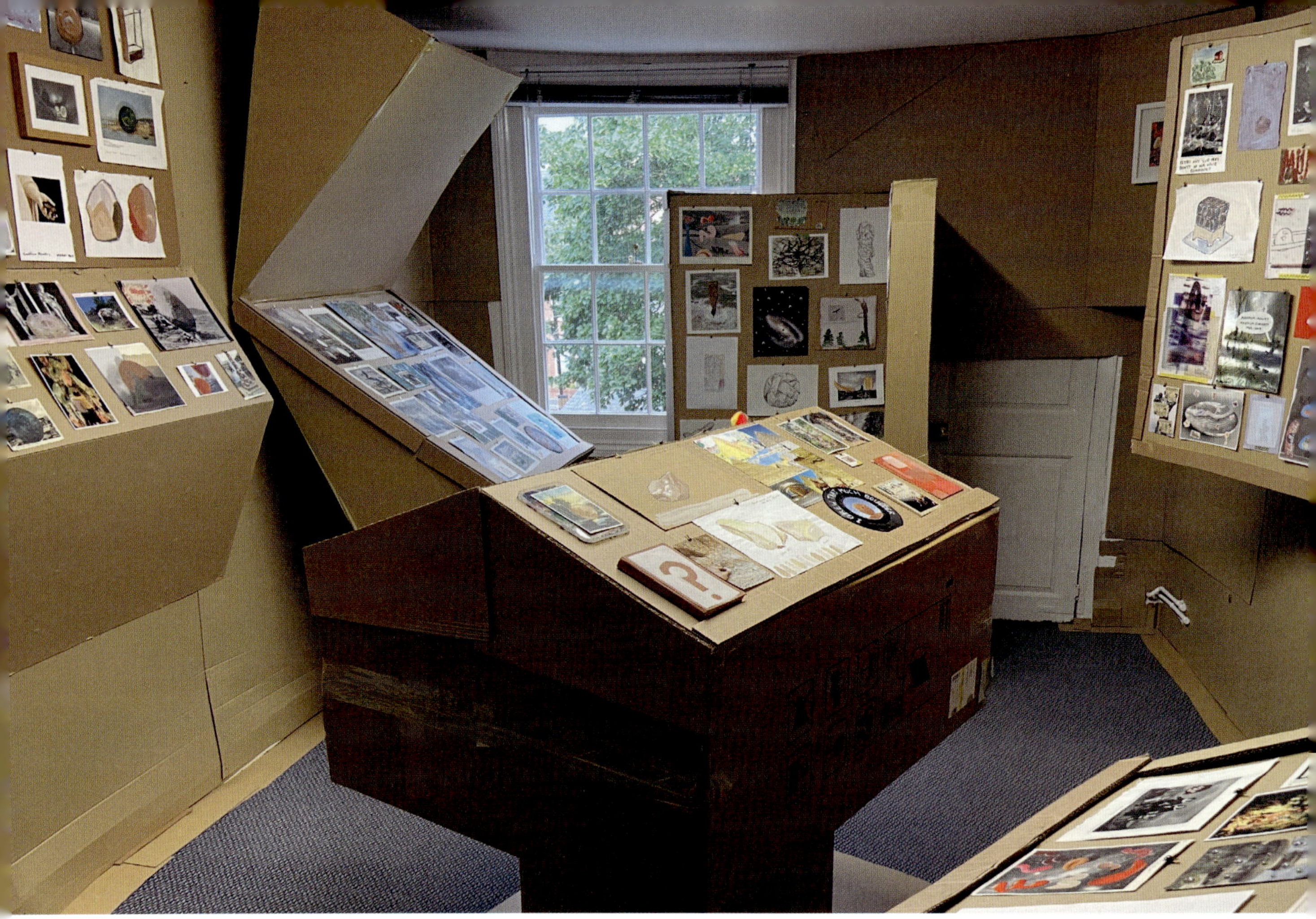

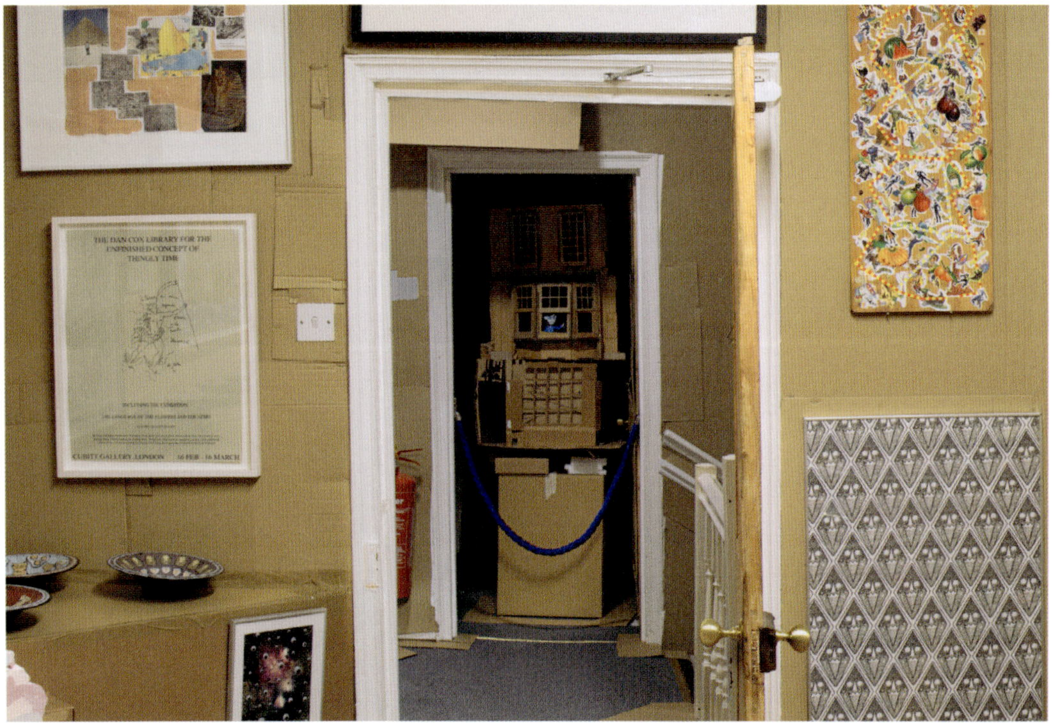
THE DAN COX LIBRARY FOR THE
UNFINISHED CONCEPT OF
THINGLY TIME
CUBITT GALLERY, LONDON
16 FEB - 16 MARCH

Including, as it does, examples of work from across Holden's varied career, 'Collected Domestic Conceptualism' could be viewed as a retrospective – one that, given its transient appearance, makes clear the fragmented processes and malleability of thinking and making that are central to being an artist. It also acknowledges how much art is now looked at online; how images are transformed when they're reduced, flattened and varnished by digital light.

Holden's use of the term 'domestic conceptualism' highlights both the intimate scale of the work and his choice of materials – from make-up, painted bowls, googly eyes, cartoons, ceramic cats, eggs, wallpaper and souvenirs to reworked charity-shop paintings, knitted objects, stickers, postcards and more. It also nods to the interconnectedness of his thinking: what the artist describes as 'a dialectical motion between house and universe'.[1]

← (both images) *Collected Domestic Conceptualism* (details), 2021, various works, cardboard and video with sound, 10 mins., variable dimensions, installation view, Pitt Studio, Worcester, UK
↓ *Among Your Other Concerns*, 2016, acrylic on found canvas, 40 × 60 cm (15 ¾ × 23 ⅝ in.)

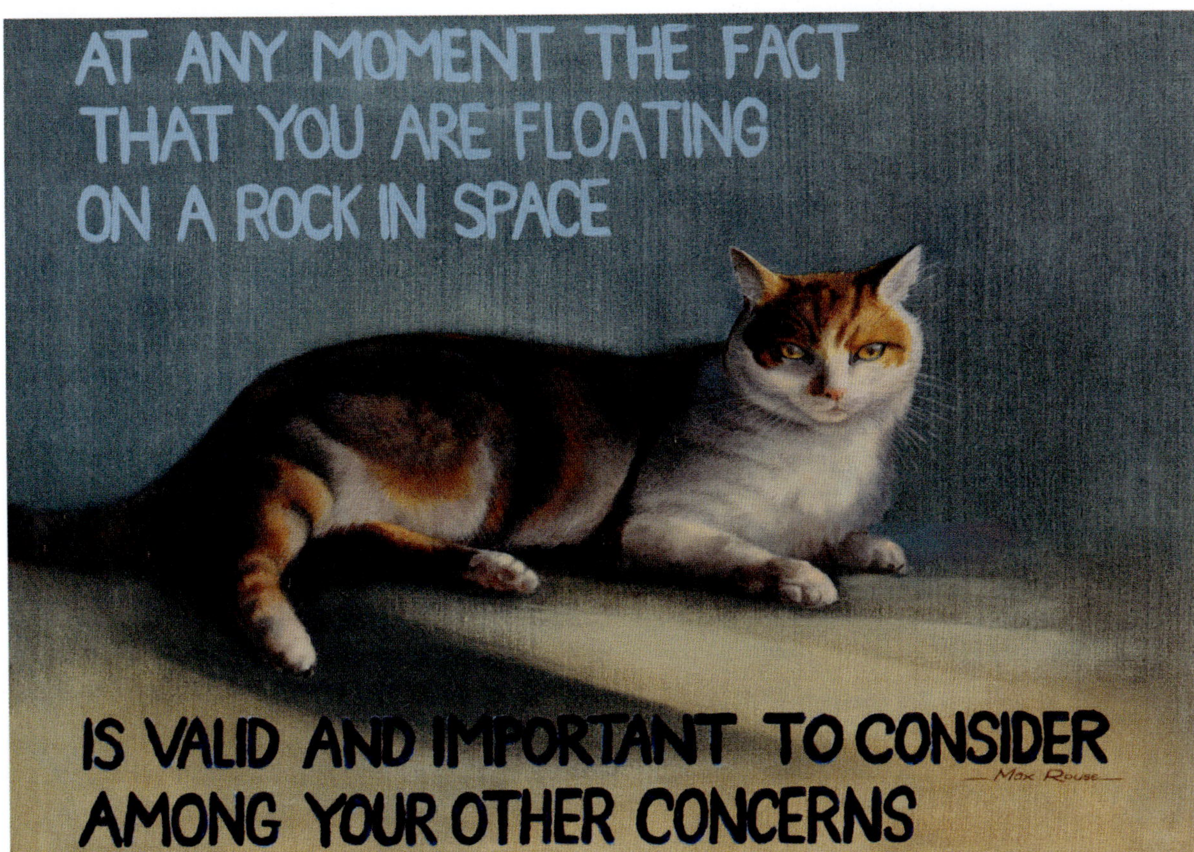

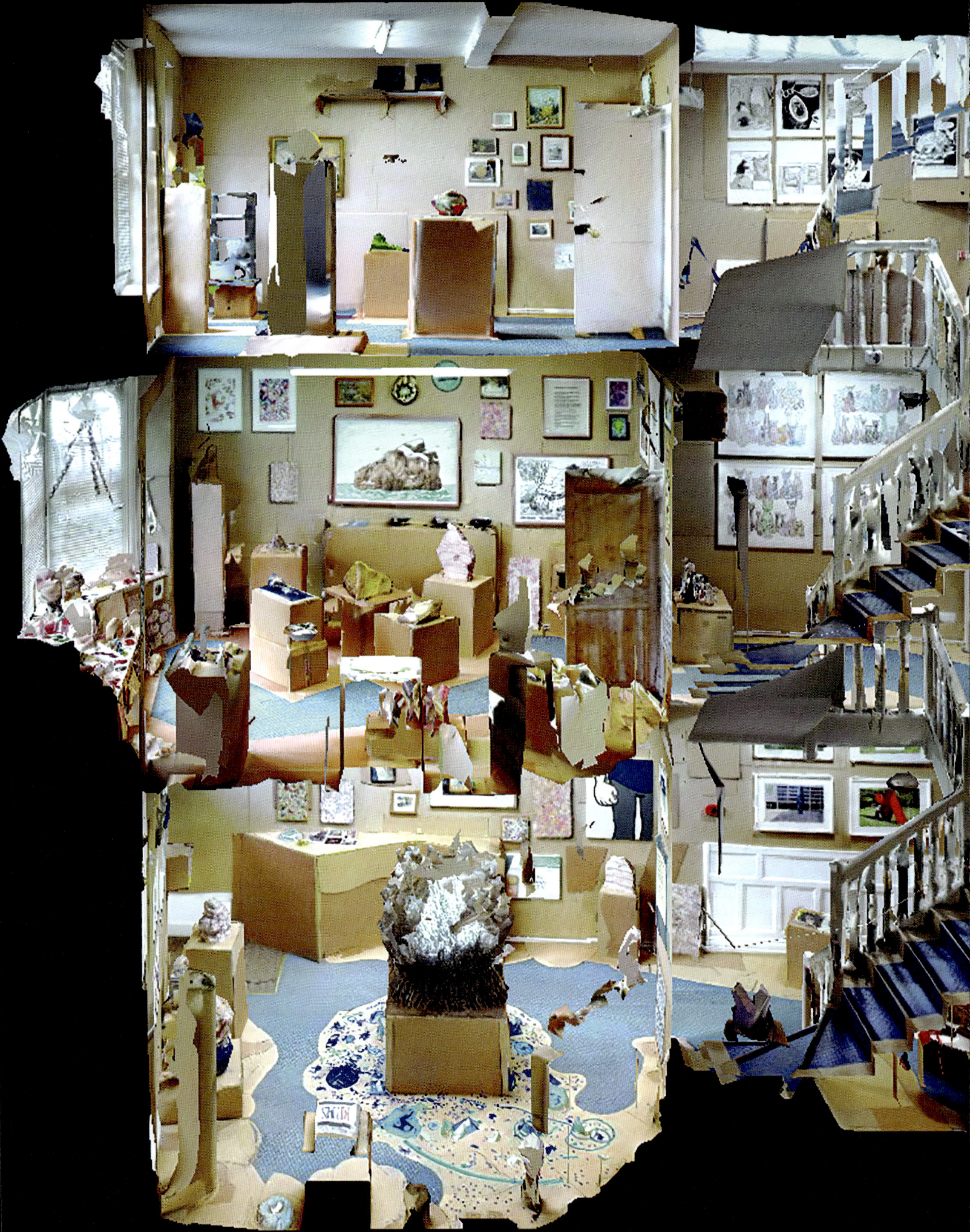

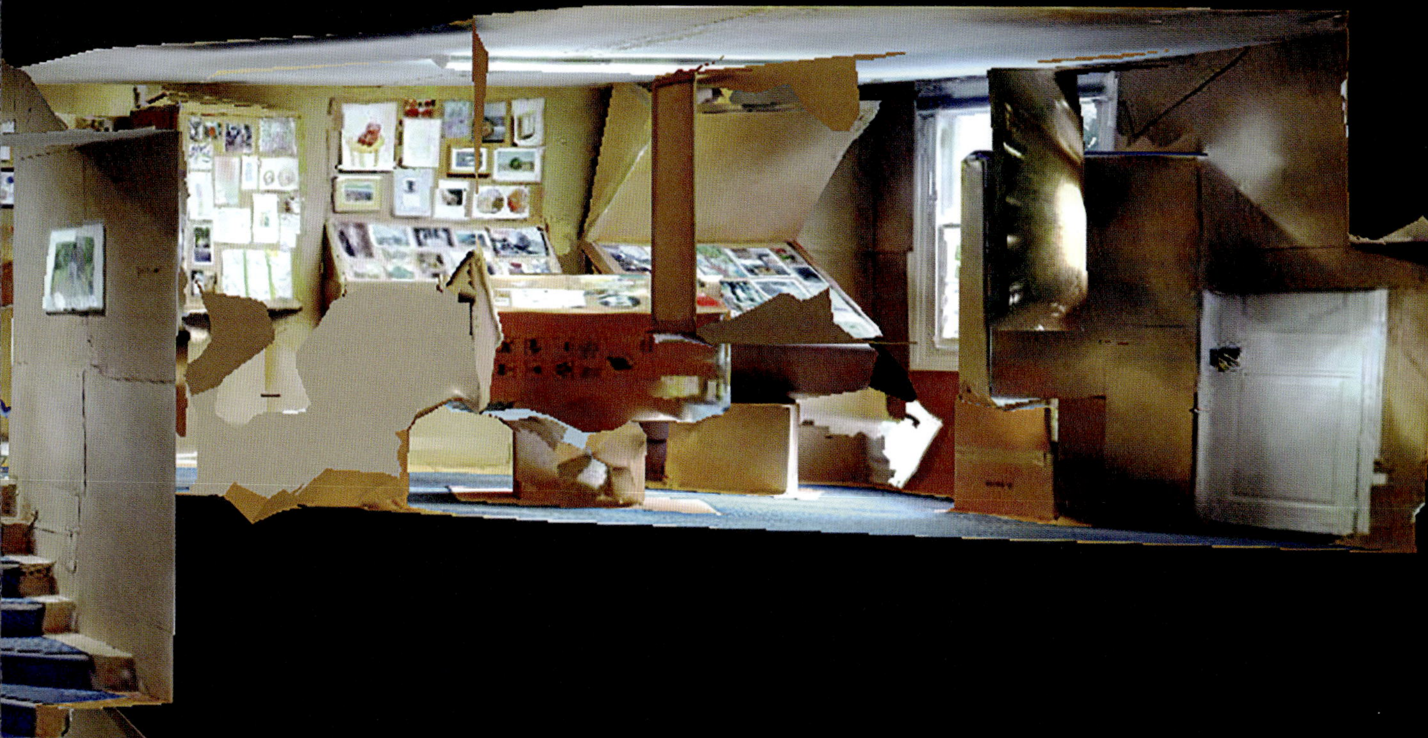

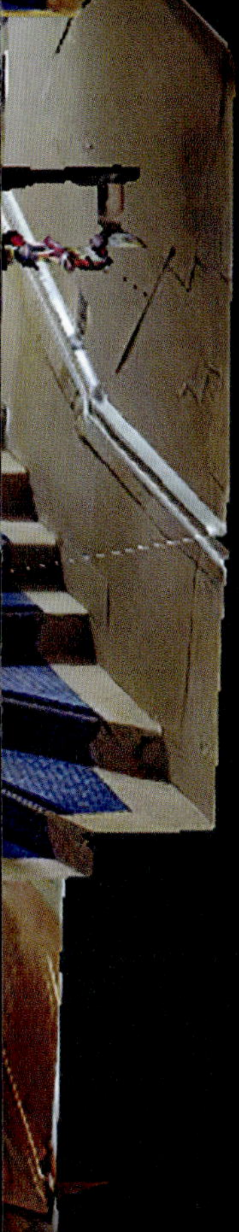

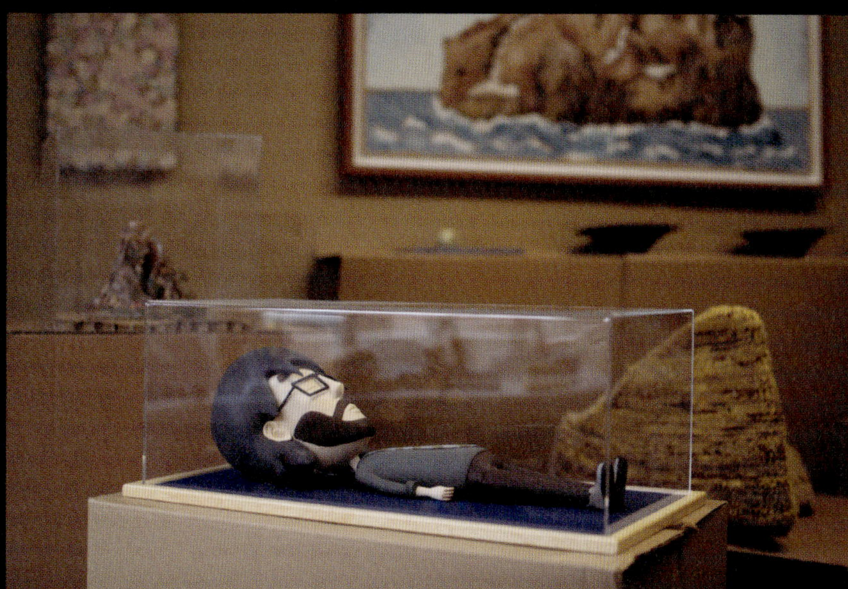

← *Collected Domestic Conceptualism*, 2021, digital scan
↑ *Collected Domestic Conceptualism* (detail), 2021, various works,

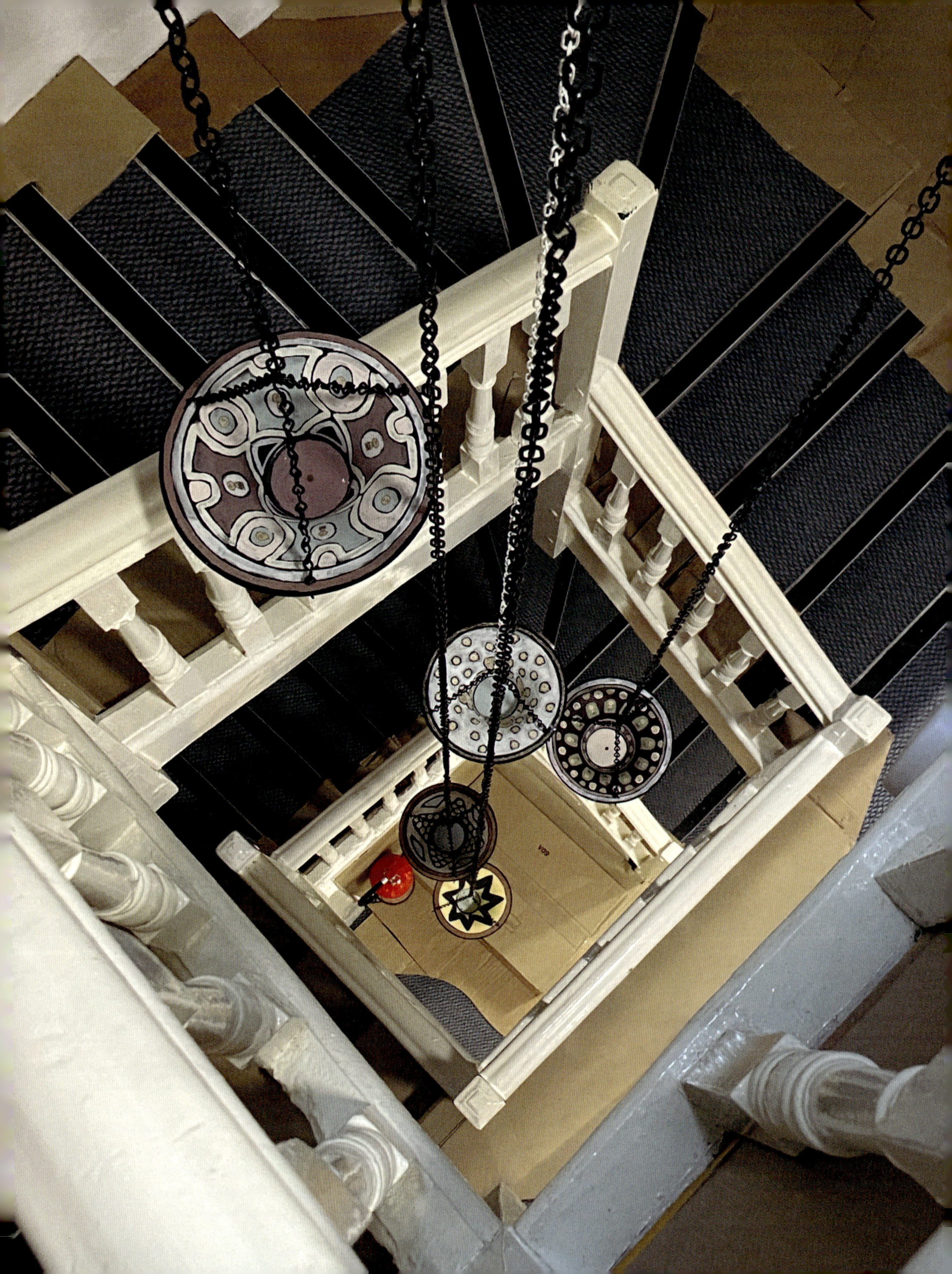

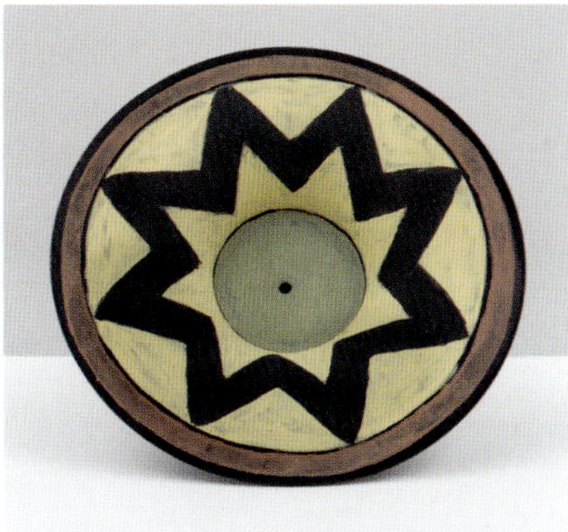

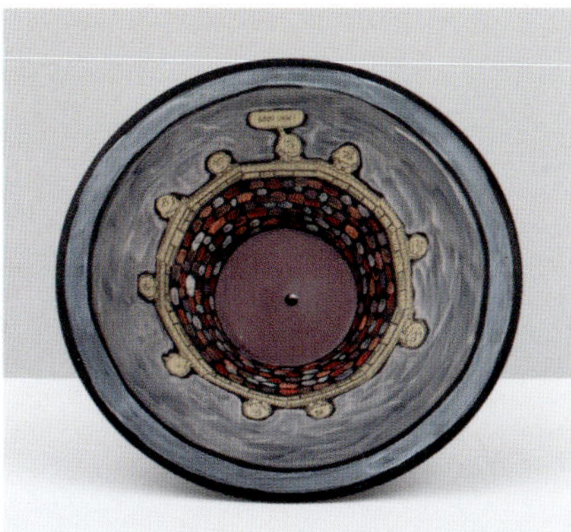

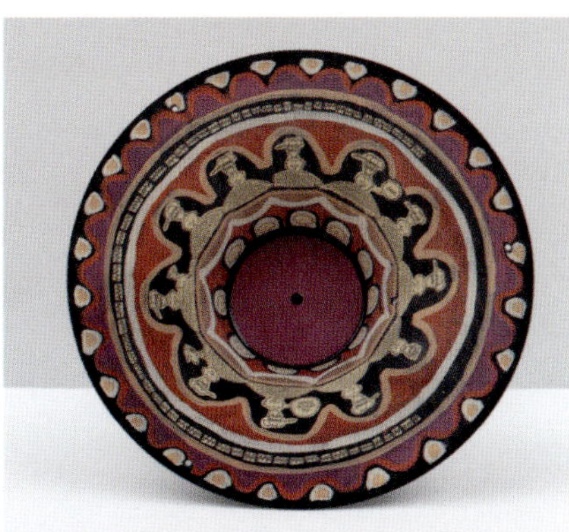

In order to group together small pieces related to larger projects, and numerous objects which had never been displayed before, the five rooms were divided into the following categories:

+ Room 1 (Living Room): Accretions, Aphorisms, Bower, Chewy Cosmos, Evolution, Manifestos, Mediated Emotions, Nests, Ornamites, Sentimental Pictures.
+ Room 2 (Study): Allusions, Archaeology, Cats, Coach trips, Decorative Bowls, Eyes, Fragments, Hermeneutics, Make-up, Ornithology, Pyramids, Reclining Figures, Souvenirs, Postcards.
+ Room 3 (Guest Room): Artist as Critic as Cartoon.
+ Room 4 (Window Room): Folly, Landscapes, Models, Over-paintings, Proposals for Public Sculptures, Relics, Unfeeling.
+ Room 5 (Library): Works on paper (from the Particular to the Universal).

The list can be read as a poetic, potted biography of the artist. It traverses the themes, objects, materials, proposals and journeys that have shaped Andy Holden's output so far, which stretch, as room five suggests, from the particular to the universal. In each of these works – which could well be called 'propositions' – lurks the seed of the next one.

No doubt it's already beginning to bloom.

1 https://andyholdenartist.com/collected-domestic-conceptualism-1. Accessed 2 Mar 2026.

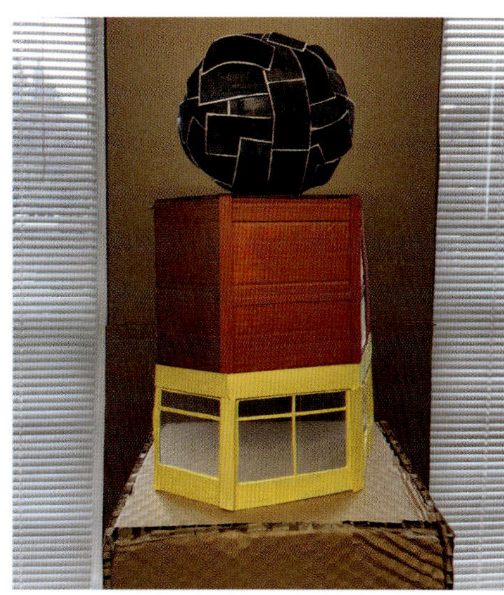

← *Collected Domestic Conceptualism* (detail), 2021, various works, cardboard and video with sound, 10 mins., variable dimensions, installation view, Pitt Studio, Worcester, UK
↑ *Pessimism of the Intellect, Optimism of the Will*, 2011, melted gramophone records with emulsion paint and collage, each: 22 × 22 × 8 cm (8 ⅝ × 8 ⅝ × 3 ⅛ in.)
→ *Study for Black Boulder Monochrome Folly*, 2020, cardboard and paint, 45 × 20 × 20 cm (17 ¾ × 7 ⅞ × 7 ⅞ in.), installation view, Pitt Studio, Worcester, UK

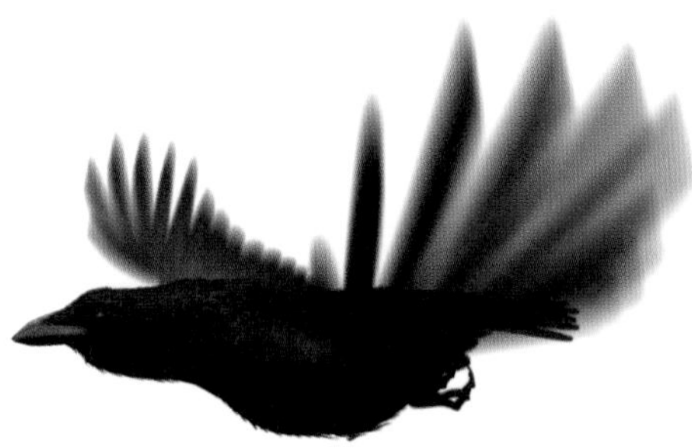

ARTIST
CHRONOLOGY

1982 Born 1982, Bedford, UK

1999 Sets up studio, 'The Utility Room' in parents' house. Begins making work that would later be considered *M!MS: Maximum Irony! Maximum Sincerity*

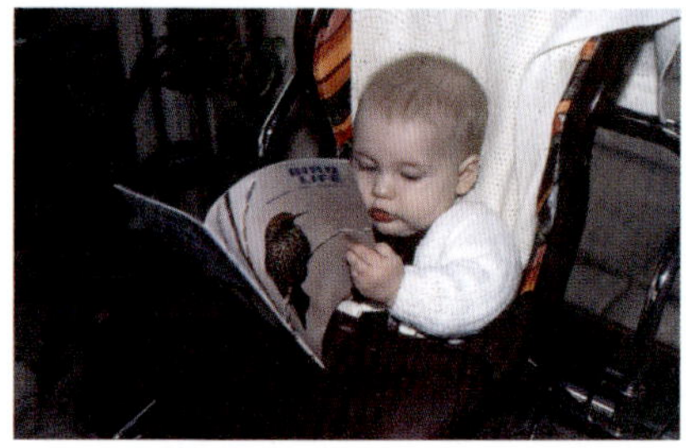

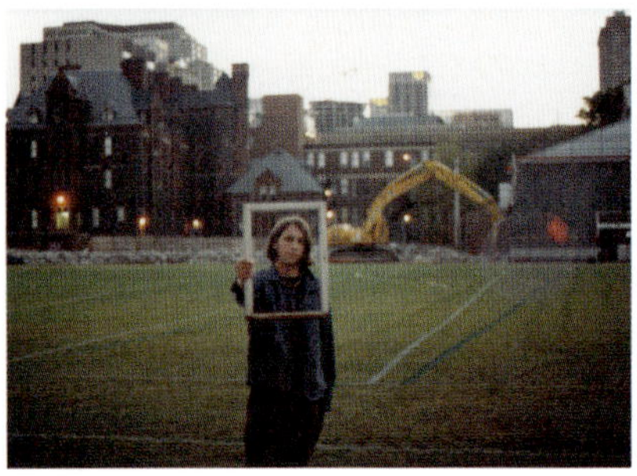

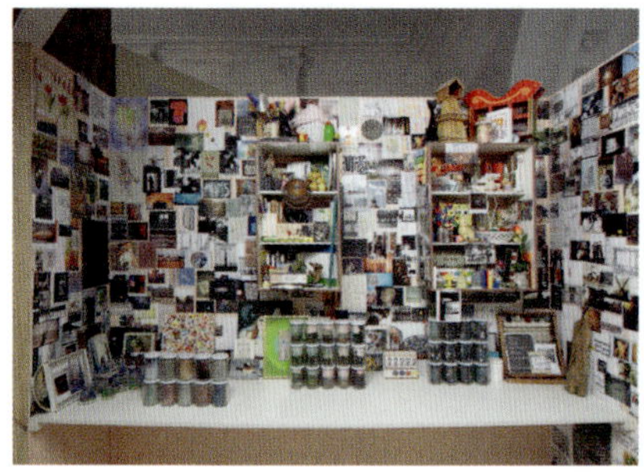

↖ Andy Holden by Peter Holden, 1982

↞ Andy Holden, Varsity Stadium, Toronto, 2000, photo by Dan Brown

← *Unstuck Studio*, Holden's teenage 'The Utility Room' studio recreated in *Towards a Unified Theory of M!MS* in 2013

2001 *Superheroes Don't Graze Their Knees*, Bird in Hand, Cambridge, UK

Last Stop for the Good Old Times, Bird in Hand, Cambridge, UK

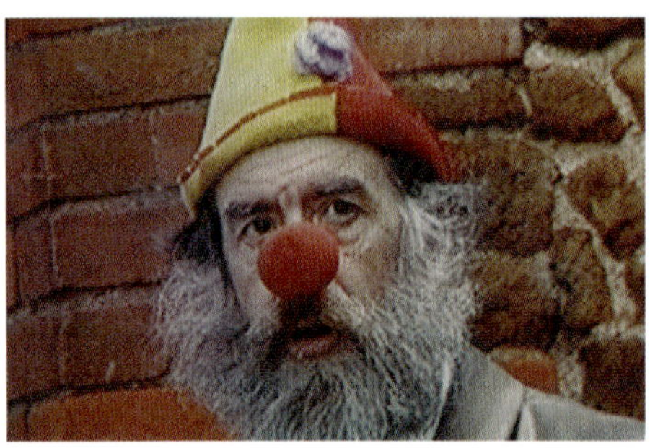

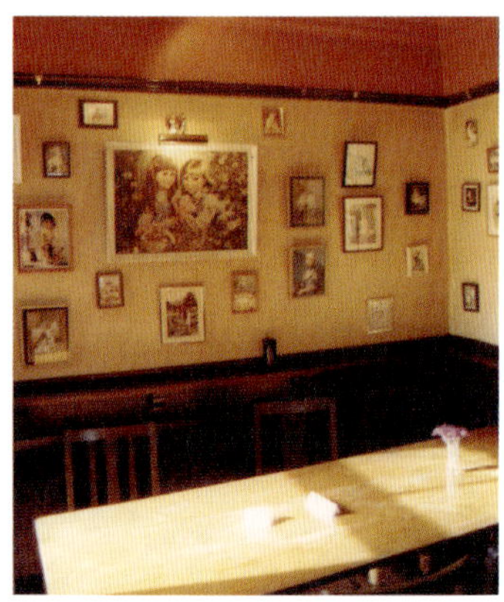

↞ *Mr Tozer the Clown*, video, 2001

← *Last Stop for the Good Old Times*, Bird in Hand, Cambridge, UK, 2001

2003 Signing of the 'MI!MS Manifesto'

Organises *Top Buzzer*, a series of group shows in a flat in New Cross, London

Album art and live visuals for Johnny Parry

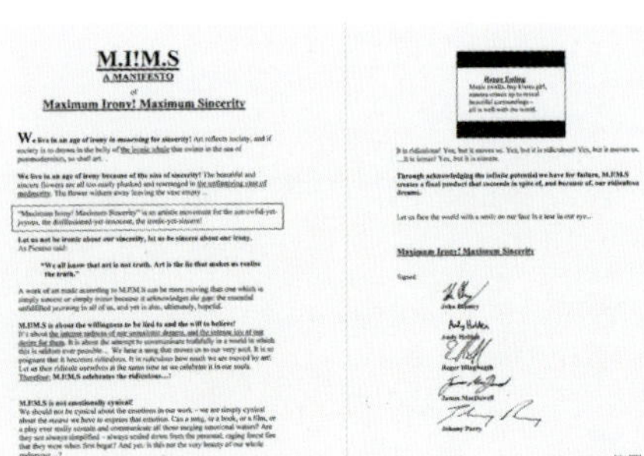
M.I!M.S

A MANIFESTO

of

Maximum Irony! Maximum Sincerity

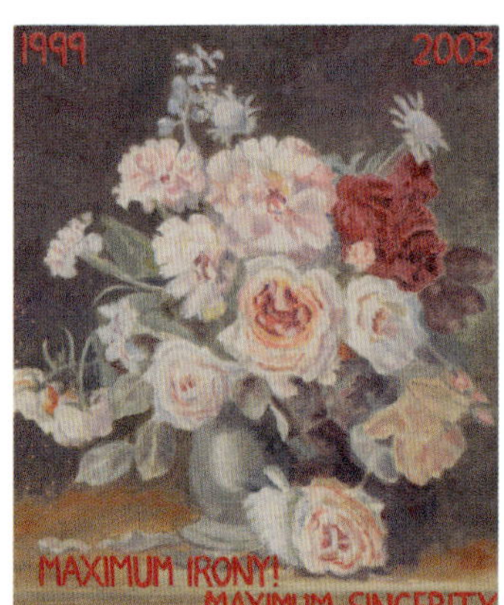

↞ MI!MS Manifesto, signed by Holden in 2003

← *Untitled*, acrylic on found painting, 2013

2004 *Guston's Boulder, Mile End*, London

2005 Graduates BA (Hons) Fine Art, Goldsmiths College, London

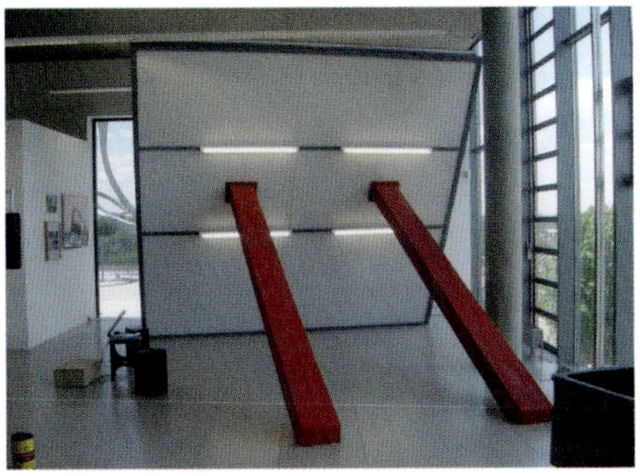

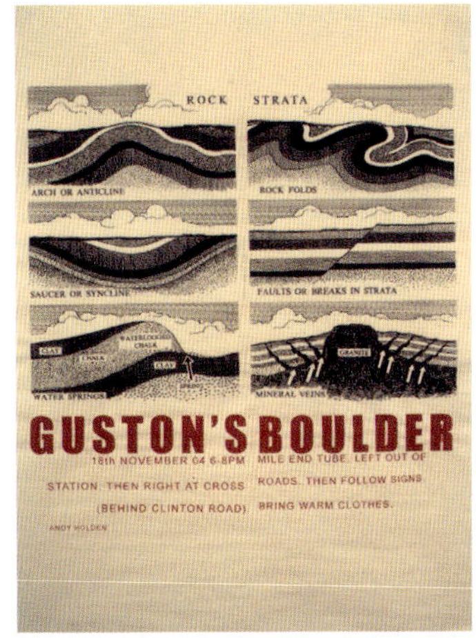

« *Standard*, installation view, Goldsmiths College, 2005

← *Guston's Boulder, Mile End*, screenprinted poster, 2004

2006 *Black Boulder Monochrome Folly, Deptford*, London
The Thing in Itself, curated by Mark Leckey, Peles Empire, London
The Grubby Mitts, *The Thing in Itself*, tape

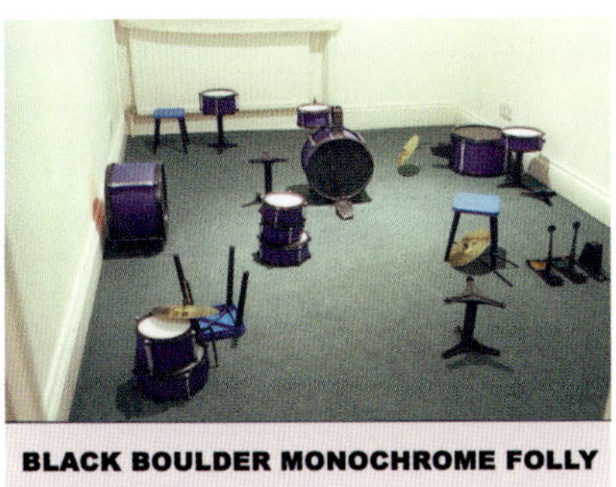

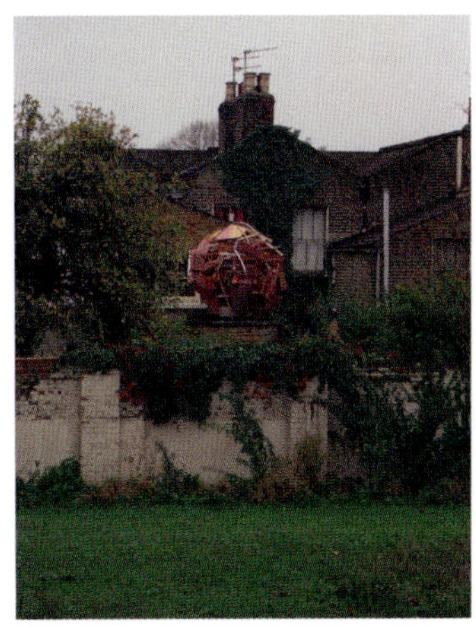

« *Black Boulder Monochrome Folly, Deptford*, poster, 2006

← *Guston's Boulder, Mile End*, installed on a roof, London, 2004

2007 *So Long See You Tomorrow / Unquiet Grave*, Hidde van Seggelen, London
Solo presentation at Vienna Fair, Austria

Cover art and music videos for Johnny Parry's album *Songs without a Purpose*
Andy Holden and Johnny Parry set up Lost Toys Records

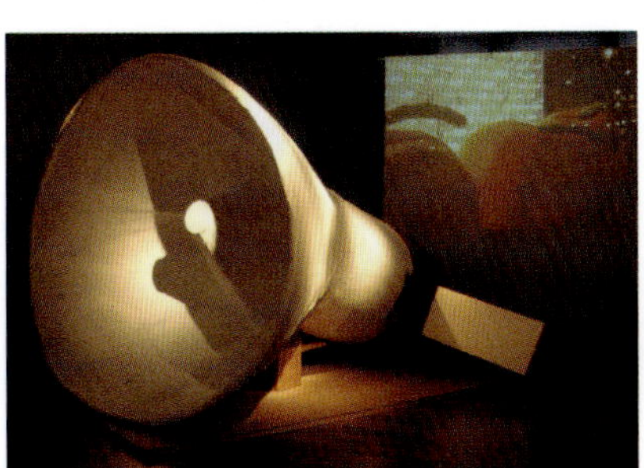

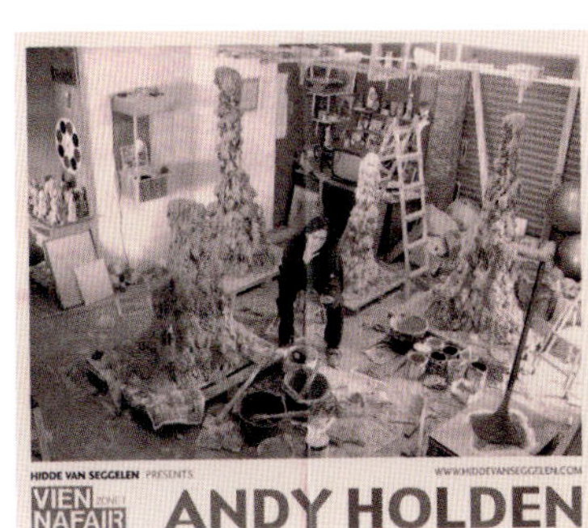

« *Unquiet Grave*, installation view, Hidde van Seggelen, London, 2007

← Poster for presentation at Vienna Fair, 2007

2008

SOLO *The World Is Round and Mr Wrigley Makes Chewing Gum*, Kunstfort Vijfhuizen, Netherlands
You Go on Without Me, Hex Projects, London

GROUP *Experimental Folklore*, Frankfurter Kunstverein, Frankfurt, Germany
Poldergeist, Kunstfort Vijfhuizen, Netherlands

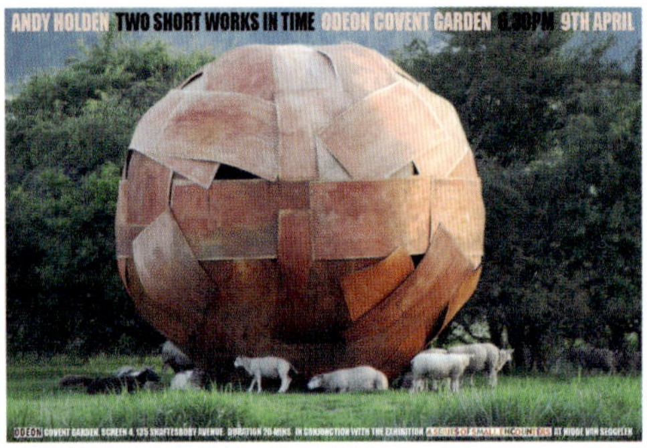

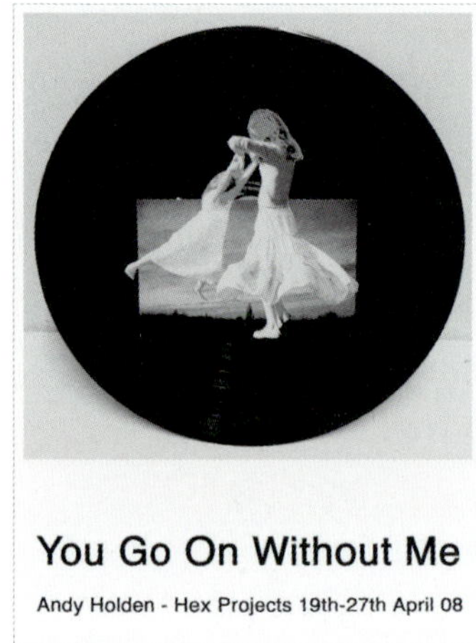

↞ *Two Short Works in Time*, poster for performance at Odeon Cinema, Covent Garden, London, 2009

← *You Go On Without Me*, poster for exhibition at Hex Projects, London, 2008

2009

SOLO *Desert Project*, Works|Projects, Bristol, UK
A Series of Small Encounters, Hidde van Seggelen, London

GROUP *Performed*, Wysing Arts Centre, Cambridge, UK
Abstract, Almost Abstract 2, Galerie van Gelder, Amsterdam

PERFORMANCES *Lecture on Migration*, Transition Gallery, London
Two Short Works in Time, Odeon Cinema, Covent Garden, London
The Grubby Mitts live at Wysing Arts Centre, Cambridge and Cube Cinema, Bristol, UK

RECORDS The Grubby Mitts, *After the Facts*, CD EP, Lost Toys Records
Cover art and music videos for Johnny Parry's album *More Love and Death*

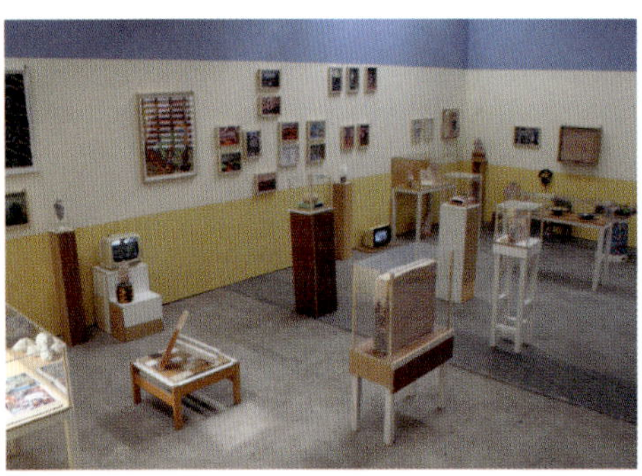

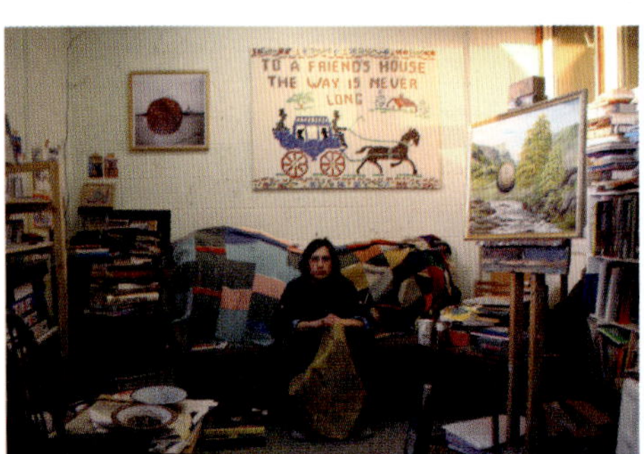

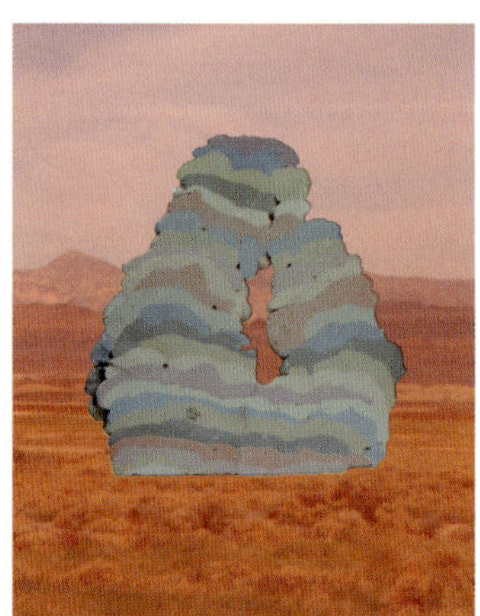

↖ Installation view, *Desert Project*, Works|Projects, Bristol, UK, 2009

↙ Andy Holden in his studio in Bedfordshire, with model for *Pyramid Piece*, 2009

← Postcard for *Desert Project*, Works|Projects, Bristol, UK, 2009

2010

SOLO *Art Now: Andy Holden*, Tate Britain, London
Permanent Vacation, Bureau, Manchester

GROUP *Props, Events and Encounters*, Hub, Athens
The Eccentric, the Idiosyncratic and the Unpredictable, Schirman & de Beaucé, Paris
Canadian Pharmacy, Neon Parc, Melbourne, Australia

PERFORMANCES *Three Short Works in Time*, Tate Britain, London
Daily, Action, Poetry, Hayward Gallery, London
Lecture on Nesting, London Festival of Architecture

CURATOR *Be Glad for the Song Has No End – A Festival of Artists' Music*, Wysing Art Centre, Cambridge, UK

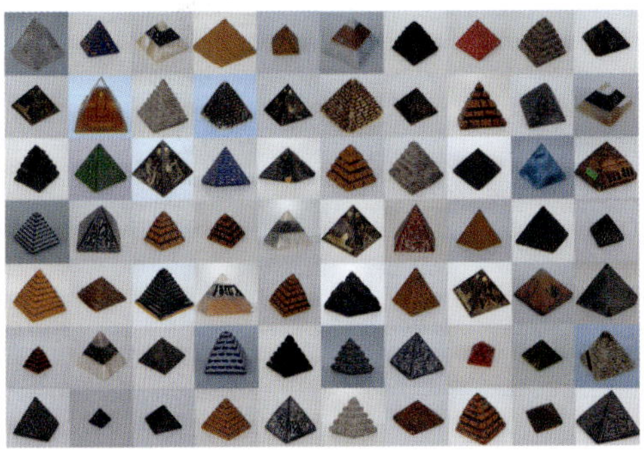

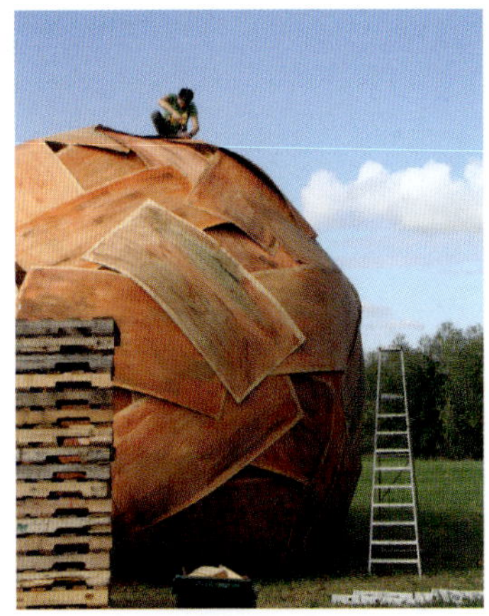

« Poster for *Art Now: Andy Holden*, Tate Britain, London, 2010

← Building the Boulder Stage at Wysing Art Centre, Cambridge, UK, for *Be Glad for the Song Has No End*, 2010

2011

SOLO *Chewy Cosmos Thingly Time*, Kettle's Yard, Cambridge, UK
Cookham Erratic, Benaki Museum, Athens

GROUP *Transcendental Empiricism*, Rob Tufnell, London
I Promise to Love You, Kunsthal Rotterdam, Netherlands
A Fire in the Master's House Is Set, Chapter, Cardiff
Off the Record, Resonance 104.4 fm, London

PERFORMANCES *Five Short Works in Time*, Kettle's Yard, Cambridge, UK
BruderKreigSoundSystem, curated by Mark Leckey, ICA, London
The Grubby Mitts at opening of *The Life of the Mind: Love, Sorrow and Obsession*, curated by Bob and Roberta Smith, New Art Gallery Walsall, UK
The Grubby Mitts, Cafe Oto, London

RECORDS The Grubby Mitts, *To a Friend's House the Way Is Never Long*, 7" white vinyl, edition of 300
Andy Holden, *Quartet for Thingly Time*, CD, edition of 100

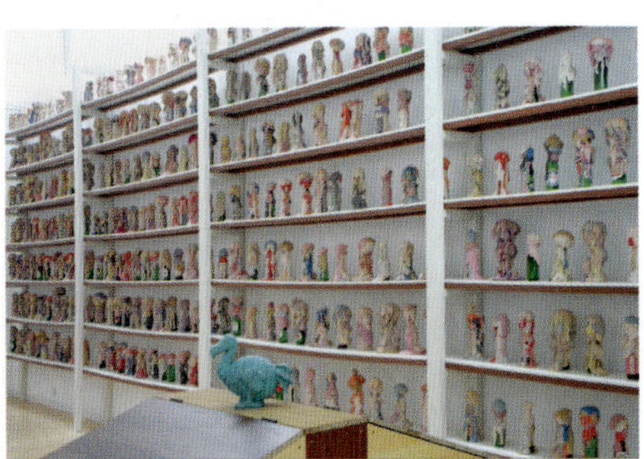

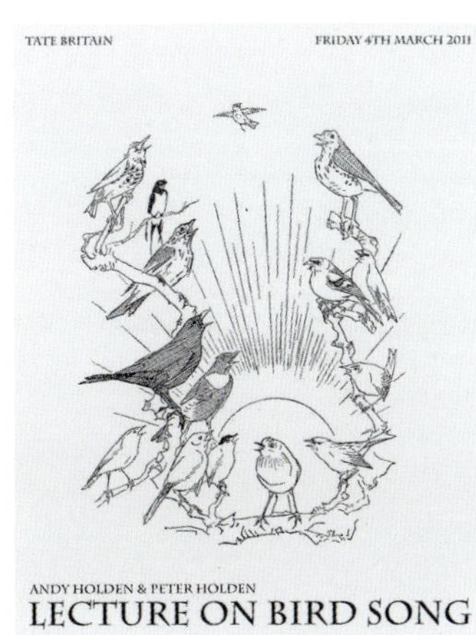

« *Chewy Cosmos, Thingly Time*, Kettle's Yard, Cambridge, UK 2011

← Screen-printed poster for *Lecture on Bird Song* at Tate Britain, with Peter Holden and music by Roger Illingworth, 2011

2012

SOLO *The Dan Cox Library for the Unfinished Concept of Thingly Time*, Cubitt Gallery, London
Stalagmite Rock Club, Art Rotterdam, Netherlands
Cookham Erratics, Works | Projects, Bristol, UK
Laws of Motion in a Cartoon Landscape, Stanley Picker Gallery, Kingston, UK

GROUP *Soundworks*, ICA, London
Nothing Like Something Happens Anywhere, Chapter, Cardiff
Latitude Contemporary Art, Latitude Festival, Henham Park, Suffolk, UK
Discussing Metamodernism, Galerie Tanja Wagner, Berlin
A Plea for Tenderness, curated by David Raymond Conroy, Seventeen, London
Human Made Things, Aspex, Portsmouth, UK
Occupants, Stanley Picker Gallery, Kingston, UK

PERFORMANCES *Brief Interviews with Hideous Men*, co-directed with David Raymond Conroy, adapted for the stage from the novel by David Foster Wallace, ICA, London
Becoming Thing, performance with Ed Atkins, Whitechapel Gallery, London
Lecture on Nesting, performance with Peter Holden, Penzance Convention, Cornwall, UK
Lecture on Bird Song, part of *House of Beasts*, Attingham Park, Shrewsbury, UK
The Grubby Mitts, Firstsite, Colchester, UK
Laws of Motion in a Cartoon Landscape, Hay Festival, Hay-on-Wye, Wales
Six Short Works in Time, Victoria Gallery & Museum, Liverpool, UK

AWARDS Paul Hamlyn Foundation Awards for Artists

RECORDS The Grubby Mitts, *Standard*, 7" white vinyl, Lost Toys Records
The Grubby Mitts, *Music of Exhaustion*, 7" vinyl, Lost Toys Records

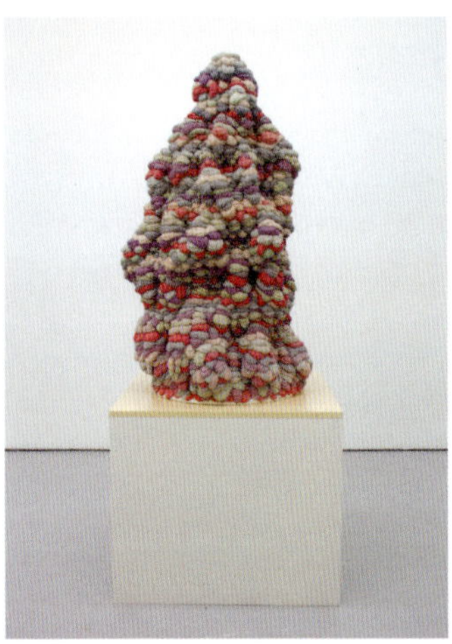

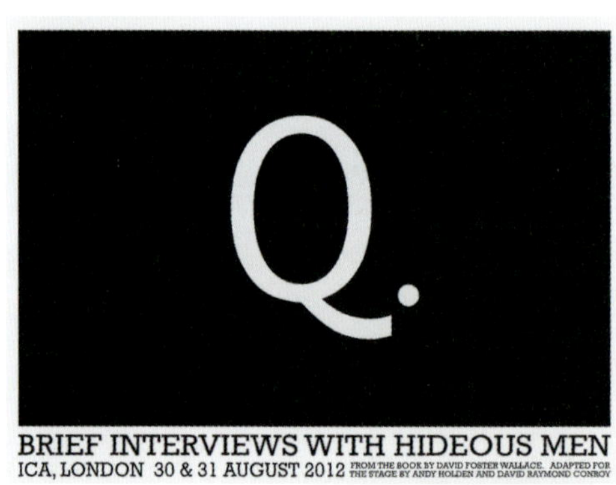

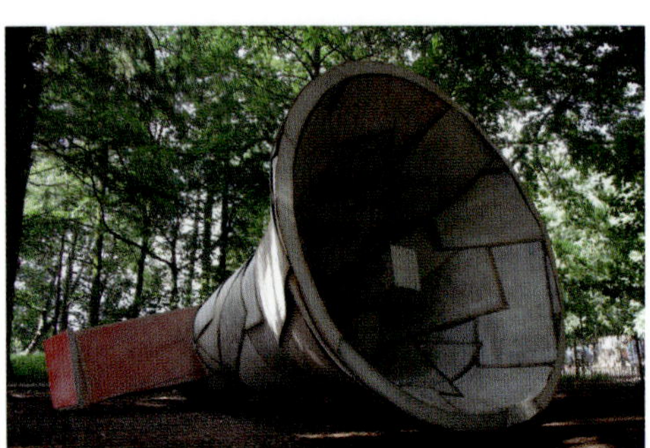

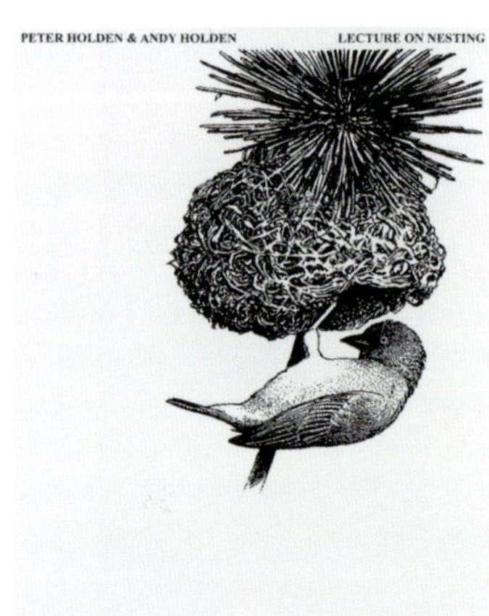

↖ *Totem for Thingly Time*, exhibition view, *A Plea for Tenderness*, Seventeen, London, 2012

↑ *Brief Interviews with Hideous Men*, poster for stage play, ICA, London, 2012

↞ *Unquiet Grave*, wood, 5 × 5 m (16½ × 16½ ft.), Latitude Festival, 2012

← *Lecture on Nesting*, with Peter Holden, Central Library, Edinburgh, 2011

2013

SOLO *Maximum Irony! Maximum Sincerity, 1999–2003: Towards a Unified Theory of M!MS*, Zabludowicz Collection, London
Folly and Landscape, Collective, Edinburgh

GROUP *Universal Addressability of Dumb Things*, curated by Mark Leckey for Hayward Gallery Touring: The Bluecoat, Liverpool; Nottingham Contemporary; De La Warr Pavilion, St Leonards-on-Sea, UK
Version Control, Arnolfini, Bristol, UK
As real as walking down the street and going to the grocery store, Rowing, London

PERFORMANCES *Seven Short Works in Time*, Hospitalfield, Arbroath, Scotland
Lecture on Nesting, Performa 13, New York
Brief Interviews with Hideous Men, with David Raymond Controy, Arnolfini, Bristol, UK
Last Stop for the Good Old Times, bus tour from London to Bedford organised by Zabludowicz Collection, London

COMMISSION *Chewy Cosmos*, Random Acts, Channel 4, commissioned by Tate Media

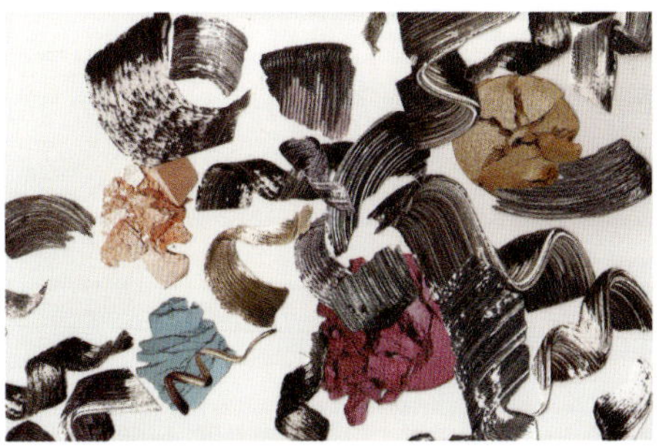

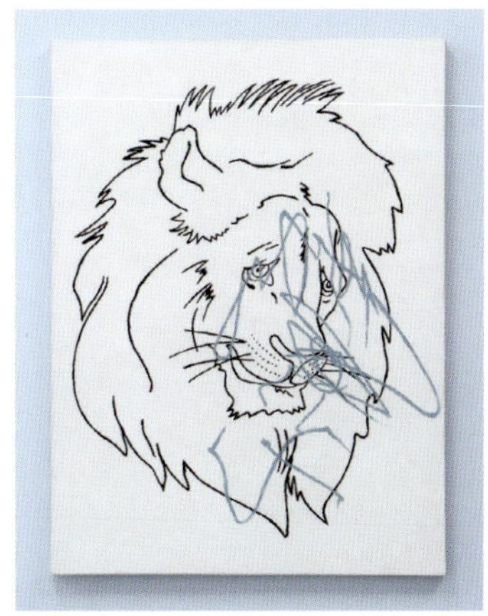

« *Chewy Cosmos*, animation still, 2013

← *Sad Lion*, acrylic on canvas, 2013

2014

SOLO *Folly (Sand Hills), Bedfordshire*, UK
Towards a Unified Theory of M!MS, Spike Island, Bristol, UK

GROUP *Anatomy of Anxieties*, Edouard Malingue Gallery, Hong Kong, China
Cacotopia / Peach Blossom Spring, Kuiyuan Gallery, Guangzhou, China
Hey I'm Mr Poetic, Wysing Arts Centre, Cambridge, UK
On the Devolution of Culture, Rob Tufnell, London

PERFORMANCES *The Politics of Friendship Tour*, tour of nine artist-run spaces around the UK with The Grubby Mitts: Primary; S1 Artspace; Rhubaba; Supercollider; Karst; Aid and Abet; Grand Union; Open School East
Hello, Welcome, Art Licks Weekend, London

RECORDS The Grubby Mitts, *What The World Needs Now Is...*, CD LP, Lost Toys Records
Various artists, *In The Golden Days of Lost Toys Records*, compilation CD, Lost Toys Records

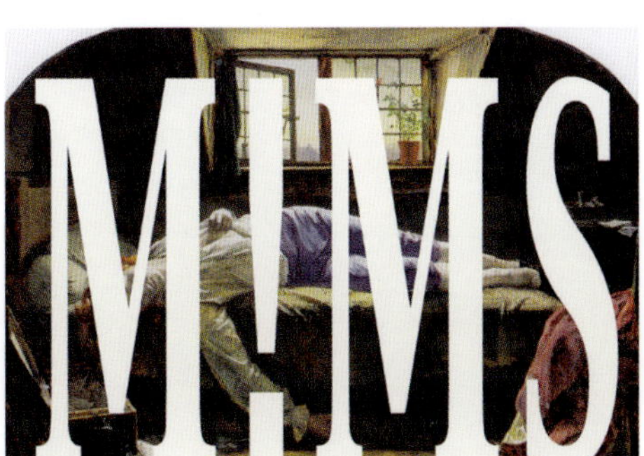

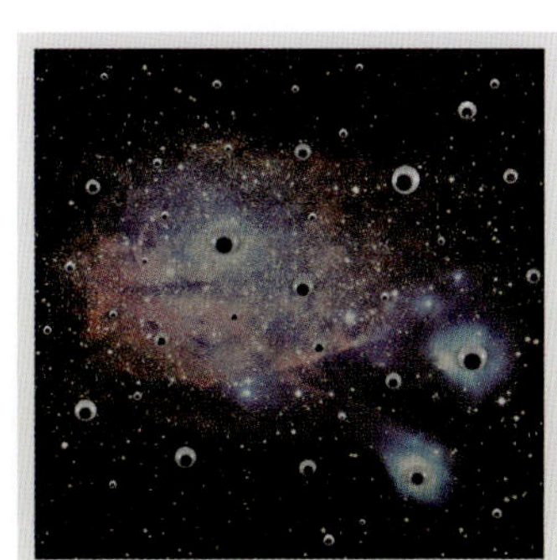

« *M!MS (Death of Chatterton)*, printed banner, 2013

← *What The World Needs Now is...* album by The Grubby Mitts, 2014

2015

SOLO *Towards a Unified Theory of M!MS,* Kunsthalle Winterthur, Switzerland
It's Only Bondage Was the Circling Sky, Stroud Valleys Artspace (SVA), UK

GROUP *20 Years*, Zabludowicz Collection, London

PERFORMANCES *Cat-tharsis,* SVA Stroud and Bedford Esquires, UK
Lecture on Nesting, Bristol Museum
The Grubby Mitts at Latitude Festival
Andy Holden with Secluded Brontë, Whitechapel Gallery, London

RECORDS *Towards a Unified Theory of M!MS*, 12" vinyl LP, Lost Toys Records
Music of Exhaustion, 7" clear vinyl with party popper pressed inside

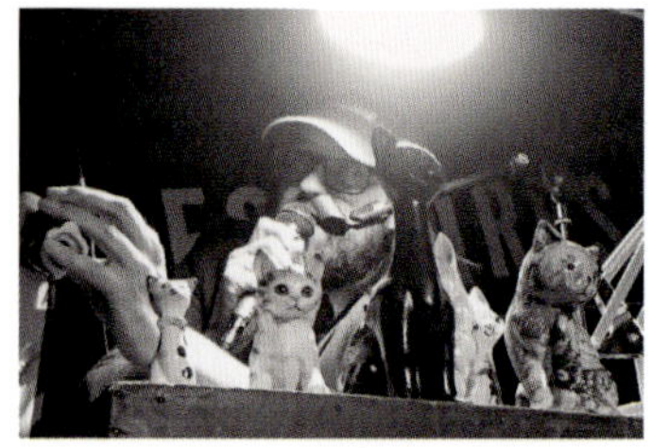

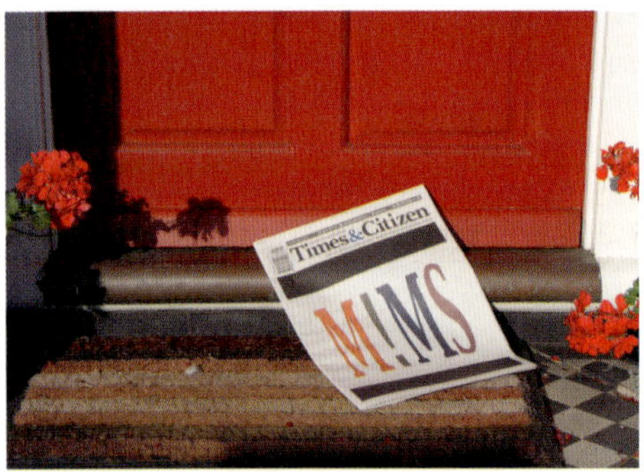

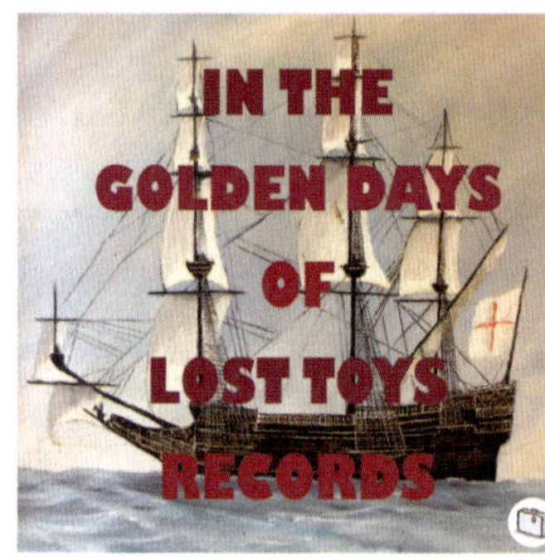

↖ Holden performing *Cat-tharsis* with The Grubby Mitts, Bedford Esquires, UK, 2015

↞ *Towards a Unified Theory of M!MS*, video still, 2013

← *In The Golden Days of Lost Toys Records*, compilation CD by Lost Toys Records, 2014

2016

SOLO *Laws of Motion in a Cartoon Landscape*, Glasgow International, Wasps Studios, UK
When U Instagram my Dead Body Use Waldon but Tag It #NoFilter, with Steve Roggenbuck, Rowing, London

GROUP *The Practice of Theories*, Wysing Arts Center, Cambridge, UK
Secret Surface, KW Institute for Contemporary Art, Berlin
Playing by the Rules, Royal Standard, Liverpool, UK
Pitt Projects: Music vs Ceramics, PULSE, New York

PERFORMANCES *Laws of Motion in a Cartoon Landscape* (live), Glasgow International, Wasps Studios, UK
The Grubby Mitts (live) Donau Festival, Austria; Whitechapel Gallery, London; MK Gallery, Milton Keynes; Bedford Esquires, UK

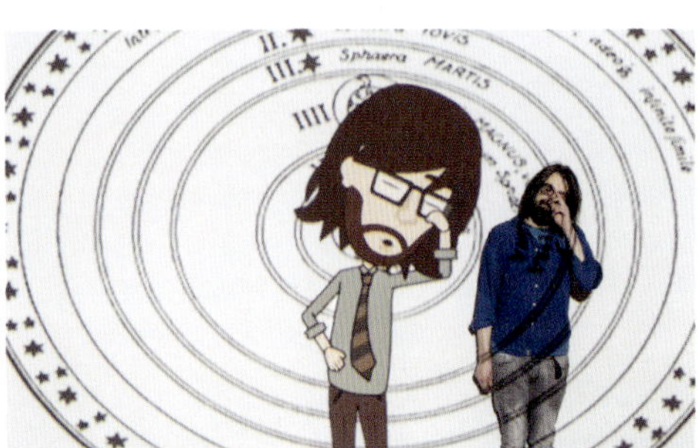

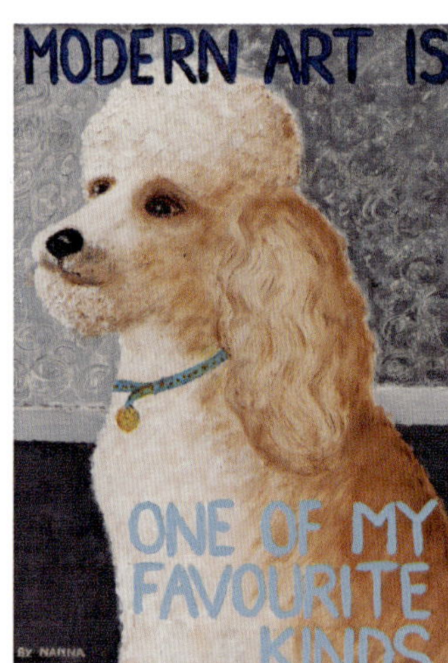

↞ Andy Holden with *Laws of Motion in a Cartoon Landscape*, Glasgow, 2016

← *Modern Art Is One of My Favourite Kinds*, print edition, 2016

2017

SOLO *Natural Selection*, Artangel commission at the former Newington Library, London
As Speed Increases Objects Can Be in Several Places at Once, Lancaster Arts, UK
Laws of Motion, Viborg Kunsthal, Denmark

GROUP *Future Generation Art Prize*, Victor Pinchuk Foundation, Kyiv, Ukraine; Palazzo Contarini Polignac, 57th Venice Biennale, Italy
Dream Sequence, MK Gallery, Milton Keynes, UK

PERFORMANCES *World as Cartoon*, Tate Britain, London
We Portal, curated by Mira Calix, V&A, London
Andy Holden & The Grubby Mitts (live), Cecil Sharp House, London

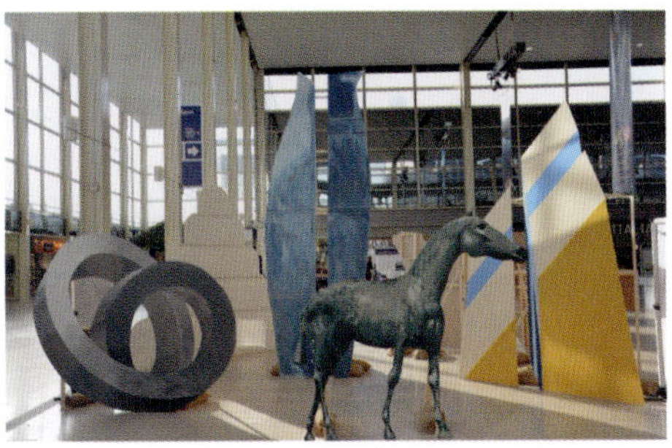

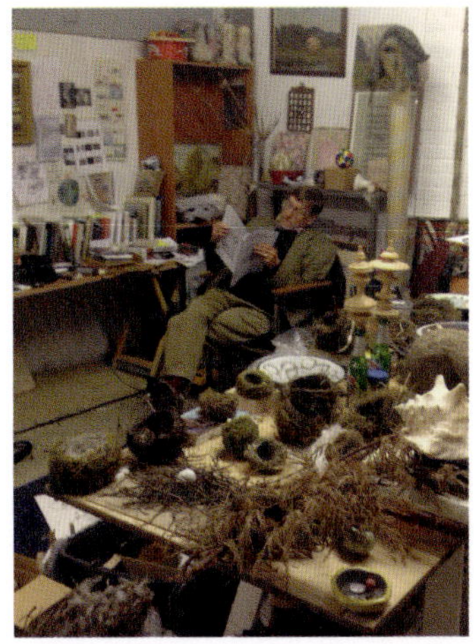

« *Dream Sequence*, Milton Keynes Shopping Centre, with MK Gallery, Milton Keynes, 2017

← Peter Holden in Andy Holden's studio, 2017

2018

SOLO *Laws of Motion in a Cartoon Landscape*, Museum of Contemporary Art, Toronto
Natural Selection, Towner Art Gallery, Eastbourne, UK
Natural Selection, Leeds Art Gallery, UK
Natural Selection, Inverleith House, Edinburgh
Natural Selection, CAST, Cornwall, UK

GROUP *Good Grief, Charlie Brown!*, Somerset House, London
Animals and Us, Turner Contemporary, Margate, UK
Rinnzekete bee bee nnz krr müü, Kunstverein Wiesbaden, Germany
1st Front Triennial, Cleveland, USA

PERFORMANCES *Opposite of Time* (live), Henry Moore Studios & Gardens, Much Hadham; Hogchester Arts, Charmouth, Dorset, UK
Laws of Motion in a Cartoon Landscape (live), *Groundwork*, Academy of Music and Theatre Arts, Falmouth University, Cornwall, UK

CURATOR Sets up Ex-Baldessarre, Bedford, UK
Estate of Hermione, Ex-Baldessarre, Bedford, UK
Silly Symphony, Ex-Baldessarre, Bedford, UK

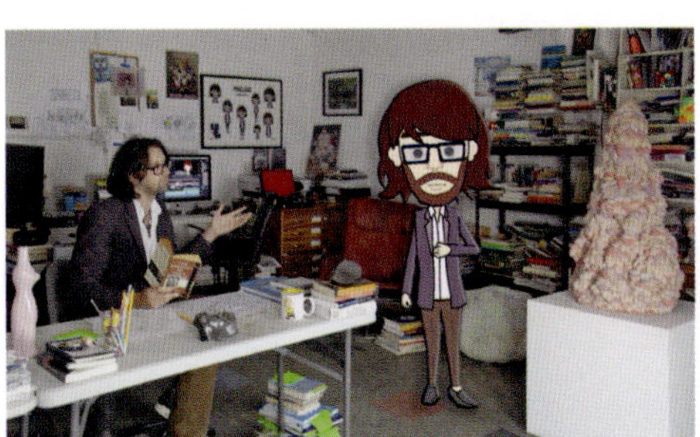

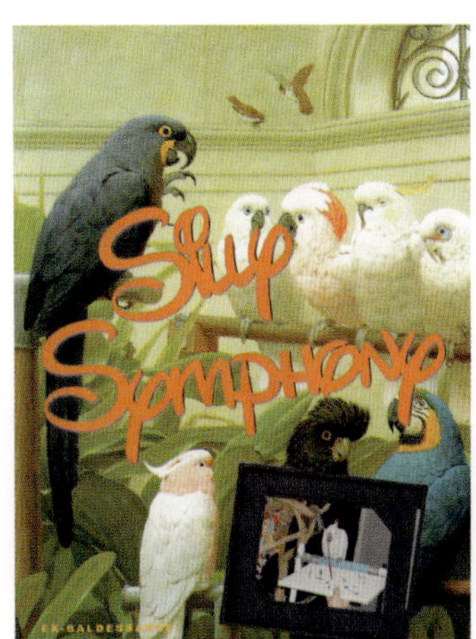

« Andy Holden studio portrait, 2018, photo by Mira Calix

← *Silly Symphony*, (with Ollie Dook and Ellie Thomas) Ex-Baldessarre, Bedford, UK, promotional postcard, 2018

2019

SOLO *Laws of Motion in a Cartoon Landscape*, Cinema Museum, London
Natural Selection, Shetland Arts, Scotland
Natural Selection, Hospitalfield at Arbroath Law Courts, Scotland
Natural Selection, Bristol Museum & Art Gallery, UK

GROUP *Fragile Earth*, MIMA (Middlesbrough Institute of Modern Art), UK
Invisible, Science Gallery, Dublin
Dark Matter, Science Gallery, London
Cartoony, New Media Gallery, Vancouver, Canada

CURATOR *Sour Persimmons Chasm*, Ex-Baldessarre, Bedford
Long Revolution, Ex-Baldessarre, Bedford

PERFORMANCES *Laws of Motion in a Cartoon Landscape* (live), Alserkal Avenue, Dubai
Laws of Motion in a Cartoon Landscape (live), Cinema Museum, London; Museum of Contemporary Art, Toronto; Viborg Kunsthal, Denmark; Science Gallery London
Cat-tharis (live), Cinema Museum, London
The Grubby Mitts (live), Cafe Oto, London

COMMISSION *What is Love?* animated film, commissioned by Google Arts & Culture for the BBC

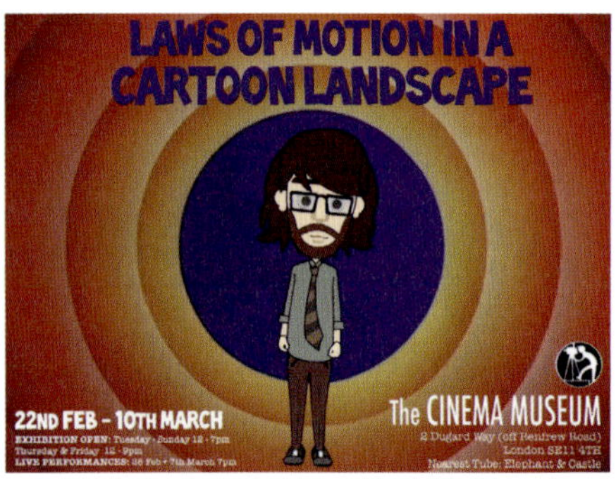

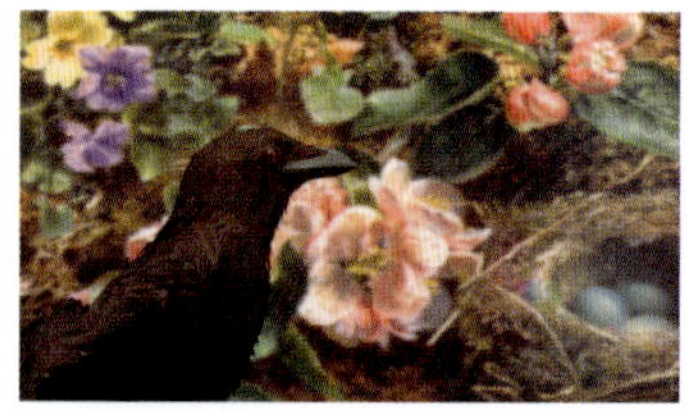

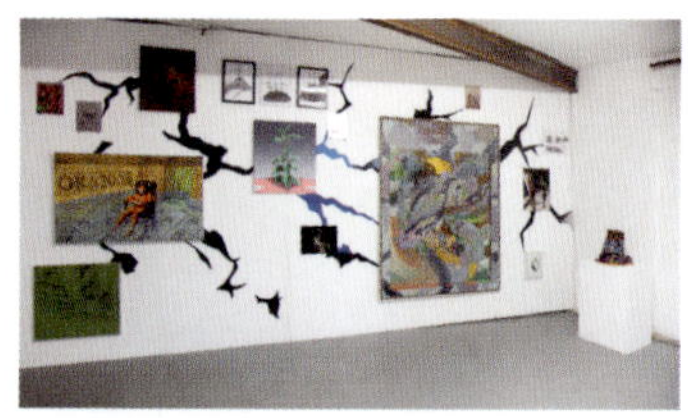

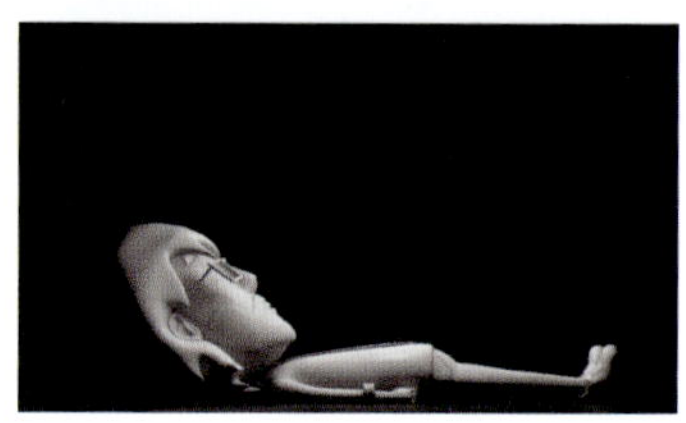

↞ Poster for *Laws of Motion in a Cartoon Landscape*, Cinema Museum, London, 2019

↖ Poster image for *Natural Selection*, Bristol Museum & Art Gallery, UK, 2019

← *Sour Persimmons Chasm*, curated by Andy Holden, installation view, Ex-Baldessarre, Bedford, UK, 2019

↙ *Structure of Feeling* production image, 2020

2020

SOLO *Structure of Feeling (Ghost Train)*, Block 336, London

CURATOR *What Am I? Simon Munnery Retrospective*, SVA, Stroud, UK
What Am I? Simon Munnery Retrospective, Ex-Baldessarre, Bedford, UK

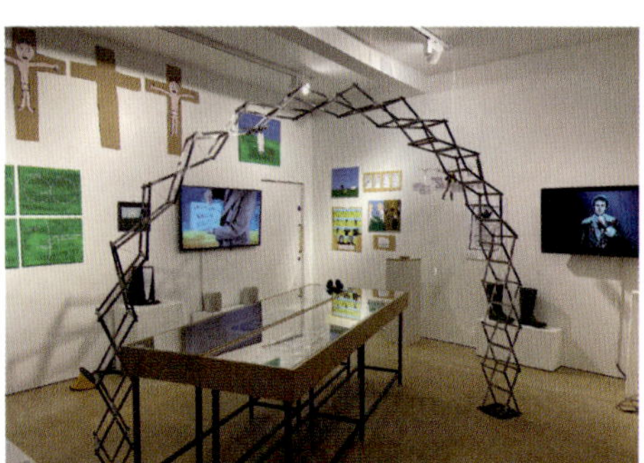

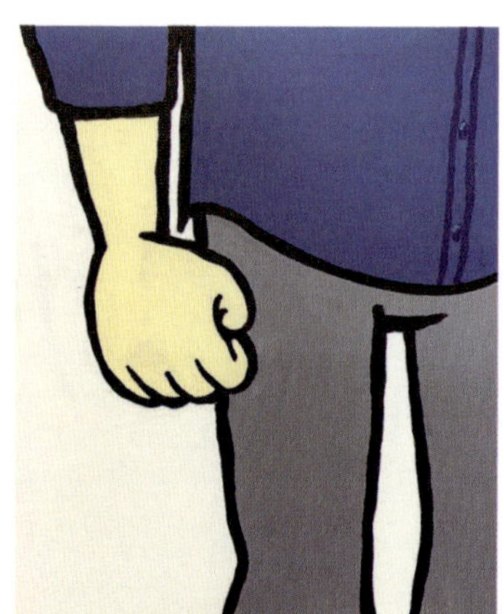

↞ *What am I? Simon Munnery Retrospective*, curated by Andy Holden, installation view, SVA Stroud, 2020

← *Structure of Feeling (Ghost Train)*, fold-out leaflet with essay by Ed Atkins, Block 336, 2020

2021

SOLO *Collected Domestic Conceptualism*, Pitt Studio, Worcester, UK

GROUP *Arcadia*, Bold Tendencies, London
To The Edge of Time, Leuven University Library, Belgium

PERFORMANCE *Unexpected Views*, National Gallery, London

CURATOR *Beano: The Art of Breaking the Rules*, Somerset House, London

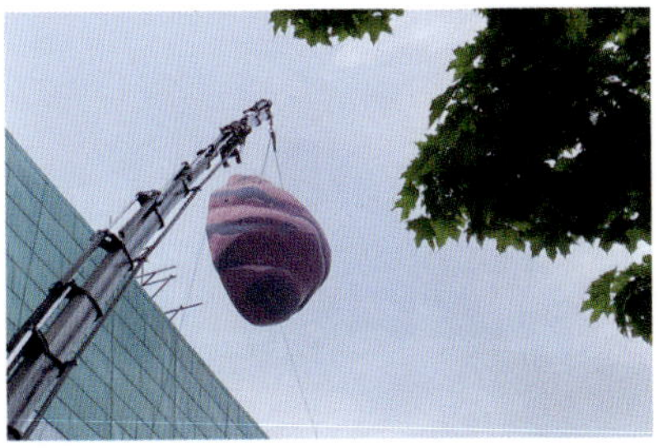

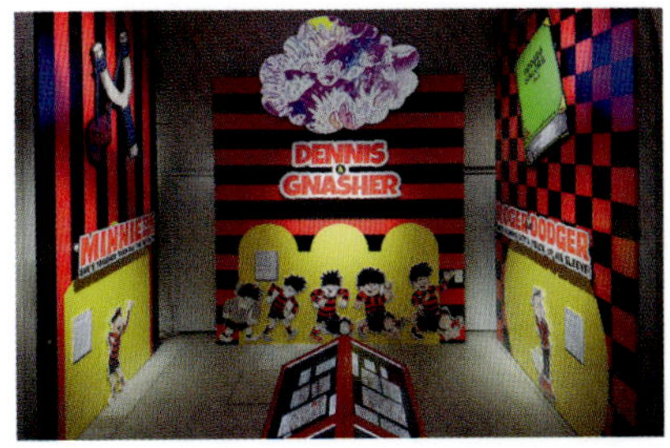

« Installing *In Praise of Folly* at the Peckham Library, for Arcadia at Bold Tendencies, 2021

← *Beano: The Art of Breaking the Rules*, installation view, Somerset House, London, 2021

2022

GROUP *British Art Show 9*, The Whitworth, Manchester; The Box, Plymouth; Wolverhampton Art Gallery, UK (organised by Hayward Gallery Touring)
Raw Nerves, Hannah Barry Gallery, London
Ghost Show, Copeland Park, London
Cubitt 30, Victoria Miro, London
Empathy for People, Empathy for Things, Art + Design Gallery, University of Hertfordshire, UK
For the Birds, Brooklyn Botanic Garden, New York

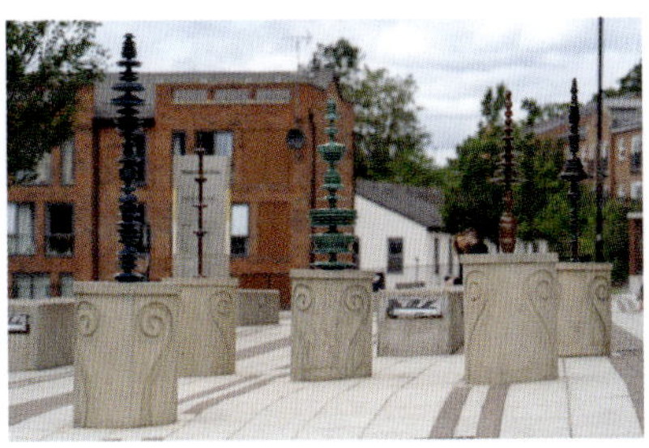

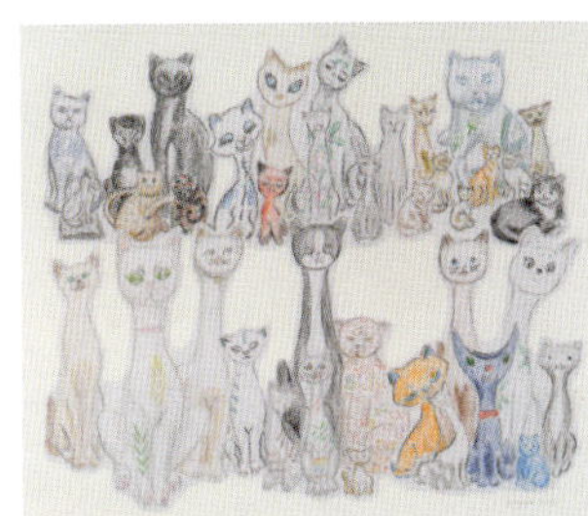

« *Auguries (Last Calls)*, Wakefield, UK, installed 2023

← *Cat-tharsis*, pencil on paper, 2020

2023

SOLO *Song of Songs*, Seventeen, London
Full of Days, Gallery of Everything, London
Full of Days, CAST, Helston, Cornwall, UK

GROUP *Behold*, Hypha Studios, London
Amber Rooms, Matt's Gallery, London

PERFORMANCE *Lecture on Birdsong*, Wakefield One, UK

COMMISSIONS *Auguries (Last Calls)*, permanent public sculpture, Wakefield, UK
I may be over there but my heart is over here, with Mira Calix, permanent mural, BCA (Bedford Creative Arts), UK
Origin of the Work of Art, private commission, UK

RECORDS Cover art for Saint Etienne, *Music for Hermione*, 10" vinyl

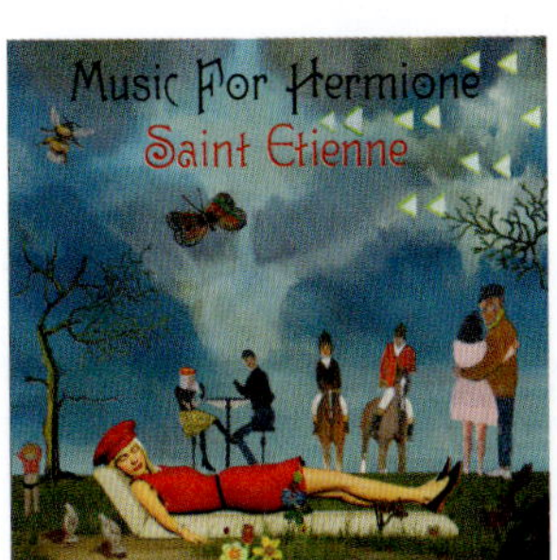

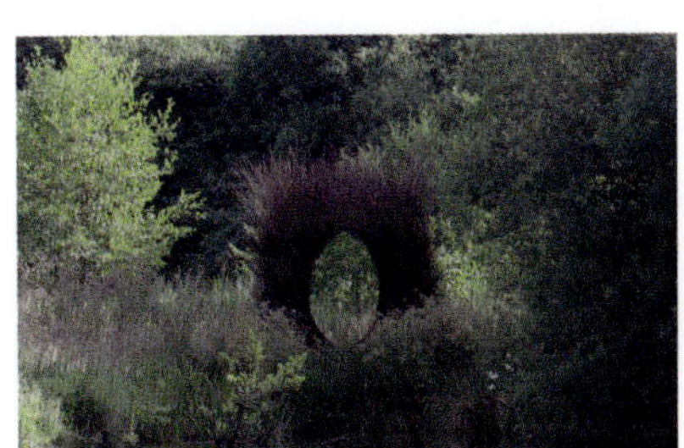

« *Music For Hermione*, soundtrack by Saint Etienne, 10" vinyl, 2023

← *Origin of the Work of Art*, private commission, 2023

2024

SOLO *Natural History of Nest Building,* Tate St Ives, Cornwall, UK
Laws of Motion in a Cartoon Landscape, The Perimeter, London
What I Was for What I Am Becoming, Charles Moffett, New York

GROUP *The Wood for the Trees*, Kröller-Müller Museum, Netherlands
Cute, Somerset House, London
Constable in Bristol 'Truth to Nature' Bristol Museum & Art Gallery, UK

PERFORMANCE *Lecture on Birdsong,* with Peter Holden and Roger Illingworth, Kröller-Müller Museum, Netherlands

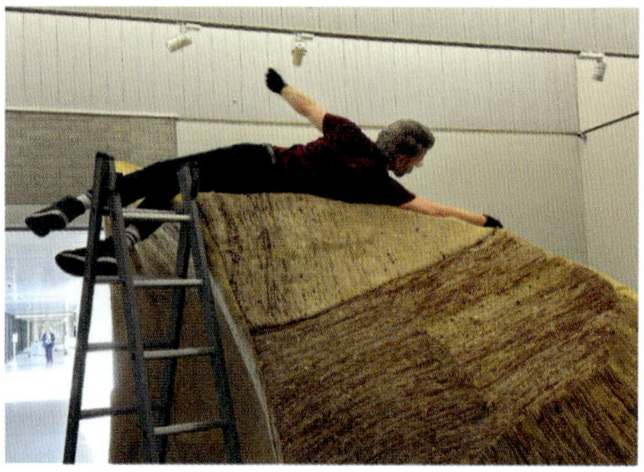

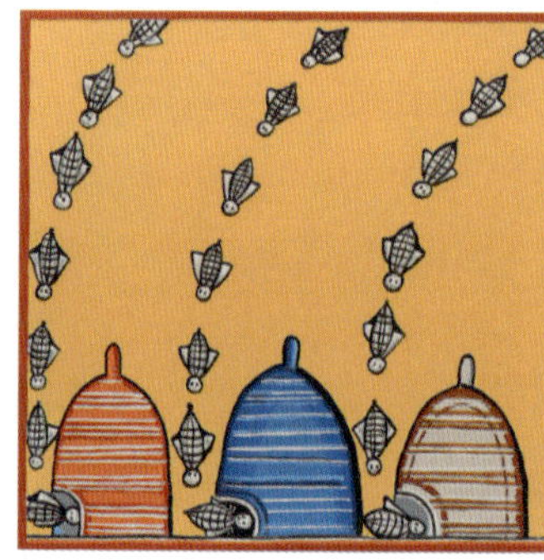

↞ Lee Farmer assisting with stitching together *Pyramid Piece,* Kröller-Müller Museum, Netherlands, 2024

← *Untitled,* 2024, emulsion on canvas, used on the cover of *Valediciton* EP by The Grubby Mitts, 2025

2025

SOLO *Love in the Misanthropocene,* Palmer Gallery, London
Natural History of Nest Building, Tolson Museum, Kirklees, UK
Cat-tharsis, Grundy Art Gallery, Blackpool, UK

GROUP *In the Shadows*: *Frieze Sculpture,* Regent's Park, London
Cute, Kunsthal Rotterdam, Netherlands
Earth Unwrapped, Pangolin London
Cat People, La Galerie, Noisy-le-Sec, France
The Pleasure of Misuse, Royal Society of Sculptors, London
Longest Way Round, Charles Moffett, New York

PERFORMANCES The Grubby Mitts (live) Bedford Esquires; New River Studios, London; ICA, London

RECORDS The Grubby Mitts, *Valediction,* 12" vinyl EP, Vibe/Anti-vibe
The Grubby Mitts, *Love in the Misanthropocene,* 12" vinyl and digital download , Vibe/Anti-vibe

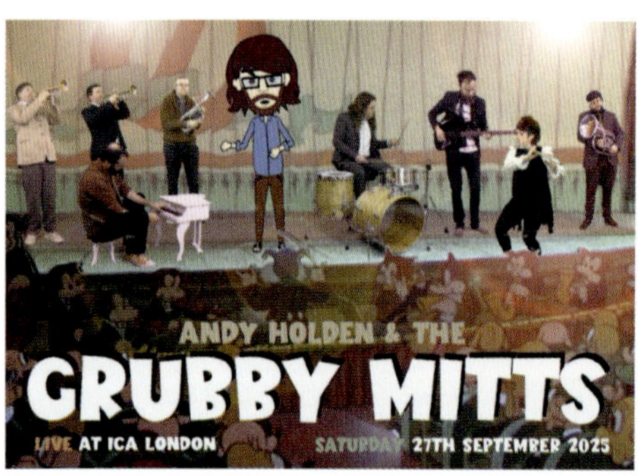

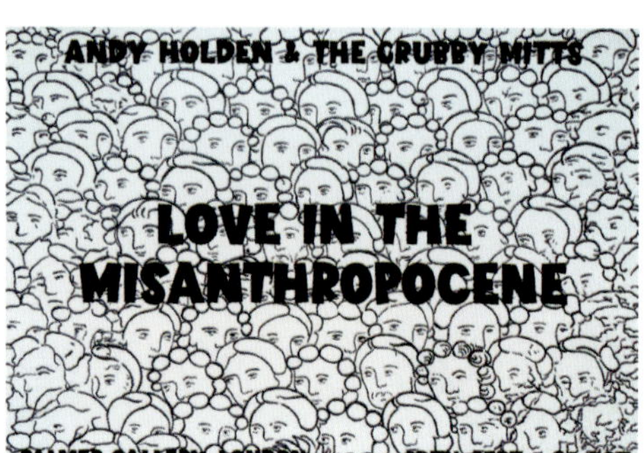

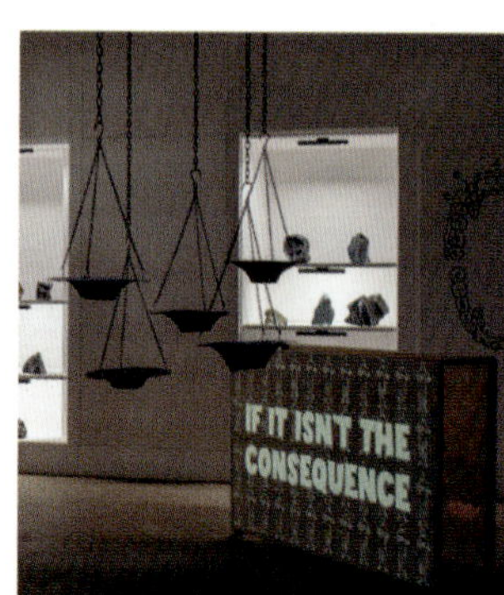

↖ Poster for Andy Holden and The Grubby Mitts (live) ICA London, 2025

↞ Poster for *Love in the Misanthropocene,* Palmer Gallery, London, 2025

← Installation view, *Love in the Misanthropocene* Palmer Gallery, London, 2025

2026

SOLO *Morning Song,* Hidde van Seggelen, Hamburg, Germany
Negative Capability, Seventeen, London

GROUP *So Cute!,* Louvre-Lens, France
Buffet d'Art, Ambika P3, London
Drive Your Plow Over the Bones of the Dead, curated by Maria Hinel, Hypha Studios, 1 Poultry, London
Where is my mind?, Quench Gallery, Margate, UK
Funny People, Lowry, Salford, UK
A Quiet Omen (Nightingale for Berkeley Square) Berkeley Square, London
Mood Swings, Norito Gallery, London
Decant (Andy Holden and Richard Wentworth), Fisher London

PERFORMANCES The Grubby Mitts, Arts Collective, Northampton, UK; The Grubby Mitts + Mozart Estate, Esquires Bedford

2027

SOLO MK Gallery, Milton Keynes, UK

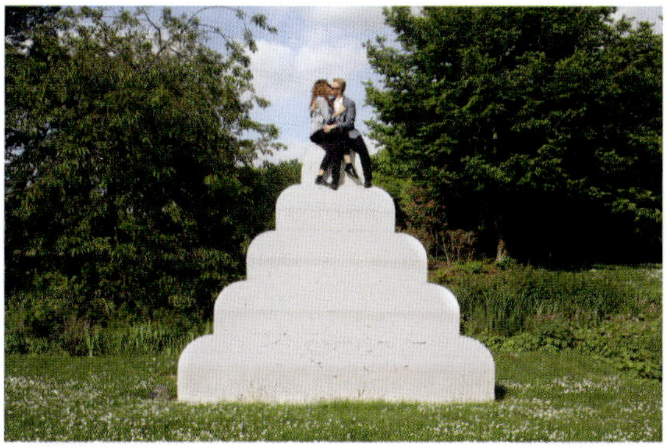

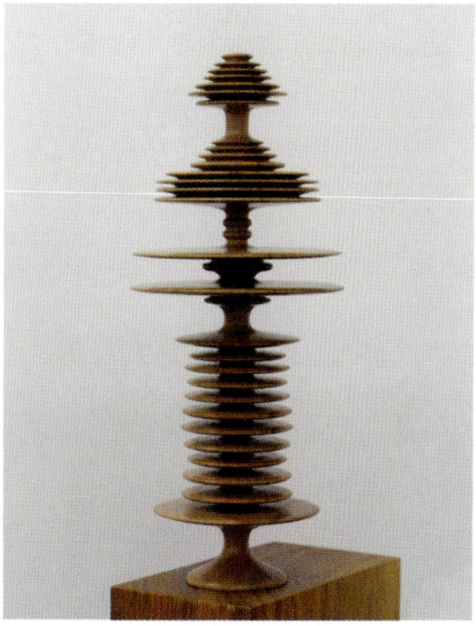

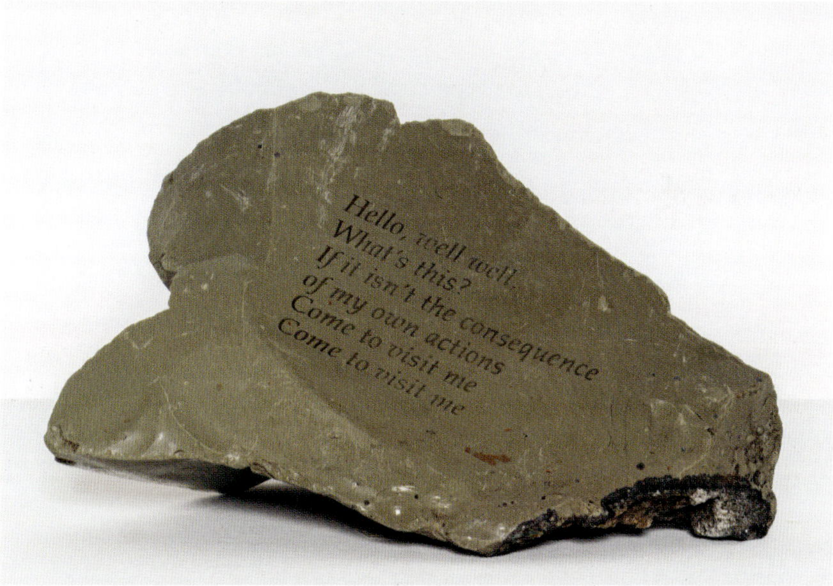

↖ Detail from *M!MS Dream Sequence (Milton Keynes)*, 2013

↑ *Nightingale*, from *Auguries*, 2025, walnut, 42 × 14 cm (16 ½ × 5 ½ in.)

← *Hello Well Well What's This? (Thames Slag)*, 2025, 22 × 12 cm (8 ⅝ × 4 ¾ in.)

SELECTED BIBLIOGRAPHY

BOOKS

Cat, Phaidon Editors (eds.) with foreword by Hannah Shaw and introduction by Leïla Jarbouai, (London/New York: Phaidon Press, 2026)

Vitamin V: Video and the Moving Image in Contemporary Art, Phaidon Editors (eds.) with introduction by Erika Balsom, (London/New York: Phaidon Press, 2025)

Birds in Art, Tim Batchelor, (London: Tate Publishing, 2024)

Contemporary Absurdities, Existential Crises, and Visual Arts, Katherine Guinness and Charlotte Kent (eds.), (Bristol: Intellect Books, 2024)

Beano: The Art of Breaking the Rules, Andy Holden (ed.), (London: Somerset House, 2022)

Bird: Exploring the Ornotholigical World, Phaidon Editors (eds.) with introduction by Katrina van Grouw, (London/New York: Phaidon Press, 2022)

Andy Holden: Collected Free Labour, (London: Slimvolume, 2021)

British Art Show 9 (group exhibition catalogue), Irene Aristizábal and Hammad Nasar, (London: Hayward Gallery Publishing, 2021)

Good Grief, Charlie Brown (group exhibition catalogue), Claire Catterall, (London: Somerset House, 2018)

Natural Selection (solo exhibition catalogue), with essays by Helen MacDonald, Darian Leader, (London: Artangel, 2017)

M!MS (solo exhibition catalogue), Andy Holden and Elizabeth Neilson (eds.), with texts by Catherine Wood, Gil Leung, Elizabeth Neilson and Fiona Parry, (Bristol/London: Spike Island/ Zabludowicz Collection, 2013)

Documents in Contemporary Art: The Object, Anthony Hudek (ed.), (London & Cambridge MA: Whitechapel Gallery & MIT Press, 2014)

The Art of Not Making: The New Artist/Artisan Relationship, Michael Petry, (London/New York: Thames & Hudson, 2011)

Chewy Cosmos Thingy Time (solo exhibition catalogue), Andy Holden and Dan Cox, (Cambridge, UK: Kettle's Yard, 2011)

SpaceCraft 2, Hideouts, & Fleeting Architectures, Lukas Feireiss, (Berlin: Gestalten, 2009)

SpaceCraft, Hideouts, & Fleeting Architectures, Lukas Feireiss, (Berlin: Gestalten, 2007)

The World is Round and Mr Wriggly Makes Chewing Gum (exhibition catalogue), text by Mark Kremer (Vijfhuizen Netherlands: Kunstfort Vijfhuizen, 2008)

ARTICLES

'These Design Cues We Spotted in Frieze Week's Coolest Projects... Gilda Bruno, *LivingEtc*, 16 Oct 2025

'Frieze Sculpture brings shade – and light – to Regent's Park', Tom Seymour, *The Art Newspaper*, 14 Oct 2025

'Andy Holden to have First Solo Exhibition in the US', Mark Westall, *Fad Magazine*, 4 Jan 2024

'When Outsider Art Entered the Mainstream', Hettie Judah, *Apollo Magazine*, July/Aug 2023

'Full of Days – review', Nuala Ernest, *Raw Vision*, 115, Summer 2023

'After Discovering a Trove of Odd, Extraordinary Paintings in a Thrift Store, Artist Andy Holden is Bringing Their Little-Known Creator to Light', Jo Lawson-Tancred, *Artnet*, 25 April 2023

'The Strange Case of the Artist Discovered in a Charity Shop', Colin Gleadell, *Telegraph*, 4 April 2023

'Full of Days review – the wonderfully strange artist...', Adrian Searle, *The Guardian*, 27 March 2023

'Andy Holden with Hermione Burton – Full of Days', Mark Westall, *Fad Magazine*, 10 March 2023

'Bringing order to the chaos of reality... Jarvis Cocker interviews six collectors', *The Observer New Review*, 8 May 2022

'How Our Critic Ended up in the Beano: The Art of Breaking the Rules – review', Adrian Searle, *The Guardian*, 20 Oct 2021

'Heartfelt, Meticulous, and Splendidly Irreverent', Arwa Halder, *Financial Times*, 2 Nov 2021

'How the Beano Encouraged Generations of Artists to Break the Rules', José da Silva, *The Art Newspaper*, 7 Oct 2021

'Andy Holden's Cartoon Ghost Train Questions the Art World's Status Quo', Alice Bucknell, *Elephant*, 27 Oct 2020

'The Mysterious Hermione...' Louisa Buck, *The Art Newspaper*, 18 Oct 2018

'Andy Holden: "A lot of my work is a fidelity to what feels right more than an objective truth"', Emily Spicer, *Studio International*, 6 March 2018

'Andy Holden and Peter Holden', Himali Singh Soin, *Artforum*, Vol 56, No.6, Feb 2018

'At Home in the World', Tom Overton, *Frieze*, 24 Nov 2017

'Why Andy Holden Flew Black to the Nest', Tim Smith-Laing, *Apollo Magazine*, 2 Nov 2017

'Natural Selection review – a risky celebration of the dastardly life of birds, Skye Sherwin, *The Guardian*, 11 Sept 2017

'Andy Holden & Peter Holden: *Natural Selection* 5* review – Artfulness is egg-shaped', Laura Cumming, *The Observer*, 10 Sept 2017

'Laws of Motion: Guilt, humour and dislocation in Andy Holden's cartoon universe', Darian Leader, *Frieze*, Issue 188, 1 June 2017

'Beyond Logic: Want to understand our messed-up, post-truth, topsy-turvy reality? If you're Andy Holden you look to cartoons', Margaret Carrigan, *Modern Painters*, March 2017

'Andy Holden's Maximum Irony! Maximum Sincerity', Elinor Morgan, *Notes on Metamodernism* 29 Sept 2014

'Life on the Outside', Augustin Macellari, *Crack Magazine*, 14 Feb 2014

'Rising stars of 2014', Skye Sherwin, *The Observer*, 5 Jan 2014

'Towards a Manifesto of Irony! Sincerity, and Nostalgia', Stephanie Bailey, *Hyperallergic*, 11 Nov 2013

'I Object', Maria Walsh, *Art Monthly*, 371, Nov 2013

'Andy Holden', James Clegg, *ArtReview*, 7 May 2013

'Interview: Andy Holden', *Frieze*, 148, 1 June 2012

'Nothing Like Something Happens Anywhere'. Cherry Smyth, *This is Tomorrow*, 13 Sept 2012

'Andy Holden: Works|Projects review', David Trigg, *Frieze*, 146, 19 March 2012

'Chewy Cosmos Thingly Time – review', David Ryan, *Art Monthly*, 348, Jul–Aug 2011

'20/20: 20 Inspirational Artists Selected by Frieze Cover Artists', *Frieze*, 133, September 2010

'Sound: Be Glad For The Song Has No End', David Ryan, *Art Monthly*, 341, Nov 2010

'Artist Andy Holden makes a marvellous mountain out of a misdemeanour', Jonathan Jones, *The Guardian*, 19 March 2010

INDEX

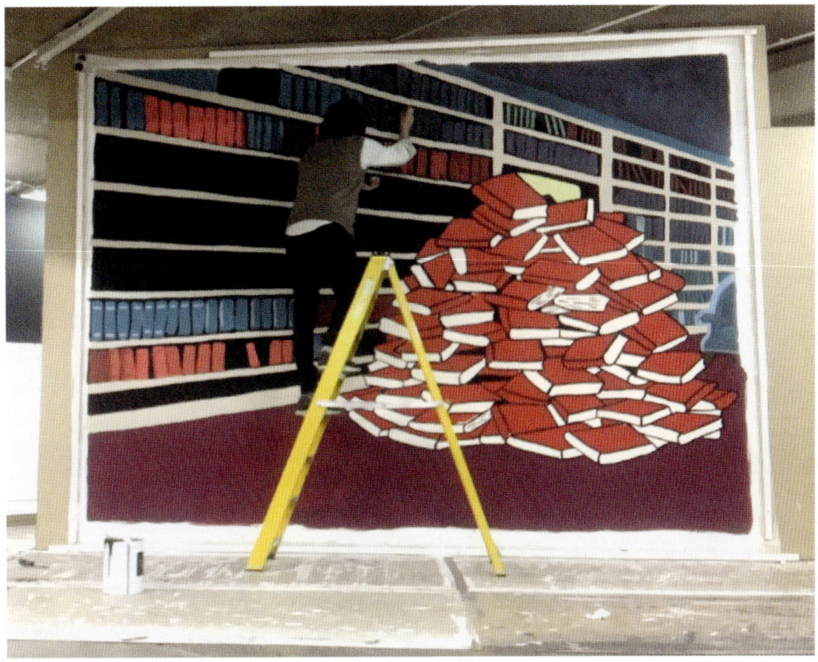

Andy Holden painting
Unpacking My Library, 2020

Page numbers in *italics* indicate illustrations

PICTURE CREDITS

Every effort has been made to contact copyright holders. The publisher will be pleased to amend in future printings any errors or omissions brought to their attention.

All works courtesy Andy Holden unless otherwise stated.

pp. 2, 25a, 25c, 25d, 26a, 26b, 27b, 28, 29a, 30, 46c, 48b, 49c, 081a, 82a–c, 83a, 94c, 94d, 94e, 112–13, 119, 123a–c, 126b, 135d, 136b and endpapers: Photo Daniel Brown.

pp. 6, 7, 8a, 9a, 9b, 25b, 37, 97b: Photo CHOREO.

pp. 7, 8a, 9a, 9b, 25b, 37, 127e: Courtesy Hidde van Seggelen, Hamburg.

pp. 10, 16, 31a–c, 38, 40a, 40b, 50e, 76–77, 78–79, 80a 80b, 81b–d, 83b, 84, 108–9, 114, 115, 116–117, 118a, 122, 127e, 126e, 126g, 127a–d, 127f, 128a–c, 128e, 129a, 129b, 129d, 130a–d, 131c, 131d, 132c, 132e, 133a, 133b, 133d, 134a–f, 135a, 135e, 135f, 136a, 136c, 136d and reverse endpaper (back): Photo Andy Holden.

pp. 11a, 11b, 12, 13, 14, 85b, 92b, 93b, 97c: Courtesy Kröller-Müller Museum. Photo © Marjon Gemmeke 2024.

pp. 19, 21, 22a, 23, 24, 27a, 34–35, 60: Photo Damien Griffiths.

p. 20: Photo Cubitt Gallery, London.

pp. 26a, 32a, 32b, 33, 36: Courtesy the artist and Seventeen, London.

p. 29b: Photo Collective Gallery, Edinburgh.

p. 31d: Photo Raffi Hentabi.

pp. 32a, 32b, 36: Photo B J Deakin Photography.

pp. 39, 40b, 40c, 41, 42–43, 46a, 46b, 47, 49a–c: Commisisoned by Zabludowicz Collection.

pp. 39, 49a, 49b: Photo R. Schwager.

p. 40a: Courtesy the artist and Zabludowicz Collection.

p. 40c: Photo Adam Jones.

pp. 41, 42–43, 47: Photo Andy Keate.

pp. 46a, 46b, 126c, 131b: Photo Stuart Whipps.

p. 46c: Courtesy Lost Toys Records.

pp. 48b, 72a–c, 73, 94a, 94b, 110–11 and front cover Photo Thomas Barratt.

p. 50a: Courtesy and photo FINN CARLOW.

p. 50b: Photo Oleksii Vyshniakov photography.

p. 50c: Courtesy Vibe/Anti-Vibe Records. Photo Craig Sharp.

p. 50d: Commissioned by Somerset House, London.

p. 50e: Courtesy Wysing Arts Centre, Cambridge.

p. 51: Courtesy and photo Eva Vermandel.

pp. 52–53, 136e and reverse endpaper (front): Photo Studio Semple.

p. 55: Courtesy the artist and Perimeter London.

p. 55: Photo Stephen James.

pp. 59, 132d: Photo Gillian Heyes / Dapple Photography.

pp. 61a, 61 b: Courtesy of Somerset House.

pp. 61a, 61b, 135b: Photo Tim Bowditch.

pp. 64–65: Groundwork, Cornwall. Photo Steve Tanner.

pp. 66-67, 68a, 69a, 70, 74–75: Photo Corey Bartle-Sanderson.

pp. 72a–c, 73, 94a, 94b, 110–11: Courtesy the artist and Charles Moffett, New York.

p. 83b: Courtesy Benaki Museum, Athens.

pp. 84a, 126a: Courtesy Andy Holden and Peter Holden. Photo Peter Holden.

p. 85a: Courtesy the artist, Spike Island, Bristol Green Capital and Artangel London. Photo Jared Schiller.

pp. 85c, 87a, 88–89, 90, 91, 92a, 92b, 93a, 95, 96, 97: *Natural Selection* was commissioned by Artangel, Bristol Museum & Art Gallery, Leeds Art Gallery and Towner Art Gallery, with the support of the National Lottery through Arts Council England, Bristol Green Capital 2015, the Henry Moore Foundation and Artangel's Guardian Angels. *Natural Selection* is part of The Artangel Collection, an initiative to bring outstanding film and video works, commissioned and produced by Artangel, to galleries and museums across the UK and internationally.

p. 85c: Photo Simon Warner.

pp. 87a, 88–89, 90, 93a, 95, 96, 97: Photo Marcus Leith.

p. 91: Photo Pete Jones. pp. 98–99: Courtesy of Frieze, London; Seventeen, London and Hidde van Seggelen, Hamburg. Photo Linda Nylind. Courtesy of Frieze.

pp. 102, 103, 104a, 104b, 105a: Courtesy the artist and Gallery of Everything.

pp. 102, 103, 105a: Photo Jorge Stride.

p. 105b: Courtesy the artist and Hayward Touring. Photo Hayward Touring / British Art Show 9.

pp. 106–7: Photo Brendan McGregor.

pp. 118b, 123d: Photo Andy Sewell.

p. 128d: Photo Rudolf Schmidt.

p. 129c: Photo Paul Allitt.

p. 132a: Photo Jim Holden.

p. 133c: Photo Mira Calix.

p. 135c: Photo Wakefield Council / Scott Merrylees.

Author Biographies

Jarvis Cocker is a musician, broadcaster and writer. He formed the band Pulp in 1978, whilst at secondary school. The band went on to become one of the most successful UK music groups of the 1990s. Between 2009 and 2017 he presented *Jarvis Cocker's Sunday Service* on BBC Radio 6Music, as well as the ongoing, award-winning BBC Radio 4 documentary series *Wireless Nights.* Cocker has honorary doctorates from both Sheffield Hallam University and Central Saint Martin's School of Art (which he attended from 1988 to 1991). His lyric collection *Mother, Brother, Lover* was published by Faber in 2011. *Good Pop, Bad Pop*, his first work of long-form prose, was published by Jonathan Cape in 2022.

Jennifer Higgie is an Australian writer, occasional curator, and former editor of *frieze* magazine who lives in London. Recent books include *The Mirror and the Palette: Revolution, Rebellion and Resilience: 500 Years of Women's Self-Portraits* (2021); *The Other Side: A Journey into Women, Art and the Spirit World* (2023); the children's book *There's Not One*, and the novel *Bedlam* (reissued in 2026). She was also the editor of *Documents of Contemporary Art: The Artist's Joke* (2007), has written numerous articles, essays and reviews, and hosted two podcasts: *Bow Down: Women in Art History* for *frieze*, and *Artists's Artists*, for the National Gallery of Australia.

Endpapers (front and back): *Chewy Cosmos*, 2011, collage, 60 × 40 cm (23 ⅝ × 15 ¾ in.). Front reverse: *After Finitude (Lucy Counting Raindrops)*, 2025, Indian ink on canvas, melted gramophone records, emulsion paint and collage, chains and hooks, painting: 100 × 200 cm (39 ⅜ × 78 ¾ in.), bowls each: diam. 25 cm (9 ⅞ in.), installation view, Palmer Gallery, London. Back reverse: Studio view, 2011

ISBN 978-1-911736-40-0

A catalogue record for this book is available from The British Library.

Commissioned and edited by Rebecca Morrill
Designed by Sylvia Ugga
Production by Sarah McLaughlin
Copy-edited by Michela Parkin
Proofread by Catalina Imizcoz
Indexed by Kevin Broccoli

Typefaces: Bradford and Traulha
Printed by Toppan Leefung, China
Publisher: HENI Publishing, London, United Kingdom

EU Authorised Representative: Easy Access System Europe - Mustamäe tee 50, 10621 Tallinn, Estonia, gpsr.requests@easproject.com

FSC www.fsc.org
MIX
Paper | Supporting responsible forestry
FSC® C104723

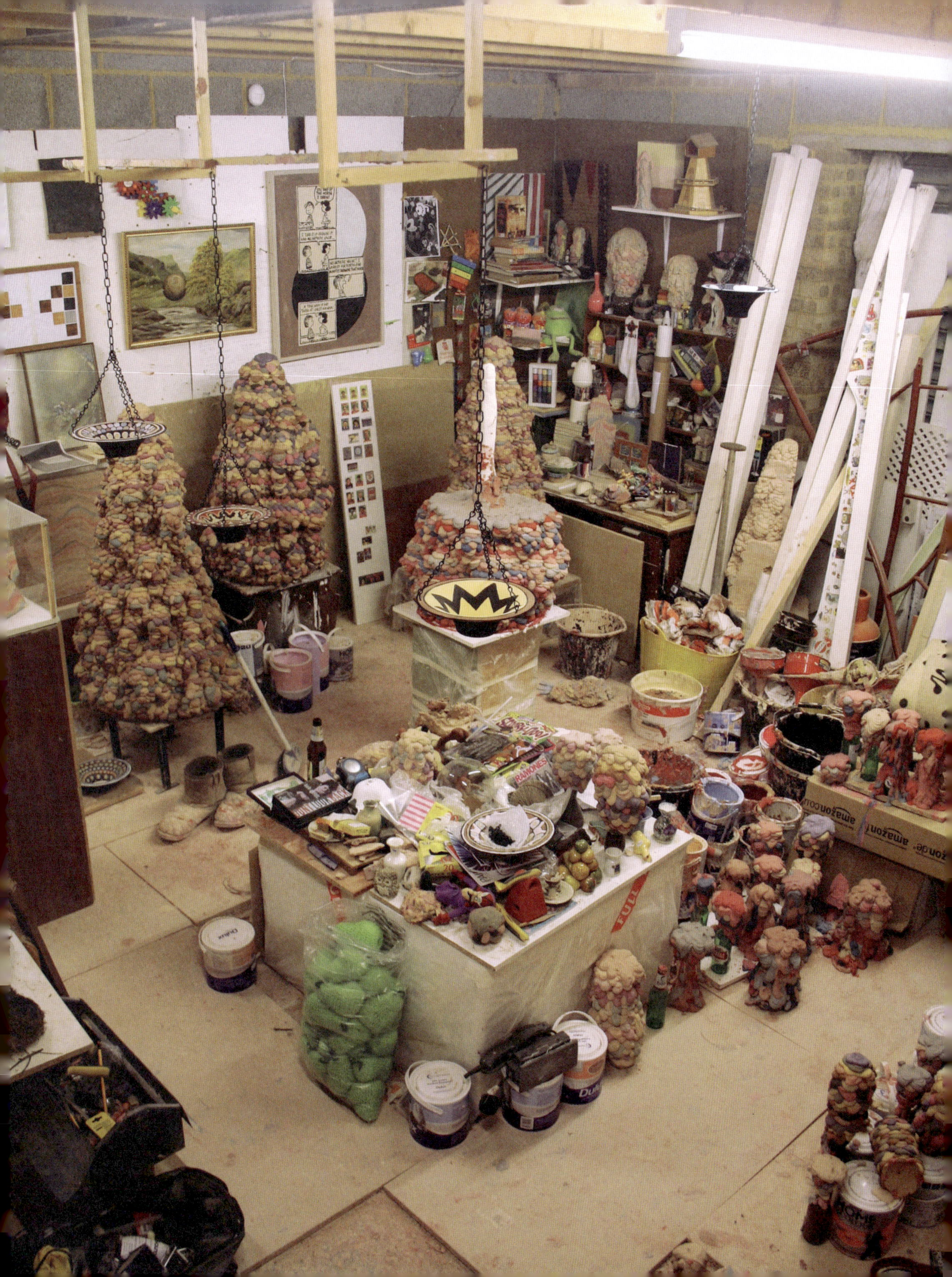

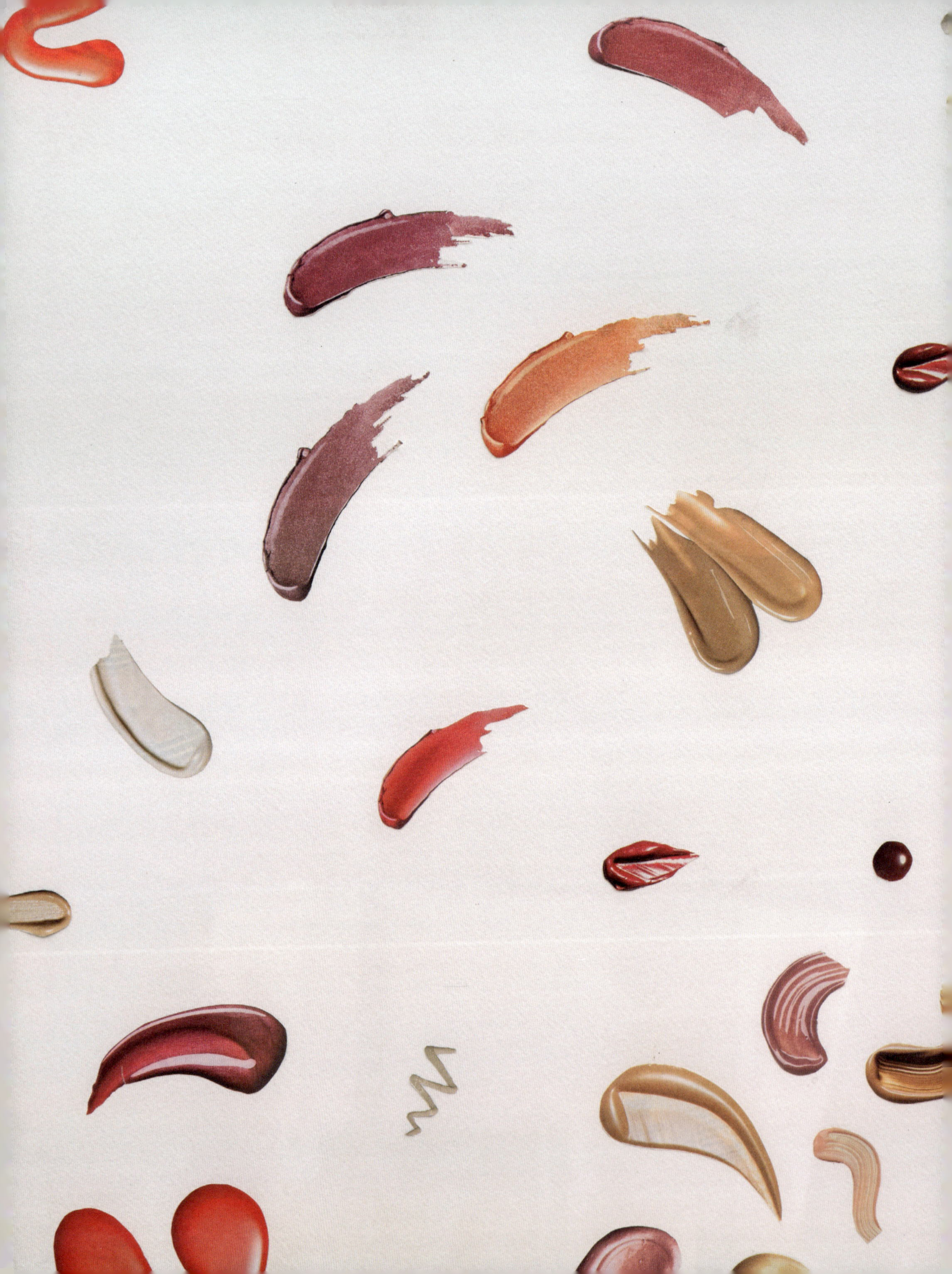